CW01084116

Allan Kardec (1804-1869)

THE GOSPEL

ACCORDING TO

SPIRITISM

Contains explanations of the moral maxims of Christ in accordance with Spiritism and their application in various circumstances in life.

by ALLAN KARDEC

Author of THE SPIRITS' BOOK

Unshakable faith is only that which can meet reason face to face in every Human epoch.

This English translation is taken from the 3rd edition of the original French, as being the one containing all of Allan Kardec's final revisions, published in 1866.

L'ÉVANGILE

SELON

LE SPIRITISME

CONTENANT

L'EXPLICATION DES MAXIMES MORALES DU CHRIST

LEUR CONCORDANCE AVEC LE SPIRITISME

ET LEUR APPLICATION AUX DIVERSES POSITIONS DE LA VIE

PAR ALLAN KARDEC

Auteur du *Livre des Esprits.*

Il n'y a de foi inébranlable que celle
qui peut regarder la raison face à face,
à tous les âges de l'humanité.

———

TROISIÈME ÉDITION

REVUE, CORRIGÉE ET MODIFIÉE.

———

PARIS

LES ÉDITEURS DU *LIVRE DES ESPRITS*

35, QUAI DES AUGUSTINS

DENTU, FRÉD. HENRI, libraires, au Palais - Royal

Et au bureau de la REVUE SPIRITE, 59, rue et passage Sainte-Anne

1866

(Facsimile of original)

Original title 'L'Évangile Selon le Spiritisme' first published in France, 1864

1st Edition of this translation 1987

ISBN 0 947823 09 3

Cover design by Helen Ann Blair

*Typesetting and Artwork by Mainline Typesetting Services
Unit 2, Millside Industrial Estate, Southmill Road, Bishop's Stortford, Herts.*

*Printed by Masterprint
Unit 4–5, The Maltings, Station Road, Newport, Essex.*

The entire proceeds of this book are donated to the ALLAN KARDEC STUDY GROUP, a non-profit organization whose workers are all voluntary, which has been set up for the purpose of the dissemination of the SPIRITIST DOCTRINE, based on the lines of the codification by Allan Kardec.

Printed in Great Britain for
THE HEADQUARTERS PUBLISHING CO LTD
5 ALEXANDRIA ROAD
LONDON W13 0NP

INDEX

NOTE: The numbers placed at the end of the various items in each chapter indicate the number(s) of the paragraph, for quick location.

PUBLISHER'S FOREWORD

Ask any Spiritualist in the United Kingdom how many branches of Spiritualism there are, most will reply two: National Spiritualists and Christian Spiritualists. Yet in Brazil there is a group of Spiritualists or, as they call themselves, Spiritists who follow the teachings of Allan Kardec who far outnumber all the Spiritualists in the U.K.

Kardec wrote a number of books on the subject of Spiritism. It has been our policy to publish all aspects of Spiritualism leaving the reader to make up his or her own mind as to which path to follow. When Janet Duncan of the ALLAN KARDEC STUDY GROUP asked us if we would be interested in publishing a new translation of The Gospel According to Spiritism, we decided yes. This volume is the result.

We hope The Gospel According to Spiritism will be the first in a series of all the Kardec works.

The Gospel According to Spiritism is the Spiritists view and explanation of the New Testament as brought to us by the Spirits and codified by Allan Kardec.

TRANSLATOR'S ACKNOWLEDGEMENTS

I am most grateful to all members of the ALLAN KARDEC STUDY GROUP and to all those who have helped in any way whatsoever, be it through prayer, advice, motivation or help with typing and most especially I wish to offer my heartfelt thanks to Martin Edmonds for hours of painstaking corrections, to Chloris Morgan our Publisher's Reader, and finally to Glaucius Oliva for undertaking the responsibility of the final verifications with the original French.

Our most grateful thanks go to the Spiritist 'brother' who generously donated the entire cost of publication. May he be eternally blessed and may his desired anonymity be respected.

We, the incarnate workers, have done our best to make this translation as authentic as is humanly possible. Our very special thanks must however, go to all the many Spiritual Helpers who have taken an active part in this translation. Many are the times I have been conscious of their presence, offering incentive and sometimes even dictating passages.

This work has brought me great joy and I can only hope that all who come to read it may likewise receive comfort and enlightenment, be strengthened and upheld along life's troubled pathways.

J. A. Duncan

TRANSLATOR'S PREFACE

This is no ordinary book. This is not a book which is usually read from cover to cover, afterwards to be placed on a book-shelf and forgotten. This is a book for daily use, for moments of trouble, when we feel in need of orientation and guidance, a bedside book, a book to be constantly on hand, to take with us in our hand-luggage when we travel. In other words this is a book offering something very special to each person who may read and study it. A book which brings peace of mind, and which comforts in times of bereavement. A book even for those who have only a faint knowledge or belief in God and Jesus. This is a book which can change lives by bringing tranquility out of chaos, certainty out of disbelief, compensation for both material and spiritual losses. But most importantly it brings us answers to many questions that we may have been asking, those famous questions such as 'Who and what am I?' 'Where did I come from?' 'What am I doing here?' 'Where am I going?' It brings us rational and logical explanations of such matters as reincarnation, inequality of wealth in the world, the reasons why we sometimes hate certain people on sight, and the many disharmonies that exist between husband and wife, brother and sister, parents and children, and many more.

Probably this book will play its greatest part in helping humanity towards a better understanding of LIFE and lead Man towards spiritual enlightenment through its usefulness when used as readings in Churches and Study Groups. It can also be of great help at times of stress, grief or when we are at a a loss to know what to do, to open the book casually, after a moments thought and read at the point where our eye first falls upon the page. Finally, but certainly not the least of its uses is that it brings the 'key' to the Bible parables in everyday language together with the deep meanings behind the teachings of Jesus.

This is the third book of the Doctrine as codified by ALLAN KARDEC whose real name was HIPPOLYTE LÉON DENIZARD RIVAIL and we offer here a brief biography of this remarkable and dedicated man.

He was born in Lyon, France on 3rd October, 1804 into a family who for many generations had been either lawyers or magistrates. He was an intelligent child and was taught high principles of honour and morals by his parents. At an early age he showed strong inclinations towards the sciences and philosophy. When he was ten years of age he was sent to the Institute of Pestalozzi at Yverdun in Switzerland, where he soon acquired the habit of investigation and learnt the art of free thinking. At the age of fourteen he began to give free lessons to school fellows who were less advanced and on occasion was asked to teach officially by Pestalozzi himself in his absence, due to his natural ability in this field. He became a fervent disciple of Pestalozzi and was much loved by the great man.

In 1822 at the age of eighteen, Hippolyte returned to France. A year later he took up residence in Paris and in 1824 published his first book entitled: 'A Theoretical & Practical Arithmetic Course.' This was so successful that it continued to be reprinted till as late as 1876. He had an instinct for methodology and this was only the beginning, for he was to publish many other books on varying subjects including 'A Classical Grammar of the French Language' (1829). Some of these were adopted by the French University and the sale of these books rendered him a sufficient income to live on, while he contined to give free lessons to school children. He taught chemistry, mathematics, astronomy, physics, rhetoric, comparative anatomy and physiology. He spoke fluent Italian and Spanish, had a profound knowledge of German, English and Dutch and some knowledge of Latin, Greek and Gallic. He also translated a number of books, choosing those which he liked best. These included several by Fénelon which he translated into German.

He opened his first school in 1825. It bore the name 'First Grade School' (École de premier degré), for superior teaching and the following year he opened 'The Rivail Technical Institute' whose teaching was based on that of Pestalozzi.

He married Amélie Gabrielle Boudet on 6th February 1832. She was nine years his senior, a writer, teacher of fine arts, poetess and artist. She was a perfect companion and helper, being dedicated and uncomplaining. She played an important part in all her husband's activities and sustained him through many financial difficulties encountered during his life, and greatly assisted him in his teaching.

This extraordinary man could have become renouned and wealthy through his various talents, but this was not to be. He was a man with a mission! Between 1848 and 1850 an explosion of spirit phenomena occured in America and even more strongly in Europe. In the last book of the codification 'Posthumous Works' published by Amélie, Kardec had written: "It was in 1854 that I heard about 'Table-turning' for the first time." His friend Mr Fortier brought him the initial news of these extraordinary happenings: "The tables also talk!" Kardec's reply to this was: "I will only believe when I see it and when it can be proved to me that a table has a brain which can think, nerves to feel with and can also become somnambulic. Until then, allow me to see nothing more than fantasy in these stories!" He had always been a disbeliever of such things as ghosts.

After various encounters with Mr Fortier, in 1855 he was finally persuaded to attend a seance and his curiosity was aroused. He then became a frequent visitor at the seances held in the house of a certain Mr Baudin. It was in fact here that he began his studies and research. He was never to become a medium, but was highly intuitive. On 30th April 1856 a medium in his group received the first indications from Spirit of his mission. His wife always accompanied him to all the meetings and eventually became his secretary, upholding him in every aspect of his work. He adopted the 'nom de plume' of ALLAN KARDEC at the suggestion of Spirit, so that the works of the codification should not be confused with his own works. The first book of the codificiation (The Spirits' Book), was published in 1857. This same year he also began meetings in his own home. A year later he founded 'The Parisiene Society for Spiritist Studies'.

The few remaining years of his life were dedicated to his work, the completion of the Codification, and to lecturing on Spiritism and its philosophy. He also made exhaustive journeys in order to take the word to as many places as possible, all of which he completed at his own expense. In 1867 he met Léon Denis, who became his disciple, and who later published a series of classic works on Spiritism.

On March 31st, 1869, having just finished drawing up the constitution and rules of a new society that he planned to form, while seated in his usual chair at his study-table in the Rue Sainte Anne, in the act of tying up a bundle of papers, his busy life was suddenly brough to an end. The passing from Earth into the Spiritual World was instantaneous, a peaceful falling asleep — a fitting end to a life well lived. But although the physical man is no longer with us he lives on in Spirit, continuing his work by inspiring, stimulating and encouraging us to continue our search for knowledge.

In his introduction to THE SPIRITS' BOOK, Allan Kardec expresses his opinion that new ideas need new terms and so he formulated the words SPIRITIST and SPIRITISM to give a clear and precise meaning to this doctrine. In his day the word Spiritualist meant the opposite to Materialist, but it did not follow that a Spiritualist believed in the existence of spirits or the possibility of communiciation with the invisible world. He employed the word Spiritism to stipulate the fundamental principle of the Spiritist theory which is the relation of the material world with spirits or the beings of the invisible world. A Spiritist is one who adheres to this doctrine. We continue to use these terms today as the ideas they represent become more fully understood. Amongst those ideas is the study of the interrelationship between the two worlds, visible and invisible; the scientific, philosophical and religious aspects of existence; the ever pressing need for man to instruct himself, to cast aside all mystery and superstition; to accept responsibility for the life he leads today and the life he is making for himself in the future by his present actions, or lack of them, as the case may be.

As life gathers momentum, as the world goes from crisis to crisis at this time, we are more and more conscious of the reality of the truths contained in Kardec's books. As the world prepares for a New Epoch, which is already dawning, we realise the need for all humanity to grow towards this knowledge, to seek enlightenment so as to be prepared. When this time will finally be upon the world then mankind will be able to appreciate the greatness of this man's vision into the future.

However, we must not forget one important fact, that in order to meet the future we must make preparations in our TODAY! Each moment that passes cannot be recovered, therefore we must make use of every instant to grow SPIRITUALLY! To open up our horizons, to broaden our minds, to seek and cultivate our SPIRITUALITY! We are Spiritual Beings, we are all immortal creatures! If we are to one day find happiness and peace then we must consider our whole being! While we go on thinking of ourselves as material people, we are only looking at half of ourselves and here lies the secret of so many mistakes, so many unhappinesses and so many failures. But in order to recognise these truths we must also be prepared to accept the responsibilities that go with them. For every person this wider and deeper knowledge of LIFE carries with it the need for self-analysis, self-correction and self-improvement. Without these things we are all standing still, marking time, going nowhere! If this book helps even one person to take just one step forward then it will have done its work.

God never demands the impossible of any one of us, nor gives us burdens for which we do not have the strength; so if we try to make a conscious effort to better ourselves then we have begun our journey into the future, towards the LIGHT, where one day victory, peace and joy will be ours.

London, 1987   *Janet Duncan*

THE CODIFICATION OF THE SPIRITIST DOCTRINE
comprises the following books:

THE SPIRITS' BOOK

THE MEDIUMS' BOOK

THE GOSPEL ACCORDING TO SPIRITISM

WHAT IS SPIRITISM

GENESIS*

HEAVEN & HELL*

POSTHUMOUS WORKS*

NOTE:
(At time of going to press.)
* — These books are not yet translated into English.

PREFACE

The Spirits of the Lord, who are the Virtues of Heaven, move as does an immense army upon receiving orders from their commander, spreading out over the face of the Earth and, similar to the stars which fall one after another from the skies, are come to illumine pathways and open the eyes of those who cannot see.

In truth I say unto you the times are come when all things will be established in their true light, when the darkness shall be dissipated, the prideful confounded and the just glorified.

The great voices of Heaven reverberate like the sound of trumpets and the choirs of angels assemble. Mankind, we are inviting you to this divine concert. Take up the harp and lift up your voices in unison so that, in a sacred chorus, the sound may extend and re-echo from one extreme of the universe to the other.

Fellow beings, beloved brothers and sisters, we are here beside you. Love one another and say from the bottom of your hearts: Lord! Lord! In so doing you fulfill the wishes of the Father who is in Heaven; then you too may enter into the Kingdom of Heaven.

THE SPIRIT OF TRUTH

NOTE: The above instructions, which were received by means of mediumship, are a precise summary of the true character of Spiritism and the finality of this work. They have been placed as the preface for this reason.
                                                                        A.K.

INTRODUCTION

1. THE OBJECTIVE OF THIS WORK

The Gospel can be divided into five parts: *the events in the life of Christ; the miracles; the prophecies; the words taken by the Church on which they based their dogmas; the moral teachings.* The first four have been the object of controversies. But the last, however, has remained constantly inviolate. Before this divine code even incredulity bows down. This is the common ground where all cults may be united, the flag under which all may gather, whatever their creeds may be, because it has never been a matter of religious dispute, which always and in all places has originated from dogmatism. Moreover, if it had been discussed, then all cults would have found their own condemnation within it, seeing that, in the majority, they have held on to the more mystical rather than the moral part, which demands an intimate reform from each one. Specially prepared for mankind, it constitutes a code of rules on how to behave in every circumstance of private and public life and offers the basic principles for all social relations, founded on rigid justice. It is, finally and above all, the infallible route to lasting happiness and the uplifting of a corner of the veil that hides the future life. This is what forms the exclusive objective of this work.

Everyone admires the moral behind the Gospel; everyone proclaims its sublimeness and the need we have of it. However, of the many who proclaim their faith, believing what others have said or relying on maxims which have become proverbs, few know the basis and even fewer understand it or are able to deduce the consequences of it. In many cases the reason for this is in the difficulty of understanding the Gospel, which for many is quite unintelligible. The allegorical form used and the intentional mysticism of the language make it something we read because we feel we ought to, because our conscience tells us to or because we are obliged to, as one would read prayers, without understanding them and consequently without taking any benefit from them. In this way the moral precepts go unnoticed, scattered here and there between a mass of narrative. This makes it impossible to get the general idea of the whole or to take these ideas as specific subjects for reading and meditation.

It is true that various works have already been written concerning the evangelic moral. But after being put into modern prose they have lost their primitive simplicity, which at the same time constitutes their charm and authenticity. Many others also deal with the best known maxims reduced to the simplest form of proverb. These then are no more than aphorisms, deprived of part of their value and interest due to the lack of accompanying accessories and the circumstances of the enunciation.

In order to avoid these undesirabilities, we have collected together in this work all the subjects, so to say, that go to form a universal moral code without distinction as to creed. In these citations we have kept all that is useful to the development of these ideas, putting aside only that which does not pertain directly to the matter. Apart from this we have kept scrupulously to the translations by Sacy (1) and to the division of the verses. But instead of following a chronological order, which would have been impossible and have made no sense, we have methodically grouped and classified the various maxims according to their respective natures so that they follow on, one from the other, as much as possible. Indication of chapters and verses permit reference to the original texts whenever desired.

These details refer only to the material side of our work, which on its own would be of secondary importance. The main objective was to put these teachings within easy reach of everybody by means of clear explanations, especially those passages which have, until now, remained obscure and so unfold the full consequences of these teachings and the manner in which they may be applied to all walks of life. This is what we have attempted to do together with the help of the Good Spirits who assist us.

Many points in the Gospel, the Bible and in the writings of the sacred authors, are in general unintelligible, some even appearing nonsensical for lack of a key which would help in understanding their true meaning. This key is to be found in its most complete form within Spiritism, as those who have already made a serious study of it can verify, and as many more in the future will also come to recognise. Spiritism is to be found throughout ancient times and repeatedly during the different epochs of humanity. We find vestiges in many places in the form of writings, in beliefs and in monuments. This is the reason why at the same time it is opening new horizons for the future, it is also projecting a no less brilliant light upon the mysteries of the past.

As a compliment to each precept we have added some well chosen instructions from amongst those dictated, in various countries and to different mediums, by the Spirits. If they had been taken from only one origin they would probably have suffered the influence either of the person or the ambient, whereas the diversification of origins proves that the Spirits give teachings without distinction and that no one person is specially privileged. (2)

---

(1) The version by Le Maistre de Sacy was always used by Kardec, but for the English translation the King James Version has been quoted. (Translator's note.)

(2) It would have been possible, without doubt, to have presented many more communications from Spirit on each subject, all of which were received in cities and centres other than those cited. We wished, however, to avoid monotony and useless repetition and so have limited our choice to

This work is for the use of everyone. From it we may all discover the means by which we may apply Christ's morals to our daily lives and how best to go about it. This applies very specially to Spiritists. Thanks to the relationship between man and the invisible world, which has henceforth been established on a permanent basis, the law of the Gospel which the Spirits have taught to all nations, will no longer be a matter of dead words because each one will be able to understand them and will see themselves incessantly compelled to put them into practice, according to the counselling of the Spiritual guides. These instructions coming from Spirit are really the voices from Heaven who have come to enlighten mankind and invite him to *put the Gospel into practice.*

2. THE AUTHORITY BEHIND THE SPIRITIST DOCTRINE

The Universal Control of the Spirit Teachings

If the Spiritist Doctrine were of a purely human conception it would offer no more guarantee than the enlightenment of those who actually conceived it. But no one on Earth could seriously contemplate the pretention of possessing the exclusive and absolute truth. If the Spirits who made these revelations had manifested to only one man we would have no guarantee of their origin since we would need to believe, on his word alone, what he said he had received as teachings from them. If we accepted perfect sincerity on his part, the most he could do would be to convince his circle of acquaintances. He would be able to form a sect, but never be able to form a world congregation.

God wished the new revelations to reach mankind by the quickest and most authentic path, so He entrusted the Spirits to deliver them from pole to pole, manifesting everywhere without conferring the exclusive privilege of hearing these words to any one individual. One person might be deceived, could even deceive themselves, but this could not happen when millions of people see and hear the same thing. This constitutes a guarantee for each one and for all. For the rest, it is possible to make one man disappear, but it is not possible to make everyone disappear. It is possible to burn books, but you cannot burn Spirits, and even if all the books were burnt, the base of the doctrine would still be inexhaustible because it is not to be found on Earth and would reappear in every place so that all might partake of it. If there is a shortage of men to diffuse it, there will always be Spirits whose action reaches everyone and even those whom no person can reach.

---

those which, from their base and form, apply more adequately within the plan of this work, reserving for future publication those we have not been able to use here.

With respect to the mediums, we have refrained from naming them. In most cases they themselves asked not to be mentioned and so we have made no exceptions. It is also a fact that the names of these mediums would not add more value to the work of the Spirits. The mentioning of them by name would only be an incentive to personal pride, to which serious mediums give no importance. They understand fully that their part in the work being merely passive, the value of the communication in no way exalts their personal merit. It would be foolish to allow oneself to become vain about an intelligent work to which one had only lent mechanical assistance.

So then, it is the Spirits themselves who do the propagating with the help of innumerable mediums, disseminating all over the world. If there had been but one interpreter, however favoured he might have been, Spiritism would barely be known. To whatever class he belonged, that interpreter would have been the object of caution to many people and not every nation would have accepted him, whereas the Spirits communicate to the four corners of the Earth, to all peoples, to all sects, to all parties and everyone accepts them. Spiritism has no nationality and does not stem from any known cult that might exist; nor is it imposed by any social class seeing that any person may receive instructions from parents, relatives and friends from the beyond. This is how it had to be accomplished if it was to lead all mankind towards brotherhood. If it did not maintain itself in neutral territory it would nurture dissensions instead of pacifying them.

The force of Spiritism, as well as the cause of its rapid spread, resides in this universal teaching. Where the word of one solitary person, even with the help of the press, would take centuries to become known by all, millions of voices are making themselves heard simultaneously in every corner of this planet. All are proclaiming the same principles and transmitting them on all levels, from the scholarly down to the most ignorant, in order that no one be disinherited. So far, this is an advantage that no other doctrine has to offer. If Spiritism then be the truth, it is not afraid of being unwanted by man, nor of modern revolutions, nor of the physical subversions of this globe, because nothing can touch the Spirits.

This is not however the only advantage which comes from this exceptional situation. It also offers an unattackable guarantee against all misgivings which might arise, be it from someone's ambition or be it through the contradictions of some Spirits. We cannot deny that these contradictions are obstacles, but they bring their own remedy with them alongside the ill.

We know that Spirits, due to differences in their various individual capacities, do not possess all the truth and do not claim to. It is not given to all to be able to penetrate certain mysteries. The knowledge of each one is proportional to their evolution. Ordinary Spirits know nothing more than does Man himself, but amongst them, as amongst men and women, are those who are presumptious and falsely wise, who think they know everything, but who in fact are ignorant; these are the systematical ones who take their own ideas to be the truth. In short, it is only the highly evolved Spirits, those who are almost completely dematerialised, who find themselves free from earthly ideas and prejudices. It is also known that less scrupulous Spirits do not hesitate to deceive by taking names which do not belong to them in order to impose their utopian ideas. As a result of all this and in relation to all that is outside the exclusive field of moral education, the revelations that any one medium may receive will have an individual character, without any stamp of authenticity, and should be considered as personal opinions, from this or that Spirit, and it would be imprudent to accept them or thoughtlessly propagate them as absolute truths.

The first corroborative test to be undertaken is without doubt that of reason, to which it is wise to submit, without exception, all that comes from Spirit. Any theory in evident contradiction to good sense, or against rigorous logic, or positive facts that have been previously acquired should be rejected, however apparently respectable be the name by which it is signed. This test will no doubt be left incomplete due to the lack of illumination of some people and the tendency of many to take their own opinions as judgements of truth. That being the case, what are those who deposit absolutely no faith in themselves to do? They should seek what seems to be the majority and take this as a guide. This then, is the manner in which you should proceed when judging what is said by the Spirits, who are the first to offer the means of so doing.

Complete concordance of Spirit teaching is the best proof of authenticity. However, it is important that this be received only under determined conditions. The weakest type of concordance is obtained when the medium, of his own accord, interrogates many different Spirits about a doubtful point. It is evident that, if the medium is under an obsessing influence or dealing with a mystifying Spirit, then that Spirit may say the same thing under different names. Neither is it any adequate guarantee to conformity when communications are received by different mediums at the same centre because they may be under the same influences.

Only one sure guarantee exists for spirit teachings: This is the concordance that exists between revelations which have been received spontaneously by a large number of mediums not known to each other and located in different places.

It is understood that we are not referring to those communications which deal with secondary interests, but those referring to the basic principles of the doctrine. Experience has taught us that when a new principle is to be presented, it always happens *spontaneously* in different places at the same time and in the same way, if not in actual form at least in general content.

On the other hand, if by any chance a Spirit formulates eccentric doctrine based exclusively on its own ideas and excluding the truth, you may be sure that this idea will remain *confined* and undoubtedly will collapse when confronted with instructions received from many other places, similar to many examples which are already known. It was this exclusiveness which destroyed all the biased doctrine which sprang up at the time of the initiation of Spiritism, when each one explained the phenomena according to their own beliefs, before the Laws that govern the relationship between the visible and invisible worlds became known.

That is what we have based ourself on when formulating a principle for the doctrine. We do not insist on it being true just because it might be in accordance with our own ideas. Neither do we have the least desire to uphold ourself as being the sole possessor of the whole truth and we have never said to anyone: "Believe in this because it is I who tell you". We consider that our own opinion is nothing more than personal, which might be true or false, as we are no more infallible than anyone else. It is not because we were taught a principle that we believe it to be true; it is due to the fact that it has received the sanction of concordance.

The position in which we find ourself is that of receiving communications from almost a thousand serious Spiritual Centres, scattered over highly diversified areas of this planet. This gives us the possibility of observing on which principles concordance is established. It is this concordance which has guided us till today, and it is the one which will go on guiding us in new fields still to be explored. We have noticed while studying these communications, coming from France and outside, that from the very special nature of the information a new path is being sought and that the moment has arrived to take a step forward. These revelations, many times given through veiled words, have frequently passed unperceived by many who receive them. Others have thought themselves to be the sole receivers. Taken in isolation, we would have given them no importance and it is only the coincidence which proves their seriousness. Later, when these new teachings reach the public, there will be many who will remember having received the same orientation. This general movement which we are studying and observing, together with the assistence of our Spiritual Guides, is what helps us to judge whether it is the correct moment to do something or not.

This universal verification constitutes the guarantee of the future unity of Spiritism and will annul all contradictory theories. It is here that in the future we shall find our criteria for the truth. The cause of the success of the doctrine as put forth in THE SPIRITS' BOOK and THE MEDIUMS' BOOK was due to the fact that everybody had received confirmation, direct from Spirit, of what these books contain. Whereas if all the Spirits had come to contradict them they would have received the same fate suffered by others who expounded imaginary concepts. Not even the support of the press would have saved them from shipwreck. But on the contrary, deprived as they were of this support, they nevertheless opened new paths and have made rapid advancement. This is because the Spirits offered their support and goodwill which not only compensated but surpassed the lack of goodwill on the part of Man. This is what will happen to all ideas, whether emanated from Man or Spirit, which prevail even in the face of this confrontation and this is the final test whose strength no one can deny.

Suppose it pleased some Spirits to dictate a book, under whatever title you choose, offering contrary teachings; let us suppose their intention was hostile, with the object of discrediting the doctrine and maliciously provoking apocryphal communications. What influence could these writings exercise if they were refuted by all other Spirits? Anyone wishing to launch a doctrine in their own name should first seek assurance in combined concordance from the Spirits. There is no comparison between a system devised by only one person to that of another devised by everyone. What can the arguments of slanderers, wishing only to belittle, achieve against the opinion of the masses, if millions of friendly voices from space make themselves heard in opposition in every corner of the Universe, as well as in family homes?

What happens to the innumerable publications which have the pretention of destroying Spiritism? Which of them has as much as caused a hesitation in its march? Till now no one has considered the matter from this point of view without forgetting the most important fact: each one has been depending on themselves, without counting on the Spirits.

The principle of concordance is also a guarantee against any alterations to which Spiritism might be subjected by other sects wishing to take possession of it for their own ends, and so change it to suit their own ideas. Whosoever tries to deviate Spiritism from its providential objective will never succeed, for the simple reason that the Spirits, as a universal body, will cause any ideas contrary to the truth to fall.

From all this stands out the main truth, which is that he who wishes to oppose the established and sanctioned ideas could, to be sure, cause a localised perturbation lasting but a short while, but could never dominate the whole, not even for a moment and certainly not over a period of time. We should also like to point out that instructions given by Spirits on points not yet elucidated by the doctrine should not be considered as law, until these instructions have been duly isolated and proven. Neither should they be accepted except with all due reserve and under the heading of 'awaiting confirmation'. From this we understand the need for greater prudence before making any such communication public. But if they are deemed fit to be publicised they should be presented as mere individual opinions, possibly true, but awaiting confirmation. It will be necessary to wait for this confirmation before proclaiming it as a complete truth, unless you wish to be accused of levity or of irreflected cruelty.

The Superior Spirits proceed with extreme wisdom in their revelations. They never touch on the most important questions, except gradually, until our intelligence shows itself to accept a more advanced truth and when circumstances show themselves to be favourable to a new idea. This is why they did not reveal everything from the outset, and still have not told everything. They never give themselves to impatience, like those who want to eat the fruit before it is ripe. It is useless to try to hurry things forward beyond the time designated by Providence for its revealing, and if you do try, the serious Spirits will always deny their assistance. Those Spirits who are frivolous are not the least preoccupied with the truth and consequently will give answers to anything and everything. So it is in this manner that whenever a question is premature, contradictory answers will always be found.

The principles mentioned above have not been formed as the result of a personal theory; they are consequences which have been forced upon us from the varying conditions within which Spirit communication is manifest. It is quite evident that if one Spirit says one thing and thousands of other Spirits say something different, we presume the t ath does not lie with the solitary communicant. For someone to imagine the) possess the truth against all the rest would be quite illogical, be it man or Spirit. The really ponderous Spirits, if they do not feel completely or sufficiently clarified about any subject *never* give a definite answer, but declare that they are merely giving their own point of view and suggest that we await the necessary confirmation.

However large, beautiful or just an idea appears, it is impossible to unite opinions right from the first moment. The conflicts which arise in this case are the inevitable consequences which such a movement would cause, and they are necessary so that the truth may be emphasized and the sooner this happens the better, so that any false ideas may be discarded. Any Spiritists who feels worried by this situation may be tranquil, as all these isolated claims will fall before the enormous and discerning force of universal concordance.

It is not the opinion of any man which will produce unity, but the unanimous voices of the Spirits; it will not be any man, least of all myself, who will destroy the Spiritist orthodoxy, neither will it be a Spirit wishing to impose whatever it may be. This unity will be accomplished by the universal gathering of Spirits who communicate throughout the world, by order of God. This is the essential character of the Spiritist Doctrine; this is its force and its authority. God desired that His Law be set upon an immovable base and so did not trust these fundamentals to only one fragile being.

Before such a powerful tribunal, where neither conspiracy, rivalries, sects or nations are known, all opposition, ambition and those who seek individual supremacy will fall. *We ourselves will fall if we try to substitute our own ideas for those of God.* He alone will decide all lawful questions, impose silence on disagreement and give reason to those who have it. Before this imposing accord, from the *voices of Heaven,* what value has an opinion of a mere man or that of one Spirit? It makes no more impression than a drop of water in the ocean and even less than a child's voice in a tempest.

Universal opinion, like that of a supreme judge, is the one which is pronounced last, being formed from all the individual opinions. If one of these contains the truth it merely shows its own relative weight in the balance and if it is false it cannot prevail against the rest. In this immense concourse all individuality disappears and this constitutes yet another disappointment for man's pride.

This harmonious assemblage is already being formed and before the turn of this century we shall see its full brightness shining forth in such a manner as to dissipate all doubt. The field is prepared and from now on potent voices will receive the mission of making themselves heard in order to congregate Man under one banner. But until this actually happens, all those who fluctuate between two opposing points of view can observe in which way general opinion forms. This will be the correct indication as to the declaration of the majority of the Spirits on the varying subjects about which they offer orientation, and is an even more accurate sign as to which of the two systems will prevail.

3. HISTORIC FACTS

In order to better understand the Gospel, it is necessary to know the true meaning of many of the words used which bear relation to the customs and the Jewish society of the time. Some of these words no longer have the same meaning and have frequently been misinterpreted, which in turn has led to uncertainty. When the full meanings are explained, it shows the real sense behind certain maxims which, at first sight, appear rather strange.

SAMARITANS — After the division of the ten tribes, Samaria became the capital of the dissident kingdom of Israel. Destroyed and rebuilt various times, under Roman rule it became the administrative head of Samaria, one of the four divisions of Palestine. Herod the Great beautified Samaria with sumptuous monuments and to gratify Augusto, gave it the name of Augusta, in Greek *Sébaste.*

The Samaritans were almost constantly at war with the kings of Judah. Profound aversion, dating from the time of the separation, perpetuated between the two tribes causing them to avoid any kind of reciprocal relations. In order to widen the schism, and to avoid going to Jerusalem for religious festivities, they built themselves a private temple and adopted some reforms. They only admitted the Pentateuch, which contained the laws of Moses, rejecting all other books to which these were annexed, and their sacred books were all written in ancient Hebrew characters. According to orthodox Jews, they were heretics and consequently despised, excommunicated and persecuted. The antagonism between the two nations was founded exclusively upon their religious divergencies, despite the fact that the origin of their belief was the same. They were the *Protestants* of their time.

Some Samaritans are still to be found in certain regions of the Lavent, especially near Nablus and in Jaffa. They observe the laws of Moses more strictly than other Jews and only marry amongst themselves.

NAZARITES — The name given in olden times to Jews who took the vow, either temporary or perpetual, to remain in perfect purity. They promised to observe chastity, abstain from alcoholic drinks and not to cut their hair. Samson, Samuel and John the Baptist were Nazarites.

Later on, the Jews gave this name to the first Christians, alluding to Jesus from Nazareth. This was also the name given to a heretical sect from the first phase of the Christian epoch and who, like the Ebonites, from whom they adopted certain principles, mixed the practice of the Mosaic Law with those of Christian dogmas. This sect disappeared during the fourth century AD.

PUBLICANS — In ancient Rome this was the name given to those who rented out the collection of public taxes and all kinds of incomes, either in Rome itself or in other parts of the Empire. They were like the general collectors and auctioneers of taxes in the ancient system in France, which still exists in some regions. The risks they ran made most people close their eyes when it came to their frequently amounted riches which for some, were the fruits of levies and scandalous gains. Later on the name 'Publican' was extended to all those who superintended public monies and their underling agents. Today, the term is employed in a disparaging way, to denote financiers and agents with very few scruples. It is said: "As greedy as a Publican" or "as rich as a Publican", referring to their ill-gotten gains.

During Roman rule the question of taxes was what the Jews found most difficult to accept, causing great irritation amongst themselves. Many revolts resulted from this problem, so turning it into a religious question, as it was considered to be against the Law. Indeed, a powerful party was formed at whose front was put a certain citizen named Judah the Gaulite, whose objective was to abolish all taxes. The Jews consequently abominated these taxes and all those entrusted with collecting them. Thence sprang up the aversion shown to Publicans of all categories, amongst whom could be found many people of esteem, but who due to their functions, were despised together with whomsoever kept company with them. Prominent Jews considered it a compromise to have any personal relationship with these people.

TAX COLLECTORS — These were the lower class of collectors, entrusted principally with the collection of tolls on entering cities. Their function corresponded more or less with those of the customs officials and the granting of passes. They shared the rejection suffered by Publicans in general. This is the reason why, in the Bible, we frequently meet the word *Publican* alongside the expression — sinful people. This did not imply debauchery or vagrancy but was a term of scorn, synonym for *people who kept bad company,* persons unworthy to mix with decent people.

PHARISEES (From the Hebrew, meaning division or separation.) — Tradition is an important part of Jewish theology. It consists of a compilation of the successive interpretations given to the Scriptures which became articles for dogmas. Amongst scholars this was the subject for interminable discussions, most of which were over simple questions as to the meaning of words and their form, just like theological disputes and subtleties of scholastics in the Middle Ages. From all this resulted different sects, each one wishing to have the monopoly of the Truth and consequently detesting one another, as so often happens.

Among these sects the most influential were the Pharisees, whose chief, Hillel, a Jewish doctor born in Babilonia some 180 or 200 years BC, was the founder of a famous school where it was taught that faith should be put only in the scriptures. The Pharisees were persecuted at different times, especially under Hyrcania (who was sovereign pontiff and king of the Jews), Aristoblus and Alexander, who was a king of Syria. However, Alexander granted them honours and restored their properties which made it possible for them to re-acquire their old powerful status. This was conserved until the ruin of Jerusalem in the year 70 AD, at which time the name disappeared in consequence of the scattering of the Jews.

The Pharisees took an active part in religious controversy. They were faithful practitioners of exterior cults and ceremonies, full of ardent zeal, proselytism, enemies of innovations, maintaining great severity of principles. But behind the cover of punctilious devotion lay dissolute habits, a great deal of pride and above all an excessive desire to dominate. Religion was actually a means to an end, rather than an object of sincere faith. It possessed nothing of virtue beyond outward appearances and ostentation. Nevertheless, they exercised a great influence over the people, in whose eyes they were sacred. This is how they became powerful in Jerusalem. They believed, or made out they believed, in Divine Providence, the immortality of the soul, eternal punishment and the resurrection of the dead (See chapter 4, item 4). But Jesus, esteeming simplicity and the qualities of the heart above all else, whose preference within the law was for the *spirit which vitalizes to the word which kills,* applied Himself throughout His mission to the unmasking of their hypocrisy, and because of this was considered by them to be their enemy. This then is the reason why the Pharisees, together with the High Priests, incited the people to eliminate Him.

THE SCRIBES — This name was given in the main to the secretaries of the kings in Judea and to certain people who understood matters relating to the Jewish army. Later it was applied to those scholars who taught the Law of Moses and interpreted it to the People. They joined in common cause with the Pharisees, sharing their principles as well as their aversion to all innovations. This is why Jesus included them when He launched criticism against the Pharisees.

SYNAGOGUE (From the Greek SUNAGOGUÊ meaning assembly, congregation.) — There was only one temple in Judah, that of Solomon in Jerusalem, where all the great ceremonies of worship were held. Every year all the Jews would go there in pilgrimage for the principal festivals, such as the Passover, the Dedication and the Feast of the Tabernacle. It was on the occasion of these feasts that Jesus would also be present. The other cities did not have temples, only synagogues, buildings where the Jewish people would collect for their Saturday meetings and public prayers, under the leadership of their Elders, the scribes, or scholars versed in the Law. It was due to this fact that Jesus, although He was not a priest, was able to teach at the synagogues on Saturdays.

Ever since the ruin of Jerusalem and the dispersal of the Jews, the synagogues, in the cities where they went to live, became temples for the celebration of their cults.

SADDUCEES — Another Jewish sect founded about 24 BC whose name came from Sadoc, its founder. They did not believe in immortality or resurrection, nor in good and bad angels. However, they did believe in God. But as they expected nothing after death, they served Him having in mind only temporary recompenses which, according to them, were limited by Divine Providence. With these thoughts in mind, their main objective in life was the satisfaction of all physical senses. As to the scriptures, they followed the texts of the old laws. They would not accept traditions or any form of interpretation. They put good works and the pure and simple observance of this law before all outward practices of worship. They were, as you see, the materialists, deists and sensualists of their time. The sect had few followers, but amongst them were some important personages and it became a political party constantly in opposition to the Pharisees.

ESSENES — They were a Jewish sect founded about the year 150 BC in the time of the Maccabeans, whose members, living in types of monastries, formed amongst themselves a kind of moral and religious association. They distinguished themselves by their pacific ways and austere virtues, taught the love of God and neighbour, the immortality of the soul, and believed in resurrection. They were celibate, condemned war and slavery, held all their worldly goods in common, and devoted themselves to agriculture. Contrary to the Sadducees, who were very sensual and denied immortality, and the Pharisees of rigid external practices and only apparent virtues, the Essenes never took part in the disputes which caused antagonism between the other two sects. In their way of life they were similar to the first Christians, and the moral principles they professed caused many people to suppose that Jesus had belonged to their community before He began His mission. It is certain that He knew them, but there is nothing to prove that He was related to them, so all that has been written to this effect is simply hypothetical.(1)

THERAPEUTS (From the Greek THÉRAPEUTAY, formed from THÉRAPEUEYN to serve, meaning: servants of God or Healers.) — These were Jewish sectarians and contemporaries of Christ, being mostly established in Alexandria in Egypt. Like the Essenes, whose principles they adopted, they also practiced all the virtues. They were extremely frugal in their eating habits, were celibate, dedicated to meditation, lived solitary lives and constituted a truly religious order. Filon, a platonic Jewish philosopher from Alexandria, was the first to speak of the Therapeuts, whom he considered as a Jewish sect. Eusebius, Saint Jerome and other originators of the Church believed them to be Christians. Whether they were, or whether they were Jewish, the fact remains that, like the Essenes, they represent a link in the union between the Jewish and Christian faiths.

4. SOCRATES AND PLATO, THE FORERUNNERS OF THE CHRISTIAN IDEA AND SPRITISM.

From the mere fact that Jesus knew the Essenes, it is erroneous to conclude that His doctrine was derived from this sect, and that if He had lived in another environment He would have professed other principles. Great ideas have never appeared suddenly. Those founded on truth have always had their predecessors, who partially prepared the path. Later, at the appointed time,

---

(1) THE DEATH OF JESUS, supposedly written by an Essene is an entirely apocryphal work, whose only objective was to serve one opinion. It carries within it the proof of its modern origin.

God sends a man who has the mission of resuming, ordinating, and completing those scattered elements and uniting them into a doctrine. In this way, when the idea arrives it finds Spirits disposed to accept it. This also happened to the Christian idea, which prognosticated many centuries previously, before either Christ or the Essenes, having had Socrates and Plato as its principle predecessors.

Socrates, like Christ, wrote nothing himself, or at least left nothing written. Like Christ, he also suffered the death of a criminal, victim of fanaticism, because he had dared to attack existing beliefs and for having put virtue above hypocrisy and the image of form, in other words, for having combatted religious prejudice. In the same manner as Jesus, Whom the Pharisees accused of corrupting the people by His teaching, Socrates was also accused by the Pharisees of his time, seeing that they have always existed in all epochs, for proclaiming the dogma of the unity of God, the immortality of the soul and the future life. Just as the doctrine of Jesus became known only through the writings of His disciples, so the doctrine of Socrates became known through his disciple Plato.

For these reasons we judge it appropriate to offer a brief summary of the most prominent points of Socrates' teachings in order to show the concordance with the Christian principles. To those who consider this parallel a profanity, claiming there can be no similarity between pagan doctrine and that of Christ, we would say that the teachings of Socrates were not pagan, because he objectively combatted paganism. As to the teachings of Jesus, which are more complete and pure, they have nothing to lose by this comparison as it is impossible to diminish the greatness of Christ's Divine mission, and that for the rest, we are dealing with historical fact which no one can obliterate. Man has now reached a point when the light emerges from beneath the bushel of its own accord, because he has reached sufficient maturity to be able to meet truth face to face, and it will be the worse for those who do not wish to see this. The time has arrived to consider matters in a more ample and evolved manner, not from the point of view of narrow and diffident interests of sects and castes. Moreover, these citations will prove that if Socrates and Plato presented Christian ideas, they also gave us the fundamental principles of Spiritism in their writings.

A SUMMARY OF THE TEACHINGS OF SOCRATES AND PLATO

1. *Man is an incarnate soul. Before his incarnation he existed united to the primordial models, to the ideas of truth, goodness and beauty; then separating from them, he incarnates, and on remembering his past is more or less tormented by the desire to return.*

The independence and distinction between the basic principle of intelligence and those of matter could not be more clearly expressed. Apart from this, it is also the doctrine of pre-existence, of man's vague intuition of another world to which he aspires; of leaving the spirit world in order to incarnate and of his return to the spirit world after death. Finally, it also expressed the doctrine of the fallen angels.

2. The soul becomes perturbed and confused when it uses the body in order to consider any object; it becomes dizzy, as if intoxicated, because it holds on to things which, by their very nature, are subject to change; whereas, when Man contemplates his very essence, he directs himself to that which is pure, eternal and immortal and seeing that his soul is of this nature, he remains joined to this state as long as he can. His perturbations then cease because he is joined to that which is immutable, and this is the state of the soul called wisdom.

Thus, the man who considers things in a down-to-earth fashion is only deceiving himself. To see things in their true perspective he must look upon them from high up, that is to say from the spiritual point of view. Those who are in possession of true wisdom then, must isolate the soul from the body in order to be able to see with the eyes of the Spirit. This is what Spiritism also teaches (see chapter 2, item 5).

3. As long as our physical body and our souls are immersed in this corruption, we can never possess the object of our desire, which is Truth. In fact, the body stirs up thousands of obstacles due to the necessity we have of caring for it. Moreover, it fills us with desires, appetites, doubts, a thousand fancies and foolish things, in such a way that we find it impossible to be sensible, even for an instant. But, if it is not possible to know anything in its entirety while the soul remains joined to the body, either we shall never know the truth, or we shall only know it after death. Freed from the misleading ideas of the body, we hope it will be permissible to talk with men and women who have also been liberated, and so understand for ourselves the essence of things. This is the reason why true philosophers prepare themselves for dying, as death represents nothing to them, and in no way is it to be feared.

Here we have the principles of the faculties of the souls being obscured by the corporeal organs and the expansion of purified souls. This does not happen to impure souls (see HEAVEN & HELL (1) 1st part, chapter 2; & 2nd part, chapter 1).

4. The soul in its impure state finds itself oppressed, and is once again attracted to the visible world by the fear of that which is invisible and immaterial. It is a mistake then, to say that the gloomy ghosts seen round tombs and monuments must be the soul of those who have left their bodies without being absolutely pure, and so still conserve part of their material form, which makes them visible to the human eye. In fact they are not good but bad souls, dragging with them the penalties of their first life, who find themselves forced to wander in such places, where they will continue to wander till their appetites, inherent to the material form with which they are clad, recalls them to another body. Then, beyond doubt, they will return to the same habits which were the object of their preferences during their first life.

_____

(1) by ALLAN KARDEC.

Not only the principle of reincarnation is clearly shown here, but also the state of those souls who maintain themselves under the yoke of matter, as described to us in spiritual communications. Furthermore, it is said that reincarnation in a material body is the consequence of the impureness of the soul, whereas the purified soul finds itself exempt from further reincarnation. This is exactly what Spiritism teaches, only adding that the soul which, having made good resolutions while in the spiritual world and possessing some acquired knowledge, brings less defects, more virtues and intuitive ideas on being reborn than it had in the preceding incarnation. In this way each existence shows both intellectual and moral progress (see HEAVEN & HELL, 2nd part, Examples).

5. After our death the genie (*Daimon, devil*), who had been assigned to us during our life, will take us to a place where all who must go to *Hades*, in order to be judged, are gathered. The souls, after having been in Hades the necessary length of time are then returned to this life, *for long periods and multiple times.*

This is the doctrine of the Guardian Angels or Protecting Spirits, and of successive reincarnations after intervals of varying lengths in the spirit world.

6. Devils occupy the space which separates Heaven from Earth; this constitutes the link which unites the Universe with itself. The Divinity never enters into direct contact with Man, which is done through the mediation of the devils with whom the gods have dealings, and who occupy themselves with him both during waking and sleeping.

In ancient times the word *daimon*, from which the term *evil* was derived, was not used in the bad sense as it is today. Nor was it used exclusively for evil beings, but for Spirits in general within which were included Superior Beings called *gods*, as well as the less elevated, the actual devils, who communicated directly with Man. Spiritism also says that Spirits inhabit space, that God only communicates with Man through the intermediary of pure Spirits who are entrusted to transmit His wishes. Spirits also communicate with Man during sleep as well as while he is awake. If we put the word *Spirit* in place of the word *devil* we have the Spiritist doctrine, and by putting the word *Angel* we have the Christian doctrine.

7. The constant preoccupation of the philosophers (as understood by Socrates and Plato) is to take great care of the soul, less with respect to the present life, which lasts but an instant, but more with respect to eternity. As the soul is immortal, would it not be more prudent to live our lives bearing this fact in mind?

Both Spiritism and the Christian faith teach the same thing.

8. If the soul is immaterial, then after this life it will have to go to a world which is equally invisible and immaterial, the same way as the body decomposes and returns to matter. It is very important, however, to clearly distinguish the pure soul which is truly immaterial and which nourishes itself, as God does, from thoughts and the sciences, from that of the soul which is more or less stained by impurities of a material nature, which impedes elevation to all that is divine and which, in fact, causes it to be retained in its earthly surroundings.

As we can see, both Socrates and Plato understood perfectly the different levels of the dematerialized soul. They insisted on the varieties of situations resulting from its *more* or *less* purified states. What they said though intuition, Spiritism proves by the numerous examples which it places before us (see HEAVEN & HELL, 2nd part).

9. If death meant the complete dissolution of man the bad Spirits would have much to gain from death as they would find themselves at one and the same time free from body, soul and vices. Only those who adorn their soul not with strange ornaments, but with those which are appropriate, may await the hour of their return to the other world with tranquility.

This is equal to saying that materialism, when it proclaims there is nothing after death, annuls all previous moral responsibility, this being consequently an inductive to badness and that badness has everything to gain from nothingness. Only the man who has divested himself of all vice and enriched himself with virtue can await the arousing in the other life with tranquility. By means of examples, which are offered to us daily, Spiritism shows how painful it is for those who are bad to pass over into this other life (see HEAVEN & HELL, 2nd part, chapter 1).

10. The body retains the well-impressed vestiges of the care it received, as well as the marks of all accidents suffered. The same applies to the soul. When it disposes of the body it maintains in evidence the features of its character, its affections, as well as the marks that have been left on it by all the various occurences during its life. Thus, the worst thing that can happen to a man or woman is to return to the other world with his or her soul laden with crimes. You see Calicles, that neither you nor Polux, nor Gorgias, can prove that we should lead a different life that can be useful when we find ourselves on the other side. From so many different opinions the only one which is unshakable is that *it is better to receive than to commit an injustice*, and that, above all else we must be careful not just to seem like, but to actually be men and women of goodness. (Taken from a dialogue between Socrates and his followers when he was in prison.)

Here we are faced with yet another point of capital importance which experience has proved to us: that the soul which is not yet purified retains the ideas, tendencies, character and passions which it had while on Earth. Is not the maxim - *It is better to receive than to commit an injustice* - entirely Christian? Jesus expressed the same thought when He said: "If someone strikes you on the cheek, then offer him the other one too" (see chapter 12, items 7 & 8).

11. One of two things — either death is the absolute destruction or it is the passing of the soul into another place. If everything is extinguished, then death would be like one of those infrequent nights when we do not dream nor have any consciousness of ourselves. However, if death is but a change of habitation, the passageway to the place where the dead must meet, what happiness to find there all those we have known! My greatest pleasure would be to closely examine the inhabitants of this other home and to distinguish there, as we do here, which of those who deem themselves worthy are actually so

considered. But it is time to part, me to my death and you to life (Socrates to his judges).

According to Socrates, those who live upon the Earth meet again after death and recognise each other. Spiritism shows that relationships continue to the extent that death is not an interruption nor the cessation of life, but rather an inevitable transformation without any discontinuity.

If Socrates and Plato had known what Christ was to teach five hundred years later, and which Spiritism now spreads, they would have said exactly the same things. There is nothing surprising in this fact, however, if we consider that all great truths are eternal and all advanced Spirits had to know them before they came to Earth in order to be able to deliver them. We may consider even further that Socrates and Plato, together with all the other great philosophers of those great times, could have later been among those chosen to uphold Christ in His Divine Mission, being chosen precisely because they were more apt to understand His sublime teachings. It also appears highly probable that today they participate in the Host of Spirits charged with teaching mankind these same truths.

12. Never return one injustice with another, nor harm anyone, whatever harm they may have caused to others. Few, however, will admit this principle and those who disagree will, beyond doubt, do nothing but despise one another.

Is this not the principle of charity, which perscribes that we do not return evil for evil and that we forgive our enemies?

13. We know the tree according to its fruit. Every action should be qualified by what it produces: qualified as evil when it causes evil and as goodness when it produces goodness.

The maxim: "It is by the fruits that we know the tree," is repeated many times throughout the Gospel.

14. Riches are a great danger. Every man who loves riches does not love himself, nor those who belong to him (see chapter 16).

15. The most beautiful prayers and the most beautiful sacrifices mean less to God than a virtuous soul who has struggled to be like Him. It has been a grave error to think that the gods dispense more attention to their offerings than to our souls. If that were the case then the greatest culprits would become favoured. But no, the truly just and upright are those who, by their words and deeds, fulfill their duties to the gods and humanity (see chapter 10, items 7 & 8).

16. We call he who loves his body more than his soul, depraved. Love is everywhere in nature and it calls us to use our intelligence; we even find it in the movements of the planets. It is love which covers nature with its richest carpet; it is a decoration and makes its home where there are flowers and perfumes. It is also love which gives peace to mankind, calms the seas, silences the storm and gives sleep to sufferers.

Love, which will unite Man through a fraternal link, is a consequence of Plato's theory on universal love as a Law of Nature. Socrates said: "Love is neither a god nor a mortal, but a great devil," that is, a great Spirit which presides over universal love. This proposition was held against him like a crime.

17. Virtue cannot be taught but comes as a gift from God to those who possess it.

This is almost the Christain doctrine of grace; but if virtue is a gift from God, then it is a favour and we may ask why it is not conceded to all. On the other hand, if it is a gift then there is no merit on the part of those who possess it. Spiritism is more explicit in saying that those who possess a virtue have acquired it through their own efforts during successive lives, by ridding themselves, little by little, of their imperfections. Grace is a force which God gives to a well meaning man or woman so that he or she may expunge their badness and so be able to practise good.

18. The natural disposition shown by all, is to perceive our own defects far less than we see those of others.

The Gospel says: "You see the mote that is in the eye of your neighbour, but you do not see the beam that is in your own eye" (see chapter 10, items 9 & 10).

19. If doctors are unsuccessful in treating the majority of ailments it is because they treat the body without treating the soul. If the whole is not in good condition then it is impossible that part of it should be well.

Spiritism offers the key to the relationship which exists between the soul and the body, so proving that one of them is constantly reacting on the other. This idea opens up a new field for science. With the possibility of showing the real cause of certain ailments, the way of curing them becomes easier. When science takes into account the spiritual element in the organism, then failures will be much less frequent.

20. All men, right from infancy, commit far more badness than goodness.

In this sentence, Socrates touches on the grave question of the predominance of badness on Earth, a question which is insoluble without knowledge of the plurality of worlds and the destiny of our planet Earth, inhabited as it is by only a fraction of humanity. Only Spiritism can resolve this question which is more fully explained further on in chapters 3, 4 & 5.

21. It is more judicious not to suppose you know that of which you are in ignorance.

This is directed at those who offer criticism about matters unknown to them, even in basic terms. Plato completes this thought of Socrates by saying: "In first place, if it is possible, we must make them more honest in their words; if they are not, we shall not bother with them, and we shall seek nothing but the truth. We shall do our best to instruct them, but shall not insult them."

This is how Spiritism should proceed in relation to those who contradict, whether in good or bad faith. If Plato were to come alive today he would find things almost as they were in his time and he would be able to use the same words. Socrates would also meet creatures who would jeer at his belief in Spirits and would believe him to be mad, together with his disciple Plato. It was for having professed these principles that Socrates saw himself ridiculed, accused of impiety and condemned to drink hemlock. So, assuredly, by reason of its controversy stirring up many interests and striking against many prejudices, these great new truths will not be accepted without a fight, nor without making martyrs.

CHAPTER 1

I HAVE NOT COME TO DESTROY THE LAW

The three revelations: Moses, Christ, Spiritism — The
Alliance of science and religion — INSTRUCTIONS FROM
THE SPIRITS: The New Era

1. *Think not that I am come to destroy the law or the prophets: I am not come to destroy, but to fulfill, for verily I say unto you, till Heaven and Earth pass, one jot or one title shall in no wise pass from the law, till all be fulfilled (Matthew, 5: 17 & 18).*

MOSES

2. There are two distinct parts to the Mosaic Law: the Law of God as promulgated on Mount Sinai and the civil or disciplinary law decreed by Moses. The first is invariable; the other, being appropriate to the customs and character of the people, modifies itself with time.

The Law of God is formulated on the following ten commandments:-

I. *I am the Lord thy God, which have brought thee out of the land of Egypt, out of the house of bondage. Thou shalt have no other gods before me. Thou shalt not make unto thee any graven image, or any likeness of anything that is in Heaven above, or that is in the Earth beneath, or that is in the water under the Earth: thou shalt not bow down thyself to them nor serve them (1).*

II. *Thou shalt not take the name of the Lord thy God in vain.*

III. *Remember the Sabbath Day, to keep it Holy.*

IV. *Honour thy father and thy mother, that thy days may be long upon the land which the Lord thy God giveth thee.*

---

(1) Allan Kardec thought fit to quote only the first part of this verse. We would therefore call attention to the great significance of this unquoted section which states that the sins of the fathers will be visited upon the third and fourth generations, according to the original translations, and not the first and second generations as is stated in some of the recent translations.
In fact this is a veiled teaching of reincarnation. By the third or fourth generation the sinner has had time to reincarnate yet again, which logically means that the one who originally sinned will pay his or her own debts. This is far more in keeping with God, Who is all loving and merciful, than the suggestion that He would vent the sins of the fathers on the children who had nothing to do with the matter.
(Translator's note.)

V.   *Thou shalt not kill.*

VI.   *Thou shalt not commit adultery.*

VII.   *Thou shalt not steal.*

VIII.   *Thou shalt not bear false witness against thy neighbour.*

IX.   *Thou shalt not covet thy neighbour's wife.*

X.   *Thou shalt not covet thy neighbour's house, nor his manservant, nor his maidservant, nor his ox nor anything that is thy neighbours.*

This Law is for all times and all countries and because of this has a divine character. All other laws were decreed by Moses, who found it necessary to restrain his people through fear due to their turbulent and undisciplined nature, and also to combat the abuses and prejudices acquired by them during the period of slavery in Egypt. To give authority to his laws, he had to give them divine origin, as did other legislators of primitive peoples. The authority of man needed to base itself on the authority of God. But only the idea of a terrible God could impress ignorant peoples in whom the sentiments of true justice and morality were very little developed. It is evident that He Who included amongst His commandments 'Thou shalt not kill or cause damage to your neighbour' could not then contradict Himself by making extermination a duty.

THE CHRIST

3. Jesus did not come to destroy the Law, that is to say God's Law. He came to fulfill and develop it, to show its real meaning and to adapt it to the degree of Man's advancement at that time. That is why we find within the Law the principle of our duty to God and our fellowmen to be the base of His doctrine. Regarding the laws devised by Moses we find that he, on the contrary, modified them profoundly, both in form and substance. While constantly combating the abuses of exterior practices and false interpretations, he was unable to make the people go through a more radical reform than that of reducing the Law to the order: 'Love God above all things and your neighbour as yourself,' adding *this is all the law and the prophets.*

By the words, 'Heaven and Earth will not pass till everything be fulfilled, even to the last jot,' Jesus wished to say it was necessary for God's Law to be completely implemented and practised over all the Earth in all its pureness, with all its amplifications and consequences. In effect, what use would it have been to promulgate the Law if it were only to benefit one nation or only a few men? Mankind, being sons and daughters of God, is without distinction and so subject to the same solicitude.

4. But Jesus was no mere moralist legislator offering His word as exclusive authority. It fell to Him to complete the prophecies which had announced His advent, by means of the exceptional nature of His Spirit and His divine

mission. Jesus came to teach mankind that true life is not the one lived here on Earth, but rather the life lived in Heaven. He came to show the pathway to this Kingdom, how to be reconciled with God and to present these facts as part of things to come which would enable mankind to fulfill its destiny. However, He did not explain everything, but limited Himself to offering only the initial part of the truth on many subjects, saying that Man as yet could not understand the whole truth. But He talked about all things in implied terms. In order for people to be able to understand the hidden meaning of His words it was necessary for new ideas and knowledge to mature, so bringing the indispensable key, as these things could not appear before the human Spirit had achieved a certain degree of maturity. Science still had to play an important part in the emergence and development of these ideas; therefore it was necessary to give time for science to progress.

SPIRITISM

5. Spiritism is the new science which has come to reveal to mankind, by means of irrefutable proofs, the existence and nature of the spiritual world and its relationship with the physical world. It appears not as something supernatural, but on the contrary, as one of the living and active forces of Nature, source of an immense number of phenomena which still today are not fully understood, and because of this they are relegated to the world of fantasy and miracles. Christ alluded to this situation on several occasions and it is the reason why much of what He said remained unintelligible or has been wrongly interpreted. Spiritism offers the key by which all can easily be explained.

6. The law of the Old Testament was personified in Moses: that of the New Testament in Christ. Spiritism is then the third revelation of God's Law. But it is personified by no one because it represents teaching given, not by Man but by the Spirits who are the *voices of Heaven,* to all parts of the world through the co-operation of innumerable intermediaries. In a manner of speaking, it is the collective work formed by all the Spirits who bring enlightenment to all mankind by offering the means of understanding their world and the destiny that awaits each individual on their return to the spiritual world.

7. Just as Christ said: 'I am not come to destroy the Law but to fulfill it,' so Spiritism says: We have not come to destroy the Christian Law but to carry it out. It teaches nothing contrary to what was taught by Christ. Rather it develops it, explains it in a manner that can be understood by all and completes that which had previously been known only in its allegoric form. Spiritism has come at the predicted time to fulfill what Christ announced and to prepare for the achievement of future things. It is then, the work of Christ Who, as He also announced, presides over the regeneration which is now taking place and which will prepare the reign of the Kingdom of God here on Earth.

THE ALLIANCE BETWEEN SCIENCE AND RELIGION

8. Science and religion are the two levers of human intelligence, one revealing the laws of the material world, the other revealing those of the moral world. *But seeing that these laws have the same principle, which is God,* they cannot contradict themselves. If they contradict one another it would stand to reason that one was right and the other wrong. However, God could not have intended the destruction of His own work. Therefore the incompatibility that apparently exists between these ideas proves that they have been incorrectly interpreted, due to excessive exclusiveness on both sides. For this reason we have a conflict which has given rise to incredulity and intolerance.

We have now reached a phase upon this planet when the teachings of Christ must be completed and the intentional veil cast over some parts of these teachings lifted. A time when science must desist in its exclusive materialism, so taking into consideration the spiritual element; when religion must cease to ignore the organic and immutable law of matter, so that both may become two forces, each leaning on the other and advancing together in mutual concourse. Then religion, no longer discredited by science and no longer being able to oppose the overwhelming logic of the facts, will acquire an unshakable power because it will be in agreement with reason.

Science and Religion could not come together till this time as they could only see matters according to their exclusive points of view, which in turn caused them to be reciprocally repelled. Something more was needed to enable them to close the gap that separated them, something which could unite them. This missing link is contained in the knowledge of the laws which govern the spiritual universe and its relationship with the world of matter. These laws are as immutable as those which govern the movement of the planet and the existence of all beings. Once this relationship could be proved by experiments, a new light would begin to shine as faith began to be directed towards reason, and reason, finding nothing illogical in faith, could finally defeat materialism.

But, as in many other matters, there are always those who remain behind until the general wave of movement towards progress drags them along. If they choose to resist instead of accompanying this movement they will eventually be crushed. So, after an elaboration which has lasted for more than eighteen centuries, a moral revolution is now in progress, operated and directed by Spirit, as humanity reaches the climax of its present potentialities and marches towards a new era. It is easy to forecast the consequences which will cause inevitable changes in social relations and be impossible to withstand, because they are determined by God and derived from the Law of Progress which is God's law.

INSTRUCTIONS FROM THE SPIRITS.
THE NEW ERA

9. God is unique, and Moses was a Spirit whom He sent on a mission to make known His presence, not only to the Hebrews but to all the pagan world. The Hebrew peoples were God's instrument to enable Him to manifest through Moses and the prophets. The vicissitudes suffered by these peoples were meant to attract their attention and so help disclose the existence of the Divinity.

God's commandments as revealed through Moses contain the essence of the most comprehensive Christian morality. However, the biblical commentaries and annotations restrict their meaning, because if they had been put into action in all their pureness they would not have been understood. Nevertheless, these ten commandments have become a brilliant frontispiece and a beacon destined to light up the pathway which humanity must follow.

The morality taught by Moses was appropriate to the state of advancement of the people he proposed to regenerate. These people, who were semi-barbaric with respect to the perfecting of the soul, would not have understood that God could be worshipped by other means than holocaust, nor that it is necessary to forgive one's enemies. From the materialistic, scientific and artistic points of view their intelligence was remarkable. But they were morally backward and would never have been converted by a wholly spiritual religion. Therefore it was necesssry that they be offered a semi-materialistic form of religion, as is represented in the Hebrew faith. The holocausts spoke to their senses at the same time that the idea of God touched their Spirits.

Christ was the initiator of the most pure and sublime morality. That is to say, the morality of the evangelical Christian, which will renew the entire world by bringing together all mankind and turning them into brothers and sisters. It will cause charity to blossom forth in all hearts as well as love for one's neighbour, so establishing a common solidarity between all peoples. Finally, from this morality, which will transform the whole Earth, the planet will become the home of far superior Spirits than inhabit it till now. This is the law of progress which will be accomplished and to which nature is submitted. Spiritism is the lever which God is using to enable humanity to advance.

The time has come in which moral ideas must be developed to bring about the progress determined by God. They will follow the same route as that taken by the ideas of liberty, its predecessor. Do not think however, that these developments will be effected without a fight. No, in order to reach maturity these ideas will need discussion and conflicts so that they may attract the attention of the masses. Once this has been achieved, the beauty and sanctity of this morality will touch all Spirits, who will in turn embrace a science which will give them the key to a future life and open the doors to eternal happiness.

Moses showed humanity the way; Jesus continued this work; Spiritism will finish it. — AN ISRAELITE SPIRIT (Mulhouse, 1861).

10. Once, in His undying charity, God permitted Man to see the truth pierce the darkness. That day was the advent of Christ. After that living Light was gone the darkness returned; having been given the alternatives of truth or obscurity the world once again lost itself. Then, similar to the prophets of the Old Testament, the Spirits began to speak and finally gave warning that the world is trembling on its very foundations and thunder will resound. Remain steady!

Spiritism is of a divine order because it is based upon the actual laws of Nature, and you may be certain that everything of a divine nature has a great and useful objective. Your world was losing itself yet again because science, developed at the cost of all that is moral, was only inducing you to material well being, resulting in benefit for the Spirit of darkness. Ah! Eighteen centuries of blood and martyrs, and still Christ's reign has not yet come! Christians! Return to the Teacher who wishes to save you! It is easy for those who believe and who love. Love fills one with indescribable happiness. Yes, my children, the world is shaking as the good Spirits have repeatedly warned. Bend with the wind that announces the storm, so that you are not thrown down. That is to say, prepare yourselves so as not to be like the foolish virgins who were taken by surprise at the arrival of their husbands!

This revolution which prepares itself is more moral than material. The great Spirits, who are divine messengers, instill faith amongst you so that all who are enlightened and zealous workers may make their humble voices heard, seeing that all humanity are like grains of sand, without which there would be no mountains. Thus the words: 'We are small' lack significance. To each his mission, to each his work. Does not the ant build his republic, and other imperceptible animals raise continents? The new crusade has begun. Apostles, not of war, but of universal peace, modern Saint Bernards, look ahead and march forward. The law of the worlds is a law of progress. — FENELON (Poitiers, 1861).

11. Saint Augustin is one of the greatest popularizers of Spiritism. He has manifested himself in almost every part. The reason for this is to be found in the life story of this great Christian philosopher. He belongs to a vigorous phalanx known as Fathers of the church, to whom Christianity owes its most solid bases. Like many others he was uprooted from Paganism, or rather from the most profound godlessness, by the splendor of truth. When suddenly, in the middle of his dissipations, he felt a strange vibration in his soul which called him to himself and made him understand that happiness was not to be found in debilitating and escapist pleasures. Finally he too had a similar experience to Paul, who heard saintly voices calling to him on the road to Damascus saying: 'Saul, Saul, why do you persecute me?' When Saint Augustin heard his voices he exclaimed: 'My God! My God! Forgive me! I believe; I am a Christian!' From this moment on he became one of the greatest

supporters of the Gospel. You may read the notable confessions left by this eminent Spirit, the characterisitic and prophetic words he uttered after the death of Saint Monica, '*I am convinced that my mother will visit me and give me advice, revealing to me what awaits us in the future life.*' What great teaching in these words! What resounding foresight of the doctrine that was to come! This is the reason why today, seeing that the time has come to spread the truth as he predicted, he has become its ardent disseminator and as it were, multiplied himself in order to be able to reply to all who call him. — ERASTUS, disciple of Saint Paul (Paris 1863).

NOTE: Would it be possible for Saint Augustin to demolish what he himself had built? Certainly not. But just as many others before him, he now sees with the eye of Spirit what he could not see while he was a man. In freedom his soul sees new brightness and understands what previously had been impossible to understand. New ideas have revealed to him the true meaning of certain words. On Earth he judged things according to the knowledge he possessed at that time. But ever since he saw the new light he can appreciate those words more judiciously. Thus he had to revise his beliefs regarding incubus and sucubus spirits, as well as the condemnation which he had launched against the theory of the antipodes. Now that he can see Christianity in its true light and in all its pureness, it is acceptable that on some points he thinks differently from when he was alive, which in no way prohibits him from continuing to be a Christian apostle. He may even establish himself as a disseminator of Spiritism without renouncing his faith, because he has seen that which was forecast come to pass. Therefore, by proclaiming this doctrine today, he only leads us towards a more correct and logical interpretation of the texts. The same also occurs with other Spirits who find themselves in a similar position.

CHAPTER 2

MY KINGDOM IS NOT OF THIS WORLD

The future life. — The regality of Jesus. — A point of view. —
INSTRUCTIONS FROM THE SPIRITS. An earthly regality.

1. *Then Pilate entered into the judgement hall again, and called Jesus, and said unto him, Art thou the king of the Jews? Jesus answered, My Kingdom is not of this world. If my Kingdom were of this world, then would my servants fight, that I should not be delivered to the Jews: but now is my Kingdom not from hence.*

Pilate therefore said unto him, Art thou a king then? Jesus answered, Thou sayest that I am a king. To this end was I born, and for this cause came I into the world, that I should bear witness unto the truth. Every one that is of the truth heareth my voice (John, 18: 33, 36 & 37).

THE FUTURE LIFE

2. With these words Jesus clearly refers to a *future life,* which He presents in all circumstances as the goal which humanity must reach and which should constitute Man's greatest preoccupation here on Earth. All of his maxims refer to this great principle. Indeed, without a future life there would be no reason to have the majority of these moral precepts. This is why those who do not believe in a future life cannot understand or think the matter foolish, because they imagine that Jesus was only speaking of the present life.

This doctrine can therefore be considered as the basis of Christ's teaching. Therefore it has been placed as the first item in this work. It must be the point to be most closely looked at, as it is the only one that justifies the anomalies and irregularities of earthly life and also shows itself to be in accordance with the justice of God.

3. The Jews had only very vague ideas as to the future life. They believed in angels, whom they considered to be privileged beings of the creation; they did not know, however, that men and women could one day become angels and so participate in the same happiness. According to them the observance of God's Law would bring worldly recompense, the supremacy of their nation and victory over their enemies. The public calamities and downfalls were a punishment for disobedience to these laws. Moses could say no more than this to those who were mostly shepherds or ignorant people who needed to be

touched, before anything else, by worldly things. Later, Jesus revealed that there existed another world where God's justice follows its course. This is the world He promises to all those who obey the commandments of God and where the good find recompense. This is His kingdom, where He will be found in all His glory and to which He returned when He left Earth.

However, when adapting His teachings to the conditions of humanity at that time, Jesus did not consider it convenient to give them all the truth, for He saw they would only be dazzled by it and unable to understand. So He limited Himself, in a manner of speaking, to the presentation of a future life as a principle, as a natural law whose action no one could escape. Therefore every Christian firmly believes in a future life. But the idea that many hold is still vague, incomplete, and because of this, quite false on various points. For the majority of people it is nothing more than a belief, void of absolute certainty, so this is why there are doubts and even incredulity.

Spiritism has come to complete this point, as well as many others touched on by the teachings of Christ, now that Man is sufficiently mature as to be able to learn the truth. With Spiritism a future life is no longer an article of faith, a mere hypothesis, but becomes a material reality as facts demonstrate, because those who have described it to us have all been eye witnesses, so that not only is doubt no longer possible, but also anyone of whatever intelligence is able to get an idea of its many varied aspects, in the same way that we can imagine what a country we have never visited is like by reading a detailed description of it. But this description of the future life is circumstanciated to such an extent, the conditions of existence for those who reside there, be they happy or unhappy, are so rational that we are bound to agree that it could not be otherwise, that it represents the true justice of God.

THE REGALITY OF JESUS

4. We can all recognise that the Kingdom of Jesus is not of this world. But could He not also have a kingdom on Earth? The title of 'King' does not always imply temporary authority. We give this title by unanimous consent to anyone who, by their own talent, rises to the highest level of whatever idea, who dominates his time or influences human progress. In this way we frequently use the expression the 'king' or 'prince' for philosophers, artists, poets, writers, etc. Does not this kind of royalty, coming from personal merit or having been consecrated by posterity, reveal in many cases a supremacy far greater than that which circles a royal crown? The first is imperishable, whereas the second is but a toy of the vicissitudes. The generations which follow the first always bless themselves, whereas sometimes those who follow the second have cause to curse. The earthly one extinguishes with life; but the sovereignty of morality continues and maintains its reign, ruling above all after death. From this aspect then, is not Jesus a mightier and more powerful King than all the sovereigns of the Earth? It was with good reason then that He said to Pilate: "I am a King, but my Kingdom is not of this world".

A POINT OF VIEW

5. The clear and precise idea which can be formed of a future life provides an unshakable faith in what is to come. This faith places enormous consequences upon the moralization of Man because it completely changes *the point of view as to how life on Earth is regarded.* For those who place themselves by means of thought in the spiritual life, which is undefined, bodily life becomes a mere temporary stay in an ungrateful country. The vicissitudes and tribulations of this life become nothing more than incidents, which can be supported with patience as they are known to be of short duration and will be followed by a more amenable state. Death no longer has terror attached to it; it ceases to be a door opening on to nothingness and becomes a door that opens to liberation, through which the exile enters into a well-blessed mansion, and there finds peace. Knowing that the place where we find ourselves at the moment is only temporary and not definite, makes us pay less attention to the preoccupations of life, resulting in less bitterness and a more peaceful Spirit.

Simply by doubting the existence of a future life, Man directs all his thoughts to earthly existence. Without any certainty of what is to come he gives everything to the present. With the mistaken idea that there is nothing more precious than earthly things, Man behaves as a child who can see only its toys and is prepared to go to any length to obtain the only possessions he judges to be solid. The loss of even the least of these causes pungent hurt. A mistake, a deception, an unsatisfied ambition, an injustice to which the person has fallen victim, hurt pride or vanity, to name but a few, are just some of the torments which turn existence into an eternal agony, so in this manner causing *self-inflicted torture at every step.* From the point of view of earthly life, in whose centre we place ourselves, everything around us begins to assume vast proportions. The harm that reaches us, as well as the good that touches others, takes on a great importance in our eyes. It is like the man, who, when in the middle of a great city sees everything on a large scale, but who, when looking down from a mountain top sees things in only minute form.

This is what happens when we look at life from the point of view of a future existence. Humanity, just as the stars in space, loses itself in the great immensity. We begin to see that great and small things are confounded, as ants on top of an ant hill, that proletarians and potentates are the same stature. We lament that so many short-lived creatures give themselves over to so much labour in order to conquer a place which will do so little to elevate them, and which they will occupy for so short a time. From this it follows that the value given to earthly things is completely in reverse to that which comes from a firm belief in a future life.

6. If everybody thought in that manner, it could be argued that everything on Earth would be endangered because no one would bother about anything. But Man instinctively looks after his own well-being, so even if he knew it was but

for a short while, he would still do his best. There is no one who, when finding a thorn in his hand, will not take it out so as not to suffer. Well then, the desire for comfort forces Man to better all things, seeing that he is impelled by the instinct of progress and conservation which are part of the Laws of Nature. Therefore, he works not only through necessity but because he wants to, and because of a sense of duty, so obeying the designs of Providence which placed him on Earth for that purpose. Only a person who occupies themself more with the future can give relative importance to the present. This person is easily consoled in all his failings and misfortunes by thinking of the destiny that awaits him.

Accordingly, God does not condemn all earthly pleasures and possessions, but only condemns the abuse of these things in detriment to the soul. All those who take these words of Jesus for themselves: *My Kingdom is not of this world,* are guarding against these abuses.

Those who identify themselves with a future life are as a rich person who loses a small sum without emotion. Those whose thoughts are concentrated on earthly things are as the poor man who loses all he has, and so becomes desperate.

7. Spiritism opens up and broadens out the thought process, so offering new horizons. In place of a short-sighted vision concentrated only on the present, which makes this fleeting moment passed on Earth the unique and fragile axis of the eternal future; Spiritism shows us that this life is nothing more than a link in the magnificent, harmonious assembly which is God's work. It also shows us the solidarity which joins together all the different existences of one being, of all beings of the same world, and all the beings of all the worlds. It offers the base and the reason for universal fraternity, whereas the doctrine of the creation of the soul at the birth of the body, makes each creature a stranger one to the other. This solidarity between parts of a whole explains what is inexplicable when only one of these parts is considered. This entirety would not have been possible to understand at the time of Christ, and for this reason He waited till later to make this knowledge known.

INSTRUCTIONS FROM THE SPIRITS.
AN EARTHLY REGALITY

8. Who better than I to understand the truth of these words of Our Lord: "My Kingdom is not of this world"? When on Earth, I lost myself through pride. Who then can understand the total lack of value of the earthly kingdom if not I? What was I able to bring with me of my earthly regality? Nothing! Absolutely nothing! And as if to make my lesson more terrible, it did not even accompany me to my tomb! A queen amongst men, I thought to enter Heaven as a queen. What a disillusion! What a humiliation when, instead of being received as a sovereign, I saw above me, a long way above me, those whom I had judged insignificant and whom I had despised because they were not of noble blood.

Oh! How I understand now the barrenness of honours and splendour so eagerly courted on Earth!

In order to win a place in this Kingdom it is necessary to show abnegation, humility, benevolence and charity in its most celestial form. They do not ask who you are, nor what position you occupied. Instead they ask what good you have done, how many tears you have dried.

Oh Jesus! You said that Your Kingdom was not of this world because it is necessary to suffer in order to reach Heaven; and one cannot reach there by means of the steps to a throne. Only the most painful paths lead one to it. Seek your path then, through briars and thorns and not amongst the flowers.

Men and women hurry to and fro with the hope of acquiring earthly possessions, as if they would be able to keep them for ever. Here however, illusions disappear and it is soon perceived that they had only been chasing shadows. Then it becomes apparent that the only really golden possessions, the only ones which can be made use of in their Heavenly home, the only ones which can offer the possibility of entry, have been despised.

Have pity on those who have not entered into Heaven. Help them with your prayers, because prayer helps mankind approach the Most High; it is what links Heaven and Earth. Do not forget! — A QUEEN OF FRANCE (Havre, 1863).

CHAPTER 3

IN MY FATHER'S HOUSE ARE MANY MANSIONS

The different states of the soul in its spiritual wanderings. —
The different categories of inhabited worlds. — Earth's
destiny. — The cause of earthly miseries. — INSTRUCTIONS
FROM THE SPIRITS: Superior and inferior worlds. —
Worlds of tests and atonement. — Regenerating worlds. —The
progression of the worlds.

1. *Let not your heart be troubled: Ye believe in God, believe also in me. In my Father's house are many mansions: If it were not so, I would have told you. I go to prepare a place for you. And if I go and prepare a place for you, I will come again, and receive you unto myself; that where I am, there ye may be also (John, 14: 1-3).*

THE DIFFERENT STATES OF THE SOUL IN ITS SPIRITUAL WANDERINGS

2. The house of the Father is the Universe. The 'different mansions' are the worlds which circulate in infinite space and offer the Spirits who incarnate on them dwelling places which correspond to their progress.

Independently from the diversity of the different worlds, the words of Jesus also refer to the fortunate or wretched states of the soul in the spirit world. Conforming to whether the soul is more or less purified and detached from material ties, the ambient in which it finds itself will vary infinietly: in the aspects of things, in the sensations it feels and in the perceptions it has. While some cannot leave the ambient where they live, others raise themselves and travel all over space and the other worlds. While some guilty Spirits wander in darkness, there are others who have earned happiness, and these rejoice in a state of shining brightness while they contemplate the sublime spectacle of the great infinity. Finally, while inferior Spirits are tormented by remorse and grief, frequently isolated without consolation, separated from those who were the object of their affections and punished by the iron gauntlet of moral suffering, the just Spirit, together with those he loves, enjoys the delights of an indescribable happiness. Also in that sense there are many mansions, although they are not circumscript or localised.

THE DIFFERENT CATEGORIES OF INHABITED WORLDS

3. As a result of Spirit teaching, we know that the conditions of the various worlds differ one from the other, with respect to the degree of elevation or inferiority of their inhabitants, amongst whom are those inferior to the inhabitants of Earth, both physically and morally; some in the same category, yet others which are more or less superior in every aspect. In the inferior worlds, existence is all material, passions are sovereign and morality is almost nil. At the same time as the soul is progressing the material influences diminish, to such an extent that in the elevated worlds life is, by way of saying, all spiritual.

4. In the intermediate worlds good is mixed with evil, one or the other predominating according to the degree of advancement of the majority of the inhabitants. Although it is not possible to make an absolute classification of the different worlds, we can at least divide them in general terms by virtue of the state in which they are in, and the destiny they bring with them, based on the most predominant features upon each planet in the following manner: primitive worlds, destined to receive the initial incarnations of the human soul; worlds of tests and atonements, where evil predominates; regenerating worlds, where souls who still have to atone may absorb new strength by resting from the fatigue of fighting; blessed worlds, where goodness outweighs evil; celestial or divine worlds, inhabited by purified Spirits, where only goodness exists. Earth belongs to the category of worlds of tests and atonements, which is why mankind lives encompassed by such misery.

5. Spirits who find themselves incarnated in any world are not bound to that same world indefinitely, nor do they go through all the phases of progress needed to achieve perfection in that one world. When they reach the maximum degree of advancement their world has to offer, they then pass on to a more elevated one, and so on successively till they reach the state of purified Spirits. These different worlds are stations where the Spirits find the elements they need for their progress that are in accordance to their degree of perfection. It is a recompense to ascend to a world of higher elevation, just as it is a punishment to prolong their stay in a miserable world, or to be relegated to another even more unhappy than the one they were forced to leave, due to persisting badness.

EARTH'S DESTINY. CAUSES OF HUMAN MISERY

6. Many are surprised that on Earth there is so much badness, so many crude passions, so many miseries and every kind of sickness. From this, they conclude, the human species is a very miserable one. This judgement comes from the very narrow point of view of those who emit it, which gives a false idea of the whole. We must consider, however, that in actual fact, the entirety of humanity is not all on Earth, but only a small fraction of the total. In effect, the

human species covers all those endowed with reason who inhabit the innumerable orbs of the Universe. What then is the mere population of the Earth when compared with the total population of all the worlds? Much less than that of a very small village when compared with a great empire. The material and moral situation of terrestrial humanity is not surprising, when we take into consideration the destiny of the Earth and the nature of its inhabitants.

7. It would be a great mistake to judge all the inhabitants of a city by those who inhabit the lowest and most sordid places. In a hospital we see none but the sick and mutilated; in a prison we find gathered together all kinds of vileness, baseness and many vices; in unhealthy regions the inhabitants are, for the most part, pale, puny and sickly. Well then, picture the Earth as a combination of a suburb, a hospital, and an unhealthy place, because it is all of these put together. Then it can be understood why afflictions outweigh pleasures, for we do not send those who are healthy to hospital, nor do we throw those who have practised no wrong into houses of correction; neither can hospitals and houses of correction be places of delight.

So in the same way that the total population of a city is not to be found in its hospitals and prisons, we do not find the total population of humanity here on Earth. Just as the sick leave hospital when they are cured and those who have served their term leave prison, when Man is cured of all his moral infirmities he will also leave the Earth environment to go to happier worlds.

INSTRUCTIONS FROM THE SPIRITS.
INFERIOR AND SUPERIOR WORLDS

8. In qualifying inferior and superior worlds there is nothing absolute. A world is relatively inferior or superior only in relation to those other worlds which may be above or below it on the scale of progression.

In taking the Earth as a comparison, we may get an idea of what an inferior world is like by supposing its inhabitants to be similar to the primitive races or members of the barbaric nations, examples of which are still to be found amongst us today, these being the remnants of the primitive state of this planet. In the most backward worlds the inhabitants are, to a certain extent, rudimentary creatures, having human form but devoid of all beauty. Their instincts have not yet softened to any sentiment of delicacy or benevolence, nor have they acquired any notions of justice or injustice. Brute force is the only known law. Without either industry or inventions, they pass their time in conquest of food. However, God does not abandon even one of His creatures; at the bottom of the darkest intelligence lurkes a seed, sometimes more, sometimes less developed, of a vague intuition of a supreme Being. This instinct is enough to make them superior one from the other and to prepare their ascension to a more complete life, for they are not degraded beings, but children who are growing.

In between the inferior and elevated levels are innumerable others. From the pure Spirits, dematerialised and brilliant with glory, it is impossible to recognise the primitive beings they once were, just as from the adult it is difficult to recognise the embryo.

9. In worlds which have reached a superior level, the moral and material state is very different from that which exists on Earth. As everwhere, the form is always human, but it is more beautiful, more perfected and above all else, purified. The body possesses nothing of the earthly materiality and consequently is not subject to the same necessities, sicknesses or deteriorations which the predominance of matter provokes. Due to the higher refinements, the senses are able to capture perceptions which the gross matter of this world obstructs. The specific lightness of body permits rapid and easy locomotion; instead of dragging painfully over the ground the body floats, as it were, above the surface or glides through the air with no effort apart from that of desire, just as the angels are depicted as doing, or as the manes on the Elysian fields. According to his wishes Man keeps the features of his past migrations and shows himself to his friends as they knew him, except for the fact that he now radiates divine light, and is transfigured by interior impressions which are always of an elevated nature. In the place of countenances discoloured and dejected by suffering and passions, life and intelligence sparkle with splendour which painters have shown through the halo or aureole of the saints.

Very advanced Spirits suffer only slight resistance to matter, thus allowing body development to be extremely rapid, making infancy short and almost non-existent. With the absence of worry and anguish, life is proportionally longer than on Earth. In principle, longevity is in proportion to the degree of advancement of each world. Death in no way conveys any horror of decomposition; far from causing terror, it is considered a happy transformation because there is no doubt as to the future. During life the soul, being no longer constricted by compact matter, expands itself and delights in a lucidity which places it in an almost constant state of emancipation and allows completely free thought transmission.

10. In these blissful worlds relationships between peoples and individuals are always friendly, never perturbed by ambition to enslave their neighbour or make war. There are no masters nor slaves, none privileged by birth, only moral and intellectual superiority which establishes all conditions and which ultimately gives supremacy. Authority receives and deserves the respect of everyone, as it is only given to those who merit it and is therefore always exercised with justice. *Man does not try to elevate himself above another but only above himself, by striving for perfection.* His objective is to ascend to the category of pure Spirit, although this desire is never a torment but rather a noble ambition which induces him to study ardently in order to become an equal. In these worlds, all the delicate and elevated sentiments of human nature find themselves exalted and purified. Hate is unknown, as are petty

jealousies and the covetous of envy. The ties of love and brotherhood bind all humanity each to the other so that the strong help the weak. Through a greater or lesser degree of intelligence, Man acquires possessions of a smaller or larger quantity. However, nobody suffers from want as no one needs to make atonement. In short, evil does not exist in these worlds.

11. Evil is still needed in your world in order to make known goodness; night in order to be able to admire light; sickness so as to be able to appreciate health. In those other worlds there is no need of these contrasts; eternal light, eternal beauty and eternal serenity of the soul offer proportional eternal happiness, free from the perturbations caused by the anguish of material life and the contact with evil creatures, who find no access to these realms. These are the things which cause the human Spirit most difficulty in understanding. Mankind has been sufficiently ingenious as to paint the torments of hell, but could never imagine the glories of Heaven. Why not? Because, being inferior, only pain and misery have been known and as yet the celestial brightness has never been seen, so one cannot speak of that which is unknown. However, while humanity is raising itself up and cleansing its soul, horizons are expanding and mankind begins to compare the goodness which is in front of him, as well as the badness which is behind him.

12. Meanwhile, the happy worlds are not specifically privileged orbs, as God is not partial to any one of His children. To each one He gives the same rights and the same opportunities wherein to reach these worlds. He makes each one start at the same point and gives no one more than another. Even the highest categories are accessible to all. It only depends upon the individual to conquer their place by means of work, so reaching it more quickly or remaining inactive for centuries and centuries in the quagmire of humanity. *(This is a summary of the teachings from all the Superior Spirits.)*

WORLDS OF TESTS AND ATONEMENTS

13. What more is there to say about worlds of atonements that you don't already know, since you have only to look at the one in which you live? The great number of superior intelligences amongst your inhabitants indicates that the Earth is not a primitive world, destined to receive beings who have recently left the hand of the Creator. The innate qualities which they bring with them constitute a proof of their having already lived and achieved a certain degree of progress. But the number of vices to which they are subject also shows their great moral imperfections. This is why God has placed them in an ungrateful world, in which they can make atonement through heavy work and the suffering of the miseries of life, until they deserve to ascend to happier planets.

14. Nevertheless, not all the Spirits who have incarnated on Earth came to atone. The races which are called savage were formed from Spirits who had only just left their infancy, and who found themselves, as it were, on an

educational course for development through contact with more advanced Spirits. Later came the semi-civilized races, made up of the same Spirits as they travelled along their paths to progress. In general, these are the indiginous races on Earth, who will raise themselves little by little through the centuries, some of whom have already managed to reach an intelligent state equal to the more enlightened.

The Spirits who are in atonement are, if we may use the term, the exotic ones of the Earth; they have already lived on other worlds where they were excluded for persisting in wickedness, or for having been the cause of perturbation to the good people in those worlds. They therefore had to be exiled for a time to an ambient of more backward Spirits, so receiving the mission of helping them to advance as they bring with them more developed intelligences and the germ of the knowledge they have acquired. This then is how Spirits under punishment are found amongst the most intelligent races, and why the misfortunes of life seem so very bitter for them. This is because they have a higher degree of sensitivity and so are more highly tested by contrarieties and sorrows than the primitive races whose moral sense is still obtuse.

15. Consequently, the Earth offers an example of a world of atonement and although the variety is infinite, they all have one thing in common: they all serve as places of exile for those Spirits who rebel against the Law of God. This means that these Spirits have at one and the same time to fight against the perversity of man and the inclemency of nature, which is doubly arduous, but which will develop the qualities of heart and intelligence simultaneously. God then, in all His goodness, allows punishment to become something which will benefit the spirit. — SAINT AUGUSTIN (Paris, 1862)

REGENERATING WORLDS

16. Among the many scintillating stars in the blue canopy of the sky, how many worlds there are like yours, destined by God to serve for atonement and probation! But although there are some that are more miserable, there are also others that are happier, like those of transition which can be called worlds of regeneration. Each planetary vortex, moving in space round a common centre, drags with it its own primitive worlds of exile, probation, regeneration and happiness. We have spoken to you of worlds where newly-born Spirits are placed, when they are still ignorant of both good and evil, but where they have the possibility of travelling towards God, being in possession of themselves through free-will. We have also revealed to you the fact that ample faculties are given to each soul to enable it to practise good. But alas, there are those who succumb! So God, Who does not desire their annihilation, permits that they go to these worlds where from one incarnation to another they are purified and regenerated, returning worthy of the glory for which they were destined.

17. Regenerating worlds serve as transition phases between those of probation and happiness. The penitent soul finds calm and rest on them and can continue the purifying process. Beyond doubt, Man still finds himself subject to the laws that rule matter: humanity still experiences your sensations and desires, but is liberated from the ungoverned passions to which you are slaves, freed from pride which silences the heart, envy which tortures and hate which suffocates. On all sides the word 'love' is written; perfect equity resides over all social relationships; everyone recognises God and tries to travel in His direction by fulfilling His laws.

However, perfect happiness still does not exist in these worlds, only the dawning of happiness. There Man is still of flesh and blood, and because of this subject to vissicitudes from which only the completely dematerialized beings are liberated. He still has to suffer tests, although without the pungent anguishes of atonement. Compared to the Earth, these worlds are very pleasant, and many of you would be happy to inhabit them because they represent the calm after the storm, convalescence after cruel sickness. Nevertheless, being less absorbed by material things, Man perceives the future better, comprehends the existence of other pleasures, promised by God to those who show themselves worthy when death has once again released them from their bodies in order to bestow upon them the true life. Free then, the soul hovers above all the horizons; no longer the feelings of gross matter, only the sensation of a pure and celestial perispirit absorbing emanations direct from God, in the fragrance of love and charity coming straight from His breast.

18. But alas! Man is still fallible even in these worlds and the spirit of evil has not completely lost its empire. Not to advance is to fall back, and if Man is not firmly placed along the pathway to righteousness he may return again to a world of atonement where new and more terrible tests await.

So at night, at the time of prayer and repose, contemplate the full canopy of the sky and the innumerable spheres which shine over your head, and ask yourself which ones lead to God and ask Him for one of these regenerating worlds to open to receive you after your atonement here on Earth. — SAINT AUGUSTIN (Paris, 1862).

THE PROGRESSION OF THE WORLDS

19. Progress is a law of nature. All beings of creation, be they animated or not, have been submitted to this law through the bounty of God, Who wishes everything to be exalted and to prosper. Even actual destruction, which appears to Man to be the end of everything, is only a means of reaching a more perfect state through transformation, seeing that everything dies only to be reborn again, suffering no consequences from the annihilation.

At the same time as living beings progress morally, so the worlds in which they live progress materially. If we were to accompany a world during its different phases, from the first instant the atoms destined to its construction began to agglomerate, we would see it travelling along on a constantly progressive scale, although these steps would be imperceptible to each generation. It would offer its inhabitants a more agreeable home as these generations passed, according to the manner in which they themsevles advanced along their pathway to progress. Nothing in nature remains stationary. So we find that together with Man, the animals who are his helpers, the vegetables, and the habitations are all constantly marching along parallel to one another. How glorious this idea is and so worthy of the grandeur of the Creator! It would be paltry and unworthy of His power if, on the contrary, He concentrated His solicitude and providence on an insignificant grain of sand, which is this planet, so restricting humanity to the few people who inhabit it!

According to this law, the world has been in a materially and morally inferior position to that which it finds itself today, and it will lift itself up in both these aspects so as to reach a more elevated degree in the future. The time has now been reached for one of these periodic transformations, which will move the Earth upwards from a world of atonement to that of a regenerating planet where men will be happy because God's laws will reign. — SAINT AUGUSTIN (Paris, 1862).

CHAPTER 4

EXCEPT A MAN BE BORN AGAIN HE CANNOT SEE THE KINGDOM OF GOD

Resurrection and reincarnation. — Reincarnation strengthens
family ties, whereas a single life would destroy them. —
INSTRUCTIONS FROM THE SPIRITS: Limits of incarnations.
— The need for incarnation.

1. *When Jesus came into the coasts of Ceasaria Philippi, He asked His disciples saying, whom do men say that I the Son of man am? And they said, some say that thou art John the Baptist: some, Elias: and others Jeremias, or one of the prophets. He saith unto them, but whom say ye that I am? And Simon Peter answered and said, thou art the Christ, the Son of the living God. And Jesus answered and said unto him blessed art thou, Simon Barjona: for the flesh and blood hath not revealed it unto thee, but my Father which is in Heaven (Matthew, 16: 13-17; Mark, 8: 27-30).*

2. *Now Herod the Tetrarch heard of all that was done by Him; and he was perplexed, because that it was said of some, that John was risen from the dead; and some, that Elias had appeared; and others, that one of the old prophets was risen again. And Herod said, John have I beheaded; but who is this, of whom I hear such things? And he desired to see Him (Luke, 9: 7-9; Mark, 6: 14-15).*

3. *(After the transfiguration) And His disciples asked Him, saying, why then say the scribes that Elias must first come? And Jesus answered and said unto them, Elias truly shall first come, and restore all things. But I say unto you, That Elias is come already, and they knew him not, but have done unto him whatsoever they listed. Likewise shall also the Son of Man suffer of them. Then the discipes understood that He spake unto them of John the Baptist (Matthew, 17: 10-13; Mark, 9: 11-13).*

RESURRECTION AND REINCARNATION

4. Reincarnation was part of the Jewish dogmas, being taught under the name of *resurrection*. Only the Sadducees, who believed that everything ended with death, did not accept the idea of reincarnation. Jewish ideas on this point, as on many others, were not clearly defined because they had only vague and incomplete notions with regard to the soul and its connection with the body.

They believed that man could live again without knowing exactly the manner by which this could happen. They used the name *resurrection* for what Spiritism more correctly calls *reincarnation.* Resurrection presupposes a return to the same physical body, whereas science demonstrates that this is materially impossible, especially when that same body has decomposed and long since been dispersed and reabsorbed. *Reincarnation* is the return of a soul, or Spirit, to physical life in another body which has been newly formed for it, and which has nothing to do with the previous one. The word 'resurrection' can be applied to Lazarus but not to Elias, nor to the other prophets. If, according to their belief, John the Baptist was Elias, then the body of John could not have been the body of Elias because John was seen as a child and his parents were known. John then could be Elias reincarnated but not resurrected.

5. *There was a man of the Pharisees, named Nicodemus, a ruler of the Jews: the same came to Jesus by night, and said unto Him, Rabbi, we know that thou art a teacher come from God: for no man can do these miracles that Thou doest, except God be with him. Jesus answered and said unto him, Verily, verily, I say unto thee, except a man be born again, he cannot see the Kingdom of God. Nicodemus saith unto Him, How can a man be born when he is old? Can he enter the second time into his mother's womb, and be born?*

Jesus answered, Verily, verily, I say unto thee, except a man be born of water and of the Spirit, he cannot enter into the Kingdom of God. That which is born of the flesh is flesh; and that which is born of the Spirit is spirit. Marvel not that I said unto thee, Ye must be born again. The wind bloweth where it listeth, and thou hearest the sound thereof, but canst not tell whence it cometh, and wither it goeth; so is everyone that is born of the Spirit. Nicodemus answered and said unto Him, How can these things be? Jesus answered and said unto him, Art thou a master of Israel, and knowest not these things? Verily, verily, I say unto you, We speak that we do know, and testify that we have seen: and ye receive not our witness. If I have told you earthly things, and ye believe not, how shall ye believe, if I tell you of heavenly things? (John, 3: 1-12).

6. The idea that John had been Elias and that the prophets could relive again on Earth is to be found in many passages of the New Testament, but is most notedly quoted in the above extract. (See verses 1, 2, & 3.) If this was an erroneous belief, Jesus would have combated it as He did many others. But from this He gave it complete sanction and authority by making it a basic principle and necessary condition by saying: 'No one may reach the Kingdom of God if he is not born again,' and further insisted when He added: *'Do not be surprised when I say it is necessary to be born again.'*

7. The words: *If man is not born again of water and of Spirit,* have been interpreted in the sense of regeneration by means of the water of Baptism. But in the original text it was said simply: *not born of water and of Spirit,* whereas in some translations the words *of spirit* have been substituted by *Holy Spirit,*

which does not correspond to the original meaning. This capital point stands out from the first comments which the Gospels raised and will one day be confirmed beyond all possible doubt. (1)

8. To enable the real meaning of these words to be reached it is also necessary to pay attention to the significance of the word *water* which is not used here in its usual sense.

The knowledge of physics was very imperfect in ancient times when it was believed that the Earth had risen out of the water. Therefore water was considered to be the exclusive primitive generating substance. This is why we read in the book of Genesis: '. . . the Spirit of God moved upon the face of the waters; it floated above the waters; . . . Let there be firmament in the midst of the waters; . . . Let the waters under the heaven be gathered together unto one place, and let the dry land appear; . . . Let the waters bring forth abundantly the moving creature that hath life, and fowl that may fly above the Earth in the open firmament of heaven.'

According then to this belief, water represented the nature of matter, just as the Spirit represented the nature of intelligence. The words: 'If man is not reborn of the waters and of the Spirit, or in water and in Spirit', thus signify — 'if man is not born with his body and his soul'. This is the manner in which these words were originally understood.

This interpretation is wholly justified by these other words: *What is born of the flesh is flesh and what is born of Spirit is Spirit.* Here Jesus established a clear distinction between body and Spirit. *What is born of the flesh* clearly indicates that *only* the body generates from the body and that the Spirit is independent.

9. The words: *'The wind blows where it wishes and you hear the sound but know not from whence it comes nor whence it goes',* are referring to the *Spirit of God,* who gives life to whom He wishes, or rather to the *soul of man.* The words 'you know not where it comes from nor where it goes', signifies that we do not know who the Spirit had been previously or who it will be in the future. If the Spirit or soul was created at the same time as the body we would know where it came from because we would know its beginning. Whichever way you look at this passage, it confirms the principle of the pre-existence of the soul and subsequently the plurality of existences.

10. *And from the days of John the Baptist until now the Kingdom of Heaven suffereth violence and the violent take it by force. For all the prophets and the law prophesied until John. And if ye will receive it, this is Elias, which was for to come. He that hath ears to hear, let him hear (Matthew, 11: 12-15).*

---

(1) The translation by Osterwald is according to the original text. It says: NOT BORN OF THE WATER AND OF THE SPIRIT. That of Sacy says: OF THE HOLY SPIRIT, that of Lamennais: OF THE HOLY SPIRIT.

11. Even if the doctrine of reincarnation as expressed re John might be interpreted in principle in a purely mystic sense, the same could not happen with this passage from Matthew, which does not permit any ambiguity: *He is Elias, who was to come.* Here there is nothing figurative, nothing allegorical, only a complete affirmation. 'Since the time of John the Baptist till today the Kingdom of Heaven is seized by violence.' What do these words mean when John the Baptist was still alive at that moment? Jesus explains them to us when He says: 'If you wish to understand what I am saying, this is Elias who was to come.' Therefore, if John was Elias, Jesus alluded to the time when John was living under the name of Elias. 'Till the present time the kingdom is seized by violence,' is another allusion to the violence of the Mosaic laws, which ordered the extermination of infidels so that the rest might attain the Promised Land, the Paradise of the Hebrews, whereas according to the new law Heaven was to be won by charity and mildness.

Jesus then added: *He that hath ears to hear, let him hear.* These words are frequently uttered by Him, telling us that not everyone was in a condition to understand certain truths.

12. *Thy dead men shall live, together with my dead body shall they arise. Awake, and sing, ye that dwell in dust: for thy dew is as the dew of herbs, and the earth shall cast out the dead (Isaiah, 26: 19).*

13. This passage from Isaiah is also explicit: 'Thy dead men shall live again.' If the prophet had wished to speak of a spiritual life, if he had intended to say that those who had been executed were not dead spiritually speaking, he would have said: 'They are still alive,' and not *'They will live again.'* In the spiritual sense these words would be a contradiction, because they imply an interruption in the life of the soul. In the sense of *moral regeneration* they would be a denial of eternal suffering because they establish in principle that *all those who are dead will one day come back to life.*

14. *But when a man hath died once, when his body, separated from his spirit, has been consumed, what happens to him? Having died once can a man live again? In the war in which I find myself, each day of my life, I await my mutation. (Job, 14: 10 & 14. Translation taken from Le Maistre de Sacy).*

When a man dies, he loses all his strength, expires, afterwards, where is he? If a man dies, will he live again? Will I wait all the days of my combat, until there comes some mutation? (Taken from the Protestant translation of Osterwald.)

When a man is dead, he lives forever: when my days of existence on Earth have finished, I will wait, seeing that I shall return again. (Taken from the Greek translation.) (1)

---

(1) The King James translation says: BUT MAN DIETH AND WASTETH AWAY: YEA, MAN GIVETH UP THE GHOST. AND WHERE IS HE? IF A MAN DIE, SHALL HE LIVE AGAIN? ALL THE DAYS OF MY APPOINTED TIME WILL I WAIT, TILL MY CHANGE COME. (Translator's addition for comparison, 1987.)

15. In these three translations the principle of the plurality of existences is clearly expressed. Nobody can imagine that Job was referring to regeneration from baptismal water, which for sure he had never heard of. 'Man having *died once,* can he *live again?'* The idea of dying once and reliving implies dying and living many times. The Greek version is even more explicit, if that is possible. 'When my days of *existence on Earth* are finished, I will wait, for *I will return again',* or return again to Earth. This is so clear, as if someone were saying: I leave my house, but I will return.

'In the war in which I find myself each day of my life, I await my mutation.' Here Job evidently was referring to his struggles against the miseries of life, 'I await my mutation' meaning he was resigned. In the Greek version, *I will wait,* seems to apply more preferably to a new existence: 'When my existence has ended, I will wait, seeing that I shall return again.' It is as if Job, after death, places himself in the interval which separates one life from another and says that it is there he will await till the moment of return.

16. So there is no doubt that under the name of resurrection, the principle of reincarnation was a fundamental belief of the Jews. A point which Jesus and the prophets in general confirm, and from which it follows that to deny reincarnation is also to deny the words of Christ. One day, however, when they have been well meditated upon, without preconceived ideas, His words will be recognised as an authority on this point, as well as on many others.

17. From the religious point of view we add to this authority the philosophical view point of the proofs resulting from the observance of the facts. When we try to discover from the effects what the causes might be, reincarnation becomes an absolute necessity, an inherent part of humanity, in a word: a Law of Nature. By its very results it becomes evident in a material manner, so to speak, in the same way that a hidden motor reveals itself by its movement. It is the only way Man can find out *where he came from, where he is going and why he is here on Earth* and still be able to justify the many abnormalities and all the apparent injustices which present themselves during life. (1)

Without the principle of the pre-existence of the soul and the plurality of existences, the maxims of the Gospel in the most part become unintelligible, which is the reason why they have given rise to so many contradictory interpretations. This is the only principle which will restore them to their true and original meaning.

---

(1) See THE SPIRITS' BOOK, chapters 4 & 5; WHAT IS SPIRITISM, chapter 2, by Allan Kardec and also LA PLURALITÉ DES EXISTENCES by Pezzani, for further information on reincarnation.

REINCARNATION STRENGTHENS FAMILY TIES WHEREAS A SINGLE LIFE WOULD DESTROY THEM

18. Family ties are not destroyed through reincarnation as some would believe. On the contrary, they become stronger and closer. The opposite principle would, on the other hand, certainly destroy them.

In space, Spirit entities form groups or families bound together by affection, sympathy towards each other, and by similar inclinations. Happy at being together, these Spirits seek each other. Incarnate life separates them only for a while, so on returning to the spiritual world they again reunite as friends who have just returned from a journey. Frequently they will even follow each other into the incarnate form, coming here to be united in the same family or the same circle of friends and acquaintances, in order to work together for their mutual progress. When some members of the same spiritual family become incarnate and others not, they then continue their contact by means of thought. Those who are free watch over those who are captive. Those who are more advanced do everything they can for the less advanced, so helping them to progress. After each physical existence all have made some advancement, even if it is only a step along the path to progress. As they become less bound by matter, their affections become more real and more spiritually refined, due to the fact that they are not perturbed by selfish or violent passions. This then allows them to live many lives in the flesh without suffering any loss of mutual esteem.

It is understood, of course, that we refer to real affection, soul to soul, being the only love which survives after the destruction of the body. So it follows that those of this world who join together because of physical attraction, will have no motive to look for each other in the spirit world. The only lasting relationships are those linked by spiritual affection, all carnal affections being extinguished together with the cause that brought them about, in other words, the physical body. Understand by this that the physical cause no longer exists in the world of Spirits, but the soul exists eternally.

With regard to those who join together exclusively out of interest, they clearly mean nothing to each other. Death separates them both on Earth and in Heaven.

19. The union and affection which can exist between relatives is an indication of former sympathies which have brought them together. This is why, when referring to someone whose character, tastes, and inclinations hold no similarity to other members of the same family, it is customary to say that they do not belong to that family. When saying this, the truth is expressed far more profoundly than suspected. God permits that in certain families these Spirits, who are uncongenial or strangers to each other, reincarnate with the dual purpose of serving as a test for some members of that family, and as a means of progress for others. In this manner, due to contact with good Spirits and the general care dispensed to them, the bad or wicked Spirits get better, little by

little. Their characters grow milder, their habits become more refined and their aversions dissipated. This is how the various fusions of different categories of Spirits are accomplished, as is done with different races and peoples on the planet.

20. The fear that some people may have with regard to the indefinite increase in relationships due to reincarnation is basically selfish; proving a lack of love sufficiently ample as to be able to embrace a large number of people. Does a father who has many children love them any less than he would if there was only one? The selfish people may be tranquil because there is no reason for such a fear. The fact that a person may have had ten incarnations does not mean that in the spirit world he will find ten fathers, ten mothers, ten wives and a prodigious number of children and relatives. There he will always encounter only those who had been the object of his affections, some of whom he would have been linked to here on Earth in various relationships, or perhaps even the same ones.

21. Let us now look at the consequences of an anti-reincarnationist doctrine. It by necessity annuls all previous existences of the soul, seeing that under these ideas the soul would be created together with the body, no previous links would exist and all would be complete strangers one to another. The father would be a stranger to his child. The relationships between families would then be reduced to mere physical relations without any spiritual links whatsoever. Therefore, there would be no motive at all for anyone to claim the honour of having had such-and-such a person for their ancestor. Whereas, with reincarnation ancestors and descendants may have known each other, lived together, loved one another and can reunite later on in order to further the links of sympathy even more.

22. All that refers to the past. So now let us look at the future. According to one of the fundamental dogmas that comes from the idea of non-reincarnation, the destiny of all souls is irrevocably determined after only one existence. This fixed and definite idea of fate implies the ending of all progress, because when there is still some form of progress, then there is no definite fate. Depending on whether we have lived a good or bad life, we should go immediately to either the home of the blessed or to eternal hell. *We should then be immediately and forever separated, without hope of ever being united again.* In this way fathers, mothers and children, husbands and wives, brothers and sisters, and even friends would never be sure of seeing each other again; this then means the absolute rupture of all family ties.

However, with the acceptance of reincarnation and consequential progress, all those who love one another will meet again on Earth and also in space, gravitating together in the direction of God. If some weaken along the path they will delay their progress and their happiness, but there will never be a total loss of hope. Helped, encouraged and sustained by those who love them, they will one day be able to extricate themselves from the quagmire into which they have allowed themselves to fall. With reincarnation there is perpetual solidarity between incarnates and discarnates constantly consolidating the links of affection.

23. In conclusion, four alternatives present themselves to Man for his future beyond the tomb. Firstly — nothingness, according to the materialist doctrine; secondly — absorbtion into the universe, according to the pantheistic idea; thirdly — individuality with a fixed and definite destiny, according to the Church; fourthly — individuality with constant progress according to the Spiritist doctrine.

In the first two of these alternatives, family ties are interrupted at the time of death, and no hope is left for these souls of ever meeting again in the future. With the third alternative, there is a possibility of meeting again, if each has gone to the same region, which might be either Heaven or Hell. But with the plurality of existences, which is inseparable from gradual progression, there is certainty of the continuity of relationships between those who love, and this is what constitutes the true family.

INSTRUCTIONS FROM THE SPIRITS.
LIMITS OF INCARNATIONS

24. *What are the limits of incarnation?*

In actual fact, incarnation does not have clearly defined limits if we are thinking only of the envelope which constitutes the physical covering of the Spirit since the materiality of this covering diminishes in proportion as the Spirit purifies itself. In certain worlds more advanced than Earth, this covering is already less compact, less heavy, more refined and consequently less subject to vicissitudes. In worlds of still higher elevation it is translucent and almost fluidic. It dematerializes by degrees and finally becomes absorbed in the perispirit. According to the kind of world in which it lives, the Spirit reclothes itself with a covering appropriate to that world.

The perispirit itself undergoes successive transformations. It becomes more and more etheric, until it reaches complete depuration which is the state of all pure Spirits. If special worlds are destined for more highly advanced Spirits, they do not remain prisoners there as in the inferior worlds. The special state of detachment in which they find themselves allows them to travel to any part of the Universe to which they may be called on missions.

If we consider incarnation from the material view point, such as can be verified here on Earth, we can say that it is limited to inferior worlds. But it depends on each Spirit to liberate itself more or less quickly, by working towards purification. We should also consider that in the discarnate state, that is to say in the intervals between bodily existences, the situation of each Spirit depends on the nature of the world to which it is linked, by the degree of advancement it has acquired. Thus in the spiritual world we are more or less happy, free or enlightened, according to the degree of dematerialization achieved. — SAINT LOUIS (Paris, 1859).

THE NEED FOR INCARNATION

25. *Is incarnation a punishment and are guilty spirits bound to suffer them?*

The passing of Spirits through corporeal life is necessary in order that they may fulfill by means of a material action the purpose to which God assigned them. This is necessary for their own good, as the activity which they are obliged to perform will help the development of their intelligence. Being just, God must distribute everything in equal parts to all His children; so it is established that everyone starts from the same point, with the same aptitudes, *the same obligations to fulfill and having the same liberty to proceed.* Any type of privilege would be an injustice. But for all Spirits incarnation is a transitory state. It is a task imposed by God at the beginning of life, as a primary experiment in the use of free-will. Those who discharge this task with zeal pass over the first steps of their initiation quickly, less painfully, and so are able to reap the fruits of their labour at an earlier date. Those who, on the contrary, make bad use of the liberty that God has granted them, delay their progress and according to the degree of obstinacy demonstrated, may prolong the need for reincarnating indefinitely, in which case it becomes a punishment. — SAINT LOUIS (Paris, 1859).

26. NOTE — A common comparison would make this difference more easily understandable. The scholar cannot reach superior studies in science if he has not passed through the series of classes which lead to that level. These classes, whatever may be the work demanded, are the means by which the student will reach his objective and are not a punishment inflicted upon him. If he is diligent he can shorten the path and consequently will encounter less thorns. However, this does not happen to the one who is negligent and lazy, which will oblige him to repeat certain lessons. It is not the work of the class which is the punishment, but the necessity to recommence the same work over again.

This is what happens to mankind on Earth. For the primitive Spirit, who is only at the beginning of his spiritual life, incarnation is the means by which he can develop his intelligence. Nevertheless, it is a punishment for an enlightened man, in whom a moral sense has been greatly developed, to be obliged to live over again the various phases of a corporeal life full of anguishes, when he could have arrived at the end of his need to stay in inferior and unhappy worlds. On the other hand, if he works actively towards his moral progress, he not only shortens the period of his material incarnations, but also may jump over the intermediate steps which separate him from the superior worlds.

Is it possible for Spirits to incarnate only once in any one world and then fulfill their other existences in different worlds? This would only be possible if every person were at exactly the same point in both intellectual and moral development. The differences between them, from the savage to civilised man, show the many degrees which must be ascended. Besides, an incarnation must have a useful purpose. But what of the short-lived incarnations of children who die at a tender age? Have they suffered to no purpose, for themselves or for others? God, Whose laws are wise, does nothing that is useless. Through reincarnating on the same globe, and by being once again in contact with each other, He wishes these same Spirits to have the desire to repair reciprocated offences. With the help of their past relationships, He wishes to establish family ties on a spiritual basis, founded on the principles of the natural laws of solidarity, fraternity and equality.

CHAPTER 5

BLESSED ARE THE AFFLICTED

The justice of afflictions. — Causes of present-day afflictions.
— Past causes of afflictions. — Forgetfulness of the past. —
Motives for resignation. — Suicide and madness. —
INSTRUCTIONS FROM THE SPIRITS: To suffer well or
badly. — Evil and its remedy. — Happiness is not of this world.
— Losing loved ones. Premature deaths. — If he had been a
good man he would have died. — Voluntary torments. True
misfortune. — Melancholy. — Voluntary trials. The true hair
shirt. — Should we end our neighbour's probation? —Would it
be licit to hasten the death of someone incurably sick who is
suffering? — Sacrificing one's own life. — Making one's own
suffering useful to others.

1. *Blessed are the meek: for they shall inherit the Earth. Blessed are they which do hunger and thirst after righteousness: for they shall be filled. Blessed are they which are persecuted for righteousness sake: for theirs is the Kingdom of Heaven (Matthew, 5: 5, 6 & 10).*

2. *And he lifted up his eyes on his disciples and said, Blessed be ye poor: for yours is the Kingdom of God. Blessed are ye that hunger now: for ye shall be filled. Blessed are ye that weep now: for ye shall laugh (Luke, 6: 20 & 21).*

But woe unto you that are rich! For ye have received your consolation. Woe unto you that are full! For ye shall hunger. Woe unto you that laugh! For ye shall mourn and weep (Luke, 6: 24 & 25).

THE JUSTICE OF AFFLICTIONS

3. The compensation promised by Jesus to the afflicted of this Earth can only be effected in a future life. Without the certainty of this future these maxims would be a contradiction; still more, they would be a decoy. Even with this certainty it is difficult to understand the convenience of suffering in order to be happy. It is said that it is to acquire greater merit. But then we ask: Why do some suffer more than others? Why are some born in misery and others in opulence without having done anything to justify this situation? Why is it that some never manage to achieve anything, while for others everything seems to smile? Yet what is even less understandable is why benefits and misfortunes are divided so unequally between vice and virtue. Why do we find virtuous

people suffering side by side with the wicked who prosper? Faith in the future can console and instil patience, but it does not explain these irregularities which appear to contradict God's justice. However, once God's existence has been admitted one cannot conceive Him as being less than infinitely perfect. He is naturally all powerful, all just and all kindness, without which He would not be God. If He is supremely good and just then He cannot act capriciously, nor yet with partiality. *The vicissitudes of life derive from a cause, and as God is just so then that cause must also be just.* This is what each one of us must convince ourselves of. Through the teachings of Jesus, God started Man on the path to find that cause, and now that Man is sufficiently mature as to be able to understand, He has revealed the cause by means of *Spiritism.* That is to say, through the words of the *Spirits.*

CAUSES OF PRESENT-DAY AFFLICTIONS

4. The vicissitudes of life are of two kinds, or if you prefer, stem from two different sources which are important to distinguish. Some have their cause in present-day life, while others arise outside this present life.

On going back to the origins of earthly misfortunes it must be recognised that many are natural consequences of character and the behaviour of those who suffer them.

How many fail through their own fault? How many are the victims of their own thoughtlessness, pride or ambition?

How many destroy themselves through lack of discipline, misconduct or from not knowing how to limit their desires!

How many disastrous marriages are due to the fact that they were built on calculated interest or vanity, in which the heart took no part!

How many disagreements and fatal disputes could have been avoided with the aid of a little moderation and less susceptibility!

How many illnesses and diseases stem from intemperance and excesses of all kinds?

How many parents are unhappy with their children because they did not combat their bad instincts from an early age! Either from weakness or indifference, they allowed the germ of pride, selfishness and stupid vanity to grow in them, so causing their hearts to dry and shrivel. Later on, when reaping what they have sown, they are surprised and afflicted by the lack of gratitude and the indifference with which they are treated.

We ask each one whose heart has been hurt by vicissitudes or deceptions, to study their own conscience closely; to go back, step by step, to the origins of each misfortune which is torturing them. Like as not they will be able to say: *if I had done, or not done, such and such a thing, I would not be where I am now.*

Who then is responsible for Man's afflictions if not Man himself? So then in a great number of cases he is the cause of his own misfortunes. But instead of recognising this fact he finds it easier and less humiliating to his vanity to accuse his bad luck, providence or even his unlucky star, when in actual fact his unlucky star is his own carelessness.

When reckoning with the misfortunes of life, suffering of this nature undoubtedly forms the greatest part of all vicissitudes. Only when Man works at bettering himself, both morally and intellectually, will he be able to avoid this category of suffering.

5. Human laws cover various faults and perscribe punishment. In these cases it is possible for the condemned man to recognise that he is suffering the consequences of the wrong committed. But the law does not or cannot, reach every wrong; it falls principally upon those who cause damage to society and not upon those who only cause damage to themselves. God, however, does not allow any detour from the straight and narrow path to go unpunished. There is no wrong or infraction of His Law, however small, which does not carry with it the inevitable consequence, which may be more or less deplorable. From this it follows that in small things, as in great matters, Man is always punished according to the manner in which he has sinned. The suffering which follows is always a warning that wrong has been done. This offers him experience and makes him feel the difference between right and wrong, good and bad, so that in the future these sources of bitterness may be avoided, but without which there would be no motive for betterment. If Man were to be confident of immunity he would only delay his own progress and therefore his future happiness.

Nevertheless, sometimes experience arrives rather late, when life has already been wasted and become disordered, when strength is already spent and the person is no longer able to remedy the wrongdoing. Then man will frequently say: If I had known then what I know now how many false steps would have been avoided! *If I had to begin again* I would act differently, but now there is no more time! Like the lazy workman who says, 'I have wasted my day', he also says, 'I have wasted my life!' As the sun rising on a new day allows the worker the possibility of repaying any lost time, so it is with Man that after a period of time in the tomb a new life shines forth which will enable advantage to be taken of past experience, and good resolutions for the future to be put into practice.

PAST CAUSES OF AFFLICTIONS

6. Although there are misfortunes in this life caused by Man himself, there are also others which seem to be completely strange to him and which touch him like fate. For example: the loss of a loved one or the bread winner of a family; accidents which no amount of foresight could have prevented; reverses in fortune which precautions and judicial counselling could not avoid; natural

disasters; infirmities from birth, specially those which make work or the earning of a livelihood impossible, such as deformities, insanity, idiocy, etc.

Those who are born with restricting conditions like those mentioned, have done nothing in their present life to deserve such a sad fate, which they could not avoid and are totally impotent to change, which leaves them at the mercy of public commiseration. Why then are there these unhappy beings, when beside them, under the same roof, in the same family, are others who have been blessed in every way? In short, what can be said of children who die at a tender age and who, during their short life, knew only suffering? These are problems which as yet no philisophy has been able to find a solution for, anomalies which no religion has been able to justify and which appear to be a contradiction of goodness, justice and God's Divine Providence. If the hypothesis of the soul being created at the same time as the body and that of destiny being irrevocably determined after but a few instants upon Earth were to be verified, this would indeed be the case. If these creatures had just left the hands of the Creator, what had caused them to come into the world to face such misery? How could they have received any recompense or punishment seeing that they had been unable to practice either good or bad?

Nevertheless, by virtue of the axiom according to which *every effect has a cause,* these miseries are effects which have to have a cause, and if we admit that God is just, then that cause must also be just. Therefore as an effect is always preceeded by a cause, and if that cause is not to be found in the present life, then it follows it must come from before this life, that is to say from a preceeding life. On the other hand, God, being unable to punish goodness that has been done or badness that has not been done, it follows that if we are being punished then wrong must have been committed. If that wrong is not of the present life then it must come from a past existence. This is an alternative that no one can avoid and where logic determines on which side God's justice lies.

Man is not always punished or completely punished in the present life, but he cannot escape the consequences of his faults indefinitely. The prospering of badness or evil is but temporary, for if he does not atone today then he will atone tomorrow. Likewise, he who suffers is atoning for his past. Misfortunes which appear at first sight to be undeserved have their reason to be. Those who find themselves in a state of suffering may always say: *"Lord forgive me, for I have sinned."*

7. Sufferings due to causes prior to the present existence, as well as those which originate from present causes, are frequently the consequences of errors which have been committed. That is to say through the action of a rigorously distributive justice, we come to suffer what we have made others suffer. If we have been hard and inhumane we may be treated with harshness and inhumanity; if we were too full of pride we may be born in humble circumstances; if we have been miserly, selfish or made bad use of our riches

we may find ourselves deprived of the necessary means of survival; if we have been a bad son or daughter we may suffer from the behaviour of our children.

It is only through the plurality of existences and the destiny of the planet as a world of atonement, which it now is, that we can explain the abnormalities in the distribution of happiness or unhappiness amongst good and bad alike. Nevertheless, these abnormalities exist only in appearance, due to the fact that they are considered solely from the point of view of the present. If we elevate ourselves, by means of thought, in such a way as to see a succession of existences, we will perceive that to each one is given what is deserved, after taking into consideration that which was gained in the spiritual world. Only then does it become apparent that God's justice is uninterrupted.

Man must never forget that he finds himself in an inferior world to which he is confined, due exclusively to his imperfections. Each time he suffers a vicissitude he must remember that if he belonged to a more advanced world these things would not happen, and that it depends on himself alone to see that he never returns to this world, by working harder to improve himself.

8. Tribulations may be imposed on Spirits who are ignorant or who have become hardened, in order to induce them to make a choice with knowledge of what they are doing. Repentant Spirits who wish to repay the evil they have committed and who desire to behave better, are free to make their own choice. Such was the understanding of one Spirit who, after having failed to complete a task, asked to be allowed to repeat it so as not to lose the benefit of his work. Therefore tribulations are at the same time atonements for the past, for which we receive the deserved retribution, and also tests relating to the future, which we are preparing. We offer thanks to God who, in His goodness, helps Man to repay his debts and does not irrevocably condemn the first fault.

9. It is not to be thought, however, that all suffering in this world denotes the existence of a determined shortcoming. Many times it is simply an ordeal requested by the Spirit, which will help it towards purification and active progress. So atonement is always a test, but a test is not always an atonement. Tests and atonements though, are always signs of a relative inferiority, as that which is perfect needs no testing. Nevertheless, it is possible that a Spirit, having reached a certain degree of elevation and being desirous of further progress, may request a mission or task to perform by means of which he or she will be more or less compensated, depending on whether or not they are victorious, and according to the difficulty of the requested test. These then are those people who have naturally good instincts, whose souls are elevated and who possess inborn sentiments. They apparently bring nothing from their past existences and who despite great torments, suffer with true Christian resignation, asking only that God help them to support their trials without complaining. On the other hand, we may consider as atonements those afflictions which provoke complaint and which cause revolt against God.

Beyond doubt the suffering which does not provoke complaint can also be considered as atonement. But this indicates it was voluntarily sought rather than imposed. This constitutes a test of our strength of resolution, which in itself is a sign of progress.

10. Spirits cannot aspire to complete happiness till they have become pure. Any kind of stain prohibits entrance into the blissful worlds. It is like the passengers on a plagued ship who find themselves prohibited from entering port until they have undergone a cleansing. The imperfections of Spirits are slowly overcome by means of various corporeal lives. The tribulations of life, when well supported, help them towards progress. They erase faults and find purification by means of atonement, which is the remedy which cleanses the sores and heals the sick. The more grave the illness, the more energetic must be the remedy. Therefore, those who suffer greatly must realise that they have most to atone for, and should rejoice in the proximity of the cure. It will depend on each one to take every advantage from suffering, by being resigned and not spoiling things with impatience, seeing that, if that be the case, they will then have to begin all over again.

FORGETFULNESS OF THE PAST

11. It is useless to object that forgetfulness constitutes a barrier against the utilization of experience acquired in past lives. If God considered it convenient that a veil be cast over the past it is because it is to our advantage that this be so. In fact, remembrance would be a very great inconvenience. It could in certain cases, cause a person great humility or perhaps make them prideful, which would interfere with their free will. In any case it would certainly cause inevitable perturbation in social relationships.

A Spirit is frequently reborn into the same ambient where it has previously lived, establishing once again the same relationships, in order to repay the evil done. Recognition of these same persons, who perhaps had been hated, would only serve to rekindle that emotion. In any case, humiliation would be felt on confronting those who had been offended. So in order that we may improve ourselves God has bestowed upon us precisely what we need, that which is sufficient and nothing more, this being none other than the voice of conscience and our instinctive tendencies. He has only deprived us of what would be prejudicial.

On being reborn, Man brings with him what he has acquired. He is born exactly the way he has made himself. In each life he begins from a new starting point. It matters little to him to know what he was before. If he finds himself being punished it is because he did wrong. His actual tendencies indicate what is still to be corrected, and it is upon this he should concentrate all his attention, seeing that no trace is left of what has been rectified. The good resolutions he feels bound to make are the voice of conscience, calling attention to what is right and what is wrong, so giving strength to resist temptation.

Moreover, this forgetfulness only occurs during bodily existence. On returning to the spiritual world the remembrance of the past is regained. So it is only temporary, a slight interruption similar to that which occurs during sleep, but which does not prevent the remembrance on the subsequent day of what was done on the previous one.

But it is not only after so-called death that the Spirit may recover remembrance of the past. It can be said that it is never lost, even whilst incarnate, as experience demonstrates that during sleep, being a period when a certain amount of liberty is enjoyed, the Spirit is conscious of its past acts. It knows why it is suffering and that it suffers justly. Memory is only extinguished during the course of exterior existence, in the life of relationships. But during these partial remembrances, which if they were otherwise might cause added suffering and harm social relations, the Spirit absorbs new strength in these moments of emancipation of the soul, if it knows how to take advantage of them.

MOTIVES FOR RESIGNATION

12. With the words: *Blessed are the afflicted for they shall be consoled,* Jesus indicates the compensation which awaits those who suffer and the resignation which leads Man to bless suffering as a prelude to the cure.

These words can also be understood in this manner: that one should be content to suffer, seeing that the pain of this world is the payment for past debts which have been incurred. Patiently supported here on Earth, these pains will save centuries of future suffering. One should be happy that God is reducing the debt by permitting payment now, thereby guaranteeing a tranquil future.

Suffering Man is like a debtor who owes a large sum and to whom the creditor says: "If you pay me even a hundredth part of your debt today, I will exonerate you and you will be free; but if you do not, then I shall torment you till you pay the very last instalment." Would not the debtor feel happy in supporting all kinds of hardships in order to liberate himself, so paying only a hundredth part of what he owed? Instead of complaining to the creditor, would he not be grateful?

This is the meaning of the words, 'Blessed are the afflicted for they shall be consoled'. They are happy because they are paying their debts and also because after payment they will be free. However, if on acquitting himself on the one side, Man becomes indebted on the other, he will never find liberation. Therefore, each new fault only increases the debt, there being not one, whatsoever, which does not entail a compelling and inevitable punishment. If not today, then tomorrow; if not in this life, then in another. Amongst the list of failings, it behoves Man to put the lack of submission to God's Will in first place. So if we complain about our afflictions, if we do not accept them with resignation, or if we accuse God of being unjust, we contract new debts which in turn make us lose the fruits which should have been gathered from these sufferings. This is why we must begin again from the start, exactly as if after paying part of a debt to a creditor who has been tormenting us, we then took out another loan.

On entering into the spiritual world, Man is like the labourer who arrives on the day of payment. To some God will say: "Here is your recompense for the days you have worked", while to others, the so-called lucky ones on Earth who have lived in idleness, or those who have built their happiness on the satisfaction of their own self-esteem, and on wordly pleasures, He will say: "There is nothing more to come: you have already received your salary on Earth. Go and begin your tasks again."

13. Man can soften or increase the bitterness of his trials according to the manner in which he regards earthly life. His suffering will be all the more depending on how long he imagines it to be. But those who can see life through a spiritual prism understand bodily existence at a glance. They see that life is but a point in eternity, comprehend the shortness of its duration, and recognise that this painful moment will soon pass. The certainty of a happier future sustains and animates them and far from complaining, they offer thanks to God for the pain which will permit them to advance. On the other hand, for all those who see only bodily life before them, the duration seems interminable and the pain oppresses with all its weight.

The result of looking at life in a spiritual way is a diminishing in importance of all worldly things, and Man feels himself compelled to moderate his desires, to content himself with his position without envying others. This in turn enables him to receive weakened impressions of reverses and deceptions that may be experienced. From these attitudes comes calmness and resignation, so useful to bodily health as well as to the soul; whereas from jealousy, envy, and ambition Man voluntarily condemns himself to tortures and increases the misery and anguish during his short existence.

SUICIDE AND MADNESS

14. The calm and resignation which can be absorbed according to the manner in which terrestrial life is viewed, together with confidence in the future, give the Spirit a serenity which is the best preventive measure against *madness and suicide*. To be sure, it is certain that the vast majority of cases of madness are due to the commotion produced by vicissitudes which Man has not had the strength to face. But if the things of this world are looked at from the point of view with which Spiritism regards them, all the reverses and deceptions which in other circumstances would cause Man to become desperate, can be received with indifference, even with happiness. It is evident then, that this inner strength puts him above these happenings, so protecting him from shocks to the mind which, if it were not for this, would cause serious disturbances.

15. The same applies to suicide. Leaving aside those which occur due to drunkenness or madness, which can be classified as unconscious, it is incontestable that in every case the cause is discontentment, whatever the private motives may be. But for those who are sure they will only be unhappy for a day, and that the days to come will be much better, it is easy to be patient. Man only becomes desperate when he can see no end to his sufferings. What is a lifetime compared to eternity? Is it not less than a day? But for those who do not believe in eternity, or who judge that everything ends with life, for the unfortunate and the afflicted who become dejected, grief-stricken or heart-broken, death appears to be the only solution for so much sorrow. Expecting to receive nothing, it seems natural and even logical to them to shorten their miseries by means of suicide.

16. Total incredulity, simply doubting as to the future or having materialistic ideas, are in fact the greatest of all incitements towards suicide because they cause *moral cowardice*. When scientists, upheld by the authority of their knowledge, do their best to prove to those who will listen or read what they write, that we have nothing to expect after death, are they not in fact leading us to deduce that if we are wretched then the best thing to do is to kill ourselves? What can they offer as a reason to turn away from this consequence? What compensation do they have to offer? What hope can they give? None at all, except nothingness! From this we should conclude that if nothingness is the only heroic remedy, the only prospective, then it would be better to seek it immediately and not later on, so as to suffer less.

So then, the dissemination of materialistic doctrine is the poison which innoculates the idea of suicide into the majority of those who actually come to commit this act, and those who become disciples of such doctrines assume tremendous responsibilities. With Spiritism, however, this doubt is impossible and the aspect of life changes completely. For the believer, existence prolongs itself after the so-called death, although in many varied conditions. From this belief stems patience and resignation which naturally leads all thought away from the idea of suicide. This then is the process which enables us to acquire *moral courage.*

17. In the same aspect, Spiritism produces yet another equally positive result, one which is perhaps even more decisive. It presents to us these actual suicides, who inform us of the unhappy situation in which they find themselves, so proving that no one violates God's laws with impunity. God prohibits Man to cut short his own life. Amongst these suicides there are those whose suffering, although temporary and not eternal, is none the less terrible and of such a nature as to make those who might be considering this act reflect, before leaving this world sooner than God ordained. The Spiritist however, has various reasons against the idea of suicide: the *certainty* of a future life in which he *knows* that his happiness will be in proportion to his misfortunes and the degree of resignation shown while on Earth; the *certainty* that if he abbreviates his life he will in fact reap the exact opposite of the desired result.

By liberating himself from a trial in this manner, he will consequently encounter another and far worse one in its place, longer and more terrible. The Spiritist knows that he is mistaken in imagining that by killing himself he will reach Heaven more quickly; he knows that suicide is an obstacle which will prevent him joining those he loves and hopes to meet on the other side. From whence the consequences of suicide, which only bring deceptions, are against his own interests. For these reasons alone the number of people already saved from suicide is quite considerable. From this we may conclude that when all men and women are Spiritists, conscious suicide will cease to exist.

When comparing the results of materialist doctrines with those of the Spiritist Doctrine, on this one point alone we are forced to recognise that whereas the logic of the first leads towards suicide, the second prevents suicide, which is a fact proven on many occasions.

INSTRUCTIONS FROM THE SPIRITS.
TO SUFFER WELL OR BADLY

18. When Christ said: "Blessed be the afflicted, for the Kingdom of Heaven belongs to them", He did not refer to all those who suffer, seeing that everyone on Earth suffers, whether they be seated upon thrones or lie upon straw. But alas! So few suffer well! A mere handful understand that only trials which have been well supported can lead to the Kingdom of God. Despondency is a fault and God will refuse consolation to those who lack courage. Prayer supports the soul; however, alone it is not enough. It is also necessary to have a firm belief in the kindness of God as the basis for deep faith. You have heard it said many times that He does not put a heavy burden on weak shoulders. The burden is always in proportion to the strength, just as the recompense depends on the degree of resignation and courage. The more painful the affliction the greater the recompense. It behoves then to make ourselves worthy and it is for this purpose that life presents itself so full of tribulations.

The soldier who is not sent to the front is discontent because by resting in camp he will never receive promotion. So then, be like soldiers and do not desire repose which will only allow the body to debilitate, and benumb the soul! Be content when God sends you into battle because this is not a battle of the fireing-line, but of the bitterness of life, where frequently the one who stands firm before an enemy weakens when confronted with the tenacity of moral suffering. Although there is no reward for this kind of courage on Earth, God will reserve the laurels of victory and a place of glory for those who withstand. When facing sufferings or obstacles, if you are able to place yourself above the situation, by managing to dominate the impulses of impatience, anger and despair, then you may say to yourself with just satisfaction, 'I was the stronger'.

So then, *blessed are the afflicted* may be translated in the following manner: blessed are those who have occasion to prove their faith, firmness, perseverance, and submission to the Will of God, because they will have multiplied a hundred times the happiness they lacked on Earth, for after labour comes repose. — LACORDIARE (Havre. 1863).

EVIL AND ITS REMEDY

19. Is the Earth a place of enjoyment and a paradise of delights? Does the voice of the prophet no longer reecho in your ears? Did He not proclaim there would be weeping and gnashing of teeth for those who were born into this valley of pain? So then, all who live here must expect bitter tears and suffering, and no matter how acute or how deep the pain, lift up your eyes to Heaven and offer thanks to the Lord for wishing to test you! . . . Oh mankind! Can you not recognise the power of our Lord except when He cures the sores of your bodies, and crowns your days with beauty and fortune? Can you not recognise His love except He adorns you with all the glories, and restores the brilliance and whiteness? You should imitate the one who was given as the example. Having reached the final degree of abjection and misery, while laying upon a dung heap, he said to God, "Lord, I have known all the delights of opulence and You have reduced me to the most absolute misery; thank you, thank you, my Lord, for wishing to test your servant!" How long will your eyes remain fixed upon the horizon limited by death? When will your soul finally decide to launch itself beyond the limits of the tomb? But even if you suffer and cry the whole of this life, what is that compared to the eternal glory reserved for those who suffer their trials with faith, love, and resignation? Seek consolation for your ills in the future which God will prepare for you, and search for the causes in the past. And you, who have suffered the most, consider yourselves the blessed of this Earth.

As discarnates, when floating in space, you chose your own trials, judging yourselves sufficiently strong to support them. Why then do you complain now? You asked for riches and glory because you wished to hold fight with temptation and overcome it. You asked to fight with body and soul against both moral and physical evil, knowing that the harder the trial the greater and more glorious the victory; that as long as you have triumphed, despite the fact of your body ending up on a dung heap at death, it will release a soul of radiant whiteness purified by the baptism of atonement and suffering.

What remedy can be prescribed for those attacked by cruel obsessions and mortifying evils? There is but one infallible way: through faith, which is the appeal to Heaven. If at the moment of highest poignancy in your suffering you intone hymns to the Lord, then the angel at your bedside will show you the sign of salvation and the place which you will one day occupy . . . Faith is the only sure remedy for suffering. It will always show the infinite horizon before which the few cloudy days of the present will vanish. Therefore, do not ask what is the remedy for ulcer or sore, temptation or trial. Remind yourselves that those who believe are strengthened through the remedy of faith, and those who doubt of its efficiency, be it even for an instant, will be immediately punished because they will quickly feel the pungent anguishes of affliction.

The Lord has put His seal upon all those who believe in Him. Christ told you that it was possible to move mountains by faith alone, and I tell you that he who suffers, yet has faith to uphold him, will remain under the protection of the Lord and will suffer no more. The moments of greatest pain will become the first happy notes of eternity. The soul will detach itself from the body in such a manner that, while the latter is still writhing in convulsions, it will be gliding into the celestial regions, singing hymns of gratitude and glory to the Lord together with the angels. Fortunate are those who suffer and weep! Happy be their souls because God will heap them with blessings. — SAINT AUGUSTIN (Paris, 1863).

HAPPINESS IS NOT OF THIS WORLD

20. Mankind in general, from all walks of society, is constantly complaining either that he is not happy, or that happiness was not made for him. This, dear brothers and sisters, proves better than any possible form of reasoning the truth of the maxim from the book of Ecclesiastes: 'Happiness is not of this world.' Indeed, not riches, power or even the blossom of youth are essential conditions for happiness. Furthermore, not even by uniting these three elements, so desired by many, can happiness be assured because we are constantly hearing of people of all ages, even those from the most priviliged classes, bitterly complaining of the situation in which they find themselves.

Before this fact it is inconceivable that the militant and working classes envy, with great anxiety, the positions of those who are apparently favoured by fortune. In this world, despite what anyone can do, each must face his own part of work and misery, his quota of suffering and deceptions, from which it is easy to reach the conclusion that the Earth is a planet of trials and atonement.

So then, those who preach that the Earth is Man's only home, and that it is here during only one existence he must reach the highest level of happiness possible to his nature, are merely deluding themselves and those who listen to them, seeing that it has been demonstrated through multi-secular experiences that only in exceptional cases can this globe offer the necessary conditions for complete happiness for any one individual. In general terms, it is possible to affirm that happiness is a Utopia, whose conquest has been striven after by successive generations without their ever having been able to reach their objective. If the sensible man or woman is a rarity in the world, then the absolutely happy person has never been found.

Happiness on Earth consists of something so fleeting for those who are not guided by wisdom, that but for a year, a month or a week of complete satisfaction the rest of their existence is a series of bitter deceptions. And note, dear children, that I refer to those who are considered the lucky ones of the Earth, those who are the envy of the masses.

Consequently, if the earthly dwelling-place is specifically for trials and atonement, then we are forced to admit that somewhere there are more favourable dwelling places where the Spirit, although still a prisoner in a material body, may possess the delights of human life in all its fullness. This is the reason why God has planted those beautiful superior planets in your vortex, towards which your efforts and tendencies will one day cause you to gravitate, when you have become sufficiently purified and perfected.

However, do not deduce from my words that the Earth is perpetually destined to remain a penitentiary. No, certainly not! From the progress that has already been achieved we may readily infer further progression, and from the various social betterments obtained, new and more fertile improvements. This is the immense task allotted to this new doctrine which the Spirits have revealed.

So then, dear children, may you be animated by a saintly emulation so that you may energetically change your ways. Everyone should dedicate themselves to the propagation of Spiritism, which has already begun your own regeneration. It is your duty to help your brothers and sisters to participate in the rays of this sacred light. Accordingly set to work, dear children! Let us hope that within this solemn reunion all hearts may aspire to this great objective, which is to prepare a world for future generations where the word happiness is no longer meaningless. — FRANÇOIS-NICOLAS-MADELEINE, Cardinal MORLOT (Paris, 1863).

LOSING LOVED ONES. PREMATURE DEATHS

21. When death cuts down someone in your family, carrying off the youngest before the oldest without discrimination, you are accustomed to say that God is not just: because He sacrifices he who is strong and has all his future before him, leaving those who have lived many years and are full of deceptions: because He takes those who are useful and leaves behind those who are no longer able to work: because He breaks the heart of a mother by depriving her of the innocent creature who was her only joy.

Humans, it is on this point that you must lift yourselves above commonplace thoughts about life in order to be able to understand that goodness is frequently where you judge there to be evil, and the wisdom of providence where you think you perceive the blind fatality of destiny. Why do you evaluate divine justice by you own ideas? Do you suppose that the Lord of the Worlds applies justice through mere caprice, in order to inflict cruel punishment? Nothing happens that has not an intelligent meaning and no matter what happens there is always a reason for it. If you scrutinize better all the pain that redounds to you then you would surely find divine reason, regenerating reason, wherein you would see the worthlessness of your interests which, as a consequence, would become so secondary as to be cast into last place.

Believe me, in the case of an incarnation of twenty years, death is preferable to any of the shameful dissipations which bring untold distress to respectable families, break the hearts of mothers and cause parents' hair to whiten before their time. Premature death is frequently a great blessing which God concedes to those who depart, so preserving them from the miseries of life or the seductions which possibly occasioned the loss of life. The person who dies in the flower of youth is not a victim of fate. God judges that it is not suitable for that person to remain longer on Earth.

What a terrible tragedy, you say, to see the thread of life that was so full of hope, cut! To what hope are you referring? That of the Earth? Where he who had gone could have perhaps shone or made his way and become rich? Always there is this restricted vision which prevents one from rising above that which is material. Who can tell what might have been the actual fate of that life which you thought so full of hope? How do you know that it would not have been saturated with bitterness? Do you then disdain the hopes offered by the future life, to the point of preferring this fleeting existence here on Earth? Do you suppose that a high position amongst men is worth more than an elevated place amongst the blessed Spirits?

Instead of complaining, rejoice when it pleases God to withdraw one of your children from this vale of miseries. Would it not be selfish to wish that they continue suffering at your side? Ah! This is the pain conceived by those lacking in faith, who see death as an eternal separation! But those of you who are Spiritists know that the soul lives better when it is separated from its material form. Mothers, know that your beloved children are near you, yes, very near. Their fluidic bodies embrace you, their thoughts protect you and the remembrances that you keep delight them with happiness; but your unreasonable pain afflicts them, because it reveals a lack of faith, so constituting a revolt against the Will of God.

Those of you who understand the meaning of spiritual life, listen to the beatings of your heart when calling to these loved ones. If you ask God to bless them, you will feel great consolation, the kind which will dry your tears; you will feel magnificent aspirations which will show you the future which our Supreme Lord has promised. — SAMSON, ex-member of the Spiritist Society of Paris, (1863).

IF HE HAD BEEN A GOOD MAN HE WOULD HAVE DIED

22. When speaking of a bad person who has escaped some danger, it is customary to say that if he had been a good man he would have died. Well then, in saying this you are speaking the truth, because it frequently comes to pass that God bestows a longer trial on a Spirit who is only commencing his path to progress than He would give a good Spirit who, by merit of his worthiness, receives the blessing of the shortest possible period of atonement. Consequently, whenever you use that aphorism you unsuspectingly commit a blasphemy.

If a good man dies, having a neighbour who is considered to be bad, it is soon remarked that it would have been better if the neighbour had died instead. By saying this you are expressing something quite atrocious, because the one who departed had completed his or her tasks and the other, who is left, has perhaps not even begun. Why should you wish the bad person to be denied the necessary time to complete their tasks, while condemning the good person to remain an unnecessary prisoner? What would you say if, after having served a prison sentence, the convict were to be kept in prison, when another person, who had no right, was set at liberty? It must be understood that true liberty for a Spirit is the breaking of the ties which keep it captive within a physical body, and that while upon Earth it is really a prisoner.

Accustom yourselves then not to censure the things you do not understand, and more especially to believe that God is just in all things, and that on many occasions what appears to be an evil is really a blessing. Due to the fact that your faculties are so limited, it is not possible to have a clear vision of the whole, nor can it be felt by your obtuse senses. However, if you strive to reach beyond your limited sphere by means of thought, you will find the importance of all material things diminishes, according to the manner in which you are able to lift up your thoughts. In this way life presents itself as a mere incident in the infinite course of spiritual existence, which is the only true life. — FÉNELON (Sens, 1861).

VOLUNTARY TORMENTS

23. Man is incessantly searching for happiness which always escapes him, because pure happiness does not exist here on Earth. However, despite the vicissitudes which form an inevitable procession throughout earthly life, he may at least enjoy relative happiness, if he does not search for it within perishable things subject to the same vicissitudes, that is to say within material enjoyments, instead of seeking it within the delights of the soul. The only real happiness of this world is to be found in *heartfelt peace.* But Man shows himself avid for all things which agitate and perturb. It is really quite strange! It seems that, while it is possible to avoid problems, Man purposely creates torments for himself.

Are there any worse torments than those created by envy and jealousy? For those who are envious or jealous there is no rest; they suffer a state of perpetual fever. The possessions of others cause sleepless nights; the success of rivals provoke giddiness; emulation, in their eyes, is epitomized in eclipsing those around them; all their happiness consists in provoking a rage of jealousy in those as imprudent as themselves. Poor foolish beings they are indeed! Never imagining that tomorrow they will perhaps have to leave behind all these trifles, the covetousness of which has poisoned their lives. The words: 'Blessed are the afflicted for they shall be consoled' certainly do not apply to these, seeing that their preoccupations are not those which receive deserving recompense in Heaven.

On the other hand, many torments will be avoided by those who are content with what they have, who can see things they do not possess without envy, and who do not try to appear better than they are. These will be constantly rich since, by looking below oneself, it is always possible to see others with less than ourselves. These kind of people are calm because they do not create imaginary necessities for themselves. Is calmness then not a happiness in the midst of the turmoil of life? — FÉNELON (Leon, 1860).

TRUE MISFORTUNE

24. Everyone talks about misfortune; everyone has experienced it and therefore judges they understand its multiple character. I have come to tell you that almost everyone is deluded, as real misfortune is absolutely not what Man, that is to say those who are unfortunate, believe it to be. They see as misfortune the unheated stove, the threatening creditor, the empty cradle, tears, the funeral procession and those following with broken hearts, the anguish of betrayal and the stripping of pride from those who would wish to be dressed in the purple, but who can barely hide their nudity beneath the ragged tatters of their vanity. To all this, and much more, Man gives the name of misfortune. Yes, it is misfortune for those who only see the present. But real misfortunes are rather in the consequeneces of these facts than in the facts themselves. Tell me then, is a happening which at the time was considered to be a happy event, but which later caused disastrous consequences, not really more calamitous than another, which initially caused contrariety, but finally produced benefits? Tell me also, is a storm which uproots trees but purifies the air and dissipates unhealthy miasmas, which can cause death, not more of a blessing than an unhappiness?

In order to be able to judge, we must first consider the consequences. Thus in order to more fully appreciate what is really fortunate or unfortunate for Man, we must transport ourselves beyond the vision of this life, for it is only there that the consequeneces can begin to be felt. So everything called unhappiness, according to the short-sightedness of human beings, ends with the body and receives its compensation in the future life.

I will reveal unhappiness to you in yet another light, in the form of beauty and colour, which is accepted and even earnestly desired by your poor deluded souls. Pleasure, commotion, unnecessary agitation and the satisfaction of stupid vanities are the true misfortunes, causing Man to ignore his conscience, prevent his thought process and leave him in a dazed state with regard to his future. These true unhappinesses, so ardently sought after, are nothing more than the opium of forgetfulness. Have hope all who cry! Tremble all who laugh because their body is satiated! It is not possible to deceive God nor to escape one's destiny. Afflictions, those creditors more pitiless than the wolf pack, unloosed by your miseries, are constantly lurking behind the illusion of repose only to suddenly emerge in the form of agony, of real unhappiness, for all who have allowed their souls to become flabby through indifference and selfishness.

Therefore, let Spiritism offer enlightenment and establish truth and error in their real formats which, till now, have been so singularly deformed by your blindness! Act like brave soldiers who, far from running away from peril, prefer the dangerous fight rather than peace, which will bring them neither glory nor promotion! What does it matter to the soldier if he loses weapons, baggage and uniform if he comes out of battle the winner, covered with glory? What does it matter to those who have faith in the future if they leave riches and their physical bodies on the battlefield of life, provided the soul enters into the celestial Kingdom full of glory? — DELPHINE DE GIRARDIN (Paris, 1861).

MELANCHOLY

25. Do you know why sometimes a vague sadness fills your heart, leading you to consider that life is bitter? This is because your Spirit, aspiring to happiness and liberty, on finding itself tied to the physical body which acts like a prison, becomes exhausted through vain efforts to seek release. On recognising that these attempts are useless, the soul becomes discouraged, and as the body suffers the influence of the Spirit, it feels itself weary, apathetic, full of despondency and it is then that you judge yourself to be unhappy.

Believe me when I tell you to resist these tendencies with all your strength, as they only weaken your will-power. Aspirations for a better life are inborn in all mankind, but do not seek them in this world. Now that God is sending His Spirits to instruct you on happiness, which He has reserved for you, await with patience for the time when the liberating angel will come to help you break away from the ties which hold your Spirit captive. Remember, during your exile here on Earth, you have a mission to fulfill that you do not even suspect; be it dedicating yourself to your family or fulfilling the various obligations bestowed upon you by God. If within the course of this exiled probation, while seeking exoneration, you feel about to collapse through anxiety, uneasiness, or tribulations, be strong and courageous enough to support these pressures. Stand up to them with resolution for they will soon pass. These are the only means by which you may reach those for whom you pine and who, jubilant at seeing you once again amongst them, will hold out their hands towards you so as to guide you to regions inaccessible to earthly afflictions. — FRANÇOIS DE GENEVE (Bordeaux).

VOLUNTARY TRIALS. THE TRUE HAIR SHIRT

26. You ask me if it is licit for a man to lessen his own probation? This is equal to other questions such as: is it licit for a drowning man to save himself? Should he take a thorn from his hand? Should he call a doctor when he is ill? The reason behind our trials is to help us to use our intelligence, patience and resignation. It may happen that a man is born into a difficult and painful situation precisely to make him look for the means of alleviating these

problems. The merit is in suffering the consequences that cannot be avoided without complaining, in persevering with the fight and in not allowing oneself to become desperate when one is not successful. It is never to be found in negligence, which is more laziness than virtue.

This quite naturally leads to another question: if Jesus said 'Blessed are the afflicted,' can merit be gained by seeking afflictions which could aggravate our trials by means of voluntary suffering? To this we can reply very decidedly: yes, there is great merit in this, provided the suffering and privation are of benefit to others; this is charity through suffering. But not when the suffering and privations are of benefit to the inflictor; this would only be fanatical selfishness.

It is necessary to make a clear distinction in this matter. Regarding yourself personally, be content with the trials and problems which God sends. Do not seek to increase this volume, as it alone may at times be extremely heavy to bear. Accept it without murmuring but with faith; that is all that God asks. Do not weaken your body with useless privations and mortifications that have no objective, because you will need all your strength if you are to fulfill your work here on Earth. To torture and martyr the body voluntarily is to go against God's Law. He has given Man the means to sustain life, so to weaken the body needlessly is true suicide. Use it, but do not abuse it; that is the law. The abuse of the best thing God has given you will bring inevitable consequences as a punishment.

But quite the contrary occurs when Man imposes suffering upon himself in order to alleviate that of others. If you support cold and hunger with the object of offering heat and sustenance to another, thereby causing your body to be affected, you are making a sacrifice which God will bless. When you leave your perfumed homes to go to an infected hovel so as to console, or dirty your hands to treat wounds, or lose sleep so as to hold vigil at the bedside of the sick, who after all are your brothers and sisters in God, or put your health in jeopardy for the purpose of practising good, then it is here that you find your hair shirt, the true and blessed hair shirt. You have not allowed the delights of this world to shrivel your heart, nor have you slept upon the voluptuous breast of riches. Rather you have become a consoling angel to the sadly deserted.

Therefore, what utility is served by those who retire from the world so as to avoid its seductions and live in isolation? Where is the courage to face their problems? They have merely run away from the fight and deserted the combat. If you wish to make a sacrifice, then apply it to your soul and not to your body. Mortify your Spirit and not your flesh; whip your pride, receive humiliations without murmur, scourge yourself of self-love, harden yourself against the pain of insult and slander which is more pungent than physical pain. It is in these things that you find your true hair shirt, whose wounds will be taken into account because they will testify to your courage and submission to God's Will. — A GUARDIAN ANGEL (Paris, 1863).

SHOULD WE END OUR NEIGHBOUR'S PROBATION

27. Should anyone put an end to another's probation when they can, or should God's purpose be respected, so leaving things to take their own course?

We have already said repeatedly that you are upon this planet of atonement for the purpose of concluding your trials, and everything that happens is a consequence of past lives. This is the interest on the debt you must pay. However, in some people this fact provokes reflections which should be combated, due to the disastrous effects that might be caused.

Some people think that by being on Earth for the purpose of atonement all probation must follow its course. Then there are others who will go to the point of believing that not only must nothing be done to alleviate the suffering, but that on the contrary, they should help others to benefit more by making these sufferings more active, more intense. This is a very big mistake. It is quite true that trials must take their course as marked by God, but, and this is the difference, how do we know what God has designed? Do we know to what extent they must reach? What if our merciful Father designated that this or another suffering should only reach a certain point? How do you know whether Divine Providence has placed you, not as an instrument of torture to aggravate the suffering of the culprit, but as the soothing balm of consolation to help heal the wounds? So therefore never say, 'It is God's justice and must follow its course.' Rather say, 'Let me see what means our merciful Father has put within my reach so that I may lessen the suffering of my brother or sister. Let me see if moral consolations, material help or advice can assist in overcoming these trials with greater energy, patience and resignation. Let me see if God has given me the means of putting an end to this suffering. Perhaps this possibility has been given to me as a test or even an atonement, so that I may allay these troubles and substitute them with peace.'

Therefore, always help each other mutually in your respective probations and never consider yourself as an instrument of torture. Every person who has a heart should revolt against such an idea, especially all Spiritists because they, more than anyone else, should understand the infinite extension of God's goodness. All Spiritists should be convinced that their whole lives must be acts of love and devotion, that although they do what they may in trying to oppose God's wishes, these will always be fulfilled. Therefore they can apply maximum strength to attenuate the bitterness of atonement without fear of the consequences, being certain that only God has the right to shorten or prolong a trial, as He sees fit.

Is it not immense pride on the part of mankind to consider that it is right, in a manner of speaking, to turn the knife in the wound or to increase the dose of poison in the viscera of one who is suffering, under the pretext that it is part of the probation? Oh, always consider yourselves as instruments for the alleviation of pain! So to summarize: all are on Earth for atonement but all, without exception, must strive to lessen the atonement of one's fellow beings, which is in accordance with the law of love and charity. — BERNADIN, a Protecting Spirit (Bordeaux, 1863).

28. *A man is agonizing under cruel suffering. His state is known to be desperate. Would it be licit to save him a few instants of anguish by hastening his end?*

Who has given you the right to prejudge God's purpose? Can He not conduct a person to the very brink of the grave and then withdraw them, in order that they may awaken and recognise the need to change their ideas? Even when a dying person has reached the last extremes no one can be absolutely sure the final hour has arrived. Has science never been wrong in its predictions?

Of course there are cases which, with good reason, can be considered desperate. But even if there is no hope of a definite return to life and health, there always exists the possibility, testified on many occasions, of a sick person recovering their faculties at the last instant. Well then, this is the hour of grace conceded by God which may be of extreme importance. You do not understand the reflections which the Spirit may have during those last agonizing convulsions, nor how a lightning repentance may save them from many torments.

The materialist, who only sees the body and does not take into consideration the Spirit, is not apt to understand these things. But the Spiritist who knows what happens in the after life, comprehends the value of these last thoughts. So mitigate the last sufferings as much as you can, but guard yourself against abbreviating life, be it even for a minute, as this minute can be the means of avoiding many tears in the future. — SAINT LOUIS (Paris, 1860).

29. *For he who finds himself tired of life, but who does not wish to extinguish it by his own hands, would he be wrong to seek death on a battlefield with the intention of making his death useful?*

Whether a person kills themself or causes another to kill them, the intention is always to cut the thread of existence. Therefore there is intent to commit suicide even if there is no actual fact. The idea that this death would serve some purpose is mere illusion, just a pretext to cover up the act and for the person to excuse themself in their own eyes. If they seriously wished to serve their country, they would do their best to stay alive so they might be able to defend it, rather than seek death, because if they are dead they can no longer be of help. Real devotion consists in not being afraid of death when it is a matter of utility, of facing danger and, when necessary, in sacrificing one's life without thinking about it. But in seeking death with a *premeditated intent* by exposing oneself to risk, even if it be in service, annuls all merit for the action. — SAINT LOUIS (Paris, 1860).

30. *If a person exposes themself to imminent danger in order to save the life of a fellow being, knowing that they will succumb, will this act be considered as suicide?*

If there is no intention to seek death in this act, then there is no suicide, only devotion and abnegation, even though there is a certainty of death. But who can be sure? Who can say that Providence has not reserved an unexpected means of salvation at the last moment? Is it not possible even to save one who is before the cannon's mouth? On many occasions it happens that Providence wishes to take a trial of resignation to the extreme limits, in which case an unexpected circumstance will ward off the fatal blow. — SAINT LOUIS (Paris, 1860).

31. *Do not those who accept suffering with resignation, because they are submissive to God's wishes and are mindful of their future happiness, work only for their own benefit? Is it not possible for them to make their suffering useful to others?*

Materially and morally these sufferings may be useful to others; in a material sense, by the work, privations and sacrifices they impose upon themselves, which can contribute to the material well-being of their fellowmen; in the moral sense, by the example they offer of their submission to God's Will. By showing the strength of the Spiritist faith many unfortunate and wretched persons can be induced to resign themselves, so being saved from despair and its disastrous consequences in the future. — SAINT LOUIS (Paris, 1860).

CHAPTER 6

CHRIST THE CONSOLER

The gentle yoke. — The promised consoler. — INSTRUCTIONS
FROM THE SPIRITS: The advent of the Spirit of Truth.

THE GENTLE YOKE

1. *Come unto me, all ye that labour and are heavy laden, and I will give you rest.
Take my yoke unto you, and learn of me, for I am meek and lowly in heart: and ye
shall find rest unto your souls. For my yoke is easy, and my burden is light —
(Matthew, 11: 28-30).*

2. All sufferings such as miseries, deceptions, physical pain and loss of loved
ones will find consolation from faith in the future and from confidence in God's
justice, all of which Christ came to teach Man. On the other hand, for those
who expect nothing after this life or who simply doubt, afflictions will seem
heavier to them as they do not have any hope of mitigating their bitterness.
This is what prompted Jesus to say: "Come unto me all who are fatigued and I
will give you rest."

Meanwhile, the assistance and happiness promised to the afflicted depends
on one condition, which is to be found in the Law He taught. His yoke is the
observance of this Law, but the yoke is light and the Law gentle because it only
imposes love and charity as its obligations.

THE PROMISED CONSOLER

3. *If ye love me keep my commandments. And I will pray the Father and He shall
give you another Comforter, that he may abide with you for ever. Even the Spirit
of Truth; whom the world cannot receive, because it seeth him not, neither
knoweth him; but ye shall know him; for he dwelleth with you, and shall be in
you. But the Comforter, which is the Holy Ghost, whom the Father will send in my
name, he shall teach you all things, and bring all things to your remembrance,
whatsoever I have said unto you (John, 14: 15-17 & 26).*

4. In this passage from John, Jesus promises another consoler: the *Spirit of
Truth,* which the world did not yet know because it was not sufficiently mature
to be able to understand. This is the consoler sent by the Father to teach
mankind all things and to call to mind all that Christ had said. Therefore, if this

Spirit of Truth was to come at a later date to teach these additional matters, then it was because Christ had not told everything. If the Spirit of Truth was to come to remind us of what Christ had said that is because it had been forgotten or not properly understood.

Spiritism has come at the predicted time to fulfill Christ's promise. Presided over by the Spirit of Truth, it calls Man to observe the law and reveals all manner of things so making understandable what Jesus had said only in parable form. Christ himself had given the warning: "Listen all those who have ears to hear." Spiritism has come to open man's eyes and ears because it speaks without figuration or allegory, so lifting up the veil which had been intentionally cast upon certain mysteries. Finally, then, it has come to bring supreme consolation to the disinherited of this Earth and to all who suffer by showing them the just cause of their suffering and the useful purpose of all pain.

Christ said: "Blessed are the afflicted for they shall be consoled." But how can anyone feel fortunate if they do not know why they suffer? Spiritism shows the cause of suffering to be in past existences and in the destiny of this planet, on which Man makes atonement for his past. It explains the object behind suffering by showing it as a salutory process which produces a cure and also as a means of purification, both of which guarantee future happiness. From this it is possible for Man to understand that he deserves all his sufferings and to believe that this is just. He also learns that his suffering and pain will help him to progress and so is able to accept it without complaining, just as a worker accepts the work which will guarantee his salary. Spiritism gives Man an unshakable faith in the future so that he is no longer troubled by this consuming doubt within his soul. He is also enabled to see things from on high, which makes the importance of his earthly vicissitudes disappear on the vast and splendid horizon which Spiritism sets before him. The prospect of the happiness which awaits therefore gives him patience, resignation and courage to continue to the end of his path.

In this manner Spiritism realises what Jesus said of the promised Consoler, by bringing knowledge of those things which allow Man to know where he came from, where he is going and why he is on Earth; so attracting mankind towards the true principles of God's law and offering consolation through faith and hope.

INSTRUCTIONS FROM THE SPIRITS.

THE ADVENT OF THE SPIRIT OF TRUTH

5. I have come, as I came on another occasion to those misguided sons and daughters of Israel, to bring the truth and to dissipate the darkness. Harken unto me! As my words in the past have done, so must Spiritism remind the incredulous that above them reigns the immutable truth which is the existence

of the good God, the great God, who causes the plants to germinate and the waves to rise up. As a reaper, I have gathered in sheaves the scattered goodness in the breasts of humanity and said: "Come unto me, all you who suffer."

But Man with ungratefulness has moved away from the straight and wide path which leads to the Kingdom of my Father and has followed the bleak pathways of impiety. My Father does not wish to annihilate the human race; He wants the living and the dead, that is to say those who are dead according to the flesh because death does not exist, to assist each other mutually and listen no more to the voice of the prophets and apostles, but listen instead to those who no longer live upon Earth and who proclaim: "Pray and believe! Death is the resurrection and life is an ordeal you seek, during which the virtues you have cultivated will grow and develop, even as the cedar tree."

Those of you who are weak and know the obscurity of your own minds, do not deviate from the beacon which divine clemency has put into your hands so as to enlighten your pathway and reconduct you, who are lost children, once again to the bosom of the Father.

I am too much overcome with compassion for your miseries and by your immense weakness not to extend a helping hand to all those unhappily misguided who, while looking up to Heaven, fall into the pit of error. Believe, love, and meditate on these things which are revealed unto you. Do not mix the chaff with the good seed, nor the Utopias with the truth.

Spiritists! Love one another, that is the first precept; educate yourselves is the second. Within Christianity you will find all the truths. The errors in which Man has become enrooted are all of human origin. Here from beyond the grave, where you thought there was nothing, voices clamour: "Brothers and sisters! Nothing perishes! Jesus Christ is the victor over all evil, you can be the victors over impiety." — THE SPIRIT OF TRUTH (Paris, 1860).

6. I have come to instruct and console the poor disinherited. I have come to tell them to raise up their resignation to the level of their trials, and to weep, since pain was consecrated in the Garden of Olives. But wait with patience, for the consoling angels will also come to them and dry their tears.

Workers, plan your path! Recommence the following day the wearisome labour of the previous day. The work done by your hands furnishes the body with earthly bread; however, your souls are not forgotten. I, the divine Gardener, cultivate them in the silence of your thoughts. When the time comes for repose and the thread of life slips through your fingers and your eyes are closed to the light, you will feel the surging within and the germination of My precious seed. Nothing is lost in the Kingdom of our Father. Your sweat and miseries form the treasure that will make you rich in the superior spheres, where light substitutes the darkness and where the most naked of you will perhaps become the most resplendent.

In truth I say unto you that those who bear their burdens and help their brothers and sisters are beloved by Me. Instruct yourselves in the precious doctrine which dissipates the error of revolt and shows the sublime object of human trials. As the wind sweeps the dust, so the breeze of the Spirits dissipates your resentment against the riches of the world, which are frequently very pitiable, since they are subject to more dangerous trials than yours. I am with you and My apostle will instruct you. So, you who are kept captive by life, drink from the living spring of love and be prepared to one day launch yourselves, free and happy, upon the bosom of He Who created you weak so that you might become perfect; Who desires that you model your own pliable clay in order to be the author of your own immortality. — THE SPIRIT OF TRUTH (Paris, 1861).

7. I am the great Physician of souls and I have come to bring you the remedy that will cure. The weak, the suffering and the sick are My favourite children and I-am come to save them. Come then unto me, you who suffer and find yourselves oppressed and you will be alleviated and consoled. Do not search for strength and consolation elsewhere as the world is impotent to offer them. God directs a supreme appeal to your hearts by means of Spiritism. Listen to Him. Eradicate impiety, lies, error and incredulity from your aching souls. They are like monsters who suck the purest of your blood and open wounds which are almost always mortal. Thus in the future when you have become humble and submissive to the Creator, you will keep His divine law. Love, pray, be gentle to the Spirits of the Lord, and call unto them from the bottom of your hearts. Then He will send His beloved son to instruct you and to say these goodly words: "I am come because you called me." — THE SPIRIT OF TRUTH (Bordeaux, 1861).

8. God consoles the humble and gives strength to the afflicted when they ask. His might covers the Earth and in every place, with each tear shed, He places a consoling remedy. Abnegation and resignation are a continuous prayer and contain profound teaching. Human wisdom resides in these two words. Would that all suffering Spirits could understand this truth, instead of clamouring against their pain and moral sufferings which it behoves them to partake. So, take these words for your motto: *devotion and abnegation* — and you will be strong as they resume all the obligations which charity and humility impose. The sentiment of fulfilled duty will give repose and resignation to your Spirit. Then your heart will beat more steadily, your soul become more tranquil and your body be protected against despondency. This is why the body feels that much weaker according to how profoundly the Spirit is stricken. — THE SPIRIT OF TRUTH (Havre, 1863).

CHAPTER 7

BLESSED ARE THE POOR IN SPIRIT

What should be understood by the words 'poor in spirit.' — He
who exalts himself shall be debased. — Mysteries that are
hidden from the learned and prudent. — INSTRUCTIONS
FROM THE SPIRITS: Pride & humility. — Mission of the
intelligent person on Earth.

WHAT SHOULD BE UNDERSTOOD BY THE WORDS 'POOR IN SPIRIT'

1. *Blessed are the poor in spirit: for theirs is the Kingdom of Heaven (Matthew, 5: 3).*

2. Skeptics have mocked this maxim, as they have mocked many other things they do not understand. By 'the poor in spirit' Jesus did not mean those devoid of intelligence, but the humble, in as much as He said that the Kingdom of Heaven would be for them and not for the prideful.

Men of knowledge and imagination, so called by public conviction, generally hold such high opinions of themselves and their superiority that they consider everything divine as being undeserving of their consideration. By concentrating all their attention upon themselves, they are then unable to lift up their eyes to God. This tendency to believe they are superior to everything else very frequently leads them to deny anything which might be above them, even Divinity itself, for fear it might belittle them. Or if they condescend to admit its existence, they then contest one of its most beautiful attributes, that of providential action over things of this world, because they think they alone are sufficient to govern. Taking the intelligence they possess as a measure for universal intelligence, and judging themselves able to understand everything, they are unable to believe in the viability of that which they do not know. They consider their judgement to be law.

If they do not admit the existence of the invisible world and of a superhuman power, it is not because it is beyond their capability, but because their pride makes them revolt against the idea of something above which they are unable to place themselves and which would bring them down from the pedestal upon which they like to contemplate. Hence they only have scorn for everything that does not belong to the visible and tangible world. They attribute to themselves such imagination and learning that they cannot believe in things which, according to their way of thinking, are only good for simple people, taking for *poor in spirit* all who take such matters seriously.

However, say what they like, they will inevitably be drawn into this invisible world they scoff at, together with everyone else. It is there that their eyes will be opened, so making them realise their errors. Nevertheless, God being just, He cannot receive those who have denied His majesty in the same manner as those who submitted to His laws with humility, nor can He give them equal share.

By saying that the Kingdom of Heaven belongs to the poor in spirit, Jesus teaches that no one will be admitted without *simplicity of heart and humility of spirit;* that the ignorant person who possesses these qualities will be preferred to the wise person who believes more in himself than in God. In all circumstances Jesus put humility into the category of virtues that bring Man near to God and pride into the category of vices that keep Man away from God. The reason for this is clear, for to be humble is an act of submission to God, whereas pride is a revolt against Him. For Man then, there is far greater value for his future happiness by being *poor in spirit,* as the world would understand it, and rich in moral qualities.

HE WHO EXALTS HIMSELF SHALL BE DEBASED

3. *At the same time came the disciples unto Jesus, saying, Who is the greatest in the Kingdom of Heaven? And Jesus called a little child unto Him, and set him in the midst of them, and said, Verily I say unto you, Except ye be converted, and become as little children, ye shall not enter into the Kingdom of Heaven. Whosoever therefore shall humble himself as this little child, the same is greatest in the Kingdom of Heaven. And who shall receive one such little child, in my name, receiveth me (Matthew 18: 1–5).*

4. *Then came to Him the mother of Zebedee's children with her sons, worshipping Him, and desiring a certain thing of Him. And He said unto her, What wilt thou? She said unto Him, Grant that these my two sons may sit, the one on Thy right hand, and the other on the left, in Thy Kingdom. But Jesus answered and said, Ye know not what ye ask. Are ye able to drink of the cup that I shall drink of, and be baptised with the baptism that I am baptised with? They say unto Him, We are able. And He said unto them, Ye shall indeed drink from my cup and be baptised with the baptism that I am baptised with, but to sit on my right hand and on my left hand, is not mine to give, but it shall be given unto them for whom it is prepared of my Father. And when the ten heard it they were moved with indignation against the two brethren. But Jesus called them unto Him and said, Ye know that the Prince of the Gentiles exercises dominion over them, and they that are great exercise authority upon them. But it shall not be so among you: but whosoever will be great among you, let him be your minister: and whosoever will be chief among you let him be your servant: even as the Son of Man came not to be ministered unto, but to minister and to give His life as ransom for many (Matthew 20: 20-28).*

5. *And it came to pass as He went into the house of one of the chief Pharisees to eat bread on the Sabbath day that they watched Him. And He put forth a parable to those which were bidden, when He marked how they chose out the chief rooms: saying unto them, When thou art bidden of any man to a wedding, sit not down in the highest room; lest a more honourable man than thou be bidden of him; and he that bade thee and him come and say to thee, Give this man place; and thou begin with shame to take the lowest room. But when thou art bidden go and sit down in the lowest room; that when he that bade thee cometh, he may say unto thee, Friend go up higher; then shalt thou have worship in the presence of them that sit at meat with thee. For whosoever exalteth himself shall be debased; and he that humbleth himself shall be exalted (Luke 14: 1 & 7-11).*

6. These maxims stem from the principle of humility that Jesus was constantly presenting as an essential condition for the happiness promised to the chosen of the Lord, which He presented in this manner: "Blessed be the poor in spirit, for theirs is the Kingdom of Heaven." He took a child as a symbol of simplicity of heart when He said: "The greatest in the Kingdom of Heaven shall be he who is humble and who *is as a little child.* "That is to say, who holds no pretension to superiority or infallibility.

We find the same fundamental idea in the following maxim: *He who desires to be the greatest amongst you, let him be your servant,* and also in this: *He that humbles himself shall be exalted and he who exalts himself shall be debased.*

Spiritism confirms its theory through examples when it shows us that those who are great in the spiritual world are those who were small on Earth, and that frequently those who were great and powerful on Earth find themselves extremely small in the spiritual world. This is because on dying, Man takes with him only that which makes for greatness in Heaven, that which is never lost, which are his virtues. All earthly greatness, such as riches, titles, glory, nobleness of birth, etc., are impossible to take. On reaching the other side, if Man has nothing apart from these qualities, he finds himself destitute of everything, as a person who is ship-wrecked loses everything, even to his clothes. The only item still retained is pride, which makes the position even worse, more humiliating, when it is found that those they trod underfoot on Earth have been raised to places of glory far above.

Spiritism also shows another side of this principle within the process of successive reincarnations, when those who in one life have raised themselves to high positions, are then born into lowly conditions in a succeeding existence, if they have allowed themselves to be dominated by pride and ambition. Therefore do not seek the highest positions on Earth nor place yourself above others if you do not wish to be obliged to descend. On the contrary, seek the most humble and modest positions, seeing that God will then give you a more elevated place in Heaven if you deserve it.

MYSTERIES ARE HIDDEN FROM THE LEARNED AND PRUDENT

7. *At that time Jesus answered and said: I thank thee, O Father, Lord of Heaven and Earth, because thou hast hid these things from the wise and prudent, and hast revealed them unto babes (Matthew, 11: 25).*

8. It may appear quite singular that Jesus gives thanks to God for having revealed these things to the *simple and humble,* who are the poor in spirit, and for having hidden them from the *learned and prudent,* who apparently are more able to understand. But we must recognise that the former are those who are submissive, who humble themselves before God and do not consider themselves superior. The latter are those who are arrogant, full of pride for their worldly knowledge, judging themselves prudent because they deny God or who, when they are not refusing to accept Him, treat Him as an equal despite the fact that in ancient times *learned* was a synonym for *wise.* This is why God has left them to discover the secrets of the Earth and revealed the secrets of Heaven only to the humble, who prostrate themselves before Him.

9. The same thing has happened today with the great truths revealed by Spiritism. Many of those who are incredulous are surprised by the fact that the Spirits take so little trouble to convince them. The reason for this being that it is preferable to look after those who seek with good faith and humility, rather than offer enlightenment to those who suppose they already possess it; who perhaps imagine that God should be very thankful for having managed to attract their attention by proving His existence to them.

The power of God manifests itself in all things, from the smallest to the greatest. He does not hide His light, but rather disperses it in constant waves to every corner of the Universe, to such an extent that only those who are blind do not see. *God does not wish their eyes to be opened by force, seeing that they desire to keep them shut.* Their time will come. But first it is necessary that they feel the anguish of darkness and so *recognise it is the Divinity and not mere chance which hurts their pride.* In order to overcome this incredulity, God uses the most convenient means according to each individual. It is not their incredulity that prescribes what is to be done, nor is it up to them to say: "If you want to convince me, then you must do this or that on a certain occasion because this is what could persuade me." Therefore those who are unbelievers should not be surprised if neither God nor the Spirits who execute His wishes, do not submit to these demands. Instead, they should ask themselves what they would say if the lowest of their servants tried to impose upon them in whatever form. God imposes the conditions and does not accept those who wish to impose conditions on Him. He listens kindly to those who direct themselves to Him with humility and not to those who judge themselves greater than He.

10. It is often asked if God could not touch these people personally by means of clearly evident manifestations before which even the most obstinate unbeliever would be convinced. Beyond all doubt He could. But in this case what merit would be gained and more importantly, what use would it be? Do we not see people every day who do not bow down even before such evidence and who say: "Even if I saw I would not believe because I *know* it is impossible"? If they deny truth in such a manner it is because their spirits have not yet reached sufficient maturity to enable them to understand, nor their hearts to feel it. *Pride is the cataract which covers their vision.* What good does it do to show a light to one who is blind? Rather it is first necessary to cure the cause of the ill. This is why, as a skillful doctor, He first of all punishes their pride. He will never abandon any of His children since sooner or later their eyes will be opened, but He wishes this to happen of their own free-will. Then defeated by the torments of incredulity, they will throw themselves of their own accord into His arms, begging to be forgiven just as the prodigal son did.

INSTRUCTIONS FROM THE SPIRITS.
PRIDE AND HUMILITY

11. My dear friends, may the peace of the Lord be with you! I am come in order to encourage you to follow the good pathway.

The humble Spirits, who in other times inhabited the Earth, have been commissioned by God to enlighten you. Blessed be the Lord for the grace that He has granted us of being able to help you improve. May the Holy Spirit illuminate me, so helping to make my words understandable and grant me the favour of being able to put them within reach of all! You who are incarnate, who undergo trials and are searching for the light, I pray that the will of God come to my aid so that I may make His teachings shine before your eyes!

Humility is a virtue much forgotten amongst you. Of the many examples given very few have been followed. However, is it possible to be charitable to your neighbour without being humble? Of course not, because this sentiment reduces mankind to the same level by telling them they are brothers and sisters who should help one another mutually, which leads then to a state of goodness. Without humility you are merely adorning yourself with virtues you do not possess, as if you used clothes especially for the purpose of hiding some physical deformity. Remember He who saved us; remember His humility which was so great as to put Him above all the prophets!

Pride is the terrible adversary of humility. If Christ promised the Kingdom of Heaven to the poor it was because the great ones of this Earth imagined their titles and riches to be recompenses, conferred upon them due to merit, and so considered themselves to be of an essence much purer than that of the poor. They judged that the titles and riches were due to them, in view of which, when God took them away, they accused Him of injustice. Oh! What a mockery of God's justice, what blindness! Does God then distinguish by means of the body? Is not the physical covering of the poor person just the same as that of the rich person? Has the Creator made two kinds of humanity? Everything made by God is wise and great. Therefore never attribute to Him those ideas created by your own prideful minds.

Oh, you who are rich! While sleeping beneath your golden ceilings safe from the cold, are you unaware that thousands of your brothers and sisters, who in God's eyes are worth just as much as you, sleep upon straw? Are not those who go hungry your equals? I know full well that your pride revolts at my words. You agree to give alms, but you will never shake their hands! "Why so!" you will say, "I, who am of the noblest blood, one of the great of this Earth, equal to those miserable wretches covered in rags! This is a vain Utopia of pseudo-philosphers! If we are equal, why would God have placed them so low and me so high?" It is quite true that your vestments are not alike, but if you undressed yourselves what difference would there be between you and them? Nevertheless, those of noble blood would say there is a chemical difference; but till today no such difference has even been discovered between the blood of a lord and that of a plebeian, or that of a master and that of his slave. Who can guarantee that in the past you too have not been wretched and unfortunate as they are now? That you too have not begged for alms? Who can say that one day in the future you will not beg alms of one you despise today? Are riches eternal? Do they disappear when the body extinguishes itself? After all, the body is nothing more than the perishable covering of the Spirit! Ah! Cover yourselves with a little humility! Cast your eyes finally on the reality of the things of this world, on what leads to greatness on the one hand and debasement on the other. Remember you will not be spared from death, for no one is; nor can your titles be preserved from its blow, which may strike today, tomorrow or at any hour. If you bury yourself in your pride, oh, how much you will have to lament! Then you will be deserving of great compassion.

You who are so full of pride, what were you before you became noble and powerful? Probably you were beneath the lowest of your servants. Therefore, bow down your haughty brows, for God can cause you to fall at the exact moment when you most exalt yourselves. All men are equal on the divine scale of justice; only virtue marks the distinction in the eyes of God. All Spirits come from the same essence and all bodies are formed from the same matter. Your titles and names modify nothing. They remain in the tomb and in no way contribute to the possibility of enjoying the fortunes of the chosen. Their titles of nobleness are based solely on acts of charity and humility.

Poor creature! You are a mother! Your children suffer! They are cold and hungry while you, bent under the burden of your cross, go out to humiliate yourself in order to bring them bread! Oh! I bow down before you! How saintly and noble you are, how great in my eyes! Pray and wait, because happiness still is not of this world. God will grant the Kingdom of Heaven to the poor and oppressed who have confidence in Him.

And you, sweet maiden, who are still but a child, thrust into work and privations. Why do you have such thoughts? Why do you cry? Lift up your eyes to God, who is serene and full of pity. He will not abandon you. The sound of parties and the joys of this world make your heart beat faster. You wish to adorn yourself and join together with the fortunate of this sphere. You say to yourself that, like the women you see passing by free of cares and full of laughter, you too could be rich. Oh! Dear child, do not say such things! If you only knew how many tears and what unspeakable pain are hidden beneath those embroidered dresses, how many sobs are muffled by the sound of that noisy orchestra, you would prefer your humble position and pauperism. Maintain yourself pure in the eyes of God if you do not want your Guardian Angel to turn from you, covering his face with his white wings, leaving you to your remorse on this planet, without a guide, without support, where you will be lost and where you will be forced to await punishment in the next world.

All you who suffer injustice from your fellow men, be indulgent with the faults of your brothers and sisters, pondering that you are not exempt from guilt. This is charity and also humility. If you suffer from slander, then bow down your head before this trial. What importance does the slander of this world have for you? If your conduct is pure, cannot God recompense you? Support courageously the humiliations put upon you by man; be humble and recognise that only God is great and powerful.

Oh dear God! Will it be necessary for Christ to return to Earth a second time in order to teach His laws because Man has forgotten them? Will He once again have to expell the merchants from the temple for defiling His house, which should have been kept exclusively for prayer? Ah, who knows? Oh mankind, if God granted this grace once more would you not reject Him yet again? Would you not accuse Him of blasphemy because He would humble the pride of modern pharisees? Perhaps it is even possible that you would make Him follow the road to Golgotha again.

When Moses climbed mount Sinai to receive God's commandments, the people of Israel left to themselves abandoned the true God. Men and women gave whatever gold they possessed in order that an idol could be made for them to worship. Civilized Man still imitates them. Christ bequeathed His doctrine to you, giving examples of all the virtues, but you have abandoned these examples and precepts. Each one of you, charged with passions, has made a god in accordance with your desires; for some, bloody and terrible, for others, indifferent to the interests of the world. Nevertheless, the god you have fabricated is still the golden calf which each adapts to his own tastes and ideas.

My friends, my brothers and sisters, awaken! Let the voices of the Spirits echo in your hearts. Be generous and charitable without ostentation, that is to say, do good with humility. Let each one, little by little, begin to demolish the altars erected by everyone to their pride. In a word, if you are a true Christian you will possess the kingdom of truth. Do not continue to doubt the goodness of God when He is giving so many proofs of this fact. We have come to prepare the way so that the prophesies may be fulfilled. At some possible future time, when the Lord gives you a more resounding demonstration of His clemency, may His celestial messenger find you gathered together in a great family. It is hoped that by then, your hearts being gentle and mild, you will be worthy to hear the divine words He would offer. May the Chosen One encounter only laurels in His path which have been laid there by your having returned to goodness, charity and fraternity amongst men. Then will your world become an earthly Paradise. However, if you remain insensible to the voices of the Spirits who have been sent to purify and renew your civilized society, which although rich in science, is so poor in noble sentiments, then sadly there will be nothing left for you but tears and groans of unhappiness. But that will not happen! You will return to God the Father, and all of us who have contributed to the fulfilling of His wishes will join together in singing a hymn of thanksgiving for His unbounding goodness, so as to glorify Him throughout all the coming ages. So be it. — LACORDAIRE (Constantine, 1863).

12. Mankind, why do you complain about the calamities which you yourselves have heaped upon your heads? You despise the saintly and divine morality of Christ, so do not be surprised that the cup of iniquity should overflow on all sides.

Trouble has become generalised. Who is to blame if not you who have unceasingly tried to crush each other? It is impossible to be happy without mutual benevolence; but how can benevolence coexist alongside pride? Pride! This is the root of all your troubles. Apply yourselves therefore to destroying it, if you do not wish continually to perpetuate these fatal consequences. There is only one way which offers itself for this purpose, but it is infallible: take Christ's law as your invariable rule of conduct, that very same law which has been spurned or falsified in its interpretation.

Why do you hold that which shines and enchants the eyes in higher esteem than that which touches the heart? Why do you make the vice of opulence the object of your adulations, whereas you are disdainful of true merit when it is obscure? Whenever a rich debauchee appears, even though he be lost in body and soul, all doors open, all rush to give him attention; whereas a godly person who lives by his work is hardly given a good-day! When the consideration dispensed to others is measured by the gold they possess or the name they use, what interest can they have in correcting their defects?

But it would be very different if the many degrading and immoral practices which are gilded over, were censured by public opinion as much as is the failing of poverty. But pride shows itself ever indulgent to all who flatter it. You say that this is the century of cupidity and money. Beyond doubt; but why allow material necessity to overshadow your good sense and reason? Why must each one wish to place themself above their brother? Society today suffers the consequences of this fact.

Never forget that this state of affairs is always a sign of moral decay and decline. When pride reaches extremes it is an indication of an imminent fall, for God never fails to punish the arrogant. If He sometimes allows them to rise, it is only in order to give time for meditation and to mend their ways under the blows which come to strike their pride from time to time, to serve as warnings. But instead of becoming humble, they rebel. Thus when the cup is full God will cause them to descend, and according to how high they have risen, the more terrible will be their fall.

Suffering humanity, whose selfishness has corrupted all things, we beg you to renew your courage despite everything. In His infinite mercy God has sent you a powerful remedy for all your ills, an unexpected help for all your miseries. Open your eyes to the light! Here are the souls of those who no longer live upon the Earth, who have come to call you to the fulfillment of your true obligations. They will tell you, with the voice of experience, that compared to eternity the vanities and grandeurs of this passing existence become mere trifles. There, the greatest is the one who has been the humblest amongst the most humble of your world; he who has most loved his fellow beings will himself be the best loved in Heaven. If the powerful on Earth abuse their authority, they will find themselves reduced to a position of obedience to their own servants and lastly, humility and charity, who are as two brothers going hand in hand, are the most efficient means of obtaining grace before He who is Eternal. — ADOLF, Bishop of Argel (Marmande, 1862).

MISSION OF THE INTELLIGENT PERSON ON EARTH

13. Never be prideful of what you know, because that knowledge has very restricted limits in the world in which you live. Supposing you were a prominent intellectual celebrity on this planet, still you would have no right to be proud. If God, within His designs, causes you to be born in an ambient where you could develop this intelligence, then it was because He wished you to use it for the benefit of everyone. You have been given a mission by the fact of God having placed an instrument in your hands, which can be used to develop the retarded intelligences around you, and so conduct them to God. Is not the nature of the instrument an indication as to the purpose it should be used for? Does not the hoe which the gardener gives to his assistant, show to what use it should be put? What would you say if instead of working with the hoe, he raised it against his master with a desire to injure him? You would say it was monstrous, that he should be expelled. Well then, is it not the same for he who uses his intelligence to destroy the idea of God and Providence amongst his fellow men? Does he not raise the hoe, which was given to him to till the soil, against his master? Has he then the right to receive the promised salary? On the contrary, does he not deserve to be expelled from the garden? Do not doubt that he will be! Then he will pass through many miserable existences full of humiliations, until he finally bows down before Him to Whom he owes everything.

Intelligence holds great riches in future merits, provided it is well employed. If all men and women who possessed it used it in conformity with God's wishes, then it would be easy for the Spirits to perform their task of helping humanity advance. Unhappily, many have become instruments of pride and perdition against themselves. Mankind abuses intelligence as it does all the other faculties. But nevertheless, there is no lack of teachings which warn of a powerful Hand that may withdraw what has been granted. — FERDINAND, a Protecting Spirit (Bordeaux, 1862).

CHAPTER 8

BLESSED ARE THE PURE IN HEART

Simplicity and pureness of heart. — Sinning by means of
thought. Adultery. — True pureness. Unwashed hands. —
Offences. If your hand is the cause of an offence, cut it off. —
INSTRUCTIONS FROM THE SPIRITS: Let little children
come unto me. — Blessed are those whose eyes are closed.

SIMPLICITY AND PURENESS OF HEART

1. *Blessed are the pure in heart: for they shall see God (Matthew, 5: 8).*

2. *And they brought young children to Him, that He should touch them: and His disciples rebuked those that brought them. But when Jesus saw it, He was much displeased, and said unto them, Suffer the little children to come unto me, and forbid them not: for such is the Kingdom of God. Verily I say unto you, Whosoever shall not receive the Kingdom of God as a little child, he shall not enter therein. And He took them up in his arms, put his hands upon them, and blessed them (Mark, 10: 13–16).*

3. Pureness of heart is inseparable from simplicity and humility. It excludes all ideas of selfishness and pride. This was why Jesus took infancy as the symbol of purity and humility.

It might appear unjust to make this comparison seeing that the Spirit of a child could be very old, and on being reborn to corporeal life might bring with it the imperfections which it had not been able to cast off during previous incarnations. Only a Spirit who has reached perfection can offer an example of true purity. However, from the point of view of our present life it offers an exact comparison because a child, having had no opportunity as yet to manifest any perverse tendencies, presents us with an image of innocence and purity. So it becomes clear that Jesus did not say the Kingdom of Heaven was meant *for children,* but *for those who resemble them.*

4. Since the Spirit of a child has lived before, why does it not show itself as it really is right from birth? Everything in God's work is full of wisdom. A child needs special care which only a mother's tenderness can bestow, tenderness which stems from the frailty and ingenuousness of the child. For a mother, her child is always an angel and this is the way it must be in order to captivate concern. She would not be able to offer the same solicitude if, in place of

ingenuousness, she saw virility and adult ideas in the infantile features, nor if she came to know the past of that incarnate Spirit.

From the time of birth ideas gradually take on shape and impulse according to the development of the organs, from which it is possible to say that during the first years the Spirit is truly a child, because all ideas which form the true character remain dormant. During this period of dormancy, in which the instincts are also latent, the Spirit is more malleable, more accessible to impressions which can modify the character and which helps the Spirit progress. All of which makes it easier for the parents to educate the child at this stage.

The Spirit then, wears a temporary tunic of innocence and so Jesus was right when, not withstanding the anteriority of the soul, He takes a child as the symbol of purity and simplicity.

SINNING BY MEANS OF THOUGHT. ADULTERY

5. *Ye have heard that it was said by them of old time, Thou shalt not commit adultery: but I say unto you, That whosoever looketh on a woman to lust after her hath committed adultery with her already in his heart (Matthew, 5: 27 & 28).*

6. Under no circumstances should the word *adultery* be accepted in the exclusive sense to which it is commonly applied, but rather it should be understood in more general terms. Jesus used it many times in an extensive sense to designate evil, sin and every type of bad thought, as for example in this passage: "Whosoever therefore, shall be ashamed of Me and My words in this *adulterous and sinful generation,* of him shall the Son of Man be ashamed, when He commeth in the glory of His Father with the holy angels" (Mark, 8: 38).

True pureness is not only in behaviour but also in thought, since the person who has a pure heart does not even think evil. Jesus wished to say that He condemned sin even in thought, because it is a sign of impurity.

7. This principle naturally leads to the following question: *Do we suffer consequences for a bad thought even if it is not followed by the actual action?*

At this point it is necessary to make an important distinction. As the soul advances along its path to evolution and spiritualization, it will slowly become enlightened, and so little by little divest itself of its imperfections according to the greater or lesser goodwill it demonstrates within its freewill.

Therefore all evil thoughts result from the imperfections of the soul. But according to the strength of the desire to purify itself, the evil thought becomes a means of advancement when it is energetically repelled. This is an indication of a positive action by the soul in order to extinguish a blemish. In this way it will not give in to the temptation to satisfy an evil desire, and having resisted, the soul feels itself to be stronger and content with the victory.

On the contrary, the person who has made no good resolutions will look for every opportunity to practice evil, and if this is not achieved it will not be for the wanting, but for the lack of opportunity. This person then will be just as guilty as if he or she had actually committed evil.

To summarize, a certain degree of progress has already been achieved by the person who does not conceive the idea of committing evil; for the person who feels the urge but constantly repells it, progress is in the process of realization; for the person who thinks in terms of evil, taking pleasure in these thoughts, then the evil still exists in all its strength. In the one the work has been done, whereas in the other it is still to be started. But being just, God takes into account all these gradations when it comes to individual responsibilities for acts and thoughts.

TRUE PURENESS. UNWASHED HANDS

8. *Then came to Jesus scribes and Pharasees, which were in Jerusalem, saying, Why do thy disciples transgress the tradition of the elders? For they wash not their hands when they eat bread. But He answered and said unto them, Why do ye also transgress the commandments of God by your tradition? For God commanded, saying, honour thy father and mother: and, he that curseth father and mother, let him die the death. But ye say, Whosoever shall say to his father or his mother, it is a gift, by whatsoever though mightest be profited by me; and honour not his father or his mother he shall be free. Thus have ye made the commandment of God of none effect by your tradition. Ye hypocrites, well did Esaias prophesy of you saying, This people draweth nigh unto me with their mouth and honoureth me with their lips; but their heart is far from me. But in vain they do worship me, teaching for doctrine the commandments of men.*

And He called the multitude, and said unto them, Hear, and understand: Not that which goeth into the mouth defileth a man; but that which cometh out of the mouth, this defileth a man. Then came his disciples, and said unto Him, Knowest thou that the Pharisees were offended, after they heard this saying? But He answered and said, every plant, which my heavenly Father hath not planted, shall be rooted up. Let them alone: they be blind leaders of the blind. And if the blind lead the blind, both shall fall into the ditch (Matthew, 15: 1-14).

9. *And as He spake, a certain Pharisee besought Him to dine with him: and He went in, and sat down to meat. And when the Pharisee saw it, he marvelled that He had not first washed before dinner, and the Lord said unto him, Now do ye Pharisees make clean the outside of the cup and the platter; but your inward part is full of ravening and wickedness. Ye fools, did not He that made that which is without make that which is within also?. (Luke 11: 37-40).*

10. The Jews had scorned God's true commandments in order to cling to the practice of regulations which had been established by man and had made the observance of these regulations a matter of conscience. The original simple substance became lost beneath complicated forms of ritual. As it was much easier to practice exterior cult than to effect moral reform, *to wash hands*

instead of cleansing the heart, Man became deluded, believing himself exonerated before God by conforming to these practices. Thus, seeing that the people were taught that God demanded nothing more of them, they remained the same as they had always been. Hence the prophet said: *'But in vain do they worship me, teaching for doctrine commandments of men."*

 The verification of this can be found in the moral doctrine of Christ, which has ended up in second place and as a result many Christians, just like the ancient Jews, consider that salvation is better guaranteed by means of external practice rather than by moral practice. It is to these man-made additions to God's law which Jesus referred to when He said *"Every plant which my heavenly Father hath not planted shall be rooted up."*

The object of religion is to conduct humanity towards God. Well, God can only be reached through perfection. Therefore every religion which does not make Man better than at the present time, will never reach its objective. Everything which Man judges will support him in committing evil, is either false or had its principles falsified. Such is the result of all religions where the form surmounts the base. Belief in the efficiency of exterior manifestation is null and void if it does not oppose the acts of murder, adultery, robbery, the causing of slander or damage in whatsoever form to whomsoever it may be. These kinds of religion never create godly men and women, only people who are superstitious, hyprocrites and fanatics.

The mere appearance of pureness is not enough, because above all else it is necessary to have a pure heart.

OFFENCES. IF YOUR HAND BE THE CAUSE OF AN OFFENCE, CUT IT OFF

11. *Woe unto the world because of offences! For it must needs be that offences come; but woe unto that man by whom the offence cometh.*

But whoso shall offend one of these little ones which believe in me, it were better for him that a millstone were hanged about his neck, and that he were drowned in the depth of the sea.

Take heed that ye despise not one of these little ones; for I say unto you, That in heaven their angels do always behold the face of my Father which is in heaven. For the Son of man is come to save that which was lost (Matthew, 18: 6–11).

And if thy right hand offends thee, cut it off, and cast it from thee: for it is profitable for thee that one of they members should perish, and not that thy whole body should be cast into hell. And if thy right eye offend thee, pluck it out, and cast it from thee: for it is profitable for thee that one of thy members should perish and not that thy whole body should be cast into hell (Matthew, 5: 30-29).

12. In its most usual sense the word *offence* means any action which goes ostensively against morality or decorum. The offence is not in the action itself

so much as in the repercussion it may cause. The word always implies a certain amount of commotion and dispute. Many people are content if they avoid causing offence in public, because this would cause them to suffer loss of prestige, so hurting their pride. They do their best to hide their mistakes as this is sufficient to quieten their consciences. They are, as Jesus said: "As white sepulchres which are full of rottenness, like vessels which are clean without, but dirty within."

But in the evangelic sense the accepted meaning of the word 'offence', used so repeatedly, is very much more generalised and this is why in certain cases its meaning is not understood. It becomes not only that which affects the conscience of another person, but also everything which is the result of vice and human imperfections, every bad reaction from one individual to another, with or without repercussion. In this case the offence is *the effective result of bad morality.*

13. Jesus said: *It is necessary that offences exist in the world,* because due to the many imperfections of those on Earth, humanity shows itself inclined to practice evil and also because bad trees only bring forth bad fruits. From these words then, we must understand that evil is the consequence of Man's imperfections and not that there exists an obligation to practice evil.

14. *It must needs be that offence comes* so that humanity, being in atonement here on Earth, may punish itself by contact with its own failings, thus becoming its first victims, from whence it will finally come to understand the inconvenience of this way of life. When people are tired of suffering due to evil, they will seek a remedy in goodness. Therefore the reactions caused by these failings serve for some as a punishment and for others as a test. This is how God gets good out of evil and how humanity makes use of badness.

15. It could be said then, that evil is necessary and that it will last forever, seeing that if it disappears God would be deprived of a powerful means of being able to correct the guilty. It could also be said that it is useless to try to better mankind. However, if we ceased to have culprits then it would be unnecessary to have any kind of punishment.

Let us suppose that mankind was transformed, so becoming composed only of good men and women, then no one would think of doing evil to his neighbour and all would be happy to be good. This is the condition found in the elevated worlds, where evil has been banished. This is what will come to pass here on Earth, when Man has made sufficient progress. But new worlds are populated by primitive Spirits and also serve as places of exile, places of atonement, for those Spirits who are imperfect, rebellious, persistent in evil or who have been expelled from worlds which have become places of happiness.

16. *But woe to that man by whom the offence comes.* That is to say, that evil always being evil, the person who without knowing serves as an instrument of Divine justice, whose bad instincts were utilized, commits no less an evil and so deserves punishment. In this manner an ungrateful child is a punishment or

trial for the parents, who are forced to suffer by its attitude. This is because the mother or father had themselves been bad children and made their parents suffer. So they pay the penalty. But the circumstances should not be an excuse for the child's behaviour, who in return will have to pay the penalty through his or her own children, or in some other manner.

17. *If your hand be the cause of offence, cut it off.* This is a very strong statement and it would be absurd for it to be taken in its literal sense. It should therefore be understood that each one must destroy within themselves everything that might cause offence, that is to say all evil, by rooting out every impure thought and every tendency towards violence, corruption or depravity. It also means that it is preferable for a man to cut off a hand rather than use it to commit an evil action, or better still, to lose one's sight rather than allow one's eyes to conceive bad thoughts. For those who take the trouble to discover the allegoric meaning of His words, Jesus never said anything that was absurd. Nevertheless, many things cannot be understood without the key to decipher them and this key is offered to us through Spiritism.

INSTRUCTIONS FROM THE SPIRITS.
LET THE LITTLE CHILDREN COME UNTO ME

18. Christ said: "Let the little children come unto me." Profound in their simplicity these words do not contain just a call to children, but also a call to the souls who gravitate in the inferior regions where misfortune knows no hope. Jesus also calls to the infantile intellectuality of the adult, to the weak, to those in slavery, to the depraved and to the wicked. He could teach nothing to the physically infantile, still bound by matter and submitted to the yoke of instinct, as these had not yet reached the superior category of reason nor of free-will, which is exercised around them and for their benefit.

Jesus wanted mankind to deliver themselves to Him with confidence, in the same way that tiny tots, with their special appeal, win over the hearts of women, who are all mothers. Then He could submit these souls to His tender and mysterious influence. He was the flame which brought light to the darkness, that dawn light which announces the sunrise. He was the initiator of Spiritism, which should in its turn attract to Him not the children, but men of goodwill. Vigorous action has begun; it is no longer a question of instinctive belief and mechanical obedience; it is necessary for Man to follow the intelligent law which shows its universality.

Dearly beloved, the time has come in which, when explained, all fallacies will become truths. We shall teach the exact meaning of the parables and show the strong correlation existing between what was and what is now. In truth I say unto you that these great spiritual manifestations will open up the horizons and that this is the messenger which will shine resplendently as the sun upon the mountain top. — JOHN THE EVANGELIST (Paris, 1863).

19. Let the little children come unto Me for I have the milk which will strengthen the weak. Let all those who are fearful, feeble, in need of help and consolation come unto Me. Let the ignorant come unto Me, so that I may

enlighten them. Let all who suffer come unto Me, together with the afflicted and the unfortunate. I will teach them the great remedy which will soften their ills, revealing unto them the secret that will cure their wounds! What is this supreme balsam, my friends, which possesses such high virtue that it may be applied to all types of wounds suffered by the heart and heal them? It is love and charity! If you possess this divine flame, what is there to be afraid of? Then every moment of your life you will say: "Dear Father, I pray that Your wish be done and not mine; if it be Your pleasure to test me through pain and tribulations, blessed be it, because I know it is for my own good. If it pleases you Lord, have mercy on this weak creature, giving justifiable happiness to this heart and blessed be it yet again. But do not allow divine love to lie sleeping in my soul; make it rise up unceasingly and present itself at Your feet as witness of my gratitude."

If you have love, then you have the most desirable thing on Earth. You possess a most precious pearl which no occurance, nor malice of those who hate and persecute, can take away. If you have love you will have placed your treasure where the worms and rust cannot attack, having extinguished everything capable of defiling the pureness of your soul. Every day you will feel the diminishing weight of matter, and like a bird in the sky which no longer remembers the Earth, will continually rise up without ceasing till your soul, full of exhilaration, fills itself with the elements of the true life in the bosom of the Lord. — A Protecting Spirit (Bordeaux, 1861).

BLESSED ARE THOSE WHOSE EYES ARE CLOSED. (1)

20. My good friends, why did you call me? Was it because you wished that I put my hands upon the unhappy sufferer that is present and cure her? Ah, what suffering, dear God! She has lost her sight and darkness envelopes her. Poor child! Let her pray and wait. I do not know how to perform miracles, if God does not wish it. All the cures that I have been able to obtain, that you have been informed about, can only be attributed to He who is our Father. In your afflictions always lift up your eyes to Heaven and say from the bottom of your hearts: "Lord, cure me, but cause my sick soul to cure itself before you cure my body; let my flesh be chastised, if this be necessary, so that my soul may rise up to Your bosom with the same whiteness it possessed when You created it." After this prayer, my friends, may the good Lord always hear you. Then you will be given strength, courage and perhaps also the cure for which you have asked, in recompense for your abnegation.

However, since I am here in this assembly which deals principally with study, I will tell you that those who are deprived of their sight should consider themselves blessed in their atonement. I would remind you that Christ said it was better to pluck out your eye if it were evil, and that it was preferable to cast it into the fire rather than allow it to become the cause of your condemnation.

---

(1) This communication was given in response to an appeal of a blind person, in whose name the Spirit of J. B. Vianney, a parish priest of Ars, was evoked.

Ah! How many there are in this world who one day, when they are in absolute darkness, will curse the time they saw the light! Oh yes, how happy are those who through atonement find they have been struck in their sight! Then their eyes will not be the cause of offence nor of their downfall. They can live the full life of the soul. They can see more than those whose vision is clear! ... When God permits that I open the eyelids of some of these sad sufferers and restitute the light, then I say to myself: Dear soul, why do you not wish to know all the delights of the Spirit who lives by love and contemplation? Then you would not ask to see images that are less pure and gentle than those you glimpse through your blindness.!

Oh! Blessed is the blind person who wishes to live with God! More fortunate than you who are here at this moment, he feels happiness; it is tangible to him; he sees the souls of men and can rise up with them to the spiritual spheres where he can perceive what even the predestined of the Earth cannot manage to see. Our eyes, when open, are always ready to cause the downfall of the soul; whilst, when shut, they are always ready to help us rise up in the direction of God. Believe me, my good and dear friends, on many occasions blindness is the true light of the heart, whereas sight is frequently the angel of darkness which leads to death.

And now, a few words directed at you, my poor sufferer. Wait and be of good faith! If I were to say: "My child, your eyes will open," how jubilant you would feel! But who knows if this joy would not be the cause of a great loss! Have faith then in the good Lord who gives us happiness and permits sadness. I will do everything for you that I am permitted, but on your side you must pray, and even more important, meditate on all that I have said.

Before I leave, may all who are here gathered together receive my blessing. — VIANNEY, parish priest of Ars (Paris, 1863).

21. REMARKS: When an affliction is not a consequence of acts committed in this life, then we must look for the cause in a previous life. Everything which we call a whim of chance is nothing more than the effect of God's justice. He does not inflict wilful punishment, but desires that every penalty be in accordance with the misdeed. If in His goodness He has cast a veil over our past actions, He has also pointed out the way by saying: "Who kills by the sword shall perish by the sword." From these words we should understand that each creature is always punished according to the way in which he or she has sinned. If someone suffers the torment of losing their sight, then it is because their sight was the cause of their downfall. It might also be that this person was the cause of someone else losing their sight, perhaps in consequence of excessive work that had been imposed upon them by the one who has now lost theirs; perhaps also through ill treatment, lack of care, negligence, etc. In these cases the person responsible always undergoes the penalty caused by his own actions. On repenting, he may have chosen this very atonement, thereby applying to himself the words of Jesus: "If your eye is the motive for offence, then cast it out."

CHAPTER 9

BLESSED ARE THE MEEK AND THE PEACEMAKERS

Insults and violence. — INSTRUCTIONS FROM THE
SPIRITS: Affability and mildness. — Patience. — Obedience
and resignation. — Anger.

INSULTS AND VIOLENCE

1. *Blessed are the meek: for they shall inherit the earth (Matthew, 5: 5).*

2. *Blessed are the peacemakers: for they shall be called the children of God (Matthew, 5: 9).*

3. *Ye have heard that it was said by them of old time, Thou shalt not kill; and whosoever shall kill shall be in danger of the judgement: but I say unto you, That whosoever is angry with his brother without a cause shall be in danger of the judgement: and whosoever shall say to his brother, Raca, shall be in danger of the council; and whosoever shall say, Thou fool, shall be in danger of hell fire (Matthew, 5: 21 & 22).*

4. By these maxims Jesus makes meekness, moderation, docility, affability and patience the Law. Consequently condemning violence, anger and all discourteous expressions towards others. For example, *Raca* was a disdainful expression amongst the Hebrews meaning *a worthless person,* and was accompanied by pronounced spitting and turning the head to one side. At one point Jesus goes so far as to threaten anyone who says to another — *you are insane* — with the fire of hell.

It therefore becomes evident that here, as in all circumstances, the intention aggravates or lessens the offence. But why should a simple word become something so grave as to warrant such severe reproof? This is because every offensive word expresses a sentiment that is contrary to the laws of love and charity, which preside over all human relationships, and between them maintain cordiality and union. By sustaining hate and animosity we are undermining reciprocated benevolence and fraternity. In short, it is because next to humility before God, charity to your neighbour is the first law of all Christians.

5. But what did Jesus mean by the words "Blessed are the meek, for they shall inherit the earth," when He had recommended that mankind renounce all worldly goods after having promised those of Heaven?

While awaiting heavenly riches, mankind has need of the Earth on which to live. Jesus is only recommending that we do not give more importance to worldly goods than to the others. By these words He wishes to say that till now worldly goods have been monopolized by those who are violent, to the detriment of the meek and pacific, who frequently lack even the necessities of life while others have superfluity. Jesus promises justice will be *done on Earth as it is in Heaven* because the meek will be called God's children. When humanity submits itself to the law of love and charity, then selfishness will cease to exist; the weak and peaceful will no longer be exploited or crushed by the strong and violent. This will be the condition of the Earth when this planet becomes a happy world because it has rid itself of all evil, according to the law of progress and the promise made by Jesus.

INSTRUCTIONS FROM THE SPIRITS.

AFFABILITY AND MILDNESS

6. Benevolence towards one's fellow-creatures, which is the result of loving your neightbour, manifests itself in the form of affability and mildness. However, it is not always a good thing to trust in appearance. Education and worldliness can give Man a thin veneer of these qualities. There are many whose feigned good-nature is nothing more than an exterior mask, like beautiful clothes hiding interior deformities! The world is full of such people with a smile on their lips but poison in their hearts; *who are mild as long as nothing irritates them, but who bite at the least provocation;* those whose tongues are made of gold when speaking face to face, but change into a poisoned dart when speaking from behind.

Still in the category of those showing benign countenance, there are those domestic tyrants who make their families and subordinates suffer the weight of their pride and despotism. As if they are trying to get even for any constraints possibly imposed upon them while away from home. Not daring to use their authority on strangers who would call them to order, they want to at least be feared by those who cannot resist them. They are proud to be able to say "I give the orders here and am obeyed." But they never think that they could also add, "And I am detested."

It is not enough for milk and honey to flow from the lips. If the heart is never associated with these sentiments then there is only hypocrisy. Those whose affability and mildness are not mere pretence are never belied, for they are always the same whether in society or in privacy. Besides, they know that although it is possible to deceive Man, no one can deceive God. — LAZARUS (Paris, 1861).

PATIENCE

7. Pain is a blessing sent by God to all His elected; so when you suffer do not allow yourself to become afflicted; rather bless the Omnipotent Who, through the pain of this world, has chosen you to receive glory in Heaven.

Be patient, because this is also a charity; everyone should practice the law of charity as taught by Christ, Who is God's Envoy. Charity given to the poor in the form of alms is the easiest of all. However, there is another kind of charity which is much more laborious and so consequently offers higher merit. That is *to forgive all those placed in your pathway by God to act as instruments for your suffering and to test your patience.*

We know full well that life is difficult, being composed of so many apparently useless, insignificant and valueless things which act as repeated pinpricks and end up hurting us. However, if on the one hand we observe with care the duties imposed upon us, and on the other recognise the consolations and compensations received, then we must admit that the blessings are far more numerous than the pains. When our eyes are raised up to Heaven our burdens appear to be less heavy than when our brow is bowed down to the earth.

Courage, my friends! Christ is your model. He suffered far more than any of you and had nothing to offer penitence for, whereas we must atone for our past and thereby fortify ourselves for the future. So be patient; be Christians! This word summarizes everything. — A Friendly Spirit (Havre, 1862).

OBEDIENCE AND RESIGNATION

8. The doctrine of Jesus constantly teaches obedience and resignation, two virtues which are the companions of mildness and activity, although man wrongly confuses them with denial of sentiment and free-will. *Obedience is the consent of reason; resignation is the consent of the heart.* Both are active forces since they carry the burden which has fallen upon them due to foolish revolt. The coward cannot be resigned, any more than the prideful and selfish can be obedient. Jesus was the very incarnation of these virtues, which were despised by material antiquity. He came to Earth at a time when Roman society was perishing in the failings of corruption. He came so that, even in the bosom of depressed humanity, the triumph of sacrifice and the renouncement of sensuality would shine forth.

Thus, each epoch is marked with the stamp of the virtue or vice which it has either to save or to lose. The virtue of this generation is intellectuality, the vice is moral indifference. We merely use the word 'activity' because a genius may suddenly rise up and discover for him or herself the horizons which will be seen by the multitude only at a later date. Whereas activity denotes the reunion of the endeavours of everyone in order to reach a somewhat less brilliant conclusion, but one which will confirm the intellectual elevation of an epoch.

Submit yourself then to the impulsion we have come to give your spirits. Obey the great law of progress which is the promise of your generation. Woe to the lazy ones, woe to all those not open to understanding! Woe unto them! Because we, who are the guides of humanity on the march, shall apply the whip and subdue the rebellion by means of the double action of brake and spur. All prideful resistance will have to be overcome sooner or later. However, blessed be all those who are mild for they will lend yielding ears to these teachings. — LAZARUS (Paris, 1863).

ANGER

9. Pride induces you to judge yourselves to be more than you are and to repel any comparison which might discredit you. You consider yourselves to be so much higher than your fellow men or women, be it in spirit, in social position or even in personal advantage, that the least parallel irritates and annoys you. What happens then? You give way to anger.

Investigate the origin of these outbursts of passing dementia, which make you resemble a savage by losing your self-possession and reason; and if you do, then you will almost always be faced with hurt pride. Perchance, is it not pride which has been hurt by a contradiction which makes you repel justifiable observations and angrily reject the wisest counsel? Even impatience originating from contrarieties, and often childish ones at that, comes from the importance which each individual gives to their own personality, before which it has been given to understand that everyone should bow down.

In their frenzy, wrathful people hurl themselves at everything, from their own savage nature to lifeless objects, breaking them because they do not obey! Ah! If they could but see themselves at these moments, looking on in cold blood! Either they would be afraid of themselves, or they would think themselves simply ridiculous! Imagine then the impression made on others! Even if it is merely out of respect for oneself, it behoves one to make an effort to overcome this inclination which only makes one into a pitiable object.

If we reflect that anger in no way helps, in fact it modifies our health even to putting our life at risk, then we would recognise that we are nothing more than our own victims. But above all, there is yet another consideration which should restrain us, that of the unhappiness this kind of behaviour brings to all those around us. If we have a heart, would not this anger be a motive for remorse for having caused those we love to suffer? What a terrible moral weight upon us if, in an excess of fury, we were to practise some act which we would deplore for the rest of our life!

To summarize, anger does not exclude certain qualities of the heart, but it stops us from doing any good and may cause us to practise great evil. This then should be sufficient to induce mankind to make the necessary effort in order to dominate this trait. Moreover, for those who are Spiritists, there is an instigation to do this for yet another motive — that of anger being against charity and Christian humility. — A Protecting Spirit (Bordeaux, 1863).

10. Because of the false idea that it is not possible for a person to reform their own nature, they judge themselves exempt from even trying to correct their defects. This applies especially to those defects in which the person willingly takes pleasure, or those which would take a great deal of perseverance to eradicate. This is why, for example, an individual who is prone to anger almost always finds excuses for this temperament. Instead of confessing themselves guilty, they accuse their organism and in this manner accuse God for their faults. This is yet one more of the consequences of pride to be found in the midst of our imperfections.

Undoubtedly there are temperaments which lend themselves more readily than others to violent acts, just as there are muscles which are more flexible than others, so lending themselves better to acts of strength. However, do not believe it is here that the first cause lies, but persuade yourself that a pacific Spirit, even when in a sickly body, will always be pacific. Just as much as a violent Spirit, even when occupying a lymphatic body will not be more mild, only that the violence will take on another aspect. In this case the anger would be more concentrated, just as in the first case the anger would be more expansive.

Therefore it is not the body which gives the anger to those who do not already possess it, in the same manner neither does it cause other vices. All virtues and vices are inherent in the Spirit. If this were not the case, where would be the merit and responsibility? The person who is bodily deformed can do nothing to remedy this situation because the Spirit takes no part in it, but what can be modified is the actual Spirit, when it wants to, by means of strong desire. Does not experience show us up to what point the power of desire can take us when we look at the truly miraculous transformations happening all around us every day? Then let us convince ourselves that Man only remains bound by vices because he so desires! Those who really wish to liberate themselves can always achieve this end. If it were not so, then the law of progress would not be able to exist. — HAHNEMANN (Paris, 1863).

CHAPTER 10

BLESSED ARE THE MERCIFUL

Forgive others so that God may forgive you. — Reconciliation with your adversaries. — The sacrifice most agreeable to God. — The mote and the beam in the eye. — Do not judge others if you do not wish to be judged in return. He that is without sin, let him be the first to cast a stone. — INSTRUCTIONS FROM THE SPIRITS: The pardoning of offences. — Indulgence. —Is it permitted to reprehend, observe imperfections or to comment on the evil in others?

FORGIVE OTHERS SO THAT GOD MAY FORGIVE YOU

1. *Blessed are the merciful: for they shall obtain mercy (Matthew, 5: 7).*

2. *For if ye forgive men their trespasses, your Heavenly Father will also forgive you: but if ye forgive not men their trespasses, neither will your Father forgive your trespasses (Matthew, 6: 14 & 15).*

3. *Moreover if they brother shall trespass against thee, go and tell him his fault between thee and him alone: if he shall hear thee, thou hast gained thy brother. Then came Peter to Him, and said, Lord, how oft shall my brother sin against me, and I forgive him? Till seven times? Jesus said unto him, I say not unto thee, Until seven times: but until seventy times seven (Matthew, 18: 15, 21 & 22).*

4. Mercy is a complement to mildness, because the person who is not merciful cannot be mild and pacific. Mercy consists of being able to forget and forgive all offence. Hate and rancour denotes a Spirit without any elevation or magnanimity. Being able to forget offences is the mark of an elevated soul, which does not perturb itself with the blows it may be dealt. The one is always anxious, of a dark susceptibility and full of bitterness; while the other is calm, full of sweetness and charity.

Woe to those who say they will never forgive! If these people are not already condemned by mankind, then God will surely condemn them. What right has a person to demand forgiveness for their own faults if they are unable to forgive those of others? Does not Jesus teach that mercy must have no limits when He says that each one must forgive their brothers and sisters not merely seven times, but seventy times seven?

However, there are two very different ways of forgiving: the first is noble and great, truly generous without any hidden thoughts, which delicately avoids hurting the self-esteem and susceptibility of the adversary, even when that same adversary has no justification for his or her acts. The second, on the other hand, is when someone who has been offended, or thinks they have been offended, imposes humiliating conditions on the supposed adversary, making felt the weight of the pardon, which can only cause further irritation instead of calming; where, upon offering a hand to the offended, this is not done with benevolence, but rather with ostentation, so that the person may say to others — look how generous I am! In these circumstances a sincere reconciliation is quite impossible for either one. No, here there is no generosity, only a form of satisfying pride. In every dispute the one who shows him or herself to be more conciliatory, who demonstrates more disinterest, charity and real greatness of soul will always attract sympathy from those who are impartial.

RECONCILIATION WITH YOUR ADVERSARIES

5. *Agree with thine adversary quickly, whilst thou art in the way with him: lest at any time the adversary deliver thee to the judge, and the judge deliver thee to the officer, and thou be cast into prison. Verily I say unto thee, Thou shalt by no means come out thence, till thou hast paid the uttermost farthing (Matthew, 5: 25 & 26).*

6. In the act of pardon, as in general practice of good, there is not only a moral effect but also a material effect. As is already known, death does not liberate us from our enemies; vengeful Spirits in the after life frequently pursue with great hate all those for whom they bear rancour. From this we understand the falsity of the proverb: *The poison dies with the beast,* when it is applied to mankind.

The evil Spirit waits for the other whom he does not like to return to a physical body, where he or she is partially captive, in order to more easily torment, hurt interests or harm affections. The cause of the majority of cases of obsession lies within this fact, especially those cases which present some gravity, such as subjugations and possession. The person who is either obsessed or possessed is almost always a victim of vengeance. The motive will be found in their past lives, in which the one who is suffering gave cause for this result. God allows this to happen in order to punish the evil which was originally committed or, if this is not the case, for the lack of indulgence and charity through the refusal to grant a pardon. Consequently, from the point of view of future tranquility, it is important that each person makes amends for all grievances which may have been caused to neighbours as soon as possible.

Before death reaches us, it is necessary that we pardon all our enemies, thereby eradicating all motives for dissension, as well as all causes for ulterior animosity. In this manner it is quite possible to make a friend in the next world out of an enemy in this world. At least all those who proceed in this manner put themselves on the right side of the Law. God will not consent to anyone who has pardoned being made to suffer from vengeance.

When Jesus recommends that we should reconcile ourselves with our adversaries as soon as possible, this is not merely with the object of pacifying any discords during the actual existence, but principally to avoid their perpetuation into the future life. Jesus said: " No one can leave this prison until the last cent of their debt has been paid," that is to say, not until God's justice has been completely satisfied.

THE SACRIFICE MOST AGREEABLE TO GOD

7. *Therefore if thou bring thy gift to the altar, and there rememberest that thy brother hath ought against thee; leave there thy gift before the altar, and go thy way; first be reconciled to thy brother, and then come and offer thy gift (Matthew, 5: 23 & 24).*

8. With the words "First be reconciled to your brother, and then come and offer your gift," Jesus teaches that what is most agreeable to God is the sacrifice of our resentments and that before Man asks for pardon he should first have pardoned others and made good any damage caused to his fellow beings. Only then will the offerings be acceptable to God because they will come from a heart expunged of all evil thoughts. Jesus explains this in the material sense of offering gifts because the Jews of those days offered sacrifices, so it was necessary that His words conform to the customs of the time. The true Christian however, does not offer material gifts to God, since all sacrifice has been spiritualised, and with this the precept has gained even more strength. He offers his soul to God and his soul has to be purified. Thus, *upon entering the temple of God, Man should leave all feelings of hate and animosity outside, including evil thoughts against his fellow men.*

Only in this manner will the angels take his prayers and place them at the Feet of the eternal Father. This is what Jesus was teaching when He said: "Leave then thy gift before the altar and go first and be reconciled with thy brother if you wish to be agreeable to the Lord."

THE MOTE AND THE BEAM IN THE EYE

9. *And why beholdest thou the mote that is in thy brother's eye, but considerest not the beam that is in thine own eye? Or how wilt thou say to thy brother, Let me pull out the mote out of thine eye; and behold, a beam is in thine own eye? Thou hypocrite, first cast out the beam out of thine own eye; and then shalt thou see clearly to cast out the mote out of thy brother's eye (Matthew, 7: 3-5).*

10. One of the follies of humanity consists in seeing wrong-doing and evil in others before seeing it in ourselves. In order to be able to judge ourselves, it is first necessary that we see ourselves intimately reflected, as in a mirror. To be

permitted, as it were, to look at oneself from the outside, as if we were someone else, so that we can ask ourselves what we would think if we saw someone doing what we do. Beyond all doubt pride is what induces us to disguise all our faults, both moral and physical, even from ourselves. Such folly is essentially against charity seeing that true charity is always modest, unadorned and indulgent. Prideful charity is a contradiction, as these two sentiments neutralize one another. With effect, how can someone who is sufficiently conceited as to believe in the importance of their own personality and the supremacy of their own qualities, at the same time possess abnegation? That is to say sufficient abnegation so as to be able to cause the goodness in others to stand out, knowing that this would eclipse them: instead of extolling the evil which only casts false glory upon themself. Pride, being the father of many vices, is also the negation of many virtues. It is found to be the motive and base for almost all human actions. Therefore, it was because pride is the principle obstacle to progress, that Jesus tried so hard to combat it.

DO NOT JUDGE OTHERS IF YOU DO NOT WISH TO BE JUDGED IN RETURN. HE THAT IS WITHOUT SIN, LET HIM BE THE FIRST TO CAST A STONE

11. *Judge not, that ye be not judged. For with what judgement ye judge, ye shall be judged: and with what measure ye mete, it shall be measured unto you again (Matthew, 7: 1 & 2).*

12. *And the scribes and the Pharisees brought unto Him a woman taken in adultery; and when they had set her in the midst, they say unto Him, Master, this woman was taken in adultery, in the very act. Now Moses in the Law commanded us that such should be stoned; but what sayest Thou? This they said, tempting Him, that they might have to accuse Him. But Jesus stooped down, and with His fingers wrote on the ground, as though He heard them not. So when they continued asking Him, He lifted up Himself, and said unto them, he that is without sin among you, let him first cast a stone at her. And again He stooped down, and wrote on the ground. And they which heard it being convicted by their own consciences, went out one by one, beginning at the eldest, even unto the last: and Jesus was left alone, and the woman standing in the midst. When Jesus had lifted up Himself, and saw none but the woman, He said unto her, Woman, where are those thine accusers? Hath no man condemned thee? She said, No man, Lord. And Jesus said unto her, Neither do I condemn thee, go and sin no more (John, 8: 3-11).*

13. With the sentence: "He that is without sin amongst you, let him cast the first stone," Jesus makes indulgence the first duty towards others because there is no one who does not need it for themself. He also teaches that we must never judge others with more severity than we would wish to be judged, nor condemn in others that which we condone in ourselves. Before chastising someone for a fault, first let us see if that same censure could be applied to ourself.

Reproach may be launched against a person for two reasons: to suppress evil or to discredit the person whose acts are criticised. In this last intention there is absolutely no excuse, because here exists only malice and slander. The first may be laudable and even becomes a duty in certain cases as good may come of it, and without it the evil in society would never be restrained. Furthermore, is it not the duty of all mankind to help every fellow creature towards progress? Therefore it is important that the principle 'Do not judge others if you have no wish to be judged,' should not be taken literally as this could be destructive, whereas the spirit of these words gives life to the concept.

It is not possible that Jesus could have prohibited the overthrowing of evil, seeing that He gives examples of having done just that Himself, in no uncertain terms. What He wished to say was that the right to censure is to be found in the moral authority of he who censures. To become guilty of that which one is condemning in another person is to renounce this authority, so depriving oneself of the right to restrain.

Furthermore, our inner conscience denies respect and voluntary submission to any person who, having been invested with some kind of authority, violates the laws and principles of which they were put in charge. *There is no legitimate authority in the eyes of God but that which is based on the examples of goodness it offers.* Likewise, this is what is emphasized by the words of Jesus.

INSTRUCTIONS FROM THE SPIRITS.
THE PARDONING OF OFFENCES

14. How many times must I forgive my brothers and sisters? Not just seven times, but seventy times seven. Here we have the teaching of Jesus which should most strike the intelligence, and speak most loudly to our hearts. If these words of mercy are compared with the prayer He taught to His disciples, that prayer so simple, so concise, yet so great in its aspirations, you will always encounter the same thought. Jesus, the pre-eminently just One, replies to Peter with these words: "You must forgive without limit; you must forgive each offence as many times as it is done to you; your brothers and sisters on Earth must be taught that it is forgetfulness of self which makes a person invulnerable to attack, misbehaviours and insults; your heart must be mild and humble without measuring out your gentleness; in short, you must do whatever you wish the Celestial Father to do for you. Is He not frequently forgiving you? Have you by any chance counted how many times His pardon has come down to erase your shortcomings?"

So pay attention to the reply given by Jesus, and like Peter apply it to yourself. Forgive freely, use your indulgence, be charitable and generous, even be lavish with your love. Give and the Lord will make restitution; forgive and the Lord will forgive you; lower yourselves and the Lord will raise you up; humble yourselves and the Lord will take you to sit on His right hand.

Dearly beloved, go forth to study and comment on these words which I have spoken on the part of He, Who, from the heights of celestial splendor is always watching over you. Proceed lovingly in the thankless task which began eighteen centuries ago. Forgive your fellow men as you would wish that they forgive you. If their acts cause you personal harm, then this is just one more motive for your indulgence, since the merit of forgiveness is in proportion to the seriousness of the wrongdoing. You will gain no merit by overlooking the errors of your fellow men if they are nothing more than simple scratches.

Spiritists, never forget that the pardoning of wrongdoing must not be an empty expression, be it either by word or by action. Since you call yourselves Spiritists, then be so with all fervour. Forget all evil that has been done to you and think of nothing save one thing: the good that you can do. Those who follow this path must not stray from it even in thought, which is known to God, seeing that each one is responsible for their thoughts. Take care therefore, to expunge from yourselves all rancorous sentiments. What remains at the bottom of the hearts of each one of His children is known to God. *So, happy is he who can sleep at night saying: I have nothing against my neighbour.* — SIMON (Bordeaux, 1862).

15. To forgive one's enemies is to ask for forgiveness for oneself. To forgive one's friends is to give them proof of your friendship. To be able to forgive offences is to show yourself better than you were. So then, my friends, forgive others in order that God may forgive you, since if you are hard, demanding, inflexible, or if you use severity even against a small offence, how can you expect God to forget that each day you have even greater necessity of indulgence? Oh! Woe to those who say: "I will never forgive," for they pronounce their own condemnation! Moreover, if you searched deeper down inside, perhaps you would find that it is yourself who is the aggressor. In the fight which began as a pinprick and ended in rupture, who knows if the first blow was not cast by you, being the one who let escape harsh words of offence, or perhaps you did not proceed with all the necessary moderation? Without doubt your adversary behaved badly by showing himself to be exceedingly susceptible, but this is yet another reason for being indulgent, so as not to allow yourself to become deserving of the tirade which was launched against you. Let us admit, for the moment, that in a given circumstance you were really offended; who is able to tell if you would not further poison the matter by means of reprisals, or that you would not cause the situation to degenerate into a grave quarrel, when in actual fact the whole matter could easily be forgotten? If the prevention of the consequences of this fact depended on you, and you did nothing to impede them, then you are truly guilty. Finally, let us admit that you do not consider yourself to be deserving of any censure; in this case your merit would be even greater if you showed yourself to be clement.

Nevertheless, there are two very different ways of forgiving, the one being of the lips and the other of the heart. Many people say to their adversary "I forgive you" while inwardly rejoicing at the evil that has returned to them, commenting that he or she has only received what they deserved. How many others say "I forgive you," hastening to add "But I will never be reconciled nor do I ever want to see you again in this life!" Is this then forgiveness according to the Gospel? Surely not! True Christian forgiveness is that which casts a veil over the past and seeing that God is not satisfied with appearances alone, this can be the only kind of forgiveness to be taken into consideration. He listens to the innermost recesses of our hearts, to our most secret thoughts and is never satisfied with mere words or pretence. Complete and absolute forgiveness of all offences is peculiar to great souls, whereas rancour is always a sign of baseness and inferiority. So then, do not forget that true pardon is recognisable for its acts, rather than by the use of mere words. — PAUL, the Apostle (Leon, 1861).

INDULGENCE

16. Spiritists, today we wish to speak of indulgence, that sweet fraternal sentiment which everyone should harbour towards their fellow creatures, but which in fact is so little used. Indulgence does not see the defects of others, or if it does, it avoids speaking of them or divulging them. On the contrary, it seeks to hide them with the object of becoming the sole possessor of this knowledge, and if malevolence discovers it, then indulgence will always have a ready and plausible excuse. However, we do not mean those excuses which only have the appearance of lessening the failing, while in actual fact making it more evident, with perfidious intention.

Indulgence will never occupy itself with the evil actions of others, unless it is to offer help. But even in this case it will take care to lessen the fault as much as possible. It will never make shocking observations, nor offer censure, but only advise and even then usually in a veiled manner.

When you criticise, what consequences should be deduced from your words? That the one who censures be not guilty of that which is being reproved, so that they may be worth more than the culprit. Humanity! When will you judge first your own hearts, thoughts and actions, without occupying yourselves with what your brothers and sisters are doing? When will you have stern eyes only for yourselves?

So then, be severe with yourselves, but indulgent to others. Remind yourself of He Who judges in the last instant, Who sees the innermost movements of each heart, consequently forgiving many times the failings which you censure and often condemning that which you condone because He knows the motive behind all action. Remember also that those who clamour in loud voices for others to be excommunicated, have perhaps themselves committed those very same faults, if not even greater ones.

Therefore my friends, always be indulgent seeing that indulgence attracts the like, calms and uplifts; whereas inclemency only disanimates, drives away all calm amd causes irritation. — JOSEPH, a Protecting Spirit (Bordeaux, 1863).

17. Be indulgent with regard to the faults of others whatever these may be. Do not judge with severity any actions but your own. Then the Lord will be indulgent towards you according to the manner in which you have shown it to others.

Uphold the strong, so stimulating them to perseverance. Strengthen the weak by showing them the goodness of God, Who takes into consideration even the smallest degree of repentance. Show to all the Angel of Penitence, stretching out her white wings over the shortcomings of humanity, veiling them from the eyes of He who cannot tolerate that which is impure. Let all understand the infinite mercy of the Father, never forgetting to say to Him, through thought, and above all through actions: "Forgive us our sins as we forgive those who sin against us." Understand well the meaning of these sublime words, wherein not only is the literal sense admirable, but most of all the teachings enclosed therein.

What is it you ask the Lord for when you implore His pardon? Is it only the oblivion of your offences? An oblivion which would leave you with nothing, if God limited Himself to merely forgetting your shortcomings. It is true that He would not punish, *but neither would He offer compensation.* A recompense cannot be offered for the good which has not been done, nor even less for the evil which has been done, although this evil may have been forgotten. When you ask God to pardon your transgressions, you are asking for the favour of His grace not to fall into relapse, together with the necessary strength so as to be able to turn into other pathways, like those of submission and love, which should then be joined to those of repentance and reparation.

When you forgive a fellow creature do not be content merely to extend a veil of oblivion across the failings, seeing that in most cases this veil is quite transparent in your eyes. Instead, simultaneously sweep away the failings with forgiveness and love. Do for all your brothers and sisters what you would have the Celestial Father do for you. That is to say, substitute anger which only defiles, with love which purifies. Preach as Jesus taught, by exemplifying active and ceaseless charity. Preach as He did during all the time He remained visible to physical eyes on this planet. Preach as He continues to do unceasingly since He became visible only to the eyes of spirit. Follow this divine Example! Walk in His footsteps, for they will conduct you to a refuge offering rest after the fight. Carry all of your crosses as He did, painfully but with courage, and go up to your Calvary upon whose peak you will find glorification. — JOHN, Bishop of Bordeaux (1862).

18. Dear friends, be severe with yourselves, but ever indulgent with the weaknesses of others. This is the practice of saintly charity; alas, observed by so few! All have evil tendencies to be overcome, defects to correct and bad habits to modify. Everyone has a burden, more or less heavy, which must be got rid of in order to be able to ascend to the summit of the mountain called Progress. Why then have you shown yourself to be so clairvoyant with regard to your neighbour and yet so blind with regard to yourself?

When will you cease to see the small mote which troubles your brother's eye and instead, pay attention to the beam in your own eye, which is blinding you and causing you to go from one fall to another? Believe what your spiritual brothers are telling you! Every man or woman sufficiently full of pride as to judge themself superior in matters of virtue and merit to their incarnate brothers and sisters, is both foolish and guilty and will therefore suffer castigation by God on their day of judgement. The true character of charity is always modesty and humility, which consists in not seeing the superficial defects of others, but rather in striving to cause their goodness and virtues to predominate. Although the human heart is an abyss of corruption, there too is always the embryo of good sentiments, which are in fact the living sparks of the spiritual essence, hidden away in its innermost folds.

Spiritism! Oh! Blessed doctrine of consolation! Happy are those who know it and take profit from the edifying teachings coming from the Spirits of the Lord! For them the pathway is illuminated and along their way they are able to read these words which will indicate how it is possible to reach the end of their journey. This can only be done by putting charity into practice, meaning charity from the heart, charity to your neighbour and to yourself. In short, charity towards every living creature and above all, love for God, because this summarizes all of mankind's obligations, thus making it impossible to really love God without practising charity, and so He has made it the Law for all creatures. — DUFÊTRE, Bishop of Nevers (Bordeaux).

19. *As no one is perfect, does it follow that no one has the right to reprehend their neighbour?*

This is certainly not the right conclusion to arrive at, seeing that each one of you must work for the progress of everyone, and above all, especially for those who have been placed in your care. But for this very reason it should be done in moderation in order to obtain a useful end and not, as is so often the case, for the mere pleasure of reviling. In this event the reprehension would be wickedness, whereas in the previous instant it is a duty demanded by charity, which must be accomplished with all possible care. For the rest, the censure that is made of others should also be directed at oneself, so trying to find out if you too are not deserving of the same repremand. — SAINT LOUIS (Paris, 1860).

20. *Is it reprehensible to make note of the imperfections of others when this cannot result in any benefit for them, seeing that it will not be disclosed to them?*

Everything depends on the intention. For sure it is not forbidden to see evil where it exists. It would also be really inconvenient to see only good in all places. This illusion would prejudice progress. The mistake would be in making the observation result in the detriment of your neighbour, so discrediting him before general opinion without need. It would be equally reprehensible to do this simply in order to give vent to a sentiment of spite and the satisfaction of catching others at fault. However, the complete opposite occurs when, on extending a veil over an evil so that the public do not see it, the person who noted the defect in his neighbour does this for his own personal gain. That is to say, in order that he or she may discipline themself to avoid what has been reproved in another. Incidentally this observation is of benefit to the moralist. How else can human defects be painted if the models are not first studied? — SAINT LOUIS (Paris, 1860).

21. *Are there cases when it is right to disclose the evil in others?*

This is a very delicate question. In order to be able to reach a conclusion it is necessary to appeal to the true understanding of charity. If a person's imperfections only cause prejudice to themself then there can be nothing useful in disclosing these facts. If however it might cause harm to others, then it is preferable to attend to the interests of the majority. According to the circumstances, it may become a duty to expose hypocrisy and lies because it is better that one person fall rather than many become his or her victims. In this case it is necessary to weigh the total sum of the advantages and disadvantages. — SAINT LOUIS (Paris, 1860).

CHAPTER 11

LOVE YOUR NEIGHBOUR AS YOURSELF

The greatest commandment. Do unto others as we would have
them do unto us. The parable of the creditors and the debtors.
— Give unto Caesar that which belongs to Caesar. —
INSTRUCTIONS FROM THE SPIRITS: The law of love. —
Selfishness. — Faith and charity. — Charity towards criminals.
— Should we risk our life for a criminal?

THE GREATEST COMMANDMENT

1. *But when the Pharisees had heard that He had put the Sadducees to silence,
they were gathered together. Then one of them, which was a lawyer, asked Him a
question, tempting Him, and saying, Master, which is the greatest commandment
in the Law? Jesus said unto him, Thou shalt love thy God with all thy heart, and
with all thy soul, and with all thy mind. This is the first and great commandment.
And the second is like unto it, Thou shalt love thy neighbour as thyself. On these
two commandments hang all the Law the prophets (Matthew, 22: 34-40).*

2. *Therefore all things whatsoever ye would that men should do to you, do ye
even so to them: for this is the Law and the prophets (Matthew, 7: 12).*

*And as ye would that men should do to you, do ye also to them likewise (Luke,
6: 31).*

3. *Therefore is the Kingdom of Heaven likened unto a certain king, which would
take account of his servants. And when he had begun to reckon, one was brought
unto him, which owed him ten thousand talents. But foreasmuch as he had not to
pay, his lord commanded him to be sold, and his wife, and children, and all that
he had, and payment to be made. The servant therefore fell down, and
worshipped him, saying, Lord, have patience with me, and I will pay thee all.
Then the lord of that servant was moved with compassion, and loosed him, and
forgave him the debt. But the same servant went out, and found one of his fellow
servants, which owed him an hundred pence: and he laid hands on him, and took
him by the throat, saying, Pay me that thou owest. And his fellow servant fell
down at his feet, and besought him saying, Have patience with me and I will pay
thee all. And he would not: but went and cast him into prison, till he should pay
the debt. So when his fellow servants saw what was done, they were very sorry,
and came and told their lord all that was done. Then his lord, after that he had*

called him, said unto him, O thou wicked servant, I forgave thee all that debt,
because thou desiredst me: shouldest not thou also have had compassion on thy
fellow servant, even as I had pity on thee? And his lord was wroth and delivered
him to the tormenters, till he should pay all that was due unto him. So likewise
shall my Heavenly Father do also unto you, if ye from your hearts forgive not
every one his brother their trespasses (Matthew, 18: 23-35).

4. "To love your neighbour as yourself: to do unto others as you would have
them do unto you," expresses the most complete form of charity because it
summarizes all of man's obligations towards his fellow men. We can find no
guide to take as an example that is more guaranteed in this respect than that
we should do to others what we would have them do to us. What right have we
to demand that they behave in any better manner, that they be more
benevolent or more devoted to us than we are to them? The practice of these
maxims leads to the destruction of selfishness. When they have been adopted
as a rule of conduct and as the base of all institutions, then Man will
understand true fraternity, and so make it possible for peace and justice to
reign on this planet. There will be no more hate nor dissensions, but only
union, concordance and mutual benevolence.

GIVE UNTO CAESAR THAT WHICH BELONGS TO CAESAR

5. *Then went the Pharisees, and took counsel how they might entangle Him in*
His talk. And they sent out unto Him their disciples with the Herodians, saying,
Master, we know that thou art true and teachest the way of God in truth, neither
carest thou for any man: for thou regardest not the person of men. Tell us
therefore, what thinkest thou? Is it lawful to give tribute unto Caesar, or not? But
Jesus perceived their wickedness, and said, Why tempt ye me, ye hyprocrites?
Shew me the tribute money. And they brought unto Him a penny. And He saith
unto them, Whose is this image and superscription? And they say unto Him,
Caesar's. Then saith He unto them, Render therefore unto Caesar the things
which are Caesar's; and unto God the things that are God's. When they heard
these words, they marveled, and left Him, and went their way (Matthew, 22: 15-
22; Mark, 12: 13-17).

6. The question that was asked of Jesus was motivated by the fact that the
Jews, who abominated the tribute imposed on them by the Romans, had made
the payment of this tribute a religious question. Numerous parties had been
set up against this tax. So this payment constituted a point of irritation
amongst them at that time. If this had not been the case there would have been
no point in the question which was asked of Jesus: "Is it licit for us to pay or not
to pay this tribute to Caesar?" There had been a trap set by this question
because those who had put it expected the reply to go against either the
Roman authority or the dissident Jews. But Jesus, 'who understood their

malice,' got round this difficulty and gave them a lesson in justice by saying that to each one should be given what was due to them. (see INTRODUCTION, under the sub-title: THE PUBLICANS.)

7. However, we should not understand the words: "Give to Caesar what belongs to Caesar," in a restrictive or absolute manner. As in everything that Jesus taught, this is a general principle which has been summarized into a practical and more customary form, taken from a certain circumstance. This principle is the consequence of the other one in which we should do to others as we would have them do to us. It condemns every kind of moral or material damage which might be caused to another, as well as all disregard of their interests. It perscribes respect for the rights of each person, as each one desires that they be respected. It extends as well to the fulfillment of our obligations towards our family, society and authority, just as much as for individuals in general.

INSTRUCTIONS FROM THE SPIRITS.

THE LAW OF LOVE

8. Through spiritual progress instincts become sentiments which are more or less elevated. Love, being the finest sentiment that exists, summarizes the complete doctrine of Jesus. At the starting point Man only had instincts; after some advancement and the onset of corruption, he has sensations; but when he becomes instructed and more purified he has sentiments. The most delicate apex of sentiment is love, not the vulgar sense of the word, but that inner sun which condenses and reconciles all aspirations and superhuman revelations at its ardent focal point. The law of love substitutes the selfishness of man with the harmonizing of all beings in brotherly love, thereby extinguishing social miseries. Blessed is the one who, having surpassed the state of being human, loves with an ample love all suffering fellow beings. Blessed are those who love because they know not the miseries of either body or soul. Their step is light and they live as if transported outside of themselves. When Jesus pronounced that divine word: 'love', it made the people tremble and the martyrs, inebriated with hope, descended into the amphitheatres.

In its turn, Spiritism has come to pronounce the second word in the divine alphabet. Pay attention, because this word 'reincarnation', lifts up the tombstones from the empty graves, and triumphant over death, reveals to astonished people its intellectual patrimony. But it is not to this that Man is conducted, but rather to the conquest of his own being, already elevated and transfigured. Blood has redeemed the Spirit and today the Spirit has to liberate the Man from matter.

I have already said that in mankind's beginning he had nothing but instincts. Therefore those in whom instincts predominate are still nearer the starting point than their goal. In order to advance towards this goal, each one must conquer their instincts to the benefit of their sentiments; that is to say, these can be perfected by suffocating all material tendencies. Instincts are the germination and the embryos of sentiments; they bring progress with them, just as the acorn contains within itself the oak tree; the less advanced creatures are those who, after emerging little by little from their chrysalises, continue to maintain themselves slaves to their instincts. The Spirit needs to be cultivated as you would a pasture. All the riches of the future depend on the present labour employed, which will earn much more than earthly goods, for it will offer glorious elevation. So, having understood the law of love which joins all creatures, you will seek to find within it the most sweet delights of the soul which are the preludes to celestial happiness. — LAZARUS (Paris, 1862).

9. Love is of a divine essence, and everyone, from the most humble to the most elevated, has a spark of this sacred fire in the bottom of their hearts. It is a many times proven fact that both men and women, however vile, base or criminal, are known to devote ardent affection to living creatures or objects. This sentiment is resistant to all attempts to diminish it and has frequently even been known to reach sublime proportions. I have purposely said that affection is given to living creatures and some objects, because amongst you are individuals whose hearts are overflowing with love, but who nevertheless expend a wealth of this sentiment upon animals, plants and even material things. These are a kind of misanthropist who, while complaining to themselves about humanity in general and resisting the natural inclinations of their souls, which is to seek sympathy and affection around themselves, they reduce the law of love to the condition of instinct. But no matter what is done, they will not succeed in suffocating the living seed which God deposits within every heart at the moment of creation. This seed will develop and grow, together with morality and intelligence, and although frequently repressed by selfishness, it will become the origin of saintly virtues which produce sincere and lasting affections, which in turn will help in crossing the rugged and arid pathways of human existence.

There are those who repudiate reincarnation, believing that others will participate in the affections and sympathies of which they are jealous. My poor brothers and sisters! Your affections have made you selfish; your love has become restricted to the intimate circle of your friends and relatives, so that you are indifferent to all others. Well then, so that you may practise the law of love as God intended, it is necessary that you learn step-by-step to love all your fellow beings without distinction. The task will be long and difficult, but it will be fulfilled because God so desires. The law of love is the first and most important precept of the new doctrine, because one day it will destroy all selfishness under whatever form it may present itself, given that apart from personal selfishness there is also that of the family, the clan and nationality.

Jesus said: "Love thy neighbour as thy self." Well, what is the limit with regard to your neighbour? Is it the family, the sect, or the nation? No, it is nothing less than the whole of humanity. In the superior spheres and planets, reciprocated love harmonizes and directs the advanced Spirits which inhabit them. Your planet, which is shortly destined to make appreciable progress, will see its inhabitants practising this sublime law, which is a reflection of Divinity, in virtue of the social transformation through which it will soon pass.

Moral betterment of the human race and happiness during terrestrial life are the results which the law of love will bring. The most rebellious and corrupt will reform themselves when they see the resulting benefits stemming from the practise of the precept: "Do not unto others that which you would not wish done unto you. On the contrary, do unto others all the good that it is within your power to do."

Do not believe then in the sterility and hardening of the human heart, for even against its own will, it must give way to true love which is like a magnet that is impossible to resist. Contact with true love revives and fertilizes the seeds latent in every heart. The Earth, being a globe of probation and exile, will then be purified by this sacred fire. Then you will see practised upon its surface the acts of charity, humility, patience, devotion, abnegation, resignation and sacrifice, all of these being the offspring of true love. So do not tire of listening to the words of John the Evangelist. As perhaps you know, when sickness and old age forced him to stop teaching, he limited himself to simply repeating these gentle words: "My children, you must love one another."

Beloved brethren, make good use of these lessons because although it is difficult to put them into practise, the soul will reap great benefit from them. Believe me when I tell you to love one another and make the sublime effort that I ask of you, then you will soon see the Earth transformed into a Paradise, where the souls of the just may come for repose. — FÉNELON (Bordeaux, 1861).

10. Esteemed fellow students, the Spirits who are here present say to you through my intermediary: "Love with all your hearts so that in turn you too may be loved." This thought is so completely just that we find within it everything which can console and alleviate the trials of each day, or better still, by putting this wisdom into practise you will so elevate yourselves above all that is material, that you will become spiritualised even before you leave this earthly body. As the study of spiritual matters has developed your understanding of the future, of one thing you can be sure, you are progressing in the direction of God and will see fulfilled all the promises which correspond to the aspirations of your soul. This is why it is necessary to elevate oneself, so we may be able to judge ourselves without the constraint of matter, and why we must never condemn our neighbour without first directing our thoughts to God.

To love, in the true sense of the word, is to be loyal, honest and conscientious; to do to others what we would have them do to us. It is to look around oneself and seach for the inner meaning behind all the pain afflicting your fellow creatures, so as to be better able to offer some relief. It is to consider the great human family as your own, because this family will, at some future date, re-encounter itself in the other more advanced worlds together with other Spirits who, like you, are also God's children destined to infinite elevation. Thus you cannot deny to your fellow men and women what God has liberally granted to you, seeing that, on your side, you should be happy that they give you what you need. Therefore always have a word of comfort and hope for all who suffer so that you may be wholly just and loving.

Believe that the wise saying: "Love greatly so as to be greatly loved," will open up the way. These words are revolutionary and follow a pathway that is sure and invariable. But those of you who listen to them have already made some progress; you are much better than you were a hundred years ago. You have changed so much for your own good that you can willingly accept a host of new ideas on liberty and fraternity which before you would have rejected. Moreover, without doubt in another hundred years or so, you will accept just as easily those ideas which now you are unable to get into your heads.

Today, when the Spiritist movement has taken such a big step forward, it is seen how quickly the ideas of justice and renovation, which are a constant in Spiritist teachings, are largely accepted by the intelligent world due to the fact that these ideas correspond to all that is divine within each one. This has come about because you were prepared by a rich and fertile sowing during the last century, when the seeds of great ideas regarding progress were implanted in the bosom of earthly society. As everything is linked together under the direction of God all lessons, when received and accepted, will be the means of bringing about the universal interchange of love for one's fellow beings. In this way all incarnate Spirits, being better able to appreciate and judge things, will join hands with those from every corner of this planet. One and all will come together to understand and love each other, to destroy all injustices and all causes of misunderstandings amongst peoples.

The great concept of renewal through Spiritism, so well presented in *The Spirits' Book,* will produce the prodigious miracles of the forthcoming century, and lead to the harmonising of all the material and spiritual interests of mankind. This will be brought about through fuller understanding of the maxim: "Love greatly so as to be greatly loved." — SAMSON, an ex-member of the Spiritist Society of Paris (1863).

SELFISHNESS

11. Selfishness, the plague of all humanity, is hindering moral progress and must disappear from the Earth. It has been reserved for Spiritism to make this planet ascend in the hierarchy of the worlds. So selfishness is the target at

which all believers should point their arms, towards which all strength and courage should be directed. I say 'courage' because this will be greatly needed by each individual if they are to triumph over themselves, rather than triumph over others. Therefore let each one use all their strength to combat their own selfishness, certain that this monstrous devourer of all intellects, this off-spring of pride, is the cause of all the miseries found in this world. It is a denial of charity and consequently the greatest obstacle to human happiness.

Jesus gave us an example of charity and Pontius Pilate an example of selfishness. While the first, the Just One, was about to traverse the holy stations of His martyrdom the second was washing his hands and saying: "What does it matter to me!" He even asked the Jews: "This is a just man, so why do you want to crucify Him?" Nevertheless, he allowed them to continue to conduct Jesus to His execution.

Due to the antagonism between charity and selfishness, that leprous invasion of the human heart, Christianity has still not completely discharged all of its mission. It is to you, who are the new apostles of the faith, that the superior Spirits are giving orientation; on whom rests the responsibility and the duty of eradicating this evil, so as to give Christianity its full force which will allow it to clear the way of all obstacles that impede its progress. Expel selfishness from the Earth so it may ascend the scale of the worlds, seeing that the time has arrived for humanity to vest its virile raiments; but for this to be able to happen, it is first necessary that selfishness be expelled from all hearts. — EMMANUEL (Paris, 1861).

12. If mankind loved one another mutually then charity would be better practised. However, for this to happen it is necessary to shed the armoured plate that covers your hearts, in order that they may become sensitive to the sufferings of others. Severity and rigidity kill all good sentiments. Christ never avoided anyone, nor did He repel those who came in search of Him, whoever they might be. He helped the adulterous woman and the criminal, never fearing that His reputation might suffer as a consequence. When will you take Him as your model for all your actions? *If charity reigned on Earth then evil could not prevail; it would fade away in shame; it would hide itself, seeing that wherever it went it would feel out of place.* Then evil would simply disappear; be quite sure of this!

Begin by giving examples yourselves: be charitable to all, without distinction, and make an effort not to heed those who look on you with disdain. Leave the task of doing justice to God, to the One who every day in His kingdom separates the wheat from the chaff.

Selfishness is a total denial of charity. Moreover, without charity there would be no rest for human society. I go even further and say there would be no safety. With selfishness and pride, both of which go hand in hand, life would always be a race in which the most cunning would be the winners. It would be a fight of interests in which the most saintly affections would be trodden underfoot, and where not even sacred family ties would be deserving of respect. — PASCAL (Sens, 1862).

FAITH AND CHARITY

13. My beloved children, but a short while ago I said to you that charity without faith is not enough to maintain social order amongst men and women and be capable of making them happy. I could have said that charity without faith is not possible. In fact, generous impulses can present themselves even amongst those of no religion at all. Nevertheless unadorned charity, which can only be practised with abnegation and the constant sacrifice of all selfish interests, can only be inspired by faith because nothing but faith can give humanity the courage and perseverance needed to carry the cross of terrestrial life.

Yes, my children it is useless for a person who is always eager for pleasure to try to delude themselves as to their destiny on this planet, by pretending that they are justified in occupying themselves exclusively with their own pleasure. Beyond doubt, God created us to be happy in eternity; meanwhile earthly life must serve solely for moral improvement, which is more readily obtained with the help of physical organs and the material world. Without taking into account the ordinary vicissitudes of life, the diversities of tastes, the inclinations and the necessities, exercising yourselves in the acts of charity is also a means of improvement. In effect, only by dint of mutual concessions and sacrifices can harmony be preserved between so many different elements.

Nevertheless, you would be right to affirm that humanity was intended to be happy in this world, as long as this was sought not in material pleasures, but in goodness. The history of Christianity tells of martyrs going happily to their execution. Today in your society there is no longer a need for Christians to face the holocaust of martyrdom nor the sacrifice of lives, but only and exclusively the sacrifice of selfishness, pride and vanity. You will triumph only if you are inspired by charity and sustained by faith. — A Protecting Spirit (Cracow, 1861).

CHARITY TOWARDS CRIMINALS

14. True charity constitutes one of the sublime teachings which God has given the world. Complete fraternity should exist amongst all true followers of His doctrine. Those who are unfortunate and wretched, by this we mean criminals, should be loved as God's creatures which they are. Pardon and mercy will be given to them, just as much as to you, if they repent of all offences committed against His law. Consider yourselves to be more reprehensible, more guilty, than those to whom you deny pardon and commiseration because, as often as not, they do not know God as you do and consequently less will be asked of them than is asked of you.

Do not judge! Oh! Never make a complete judgement, my friends. In as much as the verdict you pronounce will be applied even more severely to yourself, so you will need indulgence for those sins you so unceasingly incur. Are you ignorant of the fact that there are many actions considered as crimes in the eyes of God, who symbolizes pureness, that the world does not deem as even small offences.

True charity does not consist of only giving alms, nor even in the consoling words you may add to your donation. No, this is not the only thing God demands of you. Sublime charity, as taught by Jesus, also consists in the constant use of benevolence in all things pertaining to your neighbour. This sublime virtue can also be used in your relationships with those to whom the giving of alms would have no utility, but to whom a few words of consolation, encouragement and love would raise them up to the Lord.

The time approaches, we repeat, when a great fraternity will reign on this planet; one in which all mankind will obey the laws of Christ. These laws will offer both restraints and hopes and will conduct all souls to the happy realms. Love one another then as sons and daughters of the same Father; never establish differences between those who are unhappy, nor despise any living creature, seeing that God desires everyone to be equal. God permits great criminals to be found amongst you so that they may serve as a lesson. In the near future, when mankind finds itself submitted to the true laws of God, there will no longer be any need for these lessons, *because all impure and rebelious Spirits will have been relegated to the inferior worlds in accordance with their inclinations.*

It is your duty to help those of whom I have spoken with your prayers; that is true charity. It is not your place to say to a criminal: "You are despicable and should be purged from the face of the Earth. The death penalty is much too good for the likes of you." No! This is not the way to talk! Take note of that model on whom we should base ourselves — Jesus. What would He have said if He found one of those unfortunates at His side? He would have wept over them and considered them to be sick and therefore deserving of pity and would then have extended a helping hand. In actual fact, you cannot as yet do the same thing, but at least you can pray for them and help their Spirits during the time they still have to pass on Earth. Perhaps they will be touched by repentance if you pray with all your faith. They are our neighbours just as much as the best of mankind. Their souls, having strayed and become rebelious, were created as was your own, to be perfected. Help them then, to get out of the quagmire and pray for them. — ELIZABETH OF FRANCE (Havre, 1862).

15. *A man's life is in danger; in order to save him another person must put their life at risk. However, it is known that the person in danger is a malefactor and that, if they escape, they may commit other crimes. Despite these facts should the second person risk their own life in order to save that of the criminal?*

This is a very grave question and can naturally present itself to a Spiritist. I will reply in accordance with my moral progress, since what we are dealing with is to know if we should expose our own life, even if it be for a criminal. Devotion is blind; just as enemy soldiers are rescued we should also rescue enemies of society, or in short, malefactors. Do you suppose that in such a case, it is only death hurrying to snatch away this unhappy person? Perhaps it is all their past life. Indeed, imagine that in those rapid instants, in which the last breath of life is being swept away, the lost person returns to their past or rather it looms before them. Perchance death comes too soon; the thought of reincarnation may seem terrible to them. So rush forward! Those of you who have been enlightened by the knowledge of Spiritism should be the first to offer aid, to snatch this person from their condemnation and who knows but that they, who would have died with blasphemy on their lips, may throw themselves into your arms. In any case, do not stop to ask if they would or not, just save them, since by this act you are obeying the voice in your heart which tells you: " You can save them, so save them then!" — LAMENNAIS (Paris, 1862).

CHAPTER 12

LOVE YOUR ENEMIES

Return goodness for evil. — Discarnate enemies. — Whosoever
shall smite thee on thy right cheek, turn to him the other also.
— INSTRUCTIONS FROM THE SPIRITS: Vengeance. —
Hate. — Duelling.

RETURN GOODNESS FOR EVIL

1. *Ye have heard that it hath been said, thou shalt love thy neighbour, and hate thine enemy. But I say unto you, love your enemies, bless them that curse you, do good to them that hate you, and pray for them which despitefully use you and persecute you; that ye may be the children of your Father which is in Heaven: for He maketh his sun to rise on the evil and on the good, and sendeth rain on the just and on the unjust. For if ye love them which love you, what reward have ye? Do not even the publicans the same? And if ye salute your brethren only, what do ye more than others? Do not even the publicans so? (Matthew, 5: 43-47).*

For I say unto you, that except your righteousness shall exceed the righteousness of the Scribes and Pharisees, ye shall in no case enter into the Kingdom of Heaven (Matthew, 5: 20).

2. *For if ye love them which love you, what thank have ye? For sinners also love those that love them. And if ye do good to them which do good to you, what thank have ye? For sinners also do even the same. And if ye lend to them of whom ye hope to receive, what thank have ye? For sinners also lend to sinners, to receive as much again. But love ye your enemies, and do good, and lend, hoping for nothing again; and your reward shall be great, and ye shall be the children of the Highest: for He is kind unto the unthankful and to the evil. Be ye therefore merciful, as your Father also is merciful (Luke, 6: 32-36).*

3. If the principle of charity is to love one's neighbours, then to love one's enemies is the most sublime application of this same principle, seeing that the possession of this virtue represents one of the greatest victories which can be achieved against selfishness and pride.

However, there is usually a misunderstanding in relation to the meaning of the word 'love' in this situation. When He spoke, Jesus did not mean that each one of us should have the same tenderness for an enemy as would be felt for a brother, sister or friend. Tenderness presupposes confidence; well, no one can deposit confidence in another person knowing that they bear malice; no one can show effusive friendship knowing that the other person is likely to abuse the situation. Between people who have no confidence amongst themselves there cannot be the same manifestations of sympathy which exist between those who share the same ideas. In short, no one can feel the same pleasure when they are with an enemy as would be felt when in the company of a friend.

The diversity of feelings in these two very different circumstances is the result of a physical law, which is the assimilation and repulsion of vibrations. An evil thought produces a vibrationary current which causes an unpleasant impression. A good thought encompasses us with a very agreeable emanation. This is the reason for the different sensations which are experienced on the approximation of a friend or an enemy. So then, to love one's enemy cannot signify that there should be no difference between the affection for an enemy and that for a friend. If this precept seems difficult to put into practice, perhaps impossible, this is only because it was falsely understood that Jesus had ordered us to give both friends and enemies an equal place in our hearts. Seeing that the restrictions of the human language oblige us to use the same term to express different shades of a sentiment, it is then necessary to establish these differences according to the various cases.

Therefore, to love one's enemies does not mean showing affection which would not be within our nature, as contact with an enemy makes our heart beat in an entirely different manner to the way it beats on contact with a friend. To love one's enemy means we should not hate, nor bear rancour against them, nor desire vengeance. It means to forgive all the evil they have caused *without hidden thoughts and without conditions*. It means to not put obstacles in the way of a reconciliation and to wish them well, instead of bad things. It is to feel joy, instead of regret, at the good things that may come their way; to help them whenever possible and to abstain *by words or acts* from everything which might prejudice them. Finally, it means to always return goodness for evil *without any intention to humiliate*. Whosoever can proceed in this manner fulfills the conditions of the commandment: Love your enemies.

4. To those who are incredulous, loving an enemy is contra sense. For those to whom the present life is everything, an enemy is someone noxious, who perturbs their rest and from whom, as is thought, only death can bring liberation. This is a reason for desiring vengeance. These people are not interested in forgiving, unless it is to satisfy their pride before the world. In certain other cases the act of pardon seems to them to be a weakness to which they will not stoop, and even if they do not reap vengeance, they will certainly retain rancour and evil desires against the other person.

For the believer and above all for the Spiritist, the way of looking at this situation is very different because their vision extends over the past and into the future, between which the present life is nothing more than a point in time. The Spiritist knows that due to the peculiar destiny of this planet, meeting with evil and perverse people is to be expected. The wickedness to be faced is all part of the ordeals to be supported. From this elevated point of view, the vicissitudes are easier to bear, less bitter, whether they originate from other fellow beings or from things. *If they do not complain to themselves of their trials, neither should they complain to those who serve as instruments.* If, instead of bemoaning, Spiritists were to thank God for being put to the test, they *should also thank the hand that offers them the opportunity to demonstrate their patience and resignation.* This idea will naturally dispose them towards forgiveness. They also know that apart from this, the more generous they are the more they become elevated in their own eyes, so putting themselves beyond the reach of their enemies' darts.

The person who occupies an elevated place in this world does not feel they are offended by the insults of those whom they consider their inferiors. The same happens in the moral world to those who elevate themselves above materialistic humanity. They understand that hate and rancour only degrade and lower them. In order to be superior to their adversary, their soul must be larger, nobler and more generous than his.

DISCARNATE ENEMIES

5. The Spiritist has still other motives for being indulgent towards his enemies. In the first place, he knows that evil is not the permanent condition of mankind. This occurs due to the temporary state of imperfection, and just as children correct themselves of their defects, so the evil man or woman will one day recognise their errors and so gradually become good people.

The Spiritist also knows that death is only a relief from the material presence of the enemy, because this enemy can continue to pursue with hate even after leaving the Earth. They also know that the vengeance which was seized on fails in its objective, as it has the contrary effect of causing even more irritation, which is capable of continuing on from one existence to another. It was up to Spiritism to prove through experience and the law which governs relationships between the visible and invisible worlds, that the expression: *extinguish hate with blood* is radically wrong, and that in fact blood only feeds hate, even in the after-life. It is therefore up to the doctrine to offer a positive reason for this fact, together with a practical motive for forgiveness and for Christ's commandment: *Love your enemies.* There is no heart so perverse that it will refuse, even though reluctantly, to show itself to be sensitive to good behaviour. Through good comportment it is possible to take away all pretext for retaliation and, who knows, even make a friend out of an enemy, before and after death. Through bad behaviour Man only succeeds in irritating his enemy, *who then becomes the instrument which God's Justice will use to serve as a punishment for those who are unable to forgive.*

6. It is always possible to find enemies amongst both incarnates and discarnates. Our enemies in the invisible world manifest themselves and their

malice by means of obsession and subjugations, as can be frequently seen. These represent a kind of trial, which as in other types of trials, help in the process of advancement, and for this reason the sufferer should accept them with a certain amount of resignation. These happenings are also a consequence of the inferior nature of this globe, for if there were no evil people on this planet then there would be no evil Spirits around it either. Hence, if we are to be benevolent with our incarnate enemies, we should also treat those of them who are discarnate in a like manner.

In days gone by it was the custom to make bloody sacrifices of innocent victims, in order to appease the hellish gods who were none other than evil Spirits. These fiendish gods followed on after the devils, who are the same thing. Spiritism shows us that these devils are merely the souls of perverse men and women, who have not yet disposed of their material instincts and that *no one can succeed in appeasing them, except by sacrificing the hate that exists, that is to say, by being charitable towards them.* This has the effect of not only stopping them in their evil practices, but also of recovering them and bringing them back to the path of goodness, thus contributing to their salvation. In this way the maxim: *Love your enemies,* is not circumscribed to the Earth ambient and the present life, but rather forms part of the great universal laws of solidarity and fraternity.

WHOSOEVER SHALL SMITE THEE ON THY RIGHT CHEEK TURN TO HIM THE OTHER ALSO

7. *Ye have heard that it hath been said, an eye for an eye, and a tooth for a tooth: but I say unto you, that ye resist not evil: but whosoever shall smite thee on thy right cheek, turn to him the other also. And if any man will sue thee at the law, and take away thy coat, let him have thy cloke also. And whosoever shall compel thee to go a mile, go with him twain. Give to him that asketh thee, and from him that would borrow of thee turn not thou away (Matthew, 5: 38-42).*

8. The prejudices of the world with respect to what is commonly called 'a point of honour' produces the kind of sombre susceptibility which is born of pride and the glorification of ones own personality, which in turn leads mankind to return an injury or offence with another. This is taken as justice, by those whose moral sense is still embedded in worldly passions. This was why the law of Moses prescribed an 'eye for an eye' and a 'tooth for a tooth', in accordance with the epoch in which Moses lived. When Christ came, He said: 'Return goodness for evil,' and added: 'Do not resist the evil that they wish to do to you, if *someone shall smite thee on thy cheek, present him the other also'.* To the proud this teaching seems cowardly because they do not understand that it takes more courage to support an insult than it does to take vengeance. This is always due to the fact that their vision does not go beyond the present.

Should we then take this precept at its face value? No, no more than the other, which tells us to pluck out our eye when it is the cause of offence. If we were to take these teachings to their final consequences, it would mean the condemnation of all restraint, even legal restraint, so leaving an open field for those who are evil by absolving them from any kind of fear. If no one were to check their acts of aggression then very quickly the good would also become their victims. The very instinct of self-preservation, being one of the laws of Nature, prevents anyone from offering themselves for assassination. By enunciating that maxim, Jesus did not mean that self-defence is forbidden, but rather that He *condemned vengeance*. Telling us to offer the other cheek when one has been injured, is merely another way of saying we must not repay evil with evil. Mankind should humbly accept everything that serves as a means of weakening his pride. There is greater glory in receiving an offence, than in being the offender; of patiently suffering injustice, than practising it; in being deceived, than being the deceiver; to be ruined rather than be the one who causes the ruin. It is also the condemnation of all duelling, which in actual fact is nothing more than the manifestation of pride.

Only faith in the future life and the justice of God, who never allows evil to go unpunished, can give a person the necessasry strength to patiently support the blows dealt to either their interests or their self-respect. This is why we are constantly repeating how necessary it is to look to the future; and the more we are able to raise up our thoughts above this material life, the less we shall be hurt by the things of this world.

INSTRUCTIONS FROM THE SPIRITS.

VENGEANCE

9. Vengeance is one of the last relics of the barbaric customs, which tend to disappear from the human race. It is, like the duel, one of the last vestiges of the savage habits under which humanity was struggling at the outset of the Christian era. This is why vengeance constitutes a sure indication of the backward state of the men and women who lend themselves to it and also of the Spirits who inspire them. Accordingly, my friends, this sentiment should never vibrate in the heart of anyone who proclaims themself to be a Spiritist. You know full well that to avenge oneself is so much against Christ's precept: 'Forgive your enemies', that the person who refuses to forgive not only is not a Spiritist, but certainly is not even a Christian. Vengeance is an even more ruinous inspiration when its companions are assiduous in falseness and baseness. Indeed, they who deliver themselves to this fatal and blind passion, almost never seek vengeance openly. When they are the stronger, they fall savagely upon those they call the enemy, seeing that the mere presence of these persons inflames their spite, anger and hate. However, in most cases they assume a hypocritical attitude, concealing the evil sentiments which animate them deep in their hearts. In hidden ways they follow their

unsuspecting enemy in the shadows, awaiting an opportunity to strike without danger to themselves. While hiding from their enemy, they constantly spy on them, preparing a hateful trap and when the occasion is propitious, they put the poison in the cup.

When their hate does not reach such extremes, they attack the victim through their honour and affections; nor do they hesitate in the use of slander and perfidious insinuations, ably spread on all sides, which increase along the way. As a consequence, when the one who is being persecuted presents themself in those places where the whispers of the persecutor have past, they are astonished to receive a cold reception instead of friendly and benevolent faces from those who had previously welcomed them. They are even more surprised, when instead of outstretched hands, even these are refused. Finally they feel themselves defeated when even their greatest friends and closest relatives withdraw and avoid them. Ah! The coward who seeks vengeance in this manner is a hundred times more guilty than the one who confronts his enemy and insults him face to face! So let us do away with these primitive customs! Let us dispense with these procedures from bygone days! Every Spirit who still today lays claim to a right to seek vengeance for themselves, is no longer worthy to take part in the phalanx who hold as their motto: *Without charity there is no salvation!* But no, I can no longer detain myself in the thought that a member of this great Spiritist family would dare in the future to give in to the impulse of vengeance, instead of forgiveness. — JULES OLIVIER (Paris, 1862).

HATE

10. Love one another and you will be happy. Above all else, take to heart the need to love all those who inspire indifference, hate and scorn. Christ, who should be considered as the model, gave an example of this kind of devotion. Missionary of Love that He was, He loved so much as to give His very blood and life for Love. It is a painful sacrifice to love those who insult and torment us, but it is exactly this sacrifice which makes you superior to them. If you were to hate them, as they hate you, then you would be worth no more than they. To love them is the Immaculate Host you offer to God on the altar of your hearts, which will envelop you in its aroma as if it were a sweet perfume. If the law of Love demands that each one love all their brothers and sisters without distinction, it does not mean that the heart will be protected as if by a breastplate against evil conduct. On the contrary, it is the most anguishing of trials, which I know full well, having experienced this same torture during my last earthly existence. But God is ever present, and punishes in this life or the next all who violate the law of love. My dear children, do not forget that love draws us near to God and hate drives us away from Him. — FÉNELON (Bordeaux, 1861).

DUELLING

11. A person is only truly worthy if, when thinking of life as a journey which leads to a determined point, they take little heed of the roughness of the way and do not allow their footsteps to turn aside from the straight and narrow path. With their gaze firmly set on a distant point to be reached, it is of no importance to them that briars and thorns threaten to scratch, as these do not impede progress. To devote one's time to avenging an affront is to recoil before life's ordeals and is always a crime in the eyes of God; and if you were not beguiled, as indeed you are, by your own prejudices, you would see it as being ridiculous and supreme madness.

It is a crime to commit homicide by duelling, as even your own laws recognize. No one has the right, under any circumstances, to make an attempt against the life of a fellow creature as this is, I repeat, a crime in the eyes of God who has traced the line of conduct required to be followed. In this case, more than in any other occurance, you are your own judge. Remember, you will be pardoned only in as much as you are able to pardon others. Through the act of pardoning you draw near to the Lord, since clemency is akin to strength. While even a drop of blood drawn by the hands of Man flows upon the Earth the true Kingdom of God, wherein will reign peace and love which will banish animosity, discord and wars forever, will still not have been implanted on this planet. When this happens the word 'duel' will exist in your language only as a distant and vague remembrance of a past that is gone. Then no other antagonism will exist amongst mankind, apart from the noble rivalry of righteousness. — ADOLF, Bishop of Argel (Marmande, 1861).

12. Beyond all doubt, in certain cases duelling may constitute a test of physical courage, of disdain for life. But unquestionably it is a proof of moral cowardice, just as suicide is. The suicide has not the courage to face the vicissitudes of life, whereas the duelist cannot support offences. Was it not Christ who said there is more honour and value in presenting the left cheek to he who has hit you on the right, than in avenging an offence? Did He not say to Peter in the Garden of Olives: 'Put away your sword because he who kills with the sword shall also perish by the sword'? In so saying did He not condemn for ever the act of duelling? In fact, my children, what kind of courage comes from a violent disposition, from a bloody and wrathful temperament which bellows at the slightest offence? What greatness can be found in a person who at the least insult believes that only blood can repair the damage? Let him tremble! For, from the bottom of his conscience a voice will persist in saying: "Cain! Cain! What have you done to your brother?" And he will answer that it was necessary to spill blood in order to save his honour. Then the voice will reply: "In the few minutes that remain to you of your earthly life, you thought only to save your honour before men, but you never thought to save it before God!" Poor wretch! How much blood will Christ demand of you for all the violence He has received? Was it not enough that you injured Him with thorns and lances? That you put on Him an infamous garment, and that in the middle of His

atrocious agony, you made Him listen to the mockery and derision that was showered upon Him? How many reparations has He asked of you for your many offences? The last cry of the Shepherd was a supplication to God in favour of His torturers! Oh! Be like Him! Forgive and pray for those who offend you.

My friends, remember the precept: 'Love one another.' Then for every blow received through hate, you will be able to reply with a smile and to every affront, you will offer forgiveness. Without doubt the world will rise up in fury and treat you as a coward. So, lift your head up high and show you are not afraid to gird yourself with thorns as Christ did, and that your hand does not wish to be accomplice to an assassination authorized by false ideas of honour, that are nevertheless nothing more than pride and self-conceit. When God created Man, did He bestow the right of life and death one over the other? No, this right was given only to Nature for the purpose of reconstruction and reorganization, whereas you are not permitted to dispose even of yourselves. The duelist then, just as the suicide, will find himself marked by blood when he comes before God. For both of these the Supreme Judge will reserve long and harsh penalties. If this same Judge has threatened all who call their fellow beings by the name of *Raca,* how much more severe will be the punishment for those who reach His presence with the blood of their brothers and sisters on their hands! — SAINT AUGUSTIN (Paris, 1862).

13. The duel, once called God's justice, is one of the most barbaric customs still persisting in some human societies. What would you say, however, if you saw two adversaries being plunged into boiling water or submitted to the contact of red hot iron, in order to put an end to their dispute? The one who is right being he who best suffers the test? Would you not classify these customs as being unreasonable and senseless? Well, duelling is far worse than all this. For the dextrous duelist it is nothing short of murder, practised in cold blood with all due premeditation, since he is certain of the efficiency of the blow to be dealt. For the adversary, who is almost sure to succumb by virtue of his weakness and inability, it is suicide committed after cold reflection. I know that on many occasions the person has sought to avoid the consequences of the criminal alternative by placing the responsibility for the act upon chance. Is this not going back, under another name, to the ideas from the Middle Ages of God's Judgement? We remind you that in those times Man was infinitely less guilty. It is true that the very use of the words 'God's Judgement' reveals a naive faith, but it was always some small degree of faith in the Justice of God, Who could never allow the innocent to succumb, whereas a duel resorts to brute force to such an extent that frequently the one who was offended is the one who succumbs.

Oh, senseless conceit, foolish vanity and insane pride, when will you be substituted by Christian charity, by love of one's fellow creatures and by humility, all of which were prescribed and exemplified by Christ? This will only happen when Man ceases to be dominated by these monstrous preconceptions, which the laws are impotent to repress because it is not enough to prohibit evil. For this to occur it is necessary for the source of goodness and the horror of evil to live jointly in the hearts of all humanity. — A Protecting Spirit (Bordeaux, 1861).

14. "What will they say about me," you frequently ask, "if I refuse to make the reparation that is being demanded of me or if I do not complain about those who offend me?" Those like you who are foolish, those who are backward, will censure you. But those who have been enlightened by the beacon of intellectual and moral progress will say that you have proceeded with true wisdom. Let us reflect then for a moment. Due to a word, sometimes said without thinking or the wish to offend, coming from one of your fellow beings, your pride is hurt, so you then reply scathingly and there stems a provocation. Before the decisive moment arrives ask yourself if you are behaving like a Christian. What will you have to answer to society for if you rob it of one of its members? Think of the remorse of having deprived a woman of her husband, a mother of her child, the children of their father and with this their means of sustenance! For sure, the one who offended owes a recompense. But is it not more honourable to give this spontaneously, recognising one's errors, than to endanger the life of the one who has the right to complain? As to the offended, it so happens that sometimes, because they feel gravely injured themselves or that someone dear to them has been insulted, it is not only self-respect that is at stake, but that their heart has been hurt and is suffering. So apart from it being stupid to risk one's life by throwing oneself against a wretch who is capable of infamy, we would ask if when the person dies, does the insult or whatever it was, cease to exist? Is it not true that when blood is spilt it leaves an even deeper impression of a fact which, if false, will fall of its own accord and if true, would be better buried in silence? Then nothing more is left than the quenching of the thirst for vengeance! Ah! Unhappy satisfaction which almost always gives way, even in this life, to pungent remorse! When it is the one that was offended who succumbs, where is the retribution?

When charity finally becomes the general rule of conduct for humanity, all acts and words will be confined to this maxim: Do not do to others that which you would not wish them to do to you. When this happens all causes for dissensions will disappear and with this the duels and wars, which are only duels between nations — FRANÇOIS-XAVIER (Bordeaux, 1861).

15. Because of an offensive word, possibly something slight, a man of the world throws away his life, which came from God, or throws away the life of a fellow creature, which also belongs to God. This man is a hundred times more guilty than the scoundrel, driven by covetousness and sometimes by necessity, who enters into a residence with intent to rob and kills all those who oppose his intentions. In this case, we are usually dealing with a person of little education having an imperfect notion of good and bad; whereas the duelist, as a rule, belongs to the more cultured class. The one kills with brutality, while the other kills with method and refinement, in view of which society forgives him. I

would even add that the duelist is infinitely more guilty than the scoundrel who, on giving way to a desire for vengeance, kills in a moment of exasperation. The duelist however does not have the excuse of a frenzy of passion, because between the moment of insult and retribution there has been time for reflection. He acts coldly, with premeditation, studying and calculating everything so that he may be more sure of killing his opponent. It is true he also exposes his own life, which is what rehabilitates him in the eyes of the public, as they see only an act of courage and disregard for life. But is there any courage on the part of someone who is sure of himself? The duel, reminiscent of barbarous times in which the right of the strongest was law, will disappear as a result of a better appreciation of what a point of honour really means, and according to the extent that mankind deposits living faith in a future life. — AUGUSTIN (Bordeaux, 1861).

16. REMARKS: As time goes by, duelling is becoming more and more rare. But if from time to time a painful example still occurs, at least the number is greatly diminished compared with days gone by. In those olden days a man could not leave his house without anticipating an encounter, and so always took the necessary precautions. A characteristic sign of the habits of those times and of the people was the habitual presence, either ostensible or hidden, of arms for both attack and defence. The abolition of this custom demonstrates the softening of habits, and it is interesting to follow this graduation from the epoch in which a gentleman only rode out covered with armour plate, to the times when a sword at the waist was more an ornament or blazon than a weapon of aggression. Another indication of the modification of these customs is that formerly these strange combats were held in the middle of a thoroughfare before a mob, whereas in more recent times they were held in secret. At present, death is something which causes emotion. But in other times no one took any notice of it.

CHAPTER 13

DO NOT LET YOUR LEFT HAND KNOW WHAT YOUR RIGHT HAND IS DOING

Do good without ostentation. — Hidden misfortune. — The widow's mite. — To invite the poor and the lame. To give without thought of recompense. — INSTRUCTIONS FROM THE SPIRITS: Material charity and moral charity. — Beneficence. — Compassion. — Orphans. — Beneficence recompensed by ingratitude. — Exclusive benevolence.

DO GOOD WITHOUT OSTENTATION

1. *Take heed that ye do not your alms before men, to be seen of them: otherwise ye have no reward of your Father which is in Heaven. Therefore when thou doest thine alms, do not sound a trumpet before thee, as the hypocrites do in the synagogues and in the streets, that they may have glory of men. Verily I say unto you, They have their reward. But when thou doest alms, let not thy left hand know what thy right hand doeth: That thine alms may be in secret: and thy Father which seeth in secret Himself shall reward thee openly (Matthew, 6: 1-4).*

2. *When He was come down from the mountain, great multitudes followed him. And behold, there came a leper and worshiped Him, saying, Lord, if thou wilt, thou canst make me clean. And Jesus put forth His hand and touched him, saying, I will: Be thou clean. And immediately his leprosy was cleansed. And Jesus saith unto him, See thou tell no man; but go thy way, shew thyself to the priest, and offer the gift that Moses commanded, for the testimony unto them (Matthew, 8: 1-4).*

3. There is great merit in doing good without ostentation. But it is of even greater merit to hide the hand that gives. This is the indisputable mark of great moral superiority, since in order to regard things from a higher level than the multitude it is necessary to be able to disregard the present life, and identify oneself with the future. In a word, to place oneself above humanity so as to be able to renounce the satisfaction that comes from the recognition of one's fellow creatures, and await the approval of God. Those who prefer the approval of mankind prove they put more faith in them than in God, and value the present life more than the future one. If they say anything to the contrary, then they act as if they do not believe in what they themselves are saying.

How many there are who only give with the expectancy that the one who has received will shout it to all sides! How many there are who publicly give large sums of money, but who nevertheless would not give a penny if the fact were to be hidden! This is why Jesus declared: "Those who do good ostensibly have already received their recompense." Indeed, those who seek their glorification on Earth through the good they do, have already paid themselves; God owes them nothing more; the only thing left is punishment for their pride.

Let not your right hand know what your left hand does is an image which admirably characterizes modest beneficence. But if there is true modesty, then there is also false modesty, a mere imitation of modesty. There are certain people who hide the hand that gives, but take great care to leave a small piece showing while they look about them to see if anyone has seen them trying to hide it. This is shameful, a parody of Christ's maxim! If prideful benefactors are despised by mankind, what then must they be before God? These too have already received their recompense on Earth. They are seen and are satisfied by this fact. That is all they will have.

So then, what recompense will there be for the person who causes their benefits to weigh heavily on the shoulders of the receiver; who demands at all costs recognition for the recompense; who makes their position felt by extolling the cost of the sacrifice they have made? Oh! Here there is not even earthly recompense, seeing that this person finds themself deprived of the pleasing satisfaction of hearing their name blessed. This is the first punishment for their pride. The tears they dried in benefit of their own pride, instead of rising to Heaven will fall back upon the afflicted heart and cause it to ulcerate. For the good that was practised there will be no reward because it was deplored, and all benefit that is deplored is counterfeit and so has no value.

When beneficence is practised without ostentation it is doubly meritorious. Apart from material charity there is also moral charity, seeing that this protects the susceptibility of the beneficiary, so enabling them to receive a benefit without feeling resentment from a loss of self-respect. This safeguards human dignity, since there are those who will accept a job but refuse alms. Now depending on the manner in which it is done, converting work into alms can mean humiliating the receiver, and there is always pride and evil in the act of humiliating another. On the other hand, true charity is delicate and inventive in disguising a benefit, avoiding even a simple appearance which might cause hurt, given that all moral friction increases suffering originating from necessity. Therefore the giver of true charity will find tender affectionate words which will place the receiver at ease, especially in the presence of the benefactor, whereas prideful charity will crush the receiver. Real generosity acquires total sublimity when the benefactor, inverting the parts, finds a way of placing themself in the position of being the one who is indebted when facing the person whom they are helping. This is what is meant by the words: Let not your left hand know what your right hand does.

HIDDEN MISFORTUNES

4. When great calamities occur charity is filled with emotion, and generous impulses are seen on all sides in the repairing of these disasters. But apart from these general disasters, there are millions of private catastrophes which go unnoticed, for there are those who lie on beds of suffering without complaining. These discreet and hidden misfortunes are the ones which true generosity knows how to discover without even waiting to be asked for help.

Who is that woman with the distinctive air, simply dressed, although well cared for, who is accompanied by an equally modestly dressed young girl? They enter a sordid looking house where the lady is obviously well-known because they are greeted with respect as they enter. Where is she going? Up to the garret where a mother lies surrounded by her many children. On their arrival happiness bursts forth upon the thin faces. This is because the woman has come to soothe their pains. She has brought everything they need, tempered with gentle and consoling words which allows her protégés, who are not professional beggars, to accept these benefits without blushing. The father is in hospital and while he is there the mother is unable to provide the necessities of life with her work. By the grace of this good woman these poor children will no longer feel cold nor hungry; they will go to school well-clothed and, for the smaller ones, the mother's breasts which feed them will not go dry. If any member of this family falls sick, this good woman will not refuse the material care which they may need. From their house she will go on to the hospital to take the father some comforts and also to put his mind at rest as to his family. At the corner of the road a carriage awaits, and inside is a store of everything destined for her various protégés, for one after the other they all receive visits. She never asks what their religion is nor what their opinions are, because she considers them to be her brothers and sisters and the children of God, as are all men and women. When she has finished her rounds she can say to herself: "I have begun my day well." What is her name? Where does she come from? No one knows. To all those unhappy ones she has given a name which indicates nothing. But she is the personification of a consoling angel. Each night a host of blessings rise up to the heavens in her name from Catholics, Jews and Protestants alike.

Why such modest clothing? So as not to insult their misery with her luxury. Why does she take her daughter? So that she too may learn how to practise beneficence, for the young lady also wishes to be charitable. However, the mother says to her: "What can you give, my daughter, when you have nothing of your own? If I give you something of mine to give away, what merit will that be for you? In that case it is really I who am giving, so what good would that bring you? It would not be just. So when I visit the sick you will help me treat them. To offer care to someone is to give something of yourself. Do you not think that is sufficient to start with? Well then, nothing could be simpler; you can begin by learning how to make useful articles and clothes for the children.

In this manner you will be giving of yourself." When she is a true Christian, this is how a mother should prepare her children to practise those virtues which Christ taught. Is she a Spiritist? What does that matter!

In her own home she is a woman of the world because her position demands it of her. Those about her know nothing of what she is doing, as she does not wish for any approval other than that from God and her own conscience. However, one day an unexpected circumstance brought one of her protégés to her door, selling hand-made articles. When this woman saw her, she recognised her benefactor. The lady told her to be silent and *"Tell no one!"* Jesus also spoke in this manner.

THE WIDOW'S MITE

5. *And Jesus sat over against the treasury, and beheld how the people cast money into the treasury: and many that were rich cast in much. And there came a certain poor widow, and she threw in two mites which make a farthing. And He called unto him His disciples and saith unto them, Verily I say unto you, That this poor widow hath cast in more than all they which have cast into the treasury: for all they did cast in of their abundance: but she of her want did cast in all that she had, even all her living (Mark, 12: 41-44).*

And He looked up, and saw the rich men casting their gifts into the treasury. And He saw also a certain poor widow casting in thither two mites. And He said, Of a truth I say unto you, that this poor widow hast cast in more than they all. For all these have of their abundance cast in unto the offerings of God: but she of her penury hath cast in all the living that she had (Luke, 21: 1-4).

6. Many people deplore the fact that they are unable to do all the good they desire due to lack of financial resources. They would like to be rich in order, so they say, to be able to make good use of those funds. Their intention no doubt is laudable and in some cases even sincere. However, in the vast majority is this desire totally disinterested? Will there not be those who, whilst wishing to do good to others, would also appreciate being able to begin by doing good to themselves, of being in a position to offer themselves a few more pleasures or the enjoyment of something superfluous they lack, after this then being quite ready to offer the poor what is left over? This second thought behind the desire, perchance concealed even from their own eyes, which they would have to face if they scrutinized the depths of their hearts, annuls all merit for the intention, seeing that true charity thinks of others before it thinks of itself. The sublimity of charity, in this case, would be for each one to seek within their work the necessary resources they lack to be able to realise their generous intentions, by means of employing their strength, intelligence and aptitudes. In so doing they would be offering the kind of sacrifice most pleasing to the Lord. Unhappily the majority live out their lives dreaming of ways and means of easily and quickly acquiring riches for themselves without any effort. By running after foolish fancies like the discovery of buried treasure, or some

favourable random chance, or even the possibility of receiving an unexpected inheritance etc. What can be said then about those who expect to find spiritual helpers to second their attainment of these objectives? Certainly they know nothing at all nor do they understand the sacred finalities of Spiritism, and even less of the mission of the Spirits whom God permits to communicate with incarnate men. Hence it happens that they are punished by deceptions. (See THE MEDIUM'S BOOK (1), second part, items 294 & 295.)

Those whose intentions are totally exempt from personal interest must console themselves with the knowledge that it is impossible to do all the good that could be wished, and to remember the mite of the poor, taken from meagre resources which causes deprivation, but which weighs more on God's scales than the gold of the rich who give without depriving themselves of anything. The satisfaction of the former would truly be great if they could help all the destitute on a large scale. But if this is denied them, then they must submit to this fact and limit themselves to what is possible. Furthermore, can tears be dried only with money? Should we remain inactive because we have no money? All those who sincerely wish to be of use to their fellow beings will find thousands of ways of helping. If you look for them they will appear, if not in one way then in another, because there is no one who, having full command of their faculties, cannot help someone, offer consolation, minimise both physical and moral suffering or do something useful. While money may be lacking, do we all not have time, work and hours of repose to spare which we can offer to help others? This too is the alms of the poor, the widow's mite.

TO INVITE THE POOR AND THE LAME. TO GIVE WITHOUT THOUGHT OF RECOMPENSE

7. *Then said He also to him that bade Him, When thou makest a dinner or a supper, call not thy friends, nor thy brethren, neither thy kinsmen, nor thy rich neighbours; lest they also bid thee again, and a recompense be made thee. But when thou makest a feast, call the poor, the maimed, the lame, the blind: and thou shalt be blessed; for they cannot recompense thee: for thou shalt be recompensed at the resurrection of the just. And when one of them that sat at meat with Him heard these things, he said unto Him, Blessed is he that shall eat bread in the Kingdom of God (Luke, 14: 12-15).*

8. Jesus tells us that when we prepare a feast we should not invite our friends and relations, but instead the poor and the maimed. In their literal sense these words appear to be absurd. But if we understand their spiritual essence they are in fact sublime. It is not possible that Jesus intended us to invite the maimed and beggars from the streets to unite round our table instead of friends. His language was almost always figurative as the people of those times were not capable of understanding delicate shades of thought. Therefore it was necessary for Him to use strong words which could produce colourful

(1) by Alan Kardec

images. Nevertheless, the essence of His thought is revealed is this sentence: "And thou shalt be blessed, for they cannot recompense thee." This means that we should not do good for a calculated reward, but only for the pleasure to be felt in so doing. Using a striking comparison, Jesus says: "Invite the poor to your feast because you know they cannot recompense you." By the use of the word 'feast' we should understand not the actual repast but a participation in the abundance generally enjoyed.

However, the warning can also be applied in a more literal sense. How many of you invite to your table only those who, as is said, will honour you or will return your invitation? On the other hand, there are others who find satisfaction in receiving friends and relations less fortunate than themselves. Well, how many amongst you have people like this in your family? In this way a great service can sometimes be done without it showing. These people put into practice the teachings of Jesus without recruiting the blind and the maimed only if they do so with benevolence, without ostentation, and if they know how to dissimulate the benefit by means of sincere cordiality.

INSTRUCTIONS FROM THE SPIRITS.

MATERIAL CHARITY AND MORAL CHARITY

9. "Love one another and do unto others what we wish they would do unto us." All that is religion and moral is contained in these two precepts. If they were observed in this world then everyone would be happy and there would be no more hate or resentment. I go even further: there would be no more poverty because all the poor people would be fed from the superfluity of the rich. Neither would poor women be seen dragging wretched children along the dark and sombre streets where I lived during my last incarnation.

Those among you who are rich, think on this a while! Help to the best of your abilities all those who are less fortunate. Give, in order that one day God may recompense the good you have done; and so, on leaving your terrestrial body behind, you may encounter a host of grateful Spirits who will receive you at the threshhold to a happier world. Oh! If you could but know the joy felt when, on reaching the world beyond, I found those whom I had been given to serve!. . .

Therefore, love your neighbours; love them as you would love yourself, because you now know that by repelling even one wretched person it is always possible that perhaps you are sending away a brother, father or friends from other times. If this happens to be the case, imagine your despair when you recognise them again on reaching the spiritual world!

I wish you to understand exactly what *moral charity* really is. It is something that all can practise, that costs *nothing* materially speaking, but which is most difficult to exercise. Moral charity then comprises the giving of support to all our fellow creatures and is least done in this inferior world where you now find yourselves incarnated. Believe me, there is great merit in keeping quiet while another, perhaps less intelligent, is speaking. This is but one kind of moral charity. To play deaf when mocking words escape the lips of one accustomed to deride, or to ignore the disdainful smiles of those who are receiving you, when they quite wrongly suppose themselves to be far above you, constitutes merit. However, in actual fact it will quite often be found that in the spiritual world, the *only real life,* these same persons are far below us. The merit to be gained in these situations is not due to humility, but to charity, in as much as to ignore bad behaviour is a moral charity.

Nevertheless, this kind of charity must not be allowed to interfere with the other kind already mentioned. Therefore, be specially careful never to despise your fellow beings. Remember everything I have told you, and that if you repel a poor or needy person you may perhaps be repelling a Spirit who was once dear to you, who temporarily finds him or herself in an inferior position to you. I have found here one of the destitute from Earth whom happily I had been able to help several times and from whom, in my turn, *I must now implore help.*

I remind you that Jesus said we are all brothers and sisters. Always think of this before repelling a beggar or even someone with a contagious disease, like leprosy. Goodbye; think of those who suffer and pray for them. — SISTER ROSALIE (Paris, 1860).

10. My dear friends, there are many amongst you whom I have heard saying: How can I practise charity if I am frequently without the necessities of life?

Friends, there are thousands of ways of practising charity. You may do this by means of thought, words and actions. With thought by praying for the unfortunate who have been abandoned, for those who die without even finding conditions to enable them to see the light. A prayer from your heart will alleviate their suffering. Through words, by giving good advice to your daily companions, to those who are desperate and to all for whom privations have caused embitterment which has led them to blaspheme against God, by saying to them: "I was like you; I too suffered and felt myself wretched, but I believed in Spiritism and now I am happy." To those who are old and who say to you: "It is useless, now I am at the end of my journey. I will die as I have lived," you must say to them: "God shows equal justice to all; remember the workers of the last hour." To the children who are already corrupted by the companions who surround them, who go through life ready to succumb to evil temptations, you must say: "God is looking at you, my children," and never get tired of repeating these gentle words to them. One day they will germinate in these childlike minds, and instead of being vagabonds they will then become men and women. This too is charity.

Others amongst you may say: "Pooh! We are so numerous here on Earth that God cannot possibly see each one of us." Listen carefully, my friends. When you are on the top of a mountain do you not see the millions of grains of sand which cover it? Well then, that is how God sees you. He allows you your free-will, just as He permits the grains of sand to move with the winds which disperse them. Except for one thing, in His infinite mercy, God has put a vigilant spark in the bottom of your hearts which is called your *conscience*. Listen to it because it will give good advice. Sometimes you manage to numb it by setting the spirit of evil against it. Then it is silent. But you can be sure that as soon as you begin to have even a shadow of remorse, your poor rejected conscience will again make itself heard. So listen to it, ask it questions, and frequently you will find yourself consoled by the counsel you have received.

My friends, to every new regiment the general always offers a banner. To you I offer this maxim of Christ as your watchword: "Love one another." Observe this precept, let everyone unite under this flag, and you will have happiness and consolation. — A Protecting Spirit (Lyon, 1860).

BENEFICENCE

11. The act of beneficence in this world, my friends, gives you happiness of the heart, being the purest and sweetest delight, which neither remorse nor indifference can perturb. Oh! If only you could understand something of the greatness and enjoyment which encompasses the generosity of beauteous souls! It is a sentiment which makes people look at each other as they would look at themselves and gladly disrobe in order to clothe a fellow creature in need! If only you could have as your single occupation that of making others happy! What worldly feats can be compared to those celebrated when men and women, as Divine representatives, have taken happiness to families who have known only bitterness and vicissitudes; when they see mortified faces suddenly glow with hope because without any bread these unfortunate parents only heard their children, who were ignorant of the fact that to live is to suffer, crying out unceasingly with clenched fists the words which were as daggers penetrating the maternal hearts: "I'm hungry! . . ." Oh! You must understand then the joyous impressions of those who see happiness born again, where but a moment before there had been nothing but despair. You must understand the obligations that you owe to your brothers and sisters! Go! Go then to meet misfortune! Go and offer help! Offer help, especially against hidden miseries which are the most painful of all! Dearly beloved brethren, go remembering these words of our Saviour: "When you clothe any one of these little ones, remember it is Me that you clothe!"

Charity! That sublime word which synthesizes all the virtues, it is you who will conduct all peoples of the world towards happiness. It is only by the act of charity that infinite delights can be created for each one in the future. Yet even while you remain exiled on Earth, it will be your consolation, a foretaste of the joys to be possessed later when you find yourselves united in the bosom of the God of love. It was you, divine Virtue, that enabled me to experience the only moments of satisfaction I was to enjoy while on Earth. I hope my incarnate brothers and sisters on this planet will believe these amicable words when I say: It is within charity that you must seek peace of heart, contentment of the soul and the remedy for life's afflictions. Oh! When you are on the point of accusing God, first cast your eyes down and you will see all the miseries waiting to be alleviated, the poor children without families, the old without even a friendly hand to close their eyes when death claims them! How much good there is waiting to be done! Oh! Do not complain! On the contrary offer thanks to God and lavish handfuls of sympathy, understanding and money on all who, disinherited from wordly possessions, languish in suffering and isolation. You will reap sweet happiness in the world, and later . . . Only God knows! . . . — ADOLF, Bishop of Argel (Bordeaux, 1861).

12.   To be good and charitable, that is the key to Heaven which you hold in your hands. The entirety of eternal happiness is contained in this maxim: Love one another. The soul cannot elevate itself to the high spiritual realms except by devotion to one's fellow creatures; it will not find happiness and consolation except in charitable impulses. Be good and sustain your brothers and sisters; root out that horrible ulcer known as selfishness. In fulfilling this duty, the pathway to eternal happiness should open up before you. Besides, who amongst you has not yet felt their heart beat with jubilation and inner joy at the narration of an act of wonderful dedication or some truly charitable work? If you only seek the pleasure to be felt from a good deed, then you will remain forever on the pathway to spiritual advancement. Good examples are not wanting; what is rare is simply goodwill. Take note that history keeps pious remembrance of a multitude of good men and women.

Did not Jesus tell you everything concerning the virtues of charity and love? Why then despise His divine teaching? Why do you close your ears to His divine words and your hearts to His kindly maxims? I would wish that you demonstrate more interest, and more faith, in the reading of the New Testament. However, as you despise this book, considering it to be a compilation of hollow words, a closed letter, this admirable code has been forgotten. All your ills stem from your voluntary abandonment of this résumé of the Divine Laws. Read the scintillating pages of the devotion shown by Jesus and meditate upon them!

Those of you who are strong, prepare yourselves for battle. Those who are weak, make your gentleness and faith into your arms. Let us be more presuasive and more constant in the dissemination of your new doctrine. It is only so as to give you encouragement and to stimulate your zeal and your virtues that God has given permission for this manifestation. But if you so wished, God's help and your own free-will would be sufficient for all needs, because spiritual manifestations only produce themselves for those whose eyes are closed and those with troubled hearts.

Charity is the fundamental virtue upon which all earthly virtues are based. Without this virtue there would be no others. Without charity there would be no hope of a better life, no interest in a moral guide line. Without charity there is no faith, because faith is nothing more than pure luminosity which makes a charitable soul become brilliant with light. In all worlds charity is the eternal anchor of salvation, the purest emanation which comes direct from the Creator, part of His own virtue which He gives to all creatures. How then can we despise this supreme generosity? What heart knowing this, is so perverse as to suppress and expel this divine sentiment? What child of God is so evil as to rebel against this sweet caress, which is charity.

I do not presume to speak of what I did, because Spirits also have their modesty. Nevertheless, I believe that the work I began during my earthly life is the kind of work which will contribute most to the alleviation of our fellow beings. I frequently see Spirits who, having asked, are given the work of continuing my task as their mission in life. I see them, these generous and beloved brothers and sisters, in their pious and divine ministry, practising these virtues which I recommend with a joy that can only be derived from a life of dedication and sacrifice. It is my immeasurable good fortune to see how their condition is honoured, how they are protected and esteemed in the mission they perform. Therefore, fellow beings of good and strong will-power, unite yourselves so that you may continue the work of expanding the diffusion of charity. You will find your reward in the very exercise of this virtue, and there are no bounds as to the spiritual happiness which may be felt, even in the present life. So be united, and love one another according to the teachings of Christ. So be it! — SAINT VINCENT DE PAUL (Paris, 1858).

13. They call me 'Charity'. I follow the principal path which leads to God. Accompany me, since I know the goal for all to aim at.

This morning I went on my habitual rounds, and now I come with great anguish in my heart to say to you: Oh! My friends! How many miseries and tears! How much must be done to dry all those tears and put to rights all those miseries! In vain I tried to console some of the poor mothers by whispering in their ears: Courage! There are good souls watching over you and you will not be abandoned, have patience! God exists! You are loved by Him, you are His chosen ones! They seemed to hear me and turned their startled eyes in my direction, and I could read from the appearance of their bodies, that terrible oppressor of the spirit, that they were hungry, and even if my words brought a little serenity to their hearts it was no comfort for their stomachs. I repeated: Courage! Courage! Then one poor mother, still very young and with a small child, held it up with outstretched arms, as if asking me for protection for that small creature, who found only insufficient nourishment in those sterile breasts.

Elsewhere my friends, I saw destitute old people who, being without work, found themselves without shelter and prey to all manner of sufferings and hardships. Being ashamed of their misery and never having begged, they found themselves lacking in courage to implore pity from passers by. With my heart bursting with compassion I, who possess nothing, have turned to begging for them, and so go from place to place in order to stimulate beneficence and inspire good thoughts in generous and compassionate hearts. This is why I am come here to tell you that hereabouts there are those who are wretched, in whose hovels is no bread, whose stoves are without heat and whose beds are without blankets. I do not tell you what you must do; I leave this initiative to your kindly hearts. If I were to tell you how to proceed, you would gain no credit for your good deeds. I say only that I am Charity and I extend my hands towards you through those of your suffering brothers and sisters.

But if I ask, I also give and give generously. I am inviting you to a great banquet wherein I will furnish a tree upon which all will be satiated! See how beautiful it is, how full of flowers and fruits! Go! Go! Gather all the fruits of this magnificent tree which is called beneficence. Then, in place of the foliage and fruit you have taken away, I will fasten to it all the good deeds you have practised. Then I will take this tree to God and He will load it again, in as much as beneficence is inexhaustible. Accompany me then, my friends, so that I may count you amongst those who follow my banner! Do not fear, for I will conduct you along the pathway to salvation for I am *Charity*. — CARITA, martyred in Rome (Lyon, 1861).

14. There are various ways of practising charity, which many of you confuse with the giving of alms. However, there is considerable difference between the two. Alms, my friends, are useful sometimes because they can bring alleviation to those who are poor. But this is almost always humiliating, not only for the giver but also for the receiver. On the other hand, charity joins the benefactor to the one who is receiving the benefit because it can be disguised in so many ways! It is possible to be charitable even to friends and relations, simply by being indulgent to one another, by mutually forgiving all weaknesses and by taking care not to hurt anyone's self-respect. You who are Spiritists, can be charitable in the manner in which you behave towards others who think differently than you do, or by inducing those who are less enlightened to believe without shocking them, without attacking their own convictions. You can also attract them lovingly to our meetings, so they may listen to us and so that we may know how to discover a way into their hearts. All this is just one aspect of charity.

Listen now to what is meant by charity towards the poor, those disinherited of this world, who will be recompensed by God if they are able to accept their miseries without complaint, which in turn will depend upon you and the way in which you offer help. You will understand what I mean by the following example.

Several times each week I go to watch a meeting of ladies of all ages. For us you know, they are all sisters. What do they do? They work quickly, very quickly with their agile fingers. I see how radiant are their faces and note how their hearts all beat in unison. But what is the purpose of all this work? It is because winter approaches, which will be very hard for those who are poor. During the summer those busy ants could not put by all the necessary provisions and most of their utensils have been pawned. The needy mothers are anxious and frequently weep thinking of their children who will go cold and hungry during the long winter! Poor unfortunate women, be patient, for God has inspired others more wealthy than yourselves and they have joined together to make clothes! One of these days, when the Earth is covered with snow and you are complaining and accusing God of being unjust, which is what you always do and say every time you suffer, then you will see someone appear, sent by these good workers who have established themselves as labourers for the poor. Yes, it is for you that they work like that and your complaints will be turned into blessings, because in the hearts of those who are unhappy, love follows close behind hate.

As all workers need encouragement, communications from the good Spirits come from all sides. The menfolk also take part in this society, bringing their help in the form of readings, which are pleasing to all. As recompense for the enthusiasm of everyone, and of certain individuals in particular, we the Spirits promise to bring these hard-working labourers good customers, who will pay in the form of blessings, which after all is the only currency acceptable in Heaven. We also assure them without fear of contradictions, that this currency will never be lacking for any one of these workers. — CARITA (Lyon, 1861).

15. My dear friends, every day I hear some of those amongst you say: "I am poor, so I cannot offer any charity," and yet each day I see that you lack indulgence towards your fellow men. You forgive nothing and set yourselves up as very severe judges without even asking if you would like the same done to you. Is indulgence not a charity? You, who can do nothing more than offer the charity of indulgence, do at least this, but do it grandly. Referring to material charity, I would like to tell you a story from the other world:

Two men having just died, God was heard to say that while these men had been alive all their good deeds were to be deposited in two separate sacks, and that on their death the sacks would be weighed. When each of them reached their last hours, God sent word for them to bring their two sacks. One was crammed full, voluminous and resounding with the metal it contained. The other was so small and thin that it was possible to see the few coins it contained through the cloth. Each man recognised the sack that belonged to him: "This is mine," said the first one, "I recognise it; I was rich and gave away a great deal." The other man said: "This one is mine. I was always poor. Ah! I had almost nothing to give." But what a surprise when they were put on the scales, because the voluminous one became light in weight and the small one showed itself to be heavy, so much so that it raised the first sack high into the air! Then God spoke to the rich man: "It is true that you gave much. But you did so from ostentation and to see your name on view in all the temples of pride. Furthermore, in giving you deprived yourself of nothing. Go to the left and be satisfied that the alms you gave count for something, however small." Then God spoke to the poor man: "You gave very little, my friend, but each one of your coins which are on the scales, represents a privation for you. Even if you did not distribute alms, you were charitable and the best thing is that you did it naturally, without preoccupying yourself whether it would be put into your account. You were indulgent and did not judge your neighbours; on the contrary, you found excuses for all their actions. Go to the right and you will receive your recompense." — A Protecting Spirit (Lyon, 1861).

16. Could not the rich and happy woman, who does not have to occupy her time with household duties, dedicate some of the hours of her day to useful work in aid of her fellow beings? Could she not buy clothes from the money that is left over from her pleasures, for those less fortunate than herself, who shiver with the cold? Could she not make thick warm clothing with her delicate hands, or help a mother-to-be clothe her unborn child? If her own child goes without some ribbons and lace, at least a poor child will have something to keep it warm. By working for the poor and needy you are working in the vineyard of the Lord.

And you, the poor labourer who has nothing superfluous, but nevertheless being full of love for your fellow brothers and sisters also wish to give something from the little you have. Give then a few hours of your time, which is the only treasure you possess; make some of those elegant handicrafts which tempt those who are happy; also, try making and selling work done in your evenings. Then you too can play your part in assisting your brothers and sisters in need. Perhaps you will have a few ribbons less, but you will be giving shoes to the barefoot.

And you, the women who have vowed your lives to God, continue to work with your undertakings. But take care that these achievements are not for the exclusive adornment of your chapels, to call attention to your abilities and patience! Work, my daughters, so that the product of your undertakings be destined to help your brothers and sisters before God. The poor are His dearly beloved children; to work for them is to glorify Him. Be unto them the providence which says: God gives sustenance unto the birds of the sky. Exchange the gold and silver threads with which you embroider, for food and clothes for those who have none. Do this and your work will be blessed. To all those able to produce, then give, give of your talents, inspirations and hearts and God will bless you. Poets and literary men, you who are only read by those who are worldly, satisfy their leisure, yes, but also dedicate the product of some of your works to help the needy! Painters, sculptors, artists of all kinds! May you too use intelligence to benefit your fellow beings, for your glory will be no less and some of your sufferings will be avoided.

Everyone can give! Whatever your social standing you will always find something to share with another. From whatever it is that God has bestowed upon you, a part of what He has awarded is owed to those who lack the necessities of life, seeing that, in their place you would wish others to share with you. Perhaps your earthly treasures will be a little less. Nevertheless, your heavenly treasures will likewise be increased. It is there, in Heaven, that you will reap a hundredfold of all that you have sown as benefits to others in this world. — JOHN (Bordeaux, 1861).

COMPASSION

17. Compassion is the virtue which draws you closer to the angels. It is a sister to charity, which also conducts you to God. Ah! Allow your hearts to be moved by compassion before the spectacle of the miseries and sufferings of your fellow creatures. Your tears will act as a balm on their wounds, and when shed out of sympathy will restore their hope and resignation. Oh! What sweetness is to be felt! Nevertheless, it is true that this same sweetness has a certain bitterness about it because it springs up alongside misery. But it does not have the acrid flavour of worldly pleasures, nor does it bring with it the pungent deceptions of emptiness which these pleasures leave behind. The enveloping gentle penetration of this sentiment fills the soul with joy. Compassion and pity, when deeply felt, are acts of loving; love is devotion; devotion is the forgetfullness of self and it is this, combined with abnegation in favour of those less fortunate than ourselves, which is the height of virtue. It was that virtue which the Divine Messiah practised throughout His entire life and which He taught in His saintly and sublime doctrine. When this doctrine is fully restored to its original pureness and when mankind submits to it, then the world will become a happy place wherein will reign harmony, peace and love.

The most appropriate sentiment for making mankind progress, by dominating his selfishness and pride, which predisposes the soul towards humility, beneficence and the loving of one another, is compassion! This is the same compassion which moves deep inside when you lay eyes on the suffering of your fellow creatures, which impells you to extend a helping hand and which brings tears of sympathy to your eyes. Accordingly, never stifle this celestial emotion within your heart. Do not proceed as do those who are hard and selfish, who turn aside from the afflicted because the sight of their miseries perturbs their cheerful lives for an instant. Be fearful of remaining indifferent when you could be of help. Tranquility, bought at the expense of a guilty indifference, is like the tranquility of the Dead Sea, at the bottom of which lies a vast hidden mass of putrid corruption.

Compassion is far removed from causing disturbance and inconvenience, of which the selfish person is so afraid. Nevertheless, on contact with the misfortunes and miseries of another person, the soul, rebounding upon itself, experiences a natural and profound anguish which beyond doubt vibrates throughout the whole being and causes it to be painfully affected. But the compensation is great, however, when compassion suffices to give courage and hope to an unhappy brother or sister, who are moved by a friendly handshake and so turn to you affectionately with tear-filled eyes, perhaps from emotion and gratitude, even before they raise these same eyes to Heaven in thanks for having sent someone to console and sustain them in their hour of need. Compassion then, is the melancholic but celestial precursor of charity, being the first of all virtues, which she has for sister and whose benefits she prepares and enobles. — MICHAEL (Bordeaux, 1862).

ORPHANS

18. Brothers and sisters, you should all love the orphans. If you only knew how sad it is to be abandoned, especially in infancy! God permits there to be orphans so that we may be motivated to be their parents. What an act of divine charity it is to protect a creature who has been sadly abandoned, to stop them from being hungry and cold, and administer to their soul so they may not fall prey to vice! When someone offers a helping hand to an abandoned creature they are being agreeable to God because they have understood and practised His law. Meditate on the possibility that frequently the child you are helping may be someone who was very dear to you in a past incarnation, and that if they were able to recognise you, it would no longer be an act of charity but a simple obligation. In this way, my friends, every sufferer is your brother or sister and so has a right to your kindness. However, not the kind of charity that hurts feelings, nor yet the kind of alms that burns the hand which receives it, for unfortunately help is frequently accompanied by bitterness! How many times these sufferers would rather have refused, if it were not for the fact of sickness or death being their only other option. So, give with delicacy and together with any benefits you may offer, also give the most precious benefit of all, that of a kindly word, a loving gesture and a friendly smile. Avoid being patronizing, which only turns the dagger of suffering in the heart, so causing more bleeding. Consider that by doing good, you're working for your own benefit as well as for those whom you love. — A Family Spirit (Paris, 1860).

19. *What should be thought of those who, on receiving ingratitude in payment for benefits they have done, cease practising good because they no longer get on with those who were ungrateful?*

There is far more selfishness in these people than charity, seeing that they do good only for the purpose of receiving demonstrations of acknowledgement and consequently do not do so disinterestedly. The only act of goodness acceptable to God is the one done with complete disinterest. There is of course also pride in these people, since those who behave in this manner take pleasure in the humbleness shown by the receivers of the benefits when they come to lay before them the testimony of their gratitude. Those who seek reward on Earth for the good they have done will not then receive it in Heaven. However, God will esteem all who do not seek their rewards here on Earth.

You should always help the weak, although knowing beforehand that you will receive no thanks for your help. But you can always be sure that if the person to whom you did a service forgets, God will take this even more into account than if the beneficiary had paid their debt. *If God permits that sometimes you are paid with ingratitude, this is only to test your perseverance in the practice of goodness.*

Who knows but that a momentarily forgotten benefit will not produce good fruits in the future? You can be sure it is a seed which will germinate with time. Unfortunately, we never see anything but the present! We work for ourselves and never for others. The receiving of benefits will finally soften even the most torpid heart; they may be forgotten in this world, but after having disposed of its outergarment, the Spirit who has received will remember this fact and this remembrance will be their punishment. The Spirit will deplore its own ingratitude and desire to make reparation by paying the debt in a future life, frequently seeking an existence of dedication to its benefactor. In this way, without even suspecting, you will have contributed to the moral advancement of that Spirit. You will come to recognise the truth in the words: a benefit is never lost. Besides which you will also have worked for yourself, since you will have earned merit for having done good without self-interest, without becoming disanimated by deceptions.

Ah! My friends, if you knew of all the ties which link your present life with those of past existences! If you could see at a glance the immense number of relationships that join us, one to another, for the purpose of mutual progress, you would admire even more the wisdom and goodness of the Lord, Who allows us to relive so as to be able, one day, to reach Him. — A Protecting Guide (Senns, 1862).

20. *Is it right to practise beneficence exclusively amongst persons of the same opinions, beliefs or political parties?*

No. It is exactly this idea of sects and parties which must be abolished, because there exists a brotherhood between all mankind. The true Christian, being one who can accept that all are brothers, does not stop to enquire as to beliefs or opinions before offering to help. Would a Christian be obeying the precepts of Jesus Christ, Who told us to love our enemies, if he were to repel an unfortunate person just because they professed a different belief? Therefore help without asking that anyone give an account of themselves, because if they are enemies of religion, this is just the way to make them accept it, whereas by repelling them you only cause them to hate religion. — SAINT LOUIS (Paris, 1860).

CHAPTER 14

HONOUR YOUR FATHER AND YOUR MOTHER

Filial devotion. — Who is my mother and who are my brothers?
— Corporeal relationship and spiritual relationship. —
INSTRUCTIONS FROM THE SPIRITS: Children's ingratitude
and family ties.

1. *He said unto Him, Which commandments? Jesus said: Thou shalt do no murder, Thou shalt commit no adultery, Thou shalt not steal, Thou shalt not bear false witness, Honour thy father and thy mother: and Thou shalt love thy neighbour as thyself (Matthew, 19: 18 & 19. Mark, 10: 19 & Luke 18: 20).*

2. *Honour thy father and thy mother: that thy days may be long upon the land which the Lord thy God giveth thee (Decalogue, Exodus, 20: 12).*

FILIAL DEVOTION

3 The commandment: 'Honour your father and your mother' is an inference from the general laws of charity and love towards one's fellow beings, seeing that those who do not love their mother and father cannot then love their fellow creatures. But with regard to parents, here the word *honour* contains an extra obligation, which is filial devotion. God wishes to show us that respect, esteem, obedience, caring, submission and deference should be joined to love. All these put together involve an obligation for each person to carry out what is demanded by charity with regard to one's neighbour, and which implies an even more rigorous duty towards parents. This duty naturally extends itself to those who take the place of a mother or father, and whose merit is much greater because their devotion has nothing of obligation. God will rigorously punish all violations of this commandment.

To honour your mother and father consists in not only showing respect, but also helping them in their needs, offering them rest in their old age and surrounding them with care; just as they themselves did for us during our infancy. Above all, it is necessary to demonstrate true filial devotion to destitute parents. Do you think this commandment is being kept by those who, believing they are doing a great deal of good, offer only the strictest necessities to their parents, so as to avoid them dying from hunger, while they deprive themselves of nothing? Or when, so as not to leave them unsheltered, they relegate them to the worst rooms in the house, while reserving the best and most comfortable for themselves? The parents are even fortunate when this is not done with ill-will, or when they are obliged to pay heavily for the rest of their lives by being forced to run the home! Is it then that old and feeble parents must serve their children who are younger and stronger? Did their mother make them pay for the milk they suckled? Did she count the sleepless nights when they were ill? Or the steps she took in order to guarantee they lacked nothing? No, children do not owe their parents only the strictest necessities; they also owe them, according to their possibilities, all those little extras like thoughtfulness and loving care which are nothing more than interest on what they themselves received, the payment of a sacred debt. This then is the only filial devotion which pleases God.

Alas for those who forget what they owe to those who sustained them in their hour of weakness, who, with the giving of a physical life, also gave them moral life, and many times imposed upon themselves great privations in order to guarantee the well-being of their children! Woe unto all those who are ungrateful, for they shall be punished with ingratitude and abandonment; they will be hurt in their dearest affections, *sometimes even in the present life,* but certainly in a future one, wherein they will suffer themselves what they have made others suffer!

It is true that some parents neglect their duty and are not all they should be to their children. However, it is only God who has the competence to judge, and not the children. These are not competent to be able to judge because they have perhaps deserved their parent's behaviour. If the law of charity demands that evil be paid with goodness, that we be indulgent with the imperfections of others, that we should not speak against our neighbour, that we forget and forgive all grievances, that we love even our enemies, how much greater must be our obligations when related to our parents! Therefore children, in matters relating to their parents, should take as a rule of conduct all those principles of Jesus concerning our fellow beings. They must be aware that all reprehensible behaviour towards strangers is even more reprehensible when related to parents. Also, what might be only a small offence in the first case, may be considered as a serious crime in the second, because here the offence of lack of charity is joined to that of ingratitude.

4. God said: 'Honour your father and your mother so that you may live a long time in the land that the Lord your God shall give you.' Why did He promise earthly life as a recompense and not heavenly life? The explanation lies in the words: 'that God shall give you', which having been omitted in the modern formula of the Decalogues, has altered the meaning. But first, in order to be able to understand clearly, we must go back to the situation and the ideas existing amongst the Hebrews at that time. They still knew nothing of a future life as they were unable to see anything beyond the physical. They had then to be impressed more by what they saw than by what they could not see. So God spoke to them in a language well within their reach of understanding, and as one would expect to do with a child, put them into a perspective which could

satisfy them. At that time they were still in the desert; the land to be given by God was the Promised Land, the object of their aspirations. They wished for nothing more, and God said that they would live there for a long time. That is to say, they would possess the land for a long time if they kept His commandments.

Now by the time of the advent of Jesus, they had more advanced ideas. The time had come for them to receive less material nourishment and Jesus Himself began to teach about spiritual life by saying: "My kingdom is not of this world; it is there and not here that you will receive recompense for all the good works you have practised." With these words the Promised Land ceases to be material and transforms itself into a spiritual Homeland. This is why, when we are called upon to keep the commandments: 'Honour your father and your mother,' it is not this world that is promised, but Heaven. (See chapters 2 & 3.)

WHO IS MY MOTHER AND WHO ARE MY BROTHERS?

5. *And the multitude cometh together again, so that they could not so much as eat bread. And when His friends heard of it, they went out to lay hold on Him: for they said, He is beside Himself. There came then His brethren and his mother, and, standing without, sent unto him, calling him. And the multitude sat about Him, and they said unto Him, Behold, thy mother and thy brethren without seek for thee. And He answered them, saying, Who is my mother, or my brethren? And He looked round about on them which sat about Him, and said, Behold my mother and my brethren! For whosoever shall do the will of God, the same is my brother and my sister and mother (Mark, 3: 20-21 & 31-35; Matthew, 12: 46-50).*

6. Some of the words used by Jesus appear to be quite extraordinary when compared with His goodness, kindness and unalterable benevolence. Those who are incredulous never cease to find an argument in this fact, alleging that He contradicted Himself. However, it is undeniable that His doctrine has as its basic principle, its very foundation stone, the laws of charity and love. Well then, is it possible that He would destroy on the one side what He had built on the other? Therefore we arrive at the following precise conclusion: that if certain propositions made by Jesus are in contradiction to this basic principle, then these words attributed to Him have either been wrongly reproduced, wrongly understood, or they were never pronounced by Him at all.

7. Understandably it causes great amazement that in this passage Jesus showed so much indifference towards His relatives, and in a way repudiated even His mother.

With regard to His brothers, we know they did not greatly esteem Him. Being spirits of little evolution, they did not understand His mission; they thought Him to be eccentric in His ways and His teaching did not even touch them, to the extent that not one of them became His disciple. It was said that they shared, at least up to a point, the same preconceptions as His enemies. In short, it is a known fact that whenever He appeared in the family He was received more as a stranger than as a brother. John tells us quite clearly that they *did not believe in Him.* (See John 7: 5.)

Concerning His mother, no one dare deny the tenderness and affection He devoted to her. However, it is equally our obligation to agree that she did not fully understand her Son's mission, since it was noticed that she never followed His teachings, nor did she testify for Him as did John the Baptist. Her predominating feature was maternal solicitude. Neverthless, to suppose that He denied His mother is not to know His character. Such an idea could not have found refuge in someone who said: *Honour thy father and thy mother.* Then it is necessary to find another meaning to His words, which were almost always enveloped in a mist of allegoric form.

Never losing an opportunity to teach, He therefore takes advantage of the moment and the arrival of His family in order clearly to show the difference which exists between bodily and spiritual kinship.

CORPOREAL RELATIONSHIP AND SPIRITUAL RELATIONSHIP

8. Blood ties do not necessarily create bonds between Spirits. The body comes from the body. But the Spirit does not proceed from the Spirit, since the Spirit already existed before the formation of the body. The parents do not create the Spirit of the child; they do nothing more than supply the material wrapping, although it is their duty to help the intellectual and moral development of their child, in order to further its progress.

Those incarnated in the same family, especially as close relations, are as often as not congenial Spirits linked by past relationships, which express themselves during their earthly lives by their reciprocated affections. But it can also happen that these people are complete strangers to each other, or they may be distant from each other due to past aversions which while on Earth are translated into mutual antagonisms which serve as probations. The real family ties are not those of blood then, but those of mutual sympathy and the communion of ideas which hold spirits together, *before, during and after* their incarnations. From this it follows that two people born of different parents may be more like brothers or sisters than if they were of the same blood. They can attract each other, search for each other and so feel happy together; whereas two blood brothers may be repelled by each other, as is frequently seen. This moral problem is one that only Spiritism can resolve through the explanation of the plurality of existences. (See chapter 4, item 13.)

So, there are two kinds of families: *Families through spiritual ties and families through bodily ties.* In the first case these ties are durable and strengthen with purification, perpetuating in the spiritual worlds by means of the various migrations of the soul. In the second case, the ties are as fragile as the physical body itself, extinguishing with them and in many instances dissolving morally even in the actual existence. This was what Jesus was trying to make comprehensible when He said to His disciples: "Here is my mother and my brothers by spiritual ties, because all those who do the bidding of My Father, who is in Heaven, are my brothers, my sisters and my mother."

The hostility felt by His blood brothers is clearly expressed in this narrative from Saint Mark, when it says that they had intentions of laying their hands on Jesus, under the pretext that He had *lost His Spirit*, or gone out of His mind. On being informed of their arrival and knowing full well the sentiments they harboured against Him it was only natural for Jesus, speaking in spiritual terms, to refer to His disciples as His brothers and sisters. Although His mother was accompanying His brothers, Jesus generalised the teachings which in no way implies He intended to declare that His mother, according to the physical body, was nothing to Him in spirit nor that she deserved only indifference, as He proved on many occasions.

INSTRUCTIONS FROM THE SPIRITS.

CHILDREN'S INGRATITUDE AND FAMILY TIES

9. Ingratitude is one of the most direct results of selfishness and always causes revolt in honest hearts. But the ingratitude of children towards their parents shows an even more hateful trait of character. It is specially this point of view we are going to consider, so we may analyse the causes and effects of this attitude. In this case, as in all others, Spiritism offers enlightenment on one of the greatest problems of the human heart.

When a Spirit leaves the earth plane it takes with it all the passions and all the virtues inherent in its nature, going on to improve itself in the spirit world or to remain stationary until it desires to receive enlightenment. Accordingly many Spirits return to the spiritual world full of hate and violence, as well as full of insatiable desires for vengeance. Nevertheless, there are always some amongst them who are more advanced and so able to perceive a faint glimmer of truth enabling them to appreciate the disastrous consequences of these passions, which in turn induces them to make good resolutions for the future. These Spirits understand that in order to reach God there is only one password: *Charity*. But there can be no charity without being able to forget affronts and insults. Neither can there be any charity if there is no forgiveness or if the heart is filled with hate.

Then by unprecedented efforts, these Spirits manage to observe those they hated while upon Earth. However, on seeing them again animosity is once more aroused in their hearts, causing revolt at the idea of forgiving them and even more at the thought of personal renunciation. But above all they are revolted at the thought of loving those who had destroyed their worldly goods, their honour or perhaps even their family. Meanwhile, the hearts of these unhappy Spirits continue to be disturbed and upset. They hesitate and waver, agitated by contrasting sentiments. If their good resolutions predominate, then they pray to God and implore the good Spirits to give them strength at this the most decisive moment of their ordeal.

Finally, after years of meditation and prayer, the Spirit takes the opportunity of a physical body that is, as yet, in project in the family of the one who is detested, and then asks the Spirits designated to transmit orders, for permission to fulfill here on Earth the destiny of that body which is about to be formed. What then will be this Spirit's behaviour within the chosen family? That will depend on the greater or lesser degree of persistance in the good resolutions made by that Spirit. The incessant contact with those it hates constitutes a terrible test, under which it not infrequently succumbs if its desire to win through is not sufficiently strong. In this manner, and according to whether or not the good resolutions predominate, the Spirit will be either a friend or enemy to those it was called to live amongst. This is the explanation for the hates and instinctive repulsions often noted between certain children, and which appear to be inexplicable. In actual fact there is nothing in the present life which could have caused such antipathy; in order to find the cause it would be necessary to look back into the past.

Oh! Spiritists! You must understand the great part that humanity has to play! You must understand that when a body is produced the soul which incarnates in it has come from space in order to progress. So acquaint yourselves with your duty and then put all your love into bringing this soul nearer to God. This is the mission with which you have been entrusted and for which you will receive just recompense if you fulfill your trust faithfully. The care and education given by you to this child will help in its improvement and future well-being. Remember that God will ask every mother and father: "What have you done with the child which was entrusted to you?" If through any fault of yours it has remained backward, then as punishment you will have to watch it amongst the suffering Spirits, when it depended upon you to help it towards happiness. Thus you yourselves, assailed by remorse, will ask that it be permitted for you to remedy your errors. You will request for yourself and your child another incarnation in which you will surround that Spirit with better care, and in which, being full of gratitude, the Spirit will then reciprocate by loving you.

So then, do not reject the child who repels its parents, nor the one who is ungrateful, for it is not mere chance which has made it like that and then given it to you. An imperfect intuition of the past is revealed by these attitudes, and from this we can deduce that one or the other harbours great hate or has been mortally offended; that one or the other has come to pardon or to atone. Mothers, embrace the child which causes vexation and say to yourself: One of us is guilty! Make yourselves worthy of the Divine enjoyment which God has conjugated into maternity by teaching your children that they are on Earth in order to perfect themselves, to love and to bless others. Oh, but there are many mothers amongst you having children who have innate bad principles acquired in past lives, and instead of eliminating these traits, actually maintain and develop them due to blameworthy weaknesses or through carelessness! Later on, with hearts that are lacerated by the ingratitude of your children, you will begin your atonement, even in this life.

Nevertheless, your task is not as difficult as it may seem. It does not require the wisdom of the world. Either an ignorant or wise person may discharge this duty, and Spiritism will help you to do just that by giving you the possibility of knowing the causes of the imperfections in the human soul.

Having been brought from past existences, these good or evil instincts will manifest themselves from early childhood. It is necessary that parents study these instincts; all badness originates from selfishness and pride. So be on the lookout for the least sign which will reveal the existence of such vices, and then take care to combat them without waiting for them to take deep root. Do as the good gardener does: cut off all defective shoots as soon as they appear on the tree. If you allow selfishness and pride to develop, do not be surprised if later on you are paid back by ingratitude. When parents have done everything possible for the moral advancement of their children, even if they have not been successful, then they have nothing with which to reproach themselves and their consciences may remain tranquil. For the natural anguish resulting from the unproductiveness of their efforts, God reserves a great, an immense, consolation in the *certainty* that it is only a brief delay, that it will be given to them to conclude in another existence the work that has already begun, and one day their ungrateful child will recompense them with love. (See chapter 13, item 19.)

God never gives anyone a trial superior to the strength of the person who has asked for it. He only permits those tests which can be fulfilled. Therefore if this does not happen, it is not for lack of possibilities, but for lack of willpower. In effect, how many there are who instead of resisting their bad tendencies, actually revel in them. Alas, these revellers will find that only tears and cries of anguish have been reserved for them in their future existences. Nevertheless, we should wonder at God's unbounding goodness because He never shuts the door to repentance. The day will come when the culprit, tired of suffering and with his or her pride finally humbled, will perceive that God is holding out His Hands to receive the prodigal child who throws himself at His feet. Now listen well to what I am about to tell you — *the harshest trials are almost always the indication of the end to suffering and to a certain perfecting of the Spirit, as long as they are accepted with all thought focussed on God.* These are in fact supreme moments in which, above all else, it behoves the Spirit not to cause failure due to constant complaining or the fruits of the trial will be lost, so making it necessary to begin again from the beginning. Instead of complaining, thank God for the opportunity to triumph which He has given you, that He may bestow the prize of victory upon you. Then when you leave the vortex of this earthly world, to enter into the world of spirit, you will be acclaimed as a soldier returning triumphant from the fray.

Of all the trials that exist, the hardest to bear are those which affect the heart. A person who is able to support misery and material privation with courage frequently succumbs under the weight of domestic bitterness, goaded on by the ingratitude of members of the family. Oh, what a terribly pungent anguish this is! But in these circumstances what can more effectively renew moral courage than the knowledge of the causes of the evil? Even if there are protracted lacerations, it is certain that there are no eternal despairs, because it is not possible for God to wish that any one of His creatures suffer indefinitely. What can be more comforting and more animating than the idea that the abbreviation of suffering depends on each effort made to destroy the evil within oneself, which is the cause of all misery? But in order to be able to do this, it is necessary that mankind does not confine its vision exclusively to this planet nor to only a single existence. Humanity must lift itself up so that it becomes possible to see the infinity of both the past and the future. When this happens, then God's everlasting justice becomes apparent and so you will be able to wait patiently, because all that had previously appeared to be absolute monstrosity on this Earth will have become explainable. The various wounds which you have received will appear as mere scratches. In this rapid glance cast over the whole scene, all family ties will present themselves in their true light. You will no longer see only the fragile material ties which join various members of a family together, but also the lasting ties of the Spirit which penetrate and consolidate with the process of purification, instead of being broken by the effect of reincarnation.

Families are formed by groupings of Spirits who are induced to gather together because of their affinities of tastes, moral progress and affections. During their terrestrial migrations, these same Spirits seek each other out in order to group themselves as they do in space, so giving origin to united and homogeneous families. If during their peregrinations it so happens they are temporarily separated, then they will meet again later on, happy for the new progress which has been accomplished. But as they are not allowed to work exclusively for their own benefit, God permits that less advanced Spirits incarnate amongst them in order that these may receive good advice and examples which will help them. Sometimes these Spirits cause perturbation in the midst of the others, which constitutes a trial and a task to be fulfilled. Therefore, receive these perturbed Spirits as your brothers and sisters; help them, and afterwards, when once again they are in the spiritual world, the family will be able to congratulate itself for having saved an outcast, who in their turn may save others. — SAINT AUGUSTIN (Paris, 1862).

CHAPTER 15

WITHOUT CHARITY THERE IS NO SALVATION

What the spirit needs in order to be saved. — The parable of
the good Samaritan. — The greatest of the commandments. —
The need for charity, according to Saint Paul. — Without the
Church there is no salvation. — Without truth there is no
salvation. — INSTRUCTIONS FROM THE SPIRITS:
Without charity there is no salvation.

WHAT THE SPIRIT NEEDS IN ORDER TO BE SAVED. THE PARABLE OF THE GOOD SAMARITAN

1. *When the Son of Man shall come in his glory, and all the holy angels with
Him, then shall He sit upon the throne of His glory: and before Him shall be
gathered all nations: and He shall separate them one from another as a shepherd
divideth his sheep from the goats: and He shall set the sheep on His right hand,
but the goats on the left.*

*Then shall the King say unto them on the right hand, Come, ye blessed of my
Father, inherit the kingdom prepared for you from the foundation of the world:
for I was an hungered, and ye gave me meat: I was thirsty, and ye gave me drink: I
was a stranger, and ye took me in: naked, and ye clothed me. I was sick, and ye
visited me: I was in prison, and ye came unto me.*

*Then shall the righteous answer Him saying, Lord, when saw we thee an
hungered, and fed thee? Or thirsty, and gave thee drink? When saw we thee a
stranger, and took thee in ? Or naked and clothed thee? Or when saw we thee sick,
or in prison, and came unto thee? And the King shall answer and say unto them,
Verily I say unto you, inasmuch as ye have done it unto one of the least of these
my bretheren ye have done it unto me.*

*Then shall He say also unto them on the left hands, Depart from me ye cursed
into everlasting fire, prepared for the devil and his angels: for I was hungered and
ye gave me no meat: I was thirsty, and ye gave me no drink. I was a stranger, and
ye took me not in: naked and ye clothed me not: sick and in prison, and ye visited
me not.*

Then shall they also answer Him saying, Lord, when saw we thee an hungered, or athirst, or a stranger, or naked, or sick, or in prison and did not minister unto thee? Then shall He answer them saying, Verily I say unto you, inasmuch as ye did it not to one of the least of these, ye did it not to me.

And these shall go away into everlasting punishment: but the righteous into life eternal (Matthew, 25: 31-46).

2. *And behold, a certain lawyer stood up and tempted Him, saying, Master, what shall I do to inherit eternal life? He said unto him, What is written in the law? How readest thou? And he answering said, Thou shalt love the Lord thy God with all thy heart, and with all thy soul and with all thy strength and with all thy mind: and thy neighbour as thyself. And He said unto him, Thou hast answered right: this do, and thou shalt live.*

But he, willing to justify himself, said unto Jesus, And who is my neighbour? And Jesus answering said, A certain man went down from Jesuralem to Jericho and fell among thieves, which stripped him of his raiment and wounded him and departed, leaving him half dead, and by chance there came down a certain priest that way; and when he saw him he passed by on the other side, and likewise a Levite, when he was at the place, came and looked on him and passed by on the other side. But a certain Samaritan, as he journeyed, came where he was: and when he saw him, he had compassion on him, and went to him and bound up his wounds, pouring in oil and wine and set him on his own beast and brought him to an inn, and took care of him. And on the morrow when he departed, he took out two pence and gave them to the host and said unto him, take care of him and whatsoever thou spendest more, when I come again I will repay thee.

Which now of these thinkest thou was neighbour unto him that fell among the thieves? And he said, He that shewed mercy on him. Then said Jesus unto him, Go, and do thou likewise (Luke, 10: 25-37).

3. All the moral teaching of Christ resumes itself in the need for charity and humility, that is to say, in the two virtues which are contrary to selfishness and pride. In all of His teaching Jesus indicates these two virtues as being the ones which lead to eternal happiness. He said that the poor in spirit, that is to say the humble, were blessed because the Kingdom of Heaven would be theirs: Blessed are those who have pure hearts; Blessed are the gentle and the peacemakers; Blessed are the merciful. He also taught the need to love one's neighbour as oneself, to do unto others as we would have them do unto us, to love our enemies, to forgive all offences if we wish to receive forgiveness, to do good without ostentation and to judge ourselves before we judge others. So then charity and humility are the two things which Jesus never ceased to recommend and for which He stands as an example. He also never ceased to combat pride and selfishness. Nor did He limit Himself to the mere recommending of charity, but put it in very clear and explicit terms as being the only condition for future happiness.

With respect to the description given by Jesus of the Final Judgement, we must separate, as in many other cases, that which is only form or allegory. The people to whom Jesus spoke, being still unable to understand totally spiritual questions, made it necessary for Him to offer them material images which would both shock and impress. Therefore in order for them to better understand what was being said to them, Jesus was obliged to keep closely to the form of the ideas of those times, always reserving for the future the real interpretation of His words and the points which at that time were unable to be clearly explained. But alongside the accessory or figurative parts of this explanation, there is one dominant feature: that of the happiness reserved for the just and the unhappiness awaiting those who are evil.

What then are the considerations of sentence according to that supreme judgement? On what has the indictment been based? Does the judge perhaps ask if the person under interrogation has fulfilled this or that formality, if they have more or less observed this or that external practice? No, he will ask but one question: if charity has been practised; and then make the pronouncement: "Go to the right all who have helped their brothers and sisters. Go to the left all those who have been unyielding." Is it said, by any chance, what is the orthodoxy of their faith? Is any distinction made between those who believe in this or that manner? No, because Jesus places the Samaritan, considered by some to be a heretic, who practised love towards his fellow creature above any orthodoxy which lacks charity. So do not consider charity to be merely one of the conditons for salvation. But instead, consider it to be the only condition. If there were others to be met, then Jesus would have mentioned them. Since He put charity in first place, it is because it implicitly embraces all the other virtues such as humility, kindness, benevolence, indulgence, justice, etc., and also because it is the absolute negation of pride and selfishness.

THE GREATEST OF THE COMMANDMENTS

4. *But when the Pharisees had heard that He had put the Sadducees to silence, they were gathered together. Then one of them, which was a lawyer, asked Him a question, tempting Him, and saying, Master, which is the greatest commandment in the law? Jesus said unto him, Thou shalt love the Lord thy God with all thy heart, and with all thy soul, and with all thy mind. This is the first and great commandment. The second is like unto it, thou shalt love thy neighbour as thyself. On these two commandments hang all the law and the prophets (Matthew, 22: 34-40).*

5. Charity and humility, such is the only path to salvation. Selfishness and pride are the paths to ruin. This principle is found to be formulated on the following precise terms: "Love your God with all your soul and your neighbour as yourself; *all the law and the prophets are contained in these two commandments.*" And so there would be no mistake in the understanding of the meaning of the love for God and for our neighbour, He then added: "And there is the second commandment, which is similar to the first." This means

that it is not possible to truly love God without loving your neighbour, nor to love your neighbour without loving God. Straightaway, all that you do against your neighbour you also do against God. Therefore, as it is not possible to love God without practising charity towards one's neighbour. All of mankind's obligations are resumed in the maxim: *without charity there is no salvation.*

THE NEED FOR CHARITY ACCORDING TO SAINT PAUL

6. *Though I speak with the tongues of men and of angels, and have not charity, I am become as sounding brass, or a tinkling cymbal. And though I have the gift of prophecy, and understand all the mysteries and all knowledge; and though I have faith, so that I could remove mountains, and have not charity, I am nothing. And though I bestow all my goods to feed the poor, and though I give my body to be burned, and have not charity, it profiteth me nothing. Charity suffereth long and is kind; charity vaunteth not itself, is not puffed up, doth not behave itself unseemly, seeketh not her own, is not easily provoked, thinketh no evil; rejoiceth not in iniquity, but rejoiceth in the truth; beareth all things, believeth all things, hopeth all things, endureth all things. And now abideth faith, hope, charity, these three; but the greatest of these is charity (SAINT PAUL, I Corinthians, 13: 1-7 & 13).*

7. This is the way in which Saint Paul understood this great truth, which said: 'When I have learned the language of the Angels: When I have the gift of prophecy, which I can penetrate all the mysteries; When I have all the faith that is possible, even to the point of transporting mountains, if I do not have charity, then I am nothing. Within the three virtues: faith, hope and charity, the most superior of these is charity.' In this manner and without any possible doubt, Paul places charity above even faith. This is because charity is within the reach of everybody, from the ignorant to the wise person, from rich to poor people; it is also quite independent of any particular beliefs.

He does even more: he defines true charity by showing it as being not only beneficence, but also a collective of all the qualities of the heart, in terms of goodness and benevolence towards all of our fellow beings.

WITHOUT THE CHURCH THERE IS NO SALVATION. WITHOUT TRUTH THERE IS NO SALVATION

8. The maxim — *without charity there is no salvation* — stands upon a universal principle and opens the door to supreme happiness for all of God's children, whereas the dogma — *without the church there is no salvation* — rests not upon a fundamental faith in God and the immortality of the soul, which is a belief common to all religion, but *on a special faith, in particular dogmas,* which are exclusive and absolute. Far from uniting God's children, it separates them. Instead of inciting them to love their brothers and sisters, it feeds upon and sanctions the irritations between various sectarians of the different cults, who reciprocally consider each other to be eternally damned, despite the fact that

these same sectarians may be relations or friends. Therefore by despising the great law of equality in the presence of the tomb, it separates people one from another, even in the area of repose. The maxim — *without charity there is no salvation* — consecrates the principle of equality before God and freedom of conscience. By taking this as a norm, all men and women become brothers and sisters, whatever their way of worshiping the Creator, holding up their hands and praying for each other. But with the dogma — *without the church there is no salvation* — they excommunicate and persecute each other reciprocally, living as enemies. The father does not ask after his son, nor the son after his father, nor a friend after his friend, since they consider themselves mutually condemned without possible remission. Therefore it is a dogma which is essentially against the teaching of Christ and the evangelic laws.

9. *Without truth there is no salvation* is equal to *without the church there is no salvation,* being equally exclusive, since there is no one sect existing which does not claim to hold the privilege of truth. What man can boast of being in possession of all the truth when our sphere of knowledge is constantly enlarging and ideas are being rectified every day? The absolute truth is the patrimony of only the most elevated category of Spirits. Earthly humanity cannot allege the possession of it because it is not given to mankind to know everything. It is only permissible to aspire to relative truth which is proportionate to the level of progress. If God had made the possession of truth an express and absolute condition for future happiness, He would have pronounced a verdict of general condemnation; whereas charity, even in its most ample form, may be practised by all. Spiritism, in accordance with the Gospel, admits the possibility of salvation for every person, independently of any beliefs, granted that God's laws are observed. It does not say that *without Spiritism there is no salvation,* just as it does not intend to teach all the truth as yet. Neither does it say *without truth there is no salvation* because this maxim, instead of uniting would only separate and also perpetuate antagonisms.

INSTRUCTIONS FROM THE SPIRITS.

WITHOUT CHARITY THERE IS NO SALVATION

10. My children, within the sentence: *Without charity there is no salvation,* is enclosed the destiny of mankind, both on Earth and in Heaven. On Earth, because beneath the shadow of this banner all may live in peace, and in Heaven, because those who have practised it will find grace in God's eyes. This phrase is the celestial beacon, the luminous column, which will guide mankind in life's desert, putting all on the right path to the Promised Land. It shines in Heaven as a saintly halo on the brows of the chosen ones, and on Earth it is engraved on the hearts of those to whom Jesus has said: "Go to the right and receive the blessing of My Father". You will recognise them when they come by the aroma of charity that spreads around them. Nothing can indicate with more exactitude nor summarize so well mankind's obligations, as this divine

maxim. Spiritism could not better prove its origin than present it as its rule, because it is a reflection of the most pure Christianity. Humanity will never go astray if it takes this as its guide. So then, my dear friends, dedicate yourselves to the understanding of the deep meaning behind these words and the consequences of their application and then discover for yourselves all the many ways in which they may be applied. Submit all your activities to be administered by charity and your conscience will respond. Not only will it cause you to avoid practising evil, but it will also make you practise goodness, in as much as a negative virtue is not enough; it is necessary to possess an active virtue. Therefore in order to do good there is always the need for the action of willpower, whereas in order to not practise evil it is sufficient to be inert or unconcerned.

My friends, give thanks to God for having permitted you to enjoy the enlightenment of Spiritism. Not that those who possess this enlightenment are the only ones who will be saved, but because it helps you to understand the teachings of Christ, so making you into better Christians. Therefore make every effort so that your fellow beings, on observing you, are induced to recognise that the true Spiritist and the true Christian are one and the same, given that all those who practise charity are the disciples of Jesus, without putting any embargo on whatever sect they may belong to. — PAUL, the Apostle (Paris, 1860).

CHAPTER 16

IT IS NOT POSSIBLE TO SERVE BOTH GOD AND MAMMON

The salvation of the rich. — Preserve yourself from avarice. —
Jesus in the house of Zacchaéus. — The parable of the bad rich
man. — The parable of the talents. — The providential utility
of riches. Trials of riches and misery. — The inequality of
riches. — INSTRUCTIONS FROM THE SPIRITS: True
property. —The application of riches. — Detachment from
earthly possessions. — Transference of riches

THE SALVATION OF THE RICH

1. *No servant can serve two masters: for either he will hate the one, and love the
other; or else he will hold to the one, and despise the other. Ye cannot serve both
God and Mammon (Luke, 16: 13).*

2. *And behold, one came and said unto him, Good Master, what good things
shall I do, that I may have eternal life? And He said unto him, Why callest thou
me good? There is none good but one, that is, God: but if thou wilt enter into life,
keep the commandments. He saith unto Him, Which? Jesus said, Thou shalt do
no murder, Thou shalt not commit adultery, Thou shalt not steal, Thou shalt not
bear false witness, Honour thy father and thy mother: and, Thou shalt love thy
neighbour as thyself.*

*The young man saith unto Him, All these things have I kept from my youth up:
what lack I yet? Jesus said unto him, If thou wilt be perfect go and sell that thou
hast, and give to the poor, and thou shalt have treasure in Heaven: and come and
follow me.*

*But when the young man heard that saying, he went away sorrowful: for he
had great possessions. Then Jesus said unto His disciples, Verily I say unto you,
that a rich man shall hardly enter into the Kingdom of Heaven, and again I say
unto you, It is easier for a camel to go through the eye of a needle, than for a rich
man to enter into the Kingdom of God (1) (Matthew, 19: 16-24. This same text is
also repeated by Luke, 18: 18-25, & by Mark, 10: 17-25).*

---

(1) In the Hebrew language there exists the same word meaning both a camel and a cord. In the
translation of the Bible the first meaning was quoted, but it is possible that Jesus used the other
meaning, namely a cord. This would at least appear to be more normal. (Translator's note).

PRESERVE YOURSELF FROM AVARICE

3. *And one of the company said unto Him, Master, speak to my brother that he divide the inheritance with me. And He said unto him, Man, take heed, and beware of covetousness: for a man's life consisteth not in the abundance of the things which he possesseth. And He spake a parable unto them, saying, The ground of a certain rich man brought forth plentifully: and he thought within himself, saying, What shall I do, because I have no room where to bestow my fruits? And he said, This will I do: I will pull down my barns, and build greater; and there will I bestow all my fruits and my goods. And I will say unto my soul, Soul, thou hast much goods laid up for many years; take thine ease, eat, drink and be merry. But God said unto him, Thou fool, this night thy soul shall be required of thee: then whose shall those things be which thou hast provided?*

So is he that layeth up treasure for himself, and is not rich towards God (Luke, 12: 13-21).

JESUS IN THE HOUSE OF ZACCHAÉUS

4. *And Jesus entered and passed through Jericho. And behold, there was a man named Zacchaéus, which was the chief among the publicans, and he was rich. And he sought to see Jesus who He was; and could not for the press, because he was little in stature. And he ran before and climbed up into a sycamore tree to see Him: for He was to pass that way. And when Jesus came to the place, He looked up and saw him, and said unto him, Zacchaéus, make haste and come down; for today I must bide at thy house. And he made haste and came down and received Him joyfully. And when they saw it, they all murmered, saying, That He was gone to be the guest of a man that is a sinner. (See the 'INTRODUCTION', under the heading — PUBLICANS.)*

And Zacchaéus stood and said unto the Lord; Behold, Lord, the half of my goods I give to the poor; and if I have taken anything from any man by false accusation, I restore him fourfold. And Jesus said unto him, This day is salvation come to this house forsomuch as he is a son of Abraham. For the Son of Man is come to seek and to save that which was lost (Luke, 19: 1-10).

THE PARABLE OF THE BAD RICH MAN

5. *There was a certain rich man, which was clothed in purple and fine linen, and fared sumptuously every day: and there was a certain beggar named Lazarus, which was laid at his gate, full of sores, and desiring to be fed with the crumbs which fell from the rich man's table: moreover the dogs came and licked his sores. And it came to pass, that the beggar died, and was carried by the Angels into Abraham's bosom: the rich man also died, and was buried: and in hell he lift up his eyes, being in torment and seeth Abraham afar off, and Lazarus in his bosom. And he cried and said, Father Abraham, have mercy on me, and send Lazarus, that he may dip the tip of his finger in water and cool my tongue; for I am tormented in this flame.*

But Abraham said, Son, remember that thou in thy lifetime received thy good things, and likewise Lazarus evil things: but now he is comforted and thou art tormented. And beside all things, between us and you there is a great gulf fixed: so that they which would pass from hence to you cannot; neither can they pass to us, that would come from hence.

Then he said, I pray thee therefore, father, that thou wouldest send him to my father's house: for I have five brethren; that he may testify unto them, lest they also come into this place of torment. Abraham said unto him, They have Moses and the prophets; let them hear them: And he said, Nay, father Abraham: but if one went unto them from the dead, they would repent. And he said unto them, If they hear not Moses and the prophets, neither will they be pursuaded, though one rose from the dead (Luke, 16: 19-31).

THE PARABLE OF THE TALENTS

6. For the Kingdom of Heaven is as a man travelling into a far country, who called his servants, and delivered unto them his goods. And unto one he gave five talents, to another two, and to another one; to every man according to his several ability; and straightway took his journey. Then he that had received the five talents went and traded with the same, and made them other five talents. And likewise he that had received two, he also gained other two. But he that had received one went and digged in the earth, and hid his lord's money. After a long time the lord of those servants cometh, and reckoneth with them and so he that had received five talents came and brought other five talents, saying Lord, thou deliveredst unto me five talents: Behold, I have gained beside them five talents more. His lord said unto him, Well done, thou good and faithful servant: Thou hast been faithful over a few things, I will make thee ruler over many things: Enter thou into the joy of the Lord. He also that had received two talents came and said, Lord, thou deliveredst unto me two talents: Behold, I have gained two other talents besides them. His lord said unto him, Well done, good and faithful servant; Thou has been faithful over a few things, I will make thee ruler over many things: Enter thou into the joy of the Lord. Then he which had received the one talent came and said, Lord I knew thee that thou art a hard man, reaping where thou hast not sown, and gathering where thou hast not strawed: and I was afraid and went and hid thy talent in the earth: Lo, there thou has that is thine. His lord answered and said unto him, Thou wicked and slothful servant, thou knowest that I reap where I sowed not and gathered where I have not strawed: Thou oughtest therefore to have put my money to the exchangers and then at my coming I should have received mine own with usury. Take therefore the talent from him and give it unto him which hath ten talents. For unto every one that hath shall be given and he shall have abundance: but for him that hath not shall be taken away even that which he hath. And cast ye the unprofitable servant into outer darkness: there shall be weeping and gnashing of teeth (Matthew, 25: 14-30).

THE PROVIDENTIAL UTILITY OF RICHES. TRIALS OF RICHES AND MISERY

7. If riches were meant to constitute a total obstacle to salvation for all who possess them, as might be inferred from certain words supposedly uttered by Jesus when they are interpreted in a literal fashion instead of in their spiritual meaning, then God, who conceded them would have placed an instrument of ruination in the hands of certain people against which they could not appeal. But this idea is quite repugnant to all reason. However, it is beyond doubt that from the destruction it causes, the temptations it provokes and the fascination it holds, we may deduce that riches constitute a very dangerous trial, even more dangerous than that of misery. It is the greatest provoker of pride, selfishness and sensuality. It is the strongest tie which holds Man to Earth and distracts him from thoughts of Heaven. On many occasions it produces such a state of dizziness that those who go from misery to wealth completely forget their first condition, together with those who had shared this state with them, even those who had helped them, turning them into insensitive, selfish and futile people. Nevertheless, from the fact that riches make the journey difficult, it does not follow that it becomes impossible or that it cannot become a means of salvation for those who know how to utilize it, just as certain poisons may restitute health when employed in the correct quantities and used with discernment.

When Jesus said to the young man, who inquired how he could obtain eternal life, that he should dispose of all his worldly goods and follow Him, it did not mean that Jesus was establishing an absolute principle, that everyone should get rid of everything they possess, nor that this is the only price to be paid for salvation. It was meant to show that attachment to worldly goods was an obstacle to salvation. The young man in this case had judged himself to be released from further struggle because he had observed certain commandments, and therefore he refused the idea of abandoning all the worldly goods he possessed. His desire to obtain eternal life did not run to the extreme of acquiring it through this sacrifice.

What Jesus proposed to him was a decisive test destined to uncover the depths of his thoughts. Beyond doubt he could be a perfectly honest man in the eyes of the world, never causing harm to anyone, never cursing his neighbours, never being vain, futile or prideful, and always honouring his mother and father. But still he did not possess true charity, because his virtues did not go as far as abnegation. This is what Jesus wished to demonstrate by applying the principle: Without charity there is no salvation.

In the strict acceptance of these words, the consequence would be the abolition of riches due to their being detrimental to future happiness and the cause of a great deal of the evil on Earth; for the rest, it would be the condemnation of all work, as being the means of gain. This would be an absurd consequence which would only convey mankind back to a primitive existence which, for that very reason, would be in complete contradiction to the law of progress, which is one of God's laws.

If riches be the cause of much evil, if they aggravate so many evil passions, if they really provoke so many crimes, it is not the riches themselves that we should blame but mankind who misuses them, as he does all of God's gifts. It is through ill usage that humanity constantly turns what could be most useful into something pernicious. This is a consequence of the inferior state of earthly life. If only wrongdoing and mischief could be produced by riches, then God would not have placed them upon Earth. It is up to Man to make them produce good, and even if they are not a direct element of moral progress, then beyond doubt they are a powerful element in intellectual progress.

Indeed, Man has the mission of working for the material betterment of this planet. It is up to him to reclaim it, to make it salubrious and to make arrangements so that one day the planet may receive all the population that its area can and should contain. Therefore, so as to be able to feed this larger population, it will become imperative to increase production. If the production of one country is insufficient, then it will be brought in from outside. This is why the relationships between nations constitute a vital necessity. In order to make this easier, it behoves that all the material obstacles which separate these countries be destroyed, so that communication be made rapid. For this work, which has required centuries to complete, it was essential to extract materials from the entrails of the Earth, which made Man look to science for the means of executing these tasks with more speed and safety. But in order to do this he needed resources; this necessity caused him to create riches, just as it caused the creation of science. All these activities imposed the need to amplify and develop intelligence, which man has used primarily for the satisfaction of material necessities. Nevertheless, it is this same intelligence which will later help humanity to understand all the great moral truths. Seeing that riches are the primary means of executing these tasks, there would be no more great works without them, no activity, no stimulation nor research. It is with good reason then that riches should be considered as an element of progress.

THE INEQUALITY OF RICHES

8. The inequality of riches is one of the problems which humanity will go on trying to resolve without success as long as only the present life is considered. The first question which presents itself is: Why are we not all equally rich? For the simple reason *that we are not equally intelligent, active and industrious enough to acquire it, nor sober and careful enough to keep it.* Besides, it is a mathematically demonstrable fact that riches, if equally divided would give a minimum and insufficient portion to each one. So that, supposing this division were actually made, in a short time this equilibrium would be undone by the

diversity of characters and aptitudes. That supposing it to be possible and lasting, if each one had sufficient to live upon, then the result would be an annihilation of all great works which contribute towards progress and the wellbeing of humanity. And finally, if it were conceded that each person was given the indispensable, then there would no longer be any goad to impel men and women to make discoveries or to found useful enterprises. Therefore if God has concentrated riches in certain areas, it is in order that from there it can be expanded in sufficient quantities according to needs.

Having accepted this fact, we then ask why God has conceded riches to people who are incapable of making them bear fruit for the good of all. Here we have yet another proof of the wisdom and goodness of God. By giving Man free-will, He wishes that the position of being able to distinguish right from wrong be reached through individual experience, and that the practice of good be solely the result of effort and choice. Man should not be fatally conducted towards either good or evil, as then we would be nothing more than passive and irresponsible instruments, as are animals. Wealth is a means of being able to test one's morality. But, as it is also a powerful means of action towards progress, God does not wish it to remain unproductive over long periods of time, so He *unceasingly displaces it.* Each one possesses it sooner or later, so that they may drill themselves in utilizing it and demonstrate what uses they have learnt to put it to. Nevertheless, it is materially impossible for all to possess it at the same time, as it happens that if everyone had riches, then no one would work, which would result in the improvement of the planet being compromised. *Each one then has a turn in possessing it.* In this manner, those who do not have it today, have already had it or will have it at some future time. Likewise, those who have it now perhaps will not have it tomorrow. There are rich and poor because God, being just, prescribes work to each one in turn. For those who suffer it, poverty is a test of patience and resignation; for others, riches are a test in charity and abnegation.

It is with good reason that the very bad uses to which some people put their riches are to be deplored, as are the ignoble passions provoked by their greed. This makes us ask ourselves if God is just to give riches to such creatures. It is certain that if man had but one life nothing could justify such a division of worldy goods. However, if we keep in sight not only the present life, but also the assemblage of existences, we would see that everything is justly balanced. From this point of view, the poor person lacks a motive with which to accuse providence, just as he has no motive to be envious of the rich who, in their turn also lack a motive to glorify themselves for what they possess. On the other hand, if the application of these riches is abused it will not be by means of decree of sumptuary laws that the wrongdoing will be remedied. The law can temporarily change the exterior, but it cannot succeed in changing the heart. Hence these laws would be of fleeting duration and would then be followed by more unrestrained reactions. The origin of evil lies in pride and selfishness; therefore, all manner of abuses will cease when humanity is governed by the law of charity.

INSTRUCTIONS FROM THE SPIRITS.

TRUE PROPERTY

9. The only true property that Man can own is that which may be taken with him on leaving this world. What is found on arrival on Earth and that which is left behind on parting, is enjoyed only while living here. Therefore, as humanity is forced to abandon all worldly possessions, it can be inferred that it has no real ownership of riches, only their temporary usage. What then constitutes true property? Nothing which is for the use of the body, but everything which is for the use of the soul, such as intelligence, knowledge and moral qualities. This is what man brings and takes with him, which no one can take away and which will be far more use in the next world than in the present one. It is up to him to be richer on departure than he was on arrival in this world, seeing that his future position will depend solely on what qualities have been gained in the present life. When someone travels to a distant country they take as part of their luggage only those things which will be useful to them in that place; they do not worry about those things which will be of no use. Proceed in a like manner in relation to your future life and provide yourselves with all that can be of use to you there.

The traveller who arrives at a hostel is only given a good room if he is able to pay for it. Those who have sparse resources are forced to make do with something less agreeable. When they have nothing which belongs to them, they must sleep on a pallet bed. The same applies to Man on his arrival in the world of the spirits, for it will depend entirely on what he owns as to where he will go. Nor will payment be made in terms of gold. No one will be asked what it was they had had on Earth, or what position they had occupied, nor even if they were a pauper or a prince. Instead, they will be asked what they have brought with them. Neither worldly goods nor titles will be valuated, only the total sum of virtues acquired. Well now, looked at from this aspect, it is possible that the simple worker be far richer than the prince. In vain may the latter allege that before leaving the Earth his entrance into the next world was paid for in gold. The only reply he would receive is that no one may buy a place here; it must be conquered by each person by means of doing good to others. Earthly money may buy land, houses or palaces, but in our world everything is paid for by means of the qualities of the soul. Are you rich in these qualities? Then you are welcome and may go to one of the high places where all kinds of happinesses await you. But if you are poor in these qualities then you must go to the low places, where you will be treated according to that which you possess. — PASCAL (Geneva, 1860).

10. Earthly goods belong to God, Who distributes them in accordance with His wishes. Man is nothing more than the usufructuary, a relatively honest and intelligent administrator of these goods or properties. They belong so little to him that frequently God annuls all such provisions and these riches escape from even those who considered themselves to hold the best entitlement.

You would say perhaps that this is understandable when related to inherited property, but not to that acquired by work. Undoubtedly if there were such a thing as legitimate riches, then it would apply to the latter, when honestly gained. However, *a property is only legitimately acquired when during its acquisition there has been no harm done to anyone.* An account will have to be given of all ill-gotten gains, that is to say gains which may have injured someone. But from the fact that a person may owe the acquiring of riches to themself, does it follow that, upon dying, any advantage may be gained from this circumstance? Are not precautions that may have been taken to transfer these riches to descendants frequently inutile? This is correct, for if God does not desire them to receive certain riches, then nothing can prevail against His wishes. Can someone use and abuse what he owns during his lifetime without needing to give an account of these acts? No, because in permitting the acquisition of this property it is to be supposed that God had in mind to recompense the person, during the actual existence for their effort, courage and perseverance. If however, the property be used exclusively for the satisfaction of pride and the senses, or if they become the cause of failure, then it would have been better not to have received them seeing that what is gained on the one hand is lost on the other, so annulling all merit for the work. In this case, upon leaving the Earth, God will say that the recompense has already been received. — M. a Protecting Spirit (Brussels, 1861).

THE APPLICATION OF RICHES

11. It is not possible to serve both God and Mammon. Those of you who are dominated by the love of gold, who would sell your very souls in order to possess treasure, do not forget this reminder, because these things permit you to elevate yourselves above other men and women, so allowing you to enjoy passions which make you their slaves. No, it is not possible to serve both God and Mammon! So then, if you feel your soul to be dominated by the lust of the flesh, make haste to rid yourself of this yoke that tyrannizes you, in as much as God, who is just and strict, will say unto you: 'What did you do with the property I entrusted to you, unfaithful steward? This powerful motive for good works has been used exclusively for your own personal satisfaction!'

What then is the best way to employ riches? If you look for the answer in the words 'love one another' you will find the solution, for here lies the secret of the best way of employing riches.

Those who love their neighbour already have a line of action delineated for them in these words, because the application which most pleases God is charity. Not that cold and selfish charity which consists in distributing only that which is superfluous from their golden existence, but rather that charity full of love which seeks out misfortune, and helps raise it up without causing humiliation. You who are rich, give what you have in excess! But do even more, give something of what is necessary to you because what you consider to be necessary is, in reality, also superfluous, but give wisely. Do not reject those who weep because you may be afraid of being duped, but get to the bottom of the matter. In the first place seek to alleviate; secondly seek information and then see if the possibility of work, counselling, or even offering affection would not be more efficient than the mere giving of alms. Diffuse all around you with joy and in plenty, your love for God, for work and for your neighbour. Place your riches on a secure base which is that of good works, and you will be guaranteed great profit. The riches of intelligence should serve you just as do those of wealth; therefore disperse around you the benefits of education and scatter the treasure of your love over your brothers and sisters that they may bear fruits. — CHEVERUS (Bordeaux, 1861).

12. When I consider the brevity of life, I am painfully impressed by the incessant preoccupation placed on material well-being; whereas so little time or significance is given to moral improvement, though nevertheless, this is what is really important to eternity. From the amount of effort we put into our material welfare it would appear that we were dealing with a question of the utmost importance for humanity; when in reality it will be found that in the majority of cases, this same work is nothing other than an attempt to satisfy exaggerated needs and vanities, or is a surrender to excesses. What grief, sorrow and torments you cause yourselves! What sleepless nights, just to increase what is often a more than sufficient wealth! At the height of blindness, it is not infrequent to see those whose immoderate love of wealth and pleasures allows them to be subjected to arduous and tiring work, boasting of the life of sacrifice and merit they lead, as if they were working for others and not for themselves! What fools you are! Do you really believe that the care and effort expended will be taken into consideration when, on the one hand, you are motivated by selfishness, cupidity and pride, while on the other hand you neglect your future and the duties which fraternal solidarity imposes on all who reap the advantages which society has to offer? You have thought only of your physical bodies! Your own well-being and pleasures have been the exclusive object of your selfish solicitude. For the sake of the body that perishes you have despised the Spirit that will live forever. This is why that spoiled and flattered lord becomes your tyrant; it dominates your Spirit, thus making you its slave. Can this possibly be the objective for which God granted you life? — A Protecting Spirit (Krakow, 1861).

13. Seeing that Man is both administrator and trustee for the property which is placed in his hands by God, it will therefore be indispensable to render a strict account of the uses it has been put to by virtue of man's free-will. Bad usage consists of it being used exclusively for personal satisfaction; good usage, on the contrary, is whenever this results in benefit to others. Each person's merit is in the degree of sacrifice they impose upon themself. Beneficence is just one way of employing riches; it can be used to alleviate misery, appease hunger and offer shelter and warmth to those who have none. Nevertheless, an equally imperious obligation, which is also very noteworthy, is that of preventing misery. This, above all else, is the mission of the great fortunes, a mission to be fulfilled through the many kinds of work for which it can be used. Neither does the good resulting from these works cease to exist

because those who work in this manner take legitimate benefit from it, seeing that it develops intelligence and ennobles the dignity of Man by allowing him the satisfaction of being able to say that he earns his means of sustenance; whereas the receiving of alms only humiliates and degrades. Riches which are concentrated in one hand should be like a spring of running water which spreads fertility and well-being wherever it goes. Oh wealthy men and women! Employ your riches according to the wishes of God, Who would be the first to quench your thirst at this blessed spring! Even in this present life you could reap unequalled happiness for the soul, instead of the material pleasures of selfishness, which only produce a sensation of emptiness in the heart. Your name would be blessed on Earth and when you leave it, the Lord our God would say unto you as was said in the parable of the talents: "Good and faithful servant, enter into the happiness of your God." In this parable the servant who buried the money that was entrusted to him, represents those who are miserly and in whose hands riches remain unproductive. Meanwhile, if Jesus spoke principally of alms it was because in those days, in the country in which He lived, the kinds of work in the arts and industry in which riches could be usefully employed were not yet known. So then, to all who are able to give, be it much or little, I would say this: give money only when it is necessary, and then as often as possible convert it into wages so that the person who receives it is not ashamed. — FÉNELON (Argel, 1860).

DETACHMENT FROM EARTHLY POSSESSIONS

14. My brothers, sisters and friends, I am come to offer you my contribution with the object of helping you to advance fearlessly along the pathway to improvement into which you are entering. We are all indebted one to the other. Therefore it is only possible to achieve regeneration by means of a sincere and fraternal union between Spirits and incarnate beings.

Attachment to earthly possessions constitutes one of the strongest obstacles to both moral and spiritual advancement. Through this attachment all faculties for loving are destroyed as these are only devoted to material things. Let us be sincere with each other: do riches bring unmixed happiness? When your safes are full of money, do you still feel an emptiness in your hearts? At the bottom of this basket of flowers is there not a viper? I understand the satisfaction which is experienced, and quite justifiably so, when by means of honourable and assiduous work a fortune has been gained. But from this same satisfaction, which is very natural and has God's approval, to the attachment which absorbs all other sentiments and paralyzes the impulses felt by the heart, there is a large gap. As large as the distance which separates exaggerated extravagance from that of sordid covetousness, two vices between which God has placed charity, that saintly and cleansing virtue which teaches the rich man and woman to give without ostentation, so that the poor may receive without being debased.

Whether the fortune has come to you from your family, or whether you have earned it by working, there is something you should never forget, which is that everything proceeds from God and everything refers us to Him. Nothing belongs to you on this Earth, not even your own physical body: death strips you of it even as it does of all earthly possessions. You are merely trustees and not the owners, so do not delude yourselves. God has only lent these things to you and they must be returned. What is more, they have been lent to you under the condition that at least the surplus should go to those who lack what is necessary.

One of your friends lends you a certain sum of money. However lacking in honesty you may be, you make a point of scrupulously restituting what was lent and are grateful to that person. Well then, this is the exact position of the rich man or woman. God is the Celestial Friend who lends you riches, wishing nothing more for Himself than love and recognition for the loan. However, He does demand that in turn the rich man or woman give to the poor, who just as much as he or she, are sons and daughters of God.

Ardent and demented greed are aroused in your hearts by the possessions which God has entrusted to you. Have you ever stopped to think that when you allow yourselves to become immoderately attached to a valuable or perishable object, which is just as transitory as yourselves, that one day you will have to account to God for what has been done with that which came from Him? Have you forgotten that by means of riches, you assume a sacred mission of charity here on Earth, to be intelligent distributors? Hence, when what was entrusted to you is used only for your own benefit, does it not follow that you are unfaithful trustees? What will be the result of this voluntary forgetfullness of duty? Inflexible and inexhaustible death will tear away the veil under which you have been hiding, so forcing you to give an account to Him Who has been forgotten and Who, at that moment stands before you as Judge.

It is useless to try to delude yourselves while on Earth by covering up, under the name of virtue, what is usuallly nothing more than selfishness. It is useless to call that which is only greed and cupidity by the name of economy and foresight, or to call that which is only prodigality for your own advantage, by the name of generosity. For example, a father abstains from practising charity, economizes and accumulates wealth so that, as he puts it, he may leave his children the greatest possible amount of property in order to avoid their ever knowing misery. This is very just and fatherly, I agree, and no one can censure him for this. But is it always the only motive behind his action? Does he not frequently feel bound by his own conscience to justify this personal attachment for earthly possessions, both in his own eyes and those of the world? However, even if paternal love be the only motive, is that reason enough to forget his brothers and sisters before God? When he has a surplus, will he leave his children in misery if they have a little less? In this manner, is he not giving them a lesson in selfishness and hardening their hearts? Will it not cause their love for their neighbours to wither away? Mothers and fathers, you are labouring under a grave error if you believe this is the way to gain affection from your children. By teaching them to be selfish with others you are only teaching them to be selfish with you too.

The man who has worked very hard in his life and who by the sweat of his brow has accumulated possessions, is commonly heard to say that the value of money is better appreciated when it has been worked for. This is very true. Well then! This man who declares he knows the full value of money should practise charity; his merit will then be greater than the one who, being born to abundance, is ignorant of toil and work. But also, if this same man who remembers his own sufferings and endeavours, is selfish and unmerciful to the poor he will be more guilty than the other, since the more each one knows for themselves the hidden pains of misery, the greater tendency there should be to help others.

Unhappily, in men and women who possess riches there is always a sentiment as strong as their attachment for the riches themselves, and that is pride. Not infrequently the newly rich can be seen making someone who asked for assistance, dizzy with the tales of their successes and abilities instead of helping, and then end by saying: "Do as I did". According to their way of thinking God's goodness doesn't even enter into the matter of their having obtained these riches. The merit for having obtained them being their's alone. Their pride has blinded their eyes and deafened their ears. Despite their intelligence and aptitudes they still do not understand that with only one word God can cast them down upon the Earth.

The squandering of riches is not a demonstration of detachment from worldly goods, merely carelessness and indifference. Man, as the trustees of these goods, has no right to dissipate them, neither has he the right to confiscate them for his own benefit. Extravagance is not generosity; rather it is frequently a type of selfishness. Someone who spends money by the handful in order to satisfy a fantasy will perhaps not give even a penny to someone in need. Detachment from worldly goods consists in appreciating them according to their just value, in knowing how to make use of them for the benefit of others and not exclusively in self-benefit, in not sacrificing all interest in a future life for them, and in being able to lose them without a murmur, in case it pleases God to take them away. If due to unforeseeable circumstances, you become as Job, then say as he did: "Lord, You have given and You have taken away. Let Your Will be done." This is true detachment. Above all else be submissive and trust He Who, having given and taken away, may once again restitute what was taken. Resist disanimation and desperation with all your courage, as these paralyze your strength. When God causes you to suffer a blow, never ever forget that alongside the most painful trial He always places a consolation. Above all, ponder the point that there are possessions infinitely more precious than those to be found on Earth and this thought will help you towards detachment. The less attachment you have for something means the less sensitive you will be to its loss. The man or woman who holds on to earthly possessions is like a child, who sees only the moment, whereas the person who is able to detach themself is like an adult, who sees the more important things in life because they understand the prophetic words of the Saviour: "My kingdom is not of this world."

The Lord orders no one to dispose of what they possess, since this would condemn them to voluntary pauperism, seeing that those who did this would turn themselves into social encumberances. To proceed in this manner is to misunderstand the true meaning of detachment from worldly goods. In fact this is a selfishness of another kind, because it means that the individual exempts themself from the responsibility which riches have placed on all who possess them. God gives riches to those He considers apt to administer them for the benefit of others. The rich person is given a mission which can be beautified by him and be personally profitable. To reject riches when God has bestowed them, is to renounce the benefits of the goodness it can do, when administered with good judgement. By knowing how to do without them when you do not have them, knowing how to employ them usefully when you receive them, and by knowing how to sacrifice them when necessary, you are proceeding according to God's wishes. Well then, let those into whose hands has come what in the world is called goodly fortune, say: "My Lord, you have entrusted me with a new mission; give me the strength to fulfill it according to your wishes."

My friends, here you have what I wished to teach about detachment from worldly possessions. I would summarize what I have written by saying: Know how to be content with only a little. If you are poor, do not envy the rich, because riches are not necessarily happiness. If you are rich, then do not forget that these riches at your disposal are only entrusted to you, and that you will have to justify the use to which you put them, just as you would have to give an account of an investment for which you are responsible. Do not be an unfaithful trustee, utilizing it only for the satisfaction of your own pride and sensuality. Do not think you have the right to dispose of a loan as if it were a gift, exclusively for your own benefit. If you do not know how to make restitution then you do not have the right of request, and remember that the person who gives to the poor is settling a debt contracted with God. — LACORDAIRE (Constantina, 1863).

15. *Does the principle, according to which Man is merely the trustee for the fortune which God has permitted him to enjoy during his life-time, take away the right to transmit it to his descendants?*

Man has a perfect right to transmit after his death that which he enjoyed during his lifetime, because the effect of this right is always subordinate to the Will of God, Who can, when He deems fit, prevent those descendants from enjoying what was transferred to them. This is the reason why many apparently solid fortunes collapse. Man's will then, is impotent when he desires to maintain his fortune in the hands of his descendants. This, however, does not take away his right to transfer the loan received from God, seeing that God can take it away whenever He judges opportune. — SAINT LOUIS (Paris, 1860).

CHAPTER 17

BE PERFECT

Characteristics of Perfection. — The good person. — The good
Spiritist. — The parable of the sower. — INSTRUCTIONS
FROM THE SPIRITS: Duty. — Virtue. — Those who are
superior and those who are inferior. — The worldly person. —
Look after both body and spirit.

CHARACTERISTICS OF PERFECTION

1. *But I say unto you, Love your enemies, bless them that curse you, do good to them that hate you, and pray for them which despitefully use you, and persecute you. For if ye love them which love you, what reward have ye? Do not even the publicans the same? And if ye salute your brethren only, what do ye more than others? Do not even the publicans so? Be ye therefore perfect, even as your Father which is in Heaven is perfect (Matthew, 5: 44 & 46-48).*

2. Since God possess infinite perfection in all things, the proposition: "Be perfect as your Celestial Father is perfect," if taken literally would presuppose the possibility of attaining absolute perfection. If it were given to Man to be as perfect as his Creator, then he would become his equal, which is inadmissible. But the people to whom Jesus spoke did not understand this nuance, which caused Him to limit Himself to the presentation of a model and tell them that they must strive to reach it.

Those words then must be understood in the sense of relative perfection, that which humanity is capable of achieving and which most nearly approaches the Divinity. What does this perfection consist of? Jesus said: "In loving one's enemies, in doing good to those who hate us, in praying for those who persecute us." In this way He shows that the essence of perfection is charity in its most ample form, because it implies the practice of all the other virtues.

In fact, by observing the results of all the vices and even of simple defects, it can be recognised that there is not one which does not more or less disfigure the sentiment of charity, because all of them have their beginnings in selfishness and pride, which are the negation of it. This is due to the fact that everything which over-stimulates our self-esteem destroys, or at least weakens, the elements of true charity which are: benevolence, indulgence, abnegation and devotion. Love for one's fellow creatures, when extended to love for one's enemies, cannot be allied to any defect which is against charity. Therefore for this reason it is always an indication of a greater or lesser moral superiority. From this it follows that the degree of perfection is in direct relation to the extent of this love. It was for this reason that Jesus, after having given His Disciples the rules of charity and all that they contain of the most sublime, said to them: "Be perfect, as your Celestial Father is perfect."

THE GOOD PERSON

3. The truly good person is one who complies with the laws of justice, love and charity in their highest degree of purity. If they examine their conscience concerning their own actions they will ask themselves if they have violated those laws, if they have practised any evil, if they have done all the good *that was possible,* if they have voluntarily disregarded any occasion to be useful, if anyone has any complaint to make of them and finally, if they have done to others everything that they would wish done to themselves.

They deposit their faith in God, in His goodness, in His justice and in His wisdom. They know that without His permission nothing can happen. So they submit themselves in all things to His will.

Good people have faith in the future, which is the reason to put spiritual possessions before those of a temporary nature. They know that all vicissitudes of life, all pain and all deceptions are trials or atonements and accept them without murmuring.

Men and women who possess the sentiments of charity and love do good for the sake of goodness, without waiting for payment of any kind. They repay evil with good, take up the defence of the weak against the strong and always sacrifice their own interests in the name of justice.

These kind of people encounter satisfaction in the benefits they are able to spread, in the service they are able to render, in the happinesses they promote, in the tears they are able to dry and in the consolation they offer to those who are afflicted. Their first impulse is always to think of others before themselves and to look after these interests before looking after their own. On the other hand, the selfish person always calculates the benefits and losses arising from any generous action.

The good person is always good, humane, and benevolent with everyone, without distinction as to *race or creed,* because they see all men and women as brothers and sisters. They respect all sincere convictions in others and never launch reprobation against those who think otherwise.

Charity guides them in every circumstance, because they know that those who prejudice others with evil words, who injure others with their pride by disregarding their susceptibilities, or who knowing they could avoid it, do not draw back at the thought of causing suffering or yet a contrariety, however small, lack the obligation to love one's neighbour and so do not deserve the clemancy of the Lord.

They do not harbour rancour, hate nor yet desire vengeance. Instead they follow the example of Jesus by forgiving and forgetting all offences, only remembering the benefits received, because they know that we ourselves shall be forgiven only in as much as we are able to forgive others.

These kind of people are indulgent with the weaknesses of others because they know that they also need indulgence, remembering that Christ said: "Let he who is without sin cast the first stone." They do not take pleasure in looking for defects in others, nor in calling attention to them, and if necessity obliges them to do so, they always try to look for the good qualities so as to lessen the bad ones.

Good people study their own imperfections and work unceasingly to combat them, using all their strength, so that tomorrow they will be able to say that they are just a little better than they were the day before.

The good person never tries to emphasize the importance of their own spirit or talents at the expense of others. But on the contrary, they take every opportunity to highlight in others whatever these people may have that is useful. They are not conceited about their riches, nor of any personal advantage, knowing that everything that has been given to them may be taken away.

They use, but do not abuse, the possessions which have been conceded to them because they are only a deposit, for which they will be required to give full account. They know that the most detrimental employment that these riches can be put to is the satisfaction of their own passions.

If then, by social order, a good person has been placed in a position of command over their fellow creatures, they treat them with kindness and benevolence, because before God all men are equal. They use their authority to raise up the morale of these people and never to crush them with their own pride. They avoid everything which might cause a subordinate position to be even more painful than necessary.

On the part of those who are subordinate, let it be understood that the duties which go with this position must be clearly appreciated and conscientiuosly fulfilled. (See chapter 17, item 9.)

Finally, a good person is always one who respects the rights of their fellow beings, as assured by the laws of nature, in the same way that they would wish their own to be respected.

These are not all the qualities which distinguish a good person, but anyone who tries hard to possess those which have been mentioned will find themselves on the road which leads to all the rest.

THE GOOD SPIRITIST

4. Spiritism, when thoroughly understood and above all when deeply and sincerely felt, leads to the results already expounded, which characterize the true Spiritist just as much as the true Christian, for they are one and the same. Spiritism does not institute any new morals; it only makes it easier for mankind to understand and practise Christ's morals by giving an unshakable and enlightened faith to those who are in doubt or who waver.

Meanwhile, many of those who believe in the fact of mediumistic manifestations do not comprehend the consequences nor the far reaching moral effects, or if they do, then they do not apply them to themselves. To what is this attributed? Is it due to some failing in the clarity of the doctrine? No, because it does not contain any allegories or forms which could lead to false interpretations. Clarity is the very essence from which it gets its strength, because it touches Man's intelligence directly. There is no mystery, and those who are initiated are not in possession of any secrets hidden from the people.

Is it indispensable then to possess an outstanding intelligence in order to understand? No, in as much as there are people of notable capacities who do not understand, whereas there are many of ordinary intelligence, even young people, who grasp the meaning of even the most delicate points with remarkable precision. This proves that the so called *physical* part of science only requires eyes to be able to observe, while the *essential* part demands a certain degree of sensitivity, which can be called *maturity in the moral sense* and which is quite independent of age or level of education, because it is peculiar to the spiritual advancement of the incarnate soul.

In some people, material ties are still too strong for them to be able to release themselves from earthly things. A kind of mist with which they are surrounded, does not allow them to see into the infinite future. This results in the fact of them not being able to break away from old tendencies or habits because they cannot see that there exists something better than what they already have. They believe in Spirits as a simple fact. But this modifies none or very few of their instinctive tendencies. In a word, they perceive nothing more than a small ray of light insufficient to guide them or offer profound aspirations which would make it possible for them to overcome their inclinations. The phenomenon touches them more than the morality, which seems to them to be hackneyed and monotonous. They ask only that the Spirits unceasingly initiate new mysteries, without asking themselves if they have become worthy of penetrating the hidden secrets of the Creator as yet. These then are the imperfect Spiritists, some of whom have remained stationary in time or have turned away from their brother's and sister's faith, due to their having drawn back before the necessity of self-reform, or perhaps they have kept sympathy with those who share the same weaknesses or prejudices. Nevertheless, the acceptance of the fundamental principles of the doctrine is the first step, from which it will be easier for them to take a second step in a future life.

The person who can be justifiably classified as a true and sincere Spiritist is to be found on a superior level of moral progress. The spirit of this person almost completely dominates their physical body, so giving them a clearer perception of the future. The principles of the doctrine, which leave many untouched, cause them to feel deep inner vibrations. In short, *their heart is moved* and this is what makes their faith unshakable. It is like a musician who is touched by only a few chords, whereas another person hears only sounds. *The true Spiritist can be recognised by their moral transformation and by the efforts they employ in order to dominate their bad instincts.* While one is content with a limited horizon, the other, who understands that better things exist, makes every effort to liberate himself and always manages to do this when their desire is strong and true.

THE PARABLE OF THE SOWER

5. *The same day went Jesus out of the house, and sat by the sea side. And great multitudes were gathered unto Him, so that He went into a ship, and sat; and the whole multitude stood on the shore. And He spake many things unto them in parables, saying, Behold, a sower went forth to sow. And when he sowed, some seeds fell by the wayside, and the fowls came and devoured them up: some fell upon stony places, where they had not much earth: and forthwith they sprang up, because they had no deepness of earth. And when the sun came up, they were scorched; and because they had no root, they withered away. And some fell among thorns; and the thorns sprang up, and choked them: but others fell upon good ground,, and brought forth fruit, some an hundredfold, some sixtyfold, some thirtyfold. Who hath ears to hear, let him hear (Matthew, 13: 1-9).*

Hear ye therefore the parable of the sower. When any one heareth the Word of the Kingdom, and understandeth it not, then cometh the wicked one, and catcheth away that which was sown in his heart. This is he which received seed by the wayside. But he that received the seed into stony places, the same is he that heareth the Word, and anon with joy receiveth it; yet hath he not root in himself, but dureth for a while: for when tribulation or persecution ariseth because of the Word, by and by he is offended. He also that received seed among the thorns is he that heareth the Word; and the care of this world, and the deceitfulness of riches, choke the Word, and he becometh unfruitful. But he that received seed into the good ground is he that heareth the Word, and understandeth it; which also beareth fruit, and bringeth forth, some an hundredfold, some sixty, some thirty (Matthew, 13: 18-23).

6. The parable of the sower truly represents the various ways in which we may make use of the teachings from the New Testament. There are so many people for whom these teachings are nothing more than dead words which can be compared to seeds which fall on stony ground and produce no fruits at all.

This parable brings us a no less justifiable application of the different categories of Spiritists. Do we not find symbolised in it those who are only attracted to material phenonema, from which they are unable to learn anything, because they only see it as an object of curiosity? Does it not show us those who seek the brilliance of spirit communication merely to interest themselves as long as it satisfies their imagination and who, after listening to the messages, continue to be just as cold and indifferent as they were before? Then there are those who consider the advice very good and admire it, but only apply it to others and never to themselves. Finally there are those for whom the teachings are as seeds which fall on good soil and produce fruits.

INSTRUCTIONS FROM THE SPIRITS.

DUTY

7. Duty is a moral obligation, firstly to ourselves and then to others. Duty is a law of life encountered in the smallest details as well as in the most elevated acts. Now I wish to speak only of moral duty and not of that duty which refers to the professions.

Within the order of sentiments, duty is a very difficult one to fulfill because it finds itself in antagonism with the seductions of interest and of the heart. Its victories have no witnesses and its failures suffer no repressions. Man's intimate duty is left to his free-will. The pressure of Man's conscience, this guardian of interior integrity, alerts and sustains him, but shows itself frequently impotent against the deceptions of passion. Duty of the heart, when faithfully observed, elevates Man, but how can we define it with exactitude? Where does duty begin? Where does it end? *Duty begins exactly at the point where the happiness or tranquility of our neighbour is threatened, and therefore terminates at the limit we would not wish to be passed in relation to ourselves.*

God has created all men equal in relation to pain; whether we be small or great, ignorant or educated, we all suffer for the same motives so that each one may judge in clear consciousness the evil that can be done. With reference to goodness, in its infinite variety of expressions, the criterion is not the same. *Equality in the face of pain is God's sublime providence. He desires that all of His children, being instructed through their common experiences, should not practise evil with the excuse of not knowing its effects.*

Duty is a practical summary of all moral speculation; it is the bravery of the soul which faces the anguishes of battle. It is both austere and mild, ready to adapt itself to the most diverse complications while maintaining inflexibility before temptations. *The man who fulfills his duty loves God more than his fellow beings and loves his fellow beings more than himself.* It is at one and the same time judge and slave in its own cause.

Duty is the most beautiful laurel of reason, and is born of it as a child is born of its mother. Man should love duty, not because it protects him from the evils of life from which humanity cannot escape, but because it transmits vigour to the soul, which it needs so as to be able to develop.

Duty grows and irradiates under a constantly more elevated form in each of the superior stages of humanity. A person's moral obligations towards God never cease. They must reflect the eternal virtues, which do not accept imperfect outlines, because He wishes the grandeur of His work always to be resplendent before their eyes. — LAZARUS (Paris, 1863).

VIRTUE

8. Virtue, at its highest level is a combination of all those essential qualities which constitute a goodly person, namely to be good, charitable, hard working, sober and modest. Unfortunately these virtues are almost always accompanied by slight moral failures which tarnish and weaken them. The person who calls attention to their virtues is not virtuous, because they lack the principle quality which is modesty; but they possess the vice in greatest opposition to modesty, which is pride. Virtue that is really deserving of this name, does not like to exhibit itself. We must pay attention in order to be aware of its presence; it hides itself in the shadows and runs away from public admiration. Saint Vincent de Paul was virtuous. The dignified curate of Ars was virtuous, as are a great many others who are little known in this world, but are known to God. All of these good people were ignorant of the fact that they were virtuous. They allowed themselves to be carried along by their saintly inspirations, practising good with absolute disinterestedness and complete forgetfullness of self.

It is to this virtue, well understood and practised, that I call you, my children. It is to this really Christian and truly spiritual virtue that I invite you to commit yourselves. But remove from your hearts the sentiments of pride, vanity and self-love which always tarnish the most beautiful of these qualities. Do not imitate those people who offer themselves as models, who blow their own trumpets about their own qualities for all who are tolerant enough to listen. This ostentatious virtue almost always hides a mass of little wickednesses and hateful weaknesses.

In principle, the man or woman who exalts themself, who erect statues to their own virtues, by this very fact annul all the merits they might effectively have had. Furthermore, what can be said of those whose only value is in appearing to be what they are not? You must clearly understand that whoever does good has a feeling of intimate satisfaction in the bottom of their heart. But from the moment that satisfaction is exteriorised for the purpose of provoking praise, it degenerates into self-love.

Oh, all of you whom the Spiritist faith has reanimated with its rays, who know just how far away from perfection Man finds himself, you will never deliver yourselves over to this failing! Virtue is a blessing which I desire for all sincere Spiritists, but with this warning: It is better to have fewer virtues and to be modest than to have many and be proud. It was because of pride that the various groupings of humanity through the ages have successively lost themselves. It will be through humility that they will one day redeem themselves. — FRANÇOIS–NICOLAS–MADELEINE (Paris, 1863).

THOSE WHO ARE SUPERIOR AND THOSE WHO ARE INFERIOR

9. Authority, just as much as fortune, is delegated; and those who have received it will be required to give an account of what they have done with it. Do not believe that it has been given for the futile pleasure of command, nor even less as a right or property, as is falsely thought by the majority of powerful people on Earth. Besides, God is constantly proving that it is neither the one nor the other, since He takes it away whenever it pleases Him. If it was a privilege inherent to the person who exercised it, it would be inalienable. However, no one can say that something belongs to them, when it may be taken away without their consent. God confers authority with the title of *mission* or test, as He sees fit, and takes it back in the same manner.

For the depository of authority, whatever its extent may be, from the master over his servants to a sovereign over his peoples, it must never be forgotten that such people have souls in their charge, and will have to answer for both the good and bad directives given to these subordinates. The misdemeanours these may commit, and the vices to which they may succumb in consequence of the directives received or the *bad examples* given, will all revert to those in command; just as in the same way the fruits of the solicitudes offered in conducting these subordinates towards goodness will also revert to those in authority. Every good person on Earth has either a small or a great mission, and whatever form it may take, it is always given for the purpose of goodness. Therefore to turn it away from its purpose is to fail in the execution of the task.

If God asks the rich man: "What have you done with the fortune in your hands which should have been a source for spreading fruitfulness all around you?", He will also inquire of those who have some authority: "What have you done with your authority? What evils have you avoided? What progress have you made? If I gave you subordinates it was not so that you could turn them into slaves to your desires, or docile instruments for your whims or your greed. I made you strong and entrusted to you those who were weak, so that you could protect them and help them to climb up towards Me."

The acting superior who keeps Christ's words despises none of his subordinates, because he knows that social distinctions do not exist before God. Spiritism teaches him that if these people are obeying him today, perhaps they have already given him orders in the past, or may give them to him later on, and that then he will be treated in the same manner as when they were under him.

If the superior has duties to be fulfilled, the subaltern also has duties on his side which are no less sacred. If this person is also a Spiritist their conscience will tell them, in no uncertain terms, that they are not exempt from fulfilling these duties even when their superior does not fulfill his, because they know that you do not repay evil with evil and that the failings of some do not authorize others to fail likewise. If they suffer in their position, they will comment that without doubt they deserve it because they have perhaps abused the authority they had been given at some other time, and that now they are feeling the disadvantages that they had made others suffer. If they are obliged to support this situation for want of a better one, then Spiritism teaches them to be resigned as a test of their humility which is necessary for their advancement. Their belief guides them in their conduct; inducing them to proceed as they would wish subordinates to behave towards them, if they were the superior. For this reason they are more scrupulous in the fulfillment of their obligations, as they understand that all negligence in the work which has been confided to them would cause a loss to the one who pays them and to whom they owe their time and effort. In a word, this person is guided by their sense of duty, which their faith has instilled in them, and the certainty that all turning aside from the straight and narrow pathway will be a debt incurred that must be repaid sooner or later. — FRANÇOIS–NICOLAS–MADELEINE. Cardinal MORLOT (Paris, 1863).

THE WORLDLY PERSON

10. A sentiment of pity should always animate the hearts of those who gather together under the eye of the Lord, imploring the assistance of the Good Spirits. Therefore purify your hearts. Do not allow yourselves to be perturbed by futile and mundane thoughts. Lift up your Spirits towards those you are calling, so that they, having encountered favourable dispositions, may launch a profusion of seeds which should germinate in your hearts so as to produce the fruits of charity and justice.

Do not think, however, that in constantly urging you to pray and meditate we wish you to lead the life of a mystic, or that you should maintain yourselves outside the laws of the society in which you are condemned to reside. No. You must dwell with the people of your time in the manner in which they live. Sacrifice wants, even frivolities of the day, but sacrifice them with a pure sentiment which can sanctify them.

You are called upon to be in contact with Spirits of diverse natures and opposite characters: do not enter into conflict with anyone with whom you may find yourself. Always be happy and content, with the happiness which comes from a clear conscience and the contentment of one who will inherit Heaven and is counting the days till they receive their inheritance.

Virtue does not consist of having a severe and gloomy appearance, or in repelling the pleasures which the human condition permits. It is sufficient to refer all your acts to God, Who gave you your life. It is enough that at the commencement and at the end of each task you lift up your thoughts to the Creator, asking Him with a heartfelt impulse for His protection in order to execute the work, or His blessing on its termination. On doing anything at all, take your thoughts up to that Supreme Source. Do nothing without first thinking of God, so that this thought may come to purify and sanctify your acts.

Perfection, as Christ said, is only to be found in the practice of unlimited charity, since the duties of charity cover all social positions from the most lowly to the most elevated. The person who lives in isolation will have no means of exercising charity. It is only by being in contact with one's fellow creatures, in painful battle, that we are able to find occasion to practise it. The one who isolates himself therefore is entirely deprived of the most powerful means of perfection. In only having to think of oneself, life becomes that of a selfish person. (See chapter 5, item 26.)

Therefore do not imagine that in order to be in constant contact with us, to live under the watchful eye of God, you must wear a hair shirt and cover yourselves with ashes. No, no, and yet again no! Be happy within the picture of human needs, but in this happiness never allow a thought or an act which could offend God, or cause a shadow to fall upon the face of those who love you or direct you. God is love and He blesses all who sanctify their own love. — A Protecting Spirit (Bordeaux, 1863).

LOOK AFTER BOTH BODY AND SPIRIT

11. Does spiritual perfection depend on the mortification of the body? In order to resolve this question I will base myself on elementary principles and begin by demonstrating the need to take care of the body, which according to the alternatives of health and sickness, has a very important influence upon the soul, because we must consider it to be a prisoner of the flesh. So that this prisoner can live, move itself, and even have an illusion of liberty, the body must be sound, of good disposition, and be vigorous. Let us then make a comparison. Let us suppose that both are in perfect condition; what should be done to maintain the balance between their aptitudes and their necessities, which are so very different?

In this case two systems are confronting each other: that of the ascetics who wish to bring down the body, and that of the materialists who wish to diminish the soul. Two forms of violence, each one almost as foolish as the other. Alongside these two great parties seethe the indifferent multitudes who, without either conviction or passion, love with tepidness and are economic with their pleasure. Where then is wisdom? Where then is the science of living? Nowhere at all! And this great problem would still remain to be solved if Spiritism had not come to help the researchers and demonstrate to them the relationship which exists between the body and the soul, and to tell them that as they are both reciprocally necessary, it is indispensable that both are looked after.

So then, love your soul and also look after your body which is the instrument of the soul. To pay no attention to these needs, which Nature itself indicates, is to ignore God's laws. Do not castigate your body due to failings which your free-will can induce you to commit, and for which it is just as responsible as is the badly driven horse for the accidents it causes. Perchance, will you be more perfect if by tormenting your body you do not become less selfish, less prideful and more charitable towards your neighbours? No, perfection is not to be found in this manner, but exclusively in the reformation to which you submit your Spirit. Discipline it, subjugate it and mortify it: this is the way to make it more docile to God's will, and is the one and only way which leads to perfection — GEORGES, a Protecting Spirit (Paris, 1863).

CHAPTER 18

MANY ARE CALLED, BUT FEW ARE CHOSEN

The parable of the wedding feast. — The narrow door — Not
all those who say: Lord! Lord! will enter into the Kingdom of
Heaven. — Much will be asked of he who receives much. —
INSTRUCTIONS FROM THE SPIRITS: To those who have
will be given more. — A Christian is recognised by his
works.

THE PARABLE OF THE WEDDING FEAST

1. *And Jesus answered and spake unto them again in parables, and said, The
Kingdom of Heaven is like unto a certain king, which made a marriage for his
son, and sent forth his servants to call them that were bidden to the wedding: and
they would not come. Again he sent forth other servants saying, Tell them which
are bidden, Behold, I have prepared my dinner: my oxen and my fatlings are
killed, and all things are ready: come unto the marriage. But they made light of it,
and went their ways, one to his farm, another to his merchandise: and the
remnant took his servants, and entreated them spitefully, slew them. But when
the king heard thereof he was wroth: and he sent forth his armies, and destroyed
those murderers, and burned up their city.*

*Then saith he to his servants, The wedding is ready, but they which are bidden
were not worthy. Go ye therefore into the highways, and as many as ye shall find,
bid to the marriage. So the servants went out into the highways, and gathered
together as many as they found, both bad and good: and the wedding was
furnished with guests. And when the king came in to see the guests, he saw there a
man which had not on a wedding garment: and he saith unto him, Friend, how
comest thou in hither not having a wedding garment? And he was speechless.
Then said the king to the servants, Bind him hand and foot and take him away,
and cast him into outer darkness; there shall be weeping and gnashing of teeth,
for many were called, but few are chosen (Matthew, 22: 1-14).*

2. Those who are incredulous laugh at this parable, which seems to them to be
childishly ingenuous, because they are unable to understand that there could
be so many difficulties in going to participate in a feast and, even more so, that
the guests would resist the invitation to such a point as to massacre those who
had been sent to them by the master of the house. "Parables," say the
incredulous, "beyond doubt are figurative, but nevertheless it is not necessary
to ultra-pass the limits of plausibility."

The same may be said about allegories or ingenious fables if their respective outer coverings are not removed so as to find their hidden meaning. Jesus composed His allegories from the most common of everyday occurances and customs and then adapted these to the characters of the people to whom He talked. The vast majority of these allegories had as their objective the penetration into the minds of the masses of the idea of a spiritual life. Many appear to be unintelligible merely because those who listen do not look at them from this point of view.

In this parable, Jesus compares the Kingdom of Heaven, where everything is happiness and good fortune, to a feast. When referring to the first guests to be invited He alludes to the Hebrews, who were the earliest peoples to be called by God to know His law. Those sent by the king are the prophets who came to advise them to follow the road of true happiness. However, their words were hardly listened to and their warnings were disregarded; many were massacred, like those in the parable. The guests who declined the invitation with excuses of having to look after their pastures and their businesses symbolize those worldly people who, being absorbed in terrestrial matters, remain indifferent to the things of Heaven.

It was common belief amongst the Jews of those times that their nation had to achieve supremacy above all others. In effect, didn't God promise Abraham that his posterity would cover the face of the Earth? But as always, they paid attention only to form and not substance, believing it meant actual material domination.

Before the coming of Christ all peoples, with the exception of the Jews, were idol worshippers and polytheistics. If a few people, superior to the vast masses, conceived the idea of a unique God, that idea remained only as a personal belief. Nowhere was it received as a fundamental idea, except perhaps by a few initiates who hid their knowledge under a veil of mystery, impenetrable to the masses. The Hebrews were the first to publicly practise monotheism and it was to them that God transmitted His Law, firstly through Moses and later through Jesus. From this tiny focal point the light, which was destined to spread throughout the whole world, went forth to triumph over paganism and to give Abraham a *spiritual* posterity "as numerous as the stars that fill the skies." Nevertheless, having completely abandoned idol worship, the Jews scorned the moral law and persisted in the practise of an external cult which was easier. Evil came to a head and the nation was destroyed, enslaved and divided into sects; incredulity reached even the sanctuary. It was at this point that Jesus appeared, having been sent to call them to keep the Law and to open up new horizons of a future life. Having been the *first* to be invited to the great banquet of universal faith, they rejected the words of the Celestial Messiah and sacrificed Him. In this manner they lost the rewards which should have been reaped from their own initiatives.

Nevertheless, it would be unjust to accuse the entire population for this state of affairs. The main responsibility rests with the Pharisees and Saducees who sacrificed the nation through the pride and fanaticism of some, and the incredulity of others. Therefore it is these, above all others, whom Jesus identified among those guests who refused to appear at the wedding feast. He then added that on seeing their refusal, the master of the house told his servants to go out into the highways and gather all those they could find, good and bad. Jesus was saying in this manner that the Word would be preached to all the other peoples, pagans and idol worshippers, and that these on accepting it would be admitted to the feast in place of the initial guests.

But it is not enough to be invited; it is not enough to say you are a Christian; nor to sit at the table in order to take part in the celestial banquet; before all else it is essential, as an express condition, to be clothed in the nuptial tunic, that is to say to be pure of heart and to comply with the spirit of the law. But although all the law is contained in the words: *without charity there is no salvation,* amongst all those who hear the divine Word there are so few who keep it and make good use of it! So few become worthy to enter into the Kingdom of Heaven! This is why Jesus said: *"There will be many who are called; however, few will be chosen."*

THE NARROW DOOR

3. *Enter ye in at the strait gate: for wide is the gate, and broad is the way, that leadeth to destruction, and many there be which go in thereat: because strait is the gate, and narrow is the way, which leadeth unto life, and few there be that find it (Matthew, 7: 13-14).*

4. *Then said one unto Him, Lord, are there few that be saved? And He said unto them, Strive to enter in at the strait gate: for many, I say unto you, will seek to enter in, and shall not be able, when once the master of the house is risen up, and hath shut to the door, and ye begin to stand without, and to knock at the door, saying, Lord, Lord, open unto us; and He shall answer and say unto you, I know you not whence ye are; then shall ye begin to say, We have eaten and drunk in Thy presence, and Thou hast taught in our streets. But He shall say, I tell you, I know you not whence you are; depart from me, all ye workers of iniquity. There shall be weeping and gnashing of teeth, when ye shall see Abraham, and Isaac, and Jacob, and all the prophets, in the Kingdom of God, and you yourselves thrust out. And they shall come from the east, and from the west, and from the north, and from the south, and shall sit down in the Kingdom of God, and, behold, there are last which shall be first, and there are first which shall be last (Luke, 13: 23-30).*

5. Wide is the door to damnation, because evil passions are numerous and the vast majority of humanity follow this pathway. That of salvation is narrow, because Man is obliged to exert great control over himself in order to dominate

his evil tendencies if he wishes to pass through, and this is something that few are resigned enough to do. It complements the maxim 'Many are called, but few are chosen.'

This then is the situation of terrestrial humanity, because as the Earth is a world of atonement, evil is the predominating factor. When the planet has been transformed the pathway to goodness will be the one most frequently followed. Therefore these words should be understood in a relative manner and not as an absolute. If this was to be the permanent state of humanity then God would have condemned the great majority of His creatures to damnation, which is an inadmissable supposition since we recognise that God is all justice and all kindness.

But what crimes has humanity committed to deserve such an unhappy state of affairs, in the present and the future, if everything here on Earth is so degraded, and if the soul has had no other existences? Why are there so many obstacles placed before each one? Why is the gateway so narrow as to allow only a few to enter if the destiny of the soul is permanently determined immediately after death? In this way, with only one existence, Man would always be at odds with himself and with God's justice. But with the pre-existence of the soul and the plurality of worlds, the horizons spread out; enlightenment comes to even the most obscure points of faith; the present and the future become linked to the past and it is then that it is possible to understand the depth, truth and wisdom of those words spoken by Christ.

NOT ALL THOSE WHO SAY: LORD! LORD! WILL ENTER INTO THE KINGDOM OF HEAVEN

6. *Not everyone that saith unto me, Lord, Lord, shall enter into the Kingdom of Heaven; but he that doeth the Will of my Father which is in Heaven. Many will say to me in that day, Lord, Lord, have we not prophesied in thy name? And in thy name have cast out devils? And in thy name done many wonderful works? And then will I profess unto them, I never knew you: depart from me, ye that work iniquity (Matthew, 7: 21-23).*

7. *Therefore whosoever heareth these sayings of mine, and doeth them, I will liken him unto a wise man, which built his house upon a rock: and the rain descended, and the flood came, and the winds blew, and beat upon the house; and it fell not: for it was founded upon a rock. And everyone that heareth these sayings of mine, and doeth them not shall be likened unto a foolish man, which built his house upon sand. And the rain descended, and the floods came, and the winds blew, and beat upon the house; and it fell: and great was the fall of it (Matthew, 7: 24-27, and similarly in Luke, 6: 46-49).*

8. *Whosoever therefore shall break one of these least commandments, and shall teach men so, he shall be called the least in the Kingdom of Heaven: but whosoever shall do and teach them, the same shall be called great in the Kingdom of Heaven (Matthew, 5: 19).*

9. All who recognise the mission of Jesus say; Lord! Lord! But of what use is it to call 'Master' or 'Lord' when you do not follow His precepts? Are they Christians then, who honour Him with exterior acts of devotion while at the same time making sacrifice to pride, selfishness, greed and all the passions? Are they then His disciples, those who pass their days in prayer yet show themselves no better, nor more charitable, nor more indulgent towards their fellow beings? No, seeing that as the Pharisees, they have prayer on their lips but not in their hearts. They can impress men with their manner, but not God. In vain they can say to Jesus; "Lord! Do we not prophesy, that is to say, do we not teach in Your name? Do we not expel demons in Your name? Do we not eat and drink with You?" He will reply to them; "I know not who you are; go away from me, you who commit iniquity, you who deny by your acts what you say with your lips, who slander your neighbour, who rob widows and commit adultery. Go away from me, you whose hearts distil hate and bile, who spill the blood of your brothers and sisters in My name, who cause tears to flow instead of drying them. For you there will be weeping and gnashing of teeth, seeing that God's Kingdom is for those who are gentle, humble and charitable. Do not expect to bend God's justice by the multiplicity of your words nor the amount of your kneeling. The only pathway which is open wherein you may find grace in His sight, is by the sincere practice of the law of love and charity."

The words of Jesus are eternal because they are the truth. They constitute not only a safe conduct to celestial life, but also a pledge of peace, of tranquility and the stability of earthly things. This is why all institutions, be they human, political, social or religious, that rely on these words will always remain steadfast as the house built upon rock. They will be retained by Man because in them he will find his happiness. However, those who violate these words will be as the house built upon sand, which the wind of renewal and the river of progress will sweep away.

MUCH WILL BE ASKED OF HE WHO RECEIVES MUCH

10. *And that servant, which knew his Lord's will, and prepared not himself, neither did according to His will, shall be beaten with many stripes. But he that knew not, and did commit things worthy of stripes, shall be beaten with few stripes. For unto whomsoever much is given, of him shall much be required: and to whom men have committed much, of him they will ask the more (Luke, 12: 47 & 48).*

11. *And Jesus said, For judgement I am come into this world, that they which see not might see; and that they which see might be made blind. And some of the Pharisees which were with Him heard these words, and said unto Him, Are we blind also? Jesus said unto them, If ye were blind, ye should have no sin: but now ye say, we see; therefore your sin remaineth (John, 9: 39-41).*

12. These maxims apply even more especially to the Spiritist teachings. Whoever knows Christ's precepts and does not keep them is certainly guilty.

However, besides the fact that the Gospel which contains them is only found scattered in the bosom of the Christian sects, even amongst those, how many there are who do not read them! And even amongst those who do read them, how many there are who do not understand them! The result of all this is that the words of Jesus remain lost to the majority of men and women.

It is important to note that nothing is circumscribed within the teachings of the Spirits, who reproduce these maxims in various forms, developing and commenting on them in order to put them within the reach of all. Every person, be they learned or illiterate, believer or incredulous, Christian or not, is able to receive them because the Spirits communicate in all places. No one who receives them either directly or through an intermediary, can allege ignorance. It is not possible to excuse oneself under the pretext of lack of instruction, nor even that of the obscure allegoric meaning. Therefore those who do not take advantage of these maxims to better themselves, who admire them only as something curious or interesting, without allowing them to touch their heart, who do not become less futile, less prideful, less selfish, less attached to material things, or who are no better towards their neighbour, will be all the more guilty in proportion to the number of ways open to them to acquire knowledge of truth.

Those mediums who receive good communications but continue to persist in evil, are even more censurable because they frequently write their own condemnation. Also, because if it were not for the fact of their being blinded by pride, they would recognise that it is to them that the Spirits address themselves. But instead of taking the lessons which they write or those they read, written by others, for themselves, their only preoccupation is in applying these lessons to others. In this manner they confirm these words of Jesus: "You see the splinter in the eye of your neighbour, but you do not see the beam that is in yours." (See chapter 10, item 9.)

In the sentence: "If you were blind you would not have sinned," Jesus wished to signify that the culpability is according to how enlightened a person may or may not be. Now the Pharisees, who maintained the pretence of being to all effects the most enlightened peoples of their nation, showed themselves to be more guilty before God than those who were ignorant. The same applies today.

Much will be asked of Spiritists because they have received much; on the other hand, to those who have taken every advantage of their learning much will be given.

Therefore, the first thought of all sincere Spiritists should be to find out if in the counselling received from the Spirits there is not something which applies to themselves. Spiritism will multiply the number of those who are CALLED; likewise through growing faith the proportion of those who are CHOSEN will also be multiplied.

INSTRUCTIONS FROM THE SPIRITS.
TO THOSE WHO HAVE WILL BE GIVEN MORE

13. *And the disciples came, and said unto Him, Why speaketh Thou unto them in parables? He answered and said unto them, Because it is given unto you to know the mysteries of the Kingdom of Heaven, but to them it is not given. For whosoever hath, to him shall be given, and he shall have more abundance: but whosoever hath not, from him shall be taken away even that he hath. Therefore speak I to them in parables: because they seeing see not: and hearing they hear not, neither do they understand. And in them is fulfilled the prophecy of Esaias, which saith, By hearing ye shall hear, and shall not understand; and seeing ye shall see, and shall not perceive (Matthew, 13: 10-14).*

14. *And He said unto them, Take heed what ye hear: with what measure ye mete, it shall be measured to you: and unto you that hear shall be given more. For he that hath, to him shall be given: and he that hath not, from him shall be taken even that which he hath (Mark, 4: 24 & 25).*

15. "For whosoever hath, to him shall be given, but whosoever hath not, from him shall be taken away." Let us meditate on these great teachings which have so often seemed paradoxical. 'He who has received' signifies those who possess the meaning of the divine Word. They have received it solely because they have tried to be worthy of it and because the Lord, in His merciful love, animates the efforts of those who are inclined towards goodness. By their unceasing perseverance their efforts attract the blessing of God, which acts as a magnet calling to itself progressive betterment. It is these copious blessings which make them strong enough to scale the sacred mountain on whose pinnacle is to be found rest after labour.

"From whosoever hath not, or but little, shall be taken away." This should be understood as a figurative antithesis. God does not retract the good He has conceded. Blind and deaf humanity! Use your intelligence and your hearts; see with the eyes of your spirit; listen by means of your soul and do not interpret so coarsely and unjustly the words of He Who makes the justice of God shine resplendently before your eyes. It is not God who takes away from the one who has but little, but that Spirit itself who, by being wasteful and careless, does not know how to conserve, increase, and bring to fulfillment the mite which had been given to that heart.

The son who does not cultivate the field which the work of his father had conquered for his inheritance, will see it covered with weeds. Is it then his father who takes away the harvest he did not prepare? If through lack of care he allowed the seedlings, destined to produce the crop, to wither, is it the father he should accuse for their having produced nothing? No, it is not. Instead of accusing the one who had done all the preparing, as if he were guilty of taking it back, he should complain to the real author of his miseries. With repentance and desire to be industrious, the son should put himself to work courageously to reclaim the soil by sheer will-power, digging deeply with the help of repentance and hope. Then confidently sow the good seed, which he has separated from the bad, and water it with love and charity. Then God, the God of love and charity, will give to him who has already received. He will see his efforts crowned with success and one grain will produce a hundred and another a thousand. Courage, workers! Take up your harrows and your ploughs; work with your hearts; tear out the weeds; sow the good seed that the Lord has given and the dew of love will cause the fruits of charity to grow. — A Friendly Spirit (Bordeaux, 1862).

A CHRISTIAN IS RECOGNISABLE BY HIS WORKS

16. "Not all of those who say: Lord! Lord! will enter into Heaven, but only those who do the Will of my Father, who is in Heaven."

Listen to these words of the Master, all those who repel the Spiritist Doctrine as the work of the devil. Open your ears because the moment to listen has arrived.

Is it sufficient to carry the uniform of the Lord in order to be His faithful servant? Is it enough to say: 'I am a Christian', for anyone to be a follower of Christ? Search for the true Christians and you will recognise them by their works. "A good tree cannot give forth bad fruits, nor a bad tree good fruits." "Every tree that does not give forth good fruits will be cut down and cast into the fire." These are the words of the Master. Disciples of Christ, understand them well! What kind of fruits should be given by the tree of Christianity, which is a mighty tree, whose leafy branches cover part of the world with shade, but does not as yet shelter all who should seek refuge around it? Those from the Tree of Life are fruits of life, hope and faith. Christianity, as it has done for many centuries, continues to preach these divine virtues. It uses all its strength to distribute its fruits, but so few pick them! The Tree is always good, but the gardeners are bad. They tried to mould it to their own ideas, to prune it to their necessities. They cut it, diminished it and mutilated it. Having become sterile it does not give forth bad fruits, because it gives forth no fruits at all. The thirsty traveller who stops under its branches looking for the fruits of hope, which are capable of restoring strength and courage, sees only bare branches foretelling a coming storm. In vain he asks for the fruits from the Tree of Life. Only dry leaves fall at his feet. The hands of Man have so tampered with it that it has become scorched.

My dearly beloved, open then your hearts and ears. Cultivate this Tree of Life whose fruits give eternal life. The One who planted it incites you to treat it with love and even yet you will see it give an abundance of its divine fruits. Conserve it just as it was when Christ gave it to you. Do not mutilate it. It wants to cast its immense shade over the Universe, so do not cut its branches. Its tasty fruits fall abundantly so as to satiate the hungry traveller who wishes to reach the end of his journey. Do not gather these fruits in order to leave them to rot, so they are of no use to anyone. "Many are called, but few are chosen."

This is because there are monopolizers of the Bread of Life, as there are also of material bread. Do not be one of them: the Tree that gives good fruits must give to everyone. Go then, and seek those who are hungry, lead them under the leafy branches of the Tree of Life and share with them the shelter it offers. "You cannot collect grapes from amongst the thorns." My brothers and sisters, turn away from those who call to you in order to show you the thorns of the way; instead, follow those who will lead you under the shade of the Tree of Life.

The Divine Saviour, the Just par exellence, spoke, and His words will never die; "Not all who say: Lord! Lord! will enter into the Kingdom of Heaven, but only those who do the Will of my Father who is in Heaven."

May the Lord of blessings bless you; may the God of Light illuminate you; may the Tree of Life offer you its abundant fruits! Believe and pray. — SIMON (Bordeaux, 1863).

CHAPTER 19

FAITH TRANSPORTS MOUNTAINS

The power of faith. — Religious faith. The state of unshakable
faith. — The parable of the dry fig-tree. — INSTRUCTIONS
FROM THE SPIRITS: Faith, the mother of hope and charity.
— Human and Divine faith.

THE POWER OF FAITH

1. *And when they were come to the multitude, there came to Him a certain man, kneeling down to Him, and saying, Lord, have mercy on my son: for he is lunatic, and sore vexed: for oftimes he falleth into the fire, and oftimes into the water. And I brought him to Thy disciples, and they could not cure him. Then Jesus answered and said, O faithless and perverse generation, how long shall I be with you? How long shall I suffer you? Bring him hither to me. And Jesus rebuked the devil; and he departed out of him: and the child was cured from that very hour. Then came the disciples to Jesus apart, and said, Why could we not cast him out? And Jesus said unto them, because of your unbelief: For verily I say unto you, if ye have faith as a grain of mustard seed, ye shall say unto the mountain, remove hence to yonder place, and it shall remove; and nothing shall be impossible unto you (Matthew, 17: 14-20).*

2. In one sense it is certain that confidence in one's own strength gives Man the capacity to carry out material things which he would not be able to do if he doubted himself. However, here we wish to deal exclusively with the moral sense of these words. The mountains which faith can transport are the difficulties, the resistances, the ill will, in fact all those things which Man has to face, even when we refer to good things. The prejudices, routines, materialistic interests, selfishness, the blindness of fanaticism and the prideful passions are but a few of the mountains which block the way of those who work for human progress. Robust faith gives perseverance, energy and resources which allow us to overcome these obstacles, be they large or small. From wavering faith results only uncertainty and the kind of hesitation which those adversaries we need to combat take advantage of; this faith does not even try to find the means to win because it does not believe it can.

3. Another acceptance of the term gives us to understand that faith is the confidence we have in the realization of something, and the certainty of attaining a specific end. It gives us a kind of lucidness which permits us to see,

in thought, the goal we wish to reach and the means of getting there, so that those who have faith go forward, in a manner of speaking, with absolute security. In either one of these cases, it can give place to the realization of great things.

Faith which is real and sincere is always calm; it permits patience which knows how to wait, because having its foundation in intelligence and the understanding of life, it is certain of reaching the objective it aspires to. Vacillating faith feels its own weakness; when its interest is aroused it becomes frenzied and thinks it can supply the force it lacks by using violence. Calmness during the struggle is always a sign of strength and confidence; whereas on the contrary violence denotes weakness and self-doubt.

4. It behoves us not to confuse faith with presumption. True faith is linked to humility; those who have it, deposit more confidence in God than in themselves, as they know they are but simple instruments of Divine Purpose and can do nothing without God. This is the reason why the good Spirits come to their aid. Presumption is less faith than pride, and pride is always punished sooner or later by the deceptions and frustrations inflicted upon it.

5. The power of faith can be demonstrated in a direct and special manner in magnetic action. Through the intermediary of faith, Man acts on the fluids, which are a universal agent, modifying their qualities and giving them in a manner of speaking, irresistable impulsion. From this it follows that whoever joins a normally great fluidic power to that of ardent faith can, solely by the strength of their willpower directed towards goodness, operate those singular phenomena of healing and other occurrences known in olden times as miracles, but which are nothing more than the consequences of a Law of Nature. This is the reason for Jesus saying to His apostles that if they did not cure it was because they had no faith.

RELIGIOUS FAITH. THE STATE OF UNSHAKABLE FAITH

6. From the religious point of view faith consists of the belief in the special dogmas which constitute the various religions. All of them have their articles of faith. From this aspect faith may be either *blind or rationalized.* Blind faith examines nothing and accepts without verification both truth and falsehood, and at each step clashes with evidence and reason. Taken to the extreme it produces *fanaticism.* While sitting upon error, sooner or later it collapses. Only faith that is based on truth guarantees the future, because it has nothing to fear from the progress of enlightenment, seeing that *what is true in obscurity is also true in light.* Each religion claims to have possession of the exclusive truth. But for someone to *proclaim blind faith on a point of belief is to confess themself impotent to demonstrate that they are right.*

7. It is commonly said that *faith cannot be prescribed,* from which many people declare it is not their fault if they have no faith. Beyond doubt, faith cannot be prescribed, and what is even more certain, *it cannot be imposed.* No, it cannot

be prescribed but only acquired, and there is no one who is prevented from possessing it, even amongst those who are most refractory. We are speaking of basic spiritual truths and not of any particular belief. It is not the part of faith to seek these people out, but they who should go and seek faith, and if they search with sincerity they are bound to find. it. You can be sure that those who say: "There is nothing I should like more than to believe, but I cannot," only say this with their lips and not with their hearts, seeing that while they are saying it they close their ears. However, the proof is all around them, so why do they refuse to see? On the part of some it is indifference; of others the fear of being forced to change their habits. But in the majority there is pride which refuses to recognise the existence of a superior force because they would then have to bow down before it.

In some people faith appears to be inborn, a spark being enough to cause it to unfold. This ease of assimilation of spiritual truths is an evident sign of previous progress. On the contrary, in others there is difficulty of assimilation which is a no less evident sign of their backward natures. The first already believe and understand, having brought with them on *being reborn* the intuition of what they know. Their education is complete. The second still have everything to learn; their education is still to come. Nevertheless, come it will, and if it is not completed in this existence then it will be in another.

The resistance of the unbeliever, we must agree, is almost always due less to himself than to the manner in which things have been put to him. Faith needs a base, one that gives complete understanding of what we are asked to accept. In order to believe it is not enough to *see;* above all else it is necessary to *understand.* Blind faith is no longer of this century, so much so, that it is exactly blind dogmatic faith which produces the greatest number of unbelievers today, because it tries to impose itself, demanding the abdication of the most precious prerogatives of mankind, which are rationalization and free-will. It is principally against this kind of faith that the unbeliever rebels, so showing that it is true to say faith cannot be prescribed. Due to the non-acceptance of any proofs, blind faith leaves the Spirit with a feeling of emptiness which gives birth to doubt. Rationalized faith, when based on facts and logic, leaves no doubts. Then the person believes because they are certain; and no one can be certain unless they understand. This is why they are unshakable, because *unshakable faith is that which can stand face to face with reason in all epochs of humanity.*

This is the result to which Spiritism conducts us, so triumphing against incredulity, as long as it does not encounter systematic and preconceived opposition.

THE PARABLE OF THE DRY FIG-TREE

8.   *And on the morrow, when they were come from Bethany, He was hungry: and seeing a fig tree afar off having leaves, He came, if haply He might find*

anything thereon: and when He came to it, He found nothing but leaves: for the time of figs was not yet. And Jesus answered and said unto it, no man eat fruit of thee hereafter forever. And His disciples heard it. And in the morning, as they passed by, they saw the fig tree dried up from the roots. And Peter calling to remembrance saith unto Him, Master, behold, the fig tree which thou cursed is withered away. And Jesus answering saith unto them, Have faith in God. For verily I say unto you, That whosoever shall say unto this mountain, be thou removed, and be thou cast into the sea; and shall not doubt in his heart, but shall believe that those things which he saith shall come to pass. (Mark, 11: 12–14 & 20-23.)

9. The dried up fig-tree is a symbol of those people appearing to have a tendancy towards goodness, but who in reality produce nothing worthwhile. They are like the preachers who show more brilliance than substance, whose words have a superficial varnish to them in order to please the ear, but which on close examination reveal nothing substantial for the heart, and after having listened to them we ask ourselves of what benefit they have been.

It also symbolizes all those who can be useful but are not; of all utopias, empty orders and doctrines without solid bases. What is most lacking in the majority of cases is true faith, productive faith, the kind of faith which moves the fibres of the heart, in a word, the faith which moves mountains. These people are like trees covered in leaves but devoid of fruits. This is why Jesus condemns them to sterility, for the day will come when they will find themselves dry, even to the roots. This is to say that all orders and doctrines which have produced no good for humanity will be reduced to nothing. That all persons who are deliberately purposeless or idle, because they have not put into action the resources they have brought with them, will be treated as the fig-tree which dried up.

10. Mediums are the interpreters of the Spirits, supplying the lack of material organs through which they may transmit their instructions. Here is the reason why they are endowed with faculties for this purpose. In these present days of social renewal, they have a very special incumbency. They are like trees who are destined to supply spiritual sustenance to their brothers and sisters. Their numbers multiply so there may be abundance of nutriment. They are everywhere, in all countries, in all social classes, amongst rich and poor, great and small, so that no place may be without them to demonstrate to mankind that *all are called*. However, if they turn away from the providential objective for which this precious faculty was conceded, if they employ it for futile or prejudicial things, if they put it to the service of mundane interests, if the fruits are bad instead of being good, if they refuse to utilize it for the benefit of others, if they take no benefit from it for themselves, thereby becoming better persons, then they are like the sterile fig-tree. God will take away the gift that has become useless in their hands, that seed from which they did not know how to bring forth fruit, and will allow them to fall into the hands of evil Spirits.

INSTRUCTIONS FROM THE SPIRITS.
FAITH, THE MOTHER OF HOPE AND CHARITY

11.   In order to be profitable, faith must be active; it must not become benumbed. Mother of all the virtues which lead to God, it has a duty to attentively keep watch over the development of the children it generates. Hope and charity are inferences of faith and all three together form an inseparable trinity. Is it not faith which helps us to have hope in the realisation of God's promises? If there was no faith what would there be to hope for? Is it not faith which gives love? If you do not have faith, what would be your worth and what quality would your love have?

Faith, that divine inspiration which awakens all those noble instincts which lead Man towards goodness, is the base of all regeneration. Therefore it is necessary that this base be strong and durable, as even the smallest doubt will cause it to shake, and what then of the edifice constructed upon it? Consequently, this edifice must be raised upon immovable foundations. Your faith must be stronger than the sophisms and mockery of the incredulous, seeing that faith which cannot stand up to ridicule is not true faith.

Sincere faith is gripping and contagious; it communicates itself to those who have none or who do not even desire it. It finds persuasive words which touch the soul, whereas apparent faith only uses high sounding words which leave those who hear cold and indifferent. Preach through the example of your faith, so as to transmit it to mankind. Preach through the example of your works, so as to demonstrate the merit of faith. Preach through the firmness of your hope, so they may see the confidence which fortifies and puts one in condition to confront all life's vicissitudes.

So then, have faith with all that it contains of beauty and goodness, with its pureness and rationality. Do not accept a faith that cannot be substantiated. Love God knowing why you love Him. Believe in His promises knowing why you believe in them. Follow our counsel convinced of the end to which we direct you and the ways by which we take you in order to achieve it. Believe and wait without losing heart; miracles are the works of faith — JOSEPH, a Protecting Spirit (Bordeaux, 1862).

HUMAN AND DIVINE FAITH

12.   In Man, faith is the inherent sentiment of his future destiny; it is the consciousness he has of the immense faculties implanted in his inner-self, a source in latent state, which it is his duty to make blossom forth and grow by the action of his will.

Till today faith has only been understood in its religious sense because Christ exalted it as a powerful lever, and because He has been seen only as the Head of a religion. However, Christ, Who performed material miracles, showed us through these same miracles what Man can do when he has faith, that is to say, the *will to desire* and the certainty that this wish may be achieved.

Did not the apostles also perform miracles by following His example? Moreover, what were these miracles if not natural effects whose causes were not understood at that time, but which can be explained in great part today, and which by the study of Spiritism and magnetism will become totally comprehensible?

Faith is either human or divine, according to how Man applies his faculties, to the satisfaction of terrestrial needs or to celestial and future aspirations. A man of genius who throws himself into the realisation of a great undertaking will triumph if he has faith, because he feels sure of succeeding and that he is bound to reach the end envisaged. This certainly puts an immense force at his disposal. A good man, believing in his celestial future, desiring to fill his existence with beautiful and noble actions in the certainty of the happiness which awaits him, draws on his faith for the necessary force and so accomplishes miracles of charity, devotion, and abnegation. Finally, there are no evil tendencies which cannot be combated by faith.

Magnetism is one of the greatest proofs of the power of faith when put into action. It is through faith that it cures and produces those singular phenomena in other times called miracles.

I repeat: faith is both *human* and *divine*. If all incarnates could be persuaded of the force which they carry within themselves, and if they wished to place their will at the service of this force, they would be capable of producing these so called miracles that are nothing more than the development of a human faculty. — A Protecting Spirit (Paris, 1863).

CHAPTER 20

WORKERS OF THE LAST HOUR

INSTRUCTIONS FROM THE SPIRITS: The last shall be the first. — The mission of the Spiritists. — The workers of the Lord.

1. *For the Kingdom of Heaven is like unto a man that is an householder, which went out early in the morning to hire labourers into his vineyard. And when he had agreed with the labourers for a penny a day, he sent them into his vineyard. And he went out about the third hour and saw others standing idle in the marketplace, and said unto them; Go ye also into the vineyard, and whatsoever is right I will give you. And they went their way. Again he went out about the sixth and ninth hour, and did likewise. And about the eleventh hour he went out, and found others standing idle, and saith unto them, Why stand ye here all the day idle? They say unto him, Because no man hath hired us. He saith unto them, Go ye also into the vineyard; and whatsoever is right, that shall ye receive. So when even was come, the lord of the vineyard saith unto his steward, Call the labourers, and give them their hire, beginning from the last unto the first. And when they came that were hired about the eleventh hour, they received every man a penny. But when the first came, they supposed that they should have received more; and they likewise received every man a penny. And when they had received it, they murmured against the goodman of the house, saying, These last have wrought but one hour, and thou hast made them equal unto us, which have borne the burden and heat of the day. But he answered one of them, and said, Friend, I do thee no wrong: didst not thou agree with me for a penny? Take that thine is, and go thy way: I will give unto this last, even as unto thee. Is it not lawful for me to do what I will with mine own? Is thine eye evil, because I am good? So the last shall be first, and the first last: for many be called, but few chosen (Matthew, 20: 1–16. See also the Parable of the Wedding Feast, Chapter 18, item No. 1).*

INSTRUCTIONS FROM THE SPIRITS.
THE LAST SHALL BE THE FIRST

2. The worker of the last hour has a right to his wages; nevertheless, it is important that his lateness be not due to either laziness or reluctance, but to the fact that, although willing to work, he had been patiently waiting for someone to employ him. He has a right to his wages because, being hardworking, he has waited anxiously since dawn for someone who would finally offer work. It was only that he lacked opportunity.

However, if he had refused to work at any time during the day, or if he had said: "Wait a while, rest is very agreeable to me; when the last hour sounds then I will think about the day's wages; what necessity have I to be bothered by an employer I have no regard for and don't even know? The later the better!" Then this person, my friends, would not have received the wages of work but of laziness.

What would you say then of someone who, instead of remaining inactive, utilized those hours destined for the day's labour to practice culpable acts; who blasphemed against God, spilt the blood of his brothers, launched perturbation amongst families, ruined those who trusted in him by abusing their innocence; who, in short, satiated himself with all the ignominies of human nature? What would become of him? Is it enough for him to say at the last hour: "Master, I used my time badly. Take me on till the end of the day so I do some work, although it will be very little of what was my share, and give me the wages of a good worker"? No! No! The Lord will say to him: "I have no work for you at present. You squandered away your time; you forgot what you had learnt; you can no longer work in my vineyard. Consequently, you must recommence your learning, and when you are better disposed come again to me and I will throw open my vast fields to you, where you may work at any time."

Good Spiritists, my dearly beloved, you are all workers of the last hour. The one who says:"I began work at dawn and will only finish at nightfall," is very conceited. All of you came when you were called, some a little earlier, some a little later, to this incarnation whose shackles you now carry. For how many centuries has the Lord called you to His vineyard without you wishing to enter it? Here is the moment to pocket your wages, so put to good use the time that is left and never forget that your existence, however long it may appear to be, is nothing but a fleeting moment in the immensity of time which forms eternity.
— CONSTANTINE, a Protecting Spirit (Bordeaux, 1863).

3. Jesus liked the simplicity of symbols and in His virile language the workers who arrived at the first hour were the prophets, Moses and all the initiates, who have marked the steps of progress which continued to be signposted throughout the ages by the apostles, the martyrs, the founders of the Church, the wise men, the philosophers and finally by the Spiritists. These, who are the last to come, were announced and prophesied from the dawn of the advent of the Messiah and they will receive the same recompense or, I should say, a larger recompense. Being the last to arrive, the Spiritists take advantage of all the intellectual labours of their predecessors, because Man must inherit from Man and because human work and the subsequent results are collective: God blesses solidarity. Moreover, many who relive today, or who will relive tomorrow, are terminating work begun previously. More than one patriarch, more than one prophet, more than one disciple of Christ is to be found amongst these; nevertheless, more enlightened, more advanced, working now not at the base but at the summit of the edifice. These then will receive wages according to the value of the undertaking.

The beautiful doctrine of reincarnation is perpetual and needs spiritual affiliation. A Spirit, when called upon to give an account of its earthly mandate, sees for itself the continuity of an interrupted task, which is always resumed. It sees, it feels, it intuitively grasps the thoughts of those who have preceded. It begins the lesson anew, matured by experience, to advance yet further. And all of them, the workers of the first and last hours, with their eyes fully open to the profound justice of God, murmur no more: they simply adore.

This is one of the true meanings of this parable which holds, as do all those utilized by Jesus when speaking to the people, the rudiments of the future and also, in all forms and from all aspects, the revelation of the magnificent unity which harmonizes all things in the Universe and the solidarity which joins all present beings to the past and to the future. — HENRI HEINE (Paris, 1863).

THE MISSION OF THE SPIRITISTS

4. Do you not already hear the noise of the tempest which will sweep away the old world and destroy all the iniquities of this planet? Ah, praise the Lord, all those who have put their faith in His sovereign justice and who, as new apostles of the belief revealed by the superior prophetical voices, go forth to preach the new doctrine of *reincarnation* and the elevation of Spirits according to whether they have fulfilled their missions and supported their terrestrial trials well or badly.

Do not be afraid! The tongues of fire are above your heads. Oh, true adepts of Spiritism . . . you are God's chosen ones! Go forth and preach the Divine Word. The time has come when you should sacrifice your habits, your work, and your futile occupations to its dissemination. Go forth and preach! The elevated Spirits are with you. You will most certainly speak to those who do not wish to hear the Voice of God, because this Voice calls them unceasingly to abnegation. You will preach disinterestedness to those who are avaricious, abstenance to the dissolute, gentleness to domestic tyrants and despots! Lost words, I know, but it does not matter. It is necessary that you irrigate the land to be sown with the sweat of your labour, seeing that it will not come to fruit nor produce except under the repeated blows of the evangelical hoe and plough. Go forth and preach!

To all of you, men and women of good faith who are conscious of your inferiority before the many worlds scattered in infinite space! . . . Launch yourselves into the crusade against injustice and iniquity. Go forth and ostracize the worship of the golden calf, which spreads more and more each day. Go forth; God guides you! Simple and ignorant humanity, your tongues will be freed and you will speak as no orator speaks. Go forth then and preach, for those of the population who are heedful will happily take in your words of consolation, fraternity, hope and peace.

What matter the ambushes rigged against you along the pathway! Only wolves fall into wolf traps, since the Shepherd will know how to defend His sheep from the sacrificial butchers.

Go forth those who, great before God and more blessed than Saint Thomas, believe without demanding to see and accept the fact of mediumship even when they have not managed to obtain it for themselves. Go then, for the Spirit of God is guiding you.

March forward, magnificent phalanx of faith! Before you the great battalions of unbelievers will dissipate, as does the morning dew at the first rays of the sun.

Jesus said that faith is the virtue which moves mountains. However, heavier that the greatest mountain are the impurities and all the vices which are derived from them, which lie deposited in the hearts of men. So then, depart full of courage to remove this mountain of iniquities which future generations should only know as legend, in the same way that you know only very imperfectly of the times which preceded pagan civilization.

Moral and philosophical upheavals will be produced at all points of the globe; the hour approaches when the Divine Light will spread itself over both worlds.

THE WORKERS OF THE LORD

5. The time approaches when those things which have been announced for the transformation of humanity will be accomplished. All those who have worked in the field of the Lord with disinterestedness and no other motive than charity, will be blessed! Their working days will be paid a hundred times more than was expected. Blessed are those who have said to their fellow men: "Let us work together and unite our efforts so that when the Lord arrives He will find His work finished," seeing that the Lord will say to them: "Come unto me, you who have been good servants, you who knew how to silence your rivalries and discords so that no harm should come to the work!" But woe to those who as a result of their dissensions have held back the time of the harvest, because the tempest will come and they will be taken away in the turbulence! They will cry out: "Mercy! Mercy!" However, the Lord will say to them: "How can you implore mercy when you had none for your fellow men and refused to offer them a helping hand, trampling on the weak instead of upholding them? How can you beseech mercy when you sought your recompense in earthly pleasures and the satisfaction of your pride? You have already received your recompense, just as you wished. There is nothing more to ask for; the celestial rewards are for those who have not looked for earthly compensations."

At this very moment God is preparing a census of His faithful servants, and has already taken note of those whose devotion is only apparent, so that they may not usurp the wages of the courageous servants, because those who do not draw back from the task are the ones to whom He entrusted the most difficult positions in the great work of regeneration by means of Spiritism. These words will be fulfilled: "The first shall be the last and the last shall be the first in the Kingdom of Heaven." — THE SPIRIT OF TRUTH (Paris, 1862).

CHAPTER 21

THERE WILL BE FALSE CHRISTS AND FALSE PROPHETS

A tree is known by its fruits. — The mission of the prophets. — The prodigies of the false prophets. — Do not believe all the Spirits. — INSTRUCTIONS FROM THE SPIRITS: The false prophets. — The character of the true prophet. — The false prophets from the spiritual world. — Jeremiah and the false prophets.

A TREE IS KNOWN BY ITS FRUITS

1. *For a good tree bringeth not forth corrupt fruit; neither doth a corrupt tree bring forth good fruit. For every tree is known by his own fruit. For of thorns men do not gather figs, nor of a bramble bush gather they grapes. A good man out of the good treasure of his heart bringeth forth that which is good; and an evil man out of the evil treasure of his heart bringeth forth that which is evil: for of the abundance of the heart his mouth speaketh — (Luke, 6: 43-45).*

2. *Beware of false prophets, which come to you in sheep's clothing, but inwardly they are ravening wolves, ye shall know them by their fruits. Do men gather grapes of thorns, or figs of thistles? Even so every good tree bringeth forth good fruit; but a corrupt tree bringeth forth evil fruit. A good tree cannot bring forth evil fruit, neither can a corrupt tree bring forth good fruit. Every tree that bringeth not forth good fruit is hewn down, and cast into the fire. Wherefore by their fruits ye shall know them — (Matthew, 7: 15-20).*

3. *Take heed that no man deceive you. For many shall come in my name, saying, I am Christ; and shall deceive many.*

And many false prophets shall rise, and shall deceive many. And because iniquity shall abo⁻.nd, the love of many shall wax cold. But he that shall endure unto the end, the same shall be saved.

Then if any man shall say unto you, Lo, here is Christ, or there; believe it not. For there shall arise false Christs, and false prophets, and shall shew great signs and wonders; insomuch that, if it were possible, they shall deceive the very elect — (Matthew, 24: 4, 5, 11-13, 23 & 24. Also found in Mark, 13: 5, 6, 21 & 22).

THE MISSION OF THE PROPHETS

4. The gift of revealing the future is generally attributed to the prophets, so that the words *prophecy* and *prediction* have become synonyms. In the evangelical sense the word *prophet* has a much wider significance. This name is given to all those sent by God with the mission to instruct mankind and to reveal both that which is hidden and the mysteries of spiritual life. Therefore a person may be a prophet without making any predictions. This was the idea as understood by the Jews at the time of Jesus, and this is why when they took Him before the high priest Caiaphas, the scribes and wisemen who were there spat upon Him and hit Him with their fists saying: "Christ, prophesy to us and tell us who hit you." Nevertheless, it has happened that there have been prophets who could see into the future, be it through intuition or providential revelations, so they could transmit these warnings to mankind. Due to the fact of these predictions having been fulfilled, the gift of predicting the future was considered to be one of the attributes of being a prophet.

THE PRODIGIES OF THE FALSE PROPHETS

5. "False Christs and prophets will raise themselves up and will do great prodigies and things which will astonish, to the point of seducing even the chosen ones." These words give us the true meaning of the term prodigy. In theological interpretation, prodigies and miracles are exceptional phenomena outside the law of nature. These being the *exclusive* work of God, beyond all doubt He can annul them if He so pleases. Nevertheless, simple good sense tells us that it is not possible that He has given those who are perverse and inferior power equal to His own, nor even less the right to undo that which He himself has done. Jesus could never have sanctioned such a principle. If however, according to the sense attributed to these words, the spirit of evil has the power to perform prodigies such as these, and that even those who were chosen would be deceived, then the result would be that by being able to do what God does, then prodigies and miracles would not be the exclusive privilege of God's messengers. This then would prove nothing, because there would be no means of distinguishing the miracles of the saints from those of the devil. Therefore it is necessary that we look for a more rational meaning to these words.

To the ignorant masses all phenomena whose cause is unknown become supernatural, marvelous and miraculous. Once the cause is found, it is recognised that the phenomenon, however extraordinary it appears, is nothing more than the application of one of the laws of nature. In this manner the circle of supernatural facts becomes restricted as scientific knowledge widens. At all times men and women have exploited certain knowledge they possess for the sake of ambition, self-interest and their desire to dominate so as to gain the prestige of possessing supposedly superhuman powers, or to lay claim to divine missions. These are the false Christs and false prophets. The diffusion of knowledge in these matters annihilates their credibility and will result in diminished numbers in proportion to the rate at which Man enlightens himself. The simple fact of being able to perform what some like to call prodigies, does not in any way constitute a sign of a divine mission, seeing that these phenomena may result from acquired knowledge which is within the reach of anyone, or from special organic faculties which either those who are worthy or ignoble are able to possess. True prophets are recognised by their serious characters and total morality.

DO NOT BELIEVE ALL THE SPIRITS

6. *Beloved, believe not every spirit, but try the spirits whether they are of God: because many false prophets are gone out into the world — (1 John, 4: 1).*

7. Far from sanctioning the false Christs and false prophets, as some people take pleasure in saying, spiritual phenomena comes, on the contrary, to deal them a death blow. Do not ask Spiritism for prodigies or miracles, since it positively declares it does not perform them. In the same manner that physics, chemistry, astronomy and geology reveal the laws of the material world, so Spiritism reveals other unknown laws which govern the relationships existing between the physical and spiritual worlds; laws which just as much as those of science, are laws of Nature. By giving an explanation for certain types of phenomena, which until now had remained inexplicable, it destroys all that remains of the miraculous. Consequently those who feel tempted to exploit these phenomena for personal gain, by pretending to be messengers from God, will not be allowed to abuse the credulity of the general public for long, but will be quickly unmasked. Moreover, as has already been said, these phenomena alone prove nothing. Every mission is proved by its moral effects, and these cannot be produced by everyone. One of the results of the development of the Spiritist science is that through research into the causes of certain of these manifestations, many mysteries are explained.

Only those who prefer darkness rather than light have every interest in combating this progress. But truth is like the sun, which dissipates even the most dense clouds.

Spiritism also reveals another far more dangerous aspect of false Christs and false prophets, which is to be found not amongst men, but amongst the discarnate. These are the deceiving, hypocritical, prideful and falsely-wise Spirits, who on passing from Earth into their spiritual wanderings, have adopted venerated names as masks under which to hide, in order to facilitate the acceptance of the most strange and absurd ideas. Before mediumistic relationships were understood they acted less conspicuously, by means of inspiration and unconscious mediumship heard or spoken. There are a considerable number who in various epochs, and above all in recent times, have presented themselves as some of the old prophets, Christ, the Virgin Mary and even God himself. John warns against these Spirits by saying: "Beloved, believe not every Spirit, but try the Spirits whether they are of God, because many false prophets are gone out into the world." Spiritism offers us the means of trying them when it shows us the characteristics by which we may recognise the good spirits which are *always moral, never material.* (1) It is particularly to the manner by which the good may be distinguished from the bad that these words of Jesus may be applied. "It is by the fruits that you know the quality of the tree. A bad tree cannot produce good fruits." Spirits are judged by the quality of their works, just as a tree is judged by its fruits.

INSTRUCTIONS FROM THE SPIRITS.

THE FALSE PROPHETS

8. Where it is said: "Christ is here," do not go. On the contrary, be on guard because the false prophets there will be numerous. Do you not see that the leaves of the fig-tree are fading? Do you not see that its multiple shoots are awaiting the time of coming into flower? Did not Jesus say unto you: know the tree by its fruit? Then if the fruit is bitter you already know that the tree is evil; however, if the fruits are sweet and healthy you can say: "Nothing that is pure can come from something bad."

My brethren, this then is how you should judge. It is the works that you should examine. If those who say they are invested with divine powers reveal signs of a mission of high order — that is to say, if they possess the highest order of Christian and eternal virtues which are: charity, love, tolerance and goodness which conciliates all hearts — and if, in support of their works they also present the equivalent acts, then you may say: These are true messengers of God.

Nevertheless, be mistrustful of honeyed words; be mistrustful of the Scribes and Pharisees who pray in public places clothed in long tunics. Mistrust those who lay claim to a monopoly of the truth!

No, no, Christ is not amongst these, seeing that those He sends to propagate His sacred doctrine and regenerate His peoples will, above all else, follow His example, be gentle and humble of heart. Those who have to save humanity, which is running towards damnation, by their examples and their counselling will be essentially modest and humble. Run away from all who show even an atom of pride as you would run away from an infectious disease, which is apt to contaminate everything it touches. Remember, *each creature bears the stamp on their brow and even more especially in their actions, of their spiritual progress or their inferiority.*

---

(1) See the manner by which spirits can be identified in THE MEDIUM'S BOOK — second part, chapter 24 and subsequent chapters.

Go therefore, my beloved children, and advance without indecision or hidden thoughts along the blessed route you have accepted. Go always without fear; turn aside with great care from all that may impede your march towards the eternal objective. Travellers, it is only for a while longer that you will be in the shadows and suffer the pains of atonement if you open your heart to this sweet doctrine, which will reveal to you the eternal laws and satisfy every aspiration of your soul with regard to the unknown. You may already give embodiment to the fleeting sylph you see passing by in your dreams, and which being short-lived, only enchants your spirit without touching your heart. Now, my beloved, death disappears giving place to the radiant angel you know, the angel of re-encounter and reunion! Now, all you who have faithfully fulfilled your tasks, which the Creator confides to His creatures, have nothing more to fear from His justice, since He is the Father and always forgives those of His children who have strayed when they cry out for mercy. Accordingly, continue to advance unceasingly! Let your slogan be progress, continuous progress in all things, until finally you reach the happy termination of your journey, where all who proceeded you await. — LOUIS (Bordeaux, 1861).

THE CHARACTER OF THE TRUE PROPHET

9. *Mistrust the false prophets.* This recommendation is useful in all epochs, but above all in times of transition such as now when a transformation of humanity is occurring, because of a multitude of those who are ambitious and scheming will promote themselves as reformers and messiahs. We should be on guard against these imposters and it is the duty of all honest people to unmask them. You may well ask how they can be identified. Here are the things which point them out:

The command of an army is only confided to a capable general. Do you believe that God is less prudent than Man? You may be sure that He only confides important missions to those He knows are capable of fulfilling them, seeing that great missions are heavy burdens which crush those who are lacking in sufficient strength to carry them. In all things the teacher must know more than the disciple. In order to lead humanity to advance, both morally and intellectually, we must have men and women of superior intelligence and morality. This is why Spirits who are already advanced, having passed their tests in other existences, are always chosen for these missions, because if they were not superior to the ambient in which they are required to act, their effect would be nullified.

Having said that, we must conclude that the true missionary of God must justify his mission through superiority, virtue, magnanimity, results and by the moralizing influence of his work. We may also take into consideration yet another consequence. If, due to their character, virtues and intelligence, they show themselves to be less than the part they purport to represent, or the person under whose name they have placed themselves, then they are nothing more than storytellers of low character, who cannot even imitate their chosen model.

Another consideration is that, in the greater part, true missionaries of God are ignorant of the fact. They fulfill the mission to which they were called by the strength of character they possess, seconded by occult forces who inspire and direct them, even against their will, but without premeditation. In a word — *the true prophet reveals himself by his actions and is discovered by others, whereas the false prophet declares himself to be a messenger of God.* The first is humble and modest, the second is full of himself, speaks with arrogance, and as all who lie, appears to be always afraid he will not be believed.

Some of these imposters have passed themselves as apostles of Christ, others as Christ Himself, and to the disgrace of all humanity, they have encountered those sufficiently credulous as to believe in their baseness. However, a simple pondering is enough to open the eyes of even the most blind in this matter. That is to say, that if Christ were to reincarnate on Earth, He would come with all His power and all His virtues; unless one admits that He had degenerated, which would be absurd. Well, in the same manner, if we were to take away even one of God's attributes, we would no longer have God. So likewise, if we take away even one of Christ's virtues, we would no longer have Christ. The question is, do those who purport to be Christ have all His virtues? Observe them, scrutinize their ideas and actions and you will recognise that apart from anything else, they lack the distinctive qualities of Christ, which are charity and humility, while abounding in all those Christ does not possess, such as covetousness and pride. Furthermore, take note that at this moment in various countries there are many supposed Christs, just as there are many Elijahs, Saint Johns or Saint Peters, and clearly it is impossible for them all to be true. You may be sure they are only creatures who exploit the credulity of others and who find it convenient to live at the expense of those who listen to them.

So then, mistrust the false prophets especially at a time of renewal such as the present, because there will be many imposters who say they are from God. They try to satisfy their vanity here on Earth, but a terrible justice will befall them, of that you may be sure. — ERASTUS (Paris 1862).

THE FALSE PROPHETS OF THE SPIRITUAL WORLD

10. The false prophets are not to be found solely amongst incarnates. They are also to be found in even greater numbers amongst the prideful Spirits, who by appearing to be all love and charity, sow disunion and hold back the work of emancipating humanity by infiltrating their absurd doctrines, after having gained a medium's acceptance of them. And in order to further fascinate those whom they desire to delude, so as to give more weight to their theories, they appropriate without scruples those names which Man pronounces only with great respect.

It is these Spirits who scatter a tumult of antagonism amongst groups, impell them to isolate themselves from all others, and look upon them with suspicion. This situation alone is enough to unmask them, since by so proceeding they are the first to offer a clear denial of who they claim to be. Blind therefore are those who allow themselves to fall for so great a hoax.

But there are many other ways in which they may be recognised. The Spirits of this particular category, to which they say they belong, have to be not only very good but also eminently rational. Well then, put all their doctrines through the test of reason and good sense and see what you have left. You will then agree with me that every time a Spirit indicates things of a utopian, childish, impracticable or ridiculous nature, or formulates a dogma, which the most rudimentary notions of science contradict, as a solution for the problems of humanity, or as a means of achieving their transformation, then these ideas can only come from a very ignorant or lying Spirit.

On the other hand, you may be sure that if the individual does not always appreciate the truth, it is appreciated by the good sense of the masses, which constitutes yet one more criterion. If two principles contradict each other, we can find the measure of value inherent in both by verifying which of the two generates a greater echo and sympathy. *Apart from the fact that it would be illogical to admit to oneself that any doctrine whose number of adepts progressively diminishes is more truthful than that of another whose followers continually increase.* In desiring that the truth reaches everyone, God has not confined it to a narrow circle, but has made it appear in all places, so that the light shines alongside the darkness.

Repel all those Spirits who present themselves as exclusive counsellors, preaching separation and isolation. They are almost always vain and mediocre Spirits, who seek to impose and dictate to weak and credulous persons by lavishing exaggerated praise upon them, with the aim of fascinating and so dominating them. These are generally Spirits eager for power, who having been despots both publicly or in their own homes, still continue to look for victims to tyrannize, even after death. In general, *mistrust all communications which have a mystical and singular character or those which perscribe excentric acts and ceremonies.* In all of these cases there is always legitimate motive for suspicion.

Equally you may be sure that when a truth is to be revealed to mankind it is, by way of saying, instantly communicated to all serious groups who have at their disposal serious mediums, and not only to one group at the exclusion of all others. No one can be a perfect medium if they become obsessed, and there is manifest obsession when a medium is only able to receive communication from one specific Spirit, however elevated that spirit pretends to be. Consequently, every medium and all groups who believe themselves to be privileged by reason of the communications they alone obtain, and who moreover, are subject to practises bordering on superstition, undoubtedly find themselves caught up in a well characterized obsession; above all, when the dominating Spirit swaggers under a name which both incarnates and discarnates should honour and respect and not allow reputations to be compromised in this manner.

It is incontestable that by submitting to the crucible of reason and logic all the facts and communications received from Spirit, it becomes an easy matter to reject the errors and absurdities. A single medium may become fascinated or a group deluded; but through severe verification of what is occurring in other groups, the acquiring of knowledge within the subject matter, the analysis of all communications received by the principal mediums of each group, together with the use of logic and the verification of authenticity whenever possible of the most serious Spirit communicators, it is possible to render justice to all falsehoods and trickery from any band of deceiving or malicious Spirits. — ERASTUS, disciple of Saint Paul (Paris, 1862).

(See the second item in the Introduction of this book headed: THE UNIVERSAL VERIFICATION OF THE TEACHINGS OF THE SPIRITS, and also the second part of the THE MEDIUMS' BOOK (1), chapter 23, OBSESSION.)

JEREMIAH AND THE FALSE PROPHETS

11. *Thus said the Lord of Hosts, Harken not unto the words of the prophets that prophesy unto you: they make you vain: they speak a vision of their own heart, and not out of the mouth of the Lord. They say still unto them that despise me, The Lord hath said, Ye shall have peace; and they say unto every one that walketh after the imagination of his own heart, No evil shall come upon you. For who hath stood in the counsel of the Lord, and hath perceived and heard His Word? Who hath marked His Word, and heard it? I have not sent these prophets, yet they ran: I have not spoken to them, yet they prophesied. I have heard what the prophets said, that prophesy lies in My name, saying, I have dreamed, I have dreamed. How long shall this be in the heart of the prophets that prophesy lies? Yes, they are prophets of the deceit of their own heart. And when this people, or the prophet, or a priest, shall ask thee, saying, What is the burden of the Lord? Thou shalt then say unto them, what burden? I will even forsake you, saith the Lord (Jeremiah, 23: 16-18, 21, 25, 26 & 33).*

My friends, I wish to talk to you about this passage from the prophet Jeremiah. Speaking through his mouth, God said: "It is the vision of their own hearts which makes them speak in this manner." These words clearly indicate that already in those times the charlatans and the impassioned abused the gift of prophesy and exploited it. They consequently abused the simple and almost blind faith of the people by predicting, *for money,* both good and agreeable things. This kind of fraud was very widespread within the Jewish nation, and so it is easy to understand that the poor people, in their ignorance, had no possible means of distinguishing the good from the bad, as they were always more or less duped by the pseudo-prophets, who were nothing more than imposters and fanatics. There is nothing more significant than these words: "I did not send these prophets yet they run, I have not spoken to them

_____

(1) by Allan Kardec.

yet they prophesy." Further on it says: "I heard these prophets who prophesy lies in My Name, saying, I have dreamed, I have dreamed." This is one of the ways they used to explain the confidences they were supposedly given. The masses, being credulous, did not think to dispute the truth of these dreams and visions. They thought it quite natural and frequently invited these 'prophets' to speak.

After the words of the prophet, listen to the wise counsel of the Apostle John, when he said: "Do not believe in all the Spirits. First test them to see if they come from God." This is because among those who are invisible there are also those who take pleasure in deluding, if they have the chance. The deluded ones are, as we can see, the mediums who do not take the necessary precautions. Beyond all doubt, it is unquestionably one of the greatest stumbling blocks against which many come to grief, especially when they are new to Spiritism. For them it is a test from which they will be able to extricate themselves only by using much prudence. Therefore, before anything else, learn to distinguish the good from the bad Spirits so that you, in your turn, may not become a false prophet. — LUOZ, a Protecting Spirit (Carlsruhe, 1861).

CHAPTER 22

WHOM GOD HAS JOINED TOGETHER, LET NO MAN PUT APART

The indissolubility of marriage. — Divorce.

THE INDISSOLUBILITY OF MARRIAGE

1. *The Pharisees also came unto Him, tempting Him, saying unto Him, Is it lawful for a man to put away his wife for every cause? And He answered and said unto them, Have ye not read, that He which made them at the beginning made them male and female, and said, For this cause shall a man leave father and mother, and shall cleave to his wife: and they twain shall be one flesh? Wherefore they are no more twain, but one flesh. What therefore God hath joined together, let no man put asunder. They say unto Him, Why did Moses then command to give a writing of divorcement, and to put her away? He said unto them, Moses because of the hardness of your hearts suffered you to put away your wives: but from the beginning it was not so. And I say unto you, Whosoever shall put away his wife, except it be for fornication, and shall marry another, committeth adultery: and whoso marrieth her which is put away doth commit adultery (Matthew, 19: 3-9).*

2. The only things which are immutable are those which stem from God. Everything which is the work of Man is subject to change. The laws of Nature are the same at all times and in all countries. Human laws change according to the times, places and intellectual progress. In marriage, what is of a Divine Order is the union of the sexes, so that the substitution of those who die may be put into effect. But the conditions which regulate this union are so human in design that in the whole world there are not, even in Christendom, two countries where these laws are exactly identical, and none where in the course of time they do not suffer changes. The result of this is that according to civil law, what is legitimate in one country at a certain time is considered to be adultery in another country and at another time. This is due to the fact that civil law has as its objective the regulation of the interests of families, interests which vary according to customs and local necessities. In this manner for example, in certain countries a religious marriage is the only legitimate one; in others it is also necessary to have a civil marriage and finally there are yet other places where a civil marriage is sufficient on its own.

3. But in the union of the sexes, apart from the Divine material law common to all living creatures, there is another Divine law which is immutable, as are all of God's laws, one that is exclusively moral, which is the law of love. God wishes all beings to unite themselves not only through the ties of the flesh, but also through those of the soul, so that the mutual affection of the spouses be transmitted to the offspring and that it should be two, and not just one, who love them, look after them and help them progress. Is the law of love taken into consideration in ordinary conditions within marriage? Not in the least. The mutual sentiments of two beings who are attracted one to the other are not consulted, since in the majority of cases this sentiment is severed. What is looked for is not the satisfaction of the heart but that of pride, vanity and cupidity; in a word, all material interests. When everything goes well according to these interests, it is said to be a marriage of convenience: when the pockets are well lined, it is said that the spouses are equally harmonized and should be very happy.

However, no civil laws nor the obligations which these laws determine can replace the law of love. If this does not preside over the union it frequently happens that *those who were forcibly united separate themselves.* The oath sworn at the foot of the altar, when pronounced as a banal formula, then becomes a perjury. For that reason we have unhappy marriages which end up becoming criminal, which is a double disgrace that could have been avoided if, on establishing the conditions for that marriage, the law of love which is the only law sanctioning the union in the eyes of God, had not been abstracted. When God said: "And they twain shall be one flesh," and when Jesus said: "What God hath joined together let no man put assunder," these words should be understood as a reference to the union according to God's immutable law and not according to the mutable laws of Man.

4. Is the civil law then superfluous and should we go back to matrimony according to Nature? Certainly not. Civil law has the object of regulating social relationships and family interests in accordance with the requirements of civilization. Therefore it is useful and necessary, although variable. It must be provident because civilized Man must not live as a savage. However, there is nothing, absolutely nothing, which prevents it being an inference of God's law. All obstacles against the execution of this Divine Law stem from prejudices and not from the civil law. These prejudices, even if they are still alive, have lost much of their predominance amongst the enlightened peoples of this world. They will come to disappear with moral progress, which in fact will open the eyes of mankind to the countless evils, to the failings and even crimes which result from unions which are contracted on the exclusive basis of material interest. One day Man will ask if it is more humane, more charitable, more moral, to chain one being to another when they are unable to live together, than to restore their liberty; whether the prospect of an indissoluble prison will increase the number of irregular unions.

DIVORCE

5. Divorce is a man-made law whose objective is to legally separate those who are in fact already separated. It is not against God's law, since it only reforms what men have done and is only applicable in cases in which Divine law was not taken into account. If it was contrary to God's law the Church itself would be forced to consider as betrayers of a trust those of its heads who, by their own authority and in the name of religion, have imposed it on more than one occasion. In these cases it would have been a double betrayal of a trust because it only had worldly interests in view, and not the satisfaction of the law of love.

Even Jesus did not sanction the absolute indissolubility of marriage. Did He not say: "It was because of the hardness of your hearts that Moses permitted you to repudiate your women"? This signifies that ever since the time of Moses, when mutual affection is not the only motive for matrimony, separation could become necessary. Nevertheless, He added that: "In the beginning it was not like that," meaning that at the origin of humanity, when men were not yet perverted by selfishness and pride, and lived according to God's laws, the unions were derived from sympathy and not ambition or vanity. Therefore there was no desire to repudiate.

Jesus goes even further, because He specifies a case in which repudiation is justified: that of adultery. Well, adultery cannot exist where there is sincere reciprocated affection. It is true that He prohibited a man to marry a repudiated woman. But here we must take into consideration the customs and character of men in those times when the Mosaic law perscribed stoning to death. When wishing to abolish one barbaric custom, it was necessary to find a substitute penalty; and He found it in the disgrace which would come from the prohibition of a second marriage. It was to a certain extent one civil law being substituted by another. But like all laws of this nature, it had to pass the test of time.

CHAPTER 23

STRANGE MORAL

Hate the parents. — Abandon father, mother and children. —
Leave to the dead the care of burying their dead. — I have not
come to bring peace, but dissension.

HATE THE PARENTS

1. *And there went great multitudes with Him: and He turned, and said unto them: If any man come to me, and hate not his father, and mother, and wife, and children, and brethren, and sisters, yea, and his own life also, he cannot be my disciple. And whosoever doth not bear his cross, and come after me, cannot be my disciple. So likewise, whosoever he be of you that forsaketh not all that he hath, you cannot be my disciple (Luke, 14: 25-27 & 33).*

2. *He that loveth father or mother more than me is not worthy of me: and he that loveth son and daughter more than me is not worthy of me (Matthew, 10: 37).*

3. Very occasionaly certain words attributed to Christ make singular contrast to His habitual manner of speaking, so much so that we instinctively repel their literal sense without causing the sublimity of His doctrine to suffer damage. Written after His death, since none of the Evangelists wrote while He was alive, it is licit to believe that in cases like these the depth of His thoughts were not expressed or, which is no less possible, the original sense while having been passed from one language to another has consequently suffered some alteration. It is sufficient that a small error be committed but once, for those who copy to continue to repeat it, as frequently happens in the relating of historical facts.

The term *hate* in the phrase from Luke: *if any man come to me and hate not his father and mother and wife and children* — should be understood by the light of this hypothesis. It would not occur to anyone to attribute these words to Jesus. So then, it would be superfluous to discuss it or even less to try to justify it. For this it would be necessary first to know if He pronounced them, and if He had, whether in the idiom in which they were expressed the word in question had the same meaning as it does in our language. In this passage from John: "He who hates his life in this world will conserve himself for the eternal life," there is no doubt that Jesus did not attach the same meaning as we do to these words.

The Hebraic language was not rich in expressions and contained many words which had varied meanings. Such a one, for example, is that in Genesis used to describe the phases of creation. It also served simultaneously to express a given period of time and the period of a day. Later on, from this situation came the translation into the term *a day,* and the belief that the world was created in a period that lasted six times twenty-four hours. Another was the word used to designate both *camel* and a *rope,* since the ropes were made of camel hair. This is why they translated the word into the term 'camel' in the allegory of the eye of the needle (Chapter 16, item 2). (1)

Furthermore, it behoves us to pay attention to the customs and character of the various peoples, which have a very great influence over the particular nature of their language. Without this knowledge, the true meanings of certain words frequently escape us. The same term when passed from one language to another may gain either more or less strength. In one it may involve insult and blasphemy, while in another it may totally lack importance, according to the idea it provokes. Even in the same language some words lose their value with time. For this reason a rigorously literal translation does not always express the thought exactly, and so in order to maintain this exactitude it is sometimes necessary to use other equivalents rather than corresponding terms, or even paraphrases.

These comments will be found especially applicable in the interpretation of the blessed Scriptures, and in particular those of the Gospels. If the nature of the environment in which Jesus lived is not taken into account we shall be exposed to misunderstandings as to the meaning of certain expressions and certain facts, as a consequence of the habit we have of likening others to ourselves. In any case, it behoves us to divest the term HATE of its modern meaning, as this is contrary to the true message of the teachings of Jesus. (See also chapter 14, item 5 and subsequent items.)

ABANDON FATHER, MOTHER AND CHILDREN

4. And everyone that hath forsaken houses, or brethren, or sisters, or father, or mother, or wife, or children, or lands, for my Name's sake, shall receive an hundredfold, and shall inherit everlasting life (Matthew, 19: 29).

---

(1) NON ODIT in Latin: KAÏ or MISEÏ in Greek, do not mean *hate,* but rather TO LOVE LESS. What the Greek verb MISEÏ indicates is expressed even better by the Hebrew verb, which would have been used by Jesus. This verb does not only signify HATE, but also TO LOVE LESS, TO NOT LOVE AS MUCH AS, OR TO NOT LOVE THE SAME AS SOMEONE ELSE. In the Syrian dialect, which is said was used more frequently by Jesus, this meaning is even better accentuated. It is in this sense that GENESIS (Chapter 29: 30 & 31) says: "And Jacob loved Raquel more than Lia, and Jehova seeing that Lia was hated . . . " It is evident that the true meaning here is: was loved less. This is how it should be translated. In many other passages in Hebrew and, above all in Syrian, the same verb is used in the sense of TO NOT LOVE AS MUCH AS ANOTHER, which makes it contradictory to translate it into HATE, this having another clearly defined meaning. The text of Matthew, however, puts the matter quite clearly. (Note by M. Pezzani, in the 3rd edition of the original French.)

5. *Then Peter said, Lo, we have left all, and followed Thee. And He said unto them, Verily I say unto you, There is no man that hath left house, or parents, or brethren, or wife, or children, for the Kingdom of God's sake, who shall not receive manifold more in this present time, and in the world to come life everlasting (Luke, 18: 28-30).*

6. *And another also said, Lord, I will follow thee; but let me first go bid them farewell, which are at home at my house. And Jesus said unto him, No man, having put his hand to the plough, and looking back is fit for the Kingdom of God (Luke, 9: 61 & 62).*

Here, without arguing about words, we should look for the thought behind them which quite evidently was: The interests of the future life should take precedence over all other interests and human considerations. This thought is in accordance with the substance of the doctrine as taught by Jesus, whereas the idea of renouncing one's family would be a frank denial of this teaching.

Moreover, do we not have these maxims in mind when we consider the sacrifice of our interests and family affections for those of our homeland? Do we, by chance, censure those who leave their parents, brothers and sisters, wives and children in order to fight for their country? On the contrary, do they not gain in merit for having given up their homes and families in order to fulfill their duty? This then is because there are some duties which are greater than others. Does not the law impose that the daughter leave her parents in order to follow her husband? The world is full of thousands of cases in which painful separation is necessary. Nevertheless, affections are not broken because of this. These temporary separations do not diminish either the respect or the solicitude that children owe to their parents, nor the affection of these parents for their children. Therefore we see that even if we take these words literally, with the exception of the word *hate*, they would not be a contradiction of the commandment which prescribes that Man honours his father and mother, nor that of parental affections; and would certainly not be if they were understood in their spiritual meaning. These words had the finality then of showing through overstatement, how imperious is the duty of occupying oneself with the future life. Besides, they would have been less shocking for a people in an epoch in which, as a consequence of their customs, family ties were not so strong as they are within a society which is morally more advanced. These ties, always weak in primitive peoples, fortify themselves with the development of sensitivity and a sense of morality. Nevertheless, separation is necessary for progress. Without it families and races would become degenerate if there were no intermingling of different strains. This is a law of nature, and is as much in the interests of moral progress as it is for physical progress.

Here things are considered purely from the earthly point of view. Spiritism makes us look higher by showing us that the real ties of affection are not of the flesh but of the Spirit, and that these ties do not break with separation, nor even through the death of the physical body. In fact they become more robust in the spiritual life by means of the cleansing of the Spirit. This knowledge is a consoling truth from which great strength can be gained by all beings to help them support the vicissitudes of life (See chapter 4, item 18 and chapter 14, item 8).

LEAVE TO THE DEAD THE CARE OF BURYING THEIR DEAD

7. *And He said unto another, Follow me. But he said, Lord, suffer me first to go and bury my father. Jesus said unto him, Let the dead bury their dead: but go thou and preach the Kingdom of God (Luke, 9: 59 & 60).*

8. What can the words "leave to the dead the care of burying their dead" mean? The previous considerations show primarily that in the circumstances in which they were proffered, they could not have contained a censure for the one who considered it to be a devotional duty of children to bury their father. Therefore we have a more profound meaning here, which can only be perceived with a more complete knowledge of spiritual life.

Life in the spiritual world is in effect the real life, the normal life of a Spirit. Terrestrial existence, being transitory and passing, is a kind of death when compared to the splendours and activity of the spritual life. The body is nothing more than a gross covering which temporarily clothes the Spirit. It is a true fetter which secures it to the soil and from which the Spirit feels happy to be liberated. The respect given to the dead is not inspired by matter, but is due to the remembrance that the absent Spirit imbues. It is similar to someone who bestows an object which belonged to them and which they handled, that is kept by those who had affection for the person as a remembrance. This is what the man could not understand for himself. Jesus taught him by saying: Do not worry about the body, but think first of the Spirit; go and teach about God's Kingdom; go and tell men that their homeland is not to be found upon the Earth but in Heaven, because the true life exists only there.

I HAVE NOT COME TO BRING PEACE, BUT DISSENSION

9. *Think not that I am come to send peace on Earth: I am come not to send peace, but a sword. For I am come to set a man at variance against his father, and the daughter against her mother, and the daughter-in-law against her mother-in-law. And a man's foes shall be they of his own household (Matthew, 10: 34-36).*

10. *I am come to send fire on the Earth; and what will I, if it be already kindled? But I have a baptism to be baptized with; and how am I straitened till it be accomplished! Suppose ye that I am come to give peace on Earth? I tell you, Nay; but rather division: for from henceforth there shall be five in one house divided, three against two, and two against three. The father shall be divided against the son, and the son against the father; the mother against the daughter, and the daughter against the mother; the mother-in-law against her daughter-in-law, and the daughter-in-law against her mother-in-law (Luke, 12: 49-53).*

11. Could it really be that Jesus, the personification of gentleness and goodness, Who never ceases to preach the need to love our neighbours, could have said: "I come not to bring peace, but the sword; to separate the son from the father, the husband from his wife; I am come to set fire to the Earth and am in a hurry for this to happen"? Are not these words in flagrant contradiction to His teaching? Is it not blasphemy to attribute to Him the language of a bloody and devastating conqueror? No, there is no blasphemy nor contradiction in these words, because it was He Who pronounced them and they are testimony to His great wisdom. It is only that they are a little ambiguous and the form does not express the thought with exactitude, thus giving rise to misunderstanding as to their true meaning. Taken literally, they have a tendency to transform His mission, which was all peaceful, into one of perturbation and discord, which is absurd, and good sense repels this, seeing that Jesus could not contradict Himself (See chapter 19, item 6).

12. Every new idea inevitably encounters opposition and there is not one which is implanted without a fight. Well, in these cases the resistance is always in proportion to the importance of the *foreseen* results, because the greater these are the more numerous are the interests which are affected. If it is notoriously false, if it is taken as inconsequential, then no one becomes alarmed; everyone lets it go, being certain that it lacks vitality. If, however, it is true, if it is placed on a solid base, if it appears to have a future, then a secret presentiment alerts its antagonists to the fact that it constitutes a danger for them and to the order of things to whose maintenance they are pledged. Then they throw themselves against it and its adepts.

So we can measure the importance and the results of a new idea by the amount of emotion its appearance causes, by the violence of the opposition it provokes, as well as by the degree and persistence of the anger of its adversaries.

13. Jesus came to proclaim a doctrine which would undermine the very base of the abuses upon which the Pharisees, the Scribes and the Priests all lived. Accordingly they sacrificed Him, believing that by killing the Man they would kill the idea. Nevertheless this idea survived because it was the truth. It has augmented itself because it corresponds to God's design, and although born in a small and obscure hamlet in Judaea, it went and planted its standard in the very capital of the pagan world, right in the face of its fiercest enemies, those who had the greatest interest in combatting it because it was subverting centuries old beliefs to which they were attached, much more for personal interest than from conviction. Terrible battles awaited there for the Apostles; the victims were innumerable. However, the idea always grew and triumphed because, being the truth, it rose above those which had preceded.

14. It is worth noting that Christianity sprang up when Paganism had already entered into a decline and was struggling against the light of reason. It was practised only as a matter of form as faith had disappeared; only personal interest sustained it. Now those who are moved by interest are persistent and

never give way to evidence. They become more and more irritated as the counter arguments become more decisive and demonstrate more clearly their beliefs. These people know very well they are wrong, but this does not deter them, as true faith is not yet a part of their soul. What they most fear is the light which will give sight to those who are blind. The errors are to their advantage, so they hold on to them and give battle.

Did not Socrates also teach a doctrine very similar to that of Christ? Why then did it not prevail amongst one of the most intelligent peoples upon the planet at that time? This was because the time was not yet ripe. He sowed on land that had not been ploughed. Paganism was still not *worn out.* Christ received His mission at the propitious moment. It is true that a great deal was still lacking for mankind of that epoch to enable them to reach the level of Christian ideas; but there was a general aptitude amongst them which permitted the assimilation of this knowledge, because of the beginning of a sense of emptiness which the common beliefs did nothing to fill. Socrates and Plato opened up the way and prepared the Spirits of the people (See the INTRODUCTION, item 4, SOCRATES & PLATO, the forerunners of Christian ideas and of Spiritism).

15. Unfortunately the adepts of the new doctrine were unable to agree as to the interpretation of the words of Jesus, Whose meaning was frequently hidden by allegory and figures of speech. Because of this, numerous sects were quick to flourish, each claiming to possess the exclusive truth, and even eighteen centuries have not been sufficient for them to come to an agreement. Forgetting the most important of the divine precepts, which Jesus placed as the corner stone of His edifice as an express condition for salvation, namely charity, fraternity and love for one's neighbour; those sects launched curses at each other and cast themselves one upon the other, the strongest crushing the weakest, drowning themselves in blood and annihilating themselves by torture and fire. After having conquered Paganism, these Christians who had been the persecuted, became the persecutors. Fire and steel were used to implant the Cross of the Shepherd, despite its being unblemished in both worlds. It is a confirmed fact that religious wars have been the most cruel and produced more victims than all the political wars put together. In no other warfare are so many acts of atrocity or barbarism practised.

Is this the fault of the Christian Doctrine? Clearly not, as this formally condemns all violence. Did Jesus ever tell His disciples to go out and kill or commit massacres or burn those who did not believe? No! On the contrary, He always said that all men are brothers, that God is supremely merciful, that we must love our neighbours and our enemies, and do good to those who persecute us. He also said that all those who kill by the sword will perish by the sword. Therefore the responsibility does not lie with the Doctrine of Jesus, but rather with those who have falsely interpreted it and turned it into an instrument for the satisfaction of their own passions. It belongs to those who have despised these words: "My Kingdom is not of this world."

In His profound wisdom Jesus had foreseen these happenings. But these things were inevitable because they are inherent in the inferior nature of Man, which cannot be transformed suddenly. It was necessary for Christianity to go through this long and cruel test during all these centuries in order to show its strength, seeing that despite all the evil committed in its name it has remained pure and uncontaminated. This has never been disputed. The blame has always fallen upon those who have abused it. At every act of intolerance it has always been said that if Christianity were better understood and more widely practised this would never have happened.

When Jesus declared: "Think not that I am come to bring peace on Earth, but a sword," the thought behind this statement was as follows:

«Do not believe that My Doctrine will establish itself pacifically, because it will bring bloody battles wherein My name will be used as a pretext, because mankind will not have understood Me or will not have wanted to understand. Brothers and sisters, separated by their respective beliefs, will unsheath their swords one against the other and division will reign within the breast of families whose members do not share the same beliefs. I have come to launch fire upon the Earth so as to purge it of errors and prejudices, just as you put fire to a field in order to destroy the weeds; and I am in a hurry for the fire to start so the purification may be that much quicker, seeing that truth will come forth triumphantly from this conflict. War will be succeeded by peace, hate between two parties by universal brotherhood, the darkness of fanaticism by the clarity of enlightened faith. Then when the field is prepared I will send a *Comforter, the Spirit of Truth, which will re-establish all things.* This is to say that by understanding the meaning of My words the more enlightened people will finally comprehend and so put an end to the killing of brother by brother, which has disunited all the children of the same Father. Finally then, being tired of combat which has brought no result, only desolation and perturbation, even into the hearts of families, Man will recognise where his true interests lie in relation to this world and the next. He will see on which side are to be found the friends or enemies of his tranquility. Then all will put themselves under the same banner which is that of charity, and all things will re-establish themselves on Earth in accordance with truth and the principles which I have taught.»

17. Spiritism has come at the appointed time to realise the promises made by Christ. However, this cannot be done without first destroying all abuse. Just as happened with Jesus, Spiritism is faced with pride, selfishness, ambition, greed and blind fanaticism, which when taken to their last defences, try to block the pathway causing hinderance and persecutions. Therefore it too has to do battle. But the time of battles and bloody outrages is passing so that those to be suffered from now on will be of a moral nature, and even these are nearing the end. The first lasted for centuries, but these will last but a few years, because instead of breaking forth in only one place at a time, the light now shines from all points of the globe and will quickly open the eyes of those who are still blind.

18. These words of Jesus should be understood as referring to the wrath which His doctrine will provoke, the momentary conflicts which it will create and to the fights it will have to endure before it is established, just as happened to the Hebrews before they entered into the Promised Land. It should not be understood as inferring a predetermined design on His part to sow disorder and conflict. Evil comes from Man, never from Jesus. He was like the doctor who comes to cure, but whose medicine provokes a beneficial crisis in those who are sick.

CHAPTER 24

DO NOT HIDE THE LIGHT UNDER A BUSHEL

The light under a bushel. Why Jesus spoke in parables. —Do
not keep company with the Gentiles. — The healthy do not
need a doctor. — The courage of faith. — Carry your cross. He
who will save his life, shall lose it.

THE LIGHT UNDER A BUSHEL. WHY JESUS SPOKE IN PARABLES

1. *Neither do men light a candle, and put it under a bushel, but on a candlestick;
and it giveth light unto all that are in the house (Matthew, 5: 15).*

2. *No man, when he hath lighted a candle, covereth it with a vessel, or putteth it
under a bed; but setteth it on a candlestick that they which enter in may see the
light. For nothing is secret that shall not be made manifest; neither anything hid,
that shall not be known and come abroad (Luke, 8: 16 & 17).*

3. *And the disciples came and said unto Him, Why speaketh thou unto them in
parables? He answered and said unto them, Because it is given unto you to know
the mysteries of the Kingdom of Heaven, but to them it is not given. For whosoever
hath, to him shall be given, and he shall have more abundance: but whosoever
hath not, from him shall be taken away even that he hath. Therefore speak I to
them in parables: because they seeing see not; and hearing they hear not, neither
do they understand. And in them is fulfilled the prophecy of Esaias, which saith,
By hearing ye shall hear, and shall not understand; and seeing ye shall see, and
shall not perceive: for this people's heart is waxed gross, and their ears are dull of
hearing, and their eyes they have closed; lest at any time they should see with
their eyes, and hear with their ears, and should understand with their heart, and
should be converted, and I should heal them (Matthew, 13: 10-15).*

4. It appears strange to hear Jesus say that the light should not be covered up
when He constantly hid the meaning of His words under the veil of allegories,
which are not understood by everyone. However, He explains this when He
says to His disciples: "I speak to them in parables because they are not ready
to understand certain things. They see, they listen, but do not understand. So
it would have been useless to have told them everything at this time.
Nevertheless, I have told you, because it has been given to you to understand
these mysteries." So He treated the people as you would children whose ideas

had not yet developed. In this manner we come to comprehend the real meaning of the words: "Neither do men light a candle, and put it under a bushel, but on a candlestick, and it giveth light unto all that are in the house." This sentence does not mean that we should reveal all things, without due consideration as to the convenience of this revelation. All teaching should be proportional according to the intelligence of those to be taught, because there are certain people for whom a too brilliant light would only blind, without enlightening them in any way.

The same thing happens to mankind in general, as can happen to an individual. The generations have their infancy, their youth and their maturity. Each thing must come at the right moment; the seed when sown out of season will not germinate. But what prudence holds back momentarily, soon or later will be discovered because when the correct degree of development has been reached Man seeks for himself the living light as he feels obscurity weighing upon him. God having given him intelligence to understand and be guided amongst the things of the Earth and of Heaven, Man then seeks to rationalize his faith. It is at this point that he must not put the candle under the bushel, seeing that *without the light of reason faith becomes weak* (See chapter 19, item 7).

5. If providence then in its wise precaution only reveals the truth gradually, it is obvious that these truths are disclosed in proportion as humanity shows itself sufficiently mature to receive them. Providence holds them in reserve and not under a bushel. However as Man enters into possession of them he almost always hides them from the masses, with the intention of dominating the people. These are the ones who truly place the light under a bushel. This is why every religion has its mysteries whose examination is prohibited. But as these religions begin to become outdated, so science and intelligence have advanced and broken through the veil of mystery. Having become adult, the masses could then penetrate to the bottom of these matters and so remove from their faith that which was contrary to their observations.

Absolute mysteries cannot exist and Jesus was right when He said that there was no secret that would not come to be known. Everything which is hidden will be discovered one day, and what man still does not comprehend will be revealed in succession, in more advanced worlds, when he reaches purification. Here on Earth Man still finds himself as in a thick fog.

6. We ask ourselves what advantage can be gained from the multitude of parables whose meaning remains impenetrable? It must be noted that Jesus only expressed Himself in parables in areas which were rather abstract in the doctrine. But having declared charity to one's neighbour and humility as the basic conditions for salvation, everything He said in this respect is completely clear, explicit and without any ambiguities. This is as it should be, this being a rule of conduct, a rule that everyone had to comprehend in order to be able to observe it. This was the essential point for the ignorant masses to whom He said only: "This is what you need to do in order to reach Heaven." On other

matters He only disclosed His thoughts to His disciples. This was because they were more advanced, both morally and intellectually, so that Jesus could initiate them in the knowledge of more abstract truths. This is also why He said: *to those who already have, even more shall be given* (See chapter 18, item 15).

Nevertheless, even with the apostles He was not precise on many points, the complete understanding in these areas being reserved for later times. It was these parts which caused so many diverse interpretations until science on the one hand and Spiritism on the other hand revealed the new laws of Nature, so making the real meaning perceptible.

7. Today Spiritism projects its light over an immense number of obscure points. But it does not do this without due consideration. When the Spirits give their teachings they conduct themselves with admirable prudence. They consider gradually, one by one, the various known parts of the Doctrine, leaving the other parts to be revealed only when it will be opportune to bring them forth from obscurity. If they had presented the complete Doctrine right from the first moment fewer people would have shown themselves disposed to accept it, and those who were not prepared would have become frightened by it, so that the dissemination would have suffered as a consequence. So then if the Spirits have still not told everything outright, it is not because there are mysteries within the doctrine which only the privileged few may penetrate, nor is it because they have hidden the candle under the bushel, but because each piece of knowledge must come at the most opportune moment. They give time for each idea to mature and spread before presenting another, and for *events to prepare the way for the acceptance of new ideas.*

DO NOT KEEP COMPANY WITH THE GENTILES

8. *These twelve Jesus sent forth, and commanded them, saying, Go not into the way of the Gentiles, and into any city of the Samaritans enter ye not: but go rather to the lost sheep of the house of Israel. And as ye go, preach, saying, the Kingdom of Heaven is at hand (Matthew, 10: 5-7).*

9. On many occasions Jesus shows us that His vision was not confined to the Jewish people alone, but rather embraced all humanity. Moreover, if He told His apostles not to go to the pagans, it was not that He disdained conversing with them, which would not have been at all charitable; rather it was that the Jews, who already believed in one God and were waiting for a Messiah, were already prepared through the Laws of Moses and the Prophets to accept His Word. With the pagans, where even the base was lacking, there would have been everything to do and the apostles were not yet sufficiently enlightened for so difficult a task. This is why He said to them: "Go rather to the lost sheep of Israel," that is to say, go and sow in lands that are already cleared. Jesus knew that the conversion of the Gentiles would happen at a later date. Indeed, later on the apostles did go to plant a cross in the very heart of paganism.

10. These words can also be applied to the adepts and disseminators of Spiritism. The systematically incredulous, the obstinate mockers and the profit-seeking adversaries are today what the Gentiles were to the apostles. So to follow their example, go first to make converts amongst those of goodwill, those who desire enlightenment, where a fertile seed may be found and where there are many, without wasting time with those who do not want to see or hear, where they resist all the more out of pride the greater the importance that is put upon their conversion. It is better to open the eyes of a hundred blind people who wish to see clearly, than of only one person who takes pleasure in darkness, because by proceeding in this manner it is possible to increase in greater numbers those who will uphold the cause. Leaving some people undisturbed is not a case of showing indifference, but simply good sense. The time will come when they will have been persuaded by public opinion and by hearing the same information being constantly repeated all around them. Then they will think they have accepted the ideas voluntarily, by their own impulse and not under pressure from others. In addition, there are ideas which are like seeds that cannot germinate out of season, nor in land that has not been previously prepared. So it is better to wait for the right time and cultivate those that are the first to germinate, in order that the later germinating ones do not abort by virtue of too intensive a cultivation.

At the time of Jesus and as a consequence of the narrow-minded and materialistic ideas in vogue, everything was localized and circumscribed. The house of Israel was but a small nation, the Gentiles being other small nations around them. Today the ideas have been universalized and spiritualized. The new light is the privilege of no one nation; no barriers exist for it; the focus point is in all places and all men are brothers. The Gentiles are no longer a nation; they are only an opinion which is accepted in all places and over which truth will triumph little by little, just as Christianity triumphed over Paganism. These opinions are no longer combated with weapons of war, but with the force of ideas.

THE HEALTHY DO NOT NEED A DOCTOR

11. *As Jesus sat at meat in the house, behold, many publicans and sinners came down and sat with Him and His disciples. And when the Pharisees saw it they said unto His disciples, Why eateth your master with publicans and sinners? But when Jesus heard that, He said unto them, They that be whole need not a physician, but they that are sick (Matthew, 9: 10-12).*

12. Jesus addressed Himself most especially to those who were poor and deprived as they had the greatest need for consolation, together with the blind, the humble and those of good faith, because they asked Him to enlighten them. He did not address Himself to those who were proud or those who believed they had all the knowledge they needed and wished for no more (See the INTRODUCTION: items entitled PUBLICANS and THE TAX COLLECTORS).

These words, and many others, find their most fitting application within Spiritism. There are those who are sometimes surprised that mediumship is given to persons of little worth and capable of its misuse. They say that it seems that such a precious faculty should be given exclusively to those who are most deserving of it.

Before anything else, we must say that mediumship stems from a certain organic disposition and therefore anyone may be gifted with this ability, in the same way that we are gifted to see, hear and speak. Moreover, there is nothing that Man cannot abuse by means of his free-will. If God had only conceded speech, for example, to those capable of speaking ill, then there would be more dumb people than those able to speak. God has given Man various faculties together with the liberty of their use. But those who abuse them are also punished by Him.

If the possibility of communicating with the Spirits were to be given only to the most worthy, who would dare to make such a claim? Furthermore, where is the boundary between worthiness and unworthiness? Mediumship is conferred without distinction so that the Spirits can bring enlightenment to all walks of life, to all classes of people, to rich and poor alike, to those who are honest so they may be fortified in their goodness, and also to the corrupt so they may be corrected. Are these not the sick who need a doctor? Why then would God, Who does not wish for the death of sinners, deprive them of the help that can pull them out of the mire? The good Spirits come to their help and the personal advice which is received is of a nature which will impress them in a manner more striking than if it had been received indirectly. God, in His goodness, wishing to spare them the work of having to go out and get help from afar, puts the light straight into their hands. Are they not even more guilty for failing to notice this fact? Can they excuse themselves by claiming ignorance, when their own condemnation has been written, seen, heard and spoken by themselves? If they do not take advantage of this, then they will be punished by means of the loss or perversion of the faculty which was bestowed. In this case, evil Spirits will take hold, obsessing and deceiving them. But this will not lessen the receiving of real afflictions with which God punishes His unworthy servants and those whose hearts are hardened by pride and selfishness.

Mediumship does not necessarily imply habitual relations with Superior Spirits. It is merely an *aptitude* to serve as an instrument, which may be more or less useful to Spirits in general. So then a good medium is not one who communicates with ease, but one who is agreeable to the good Spirits and who is helped only by them. It is solely in this sense that the excellence of moral qualities becomes the all-powerful influence in mediumship.

THE COURAGE OF FAITH

13. *Whosoever therefore shall confess me before men, him will I confess also before My Father which is in Heaven. But whosoever shall deny me before men, him will I also deny before My Father which is in Heaven (Matthew, 10: 32 & 33).*

14. *For whosoever shall be ashamed of me and my words, of him shall the Son of Man be ashamed, when He shall come in His own glory, and in His Father's, and of the holy angels (Luke, 9: 26).*

15. To have the courage of one's beliefs has always been held in great esteem by mankind. This is because there is merit in facing dangers, persecutions, contradictions and even simple sarcasms, to which all those who openly proclaim their ideas are almost always exposed, especially when those ideas are not to the general liking. Here as in everything, the merit is in proportion to the circumstances and the importance of the result. There is always weakness in drawing back from the consequences entailed by opinions, and in denying them. But there are some cases in which this constitutes an act of cowardice as great as the one committed by fleeing from the moment of battle.

Jesus denounced this kind of cowardice from the particular point of view of His doctrine, by saying that if anyone was ashamed of His words then He too would be ashamed of them; that He would disown the person who repudiated Him and would only acknowledge before the Father, Who is in Heaven, those who publicly acknowledge Him. In other words *those who are afraid to confess themselves as disciples of truth are not worthy to be admitted into the kingdom of truth.* In this way they will lose the advantages of faith, because it is a selfish faith which they keep for themselves, hiding it for fear of the prejudice they may come to suffer in the world. Meanwhile those who put truth above all material interests and openly proclaim it, are working both for their own future and for that of others.

16. This is how it will be for the followers of Spiritism, because the Doctrine they profess is nothing more than the development and application of the Gospel teachings. Christ's words were also directed to them. They plant on Earth what will be harvested in the Spiritual world; and it is there that they will gather all the fruits of their courage and weaknesses.

CARRY YOUR CROSS. HE WHO WILL SAVE HIS LIFE SHALL LOSE IT

17. *Blessed are ye, when men shall hate you, and when they shall separate you from their company, and shall reproach you, and cast out your name as evil, for the Son of Man's sake. Rejoice ye in that day, and leap for joy: for, behold, your reward is great in heaven: for in the like manner did their fathers unto the Prophets (Luke, 6: 22 & 23).*

18. *And when He had called the people unto Him with His disciples also, He said unto them, Whosoever will come after me, let him deny himself, and take up his cross, and follow me. For whosoever will save his life shall lose it; but whosoever shall lose his life for My sake and the Gospel's, the same shall save it. For what shall it profit a man, if he shall gain the whole world and lose his own soul? (Mark, 8: 34-36. Also Luke, 9: 23-25; Matthew, 10: 39; John 12: 24 & 25).*

19. Jesus said: "Rejoice when men hate and persecute you for My sake, seeing that you will be recompensed in Heaven." These words should be understood in the following manner: Consider yourself blessed when there are fellow creatures who, by their ill-will towards you, give you the opportunity to prove the sincerity of your faith, seeing that the evil they do to you will only result in your benefit. Lament their blindness; however, do not curse them.

Then He added: "Take up your cross, all those who wish to follow Me," by which He meant that you must courageously support the trials and tribulations which your faith may bring about, since the one who wishes to save their life and their property by renouncing Christ will lose all the advantages of Heaven; while those who lose everything here in this world, even to their life, for the sake of truth, will receive a prize for courage, perseverance and abnegation in the future life. But to those who have sacrificed the heavenly benefits for earthly pleasures God will say: "You have already received your recompense."

CHAPTER 25

SEEK AND YOU WILL FIND

If you help yourself then Heaven will come to your aid. — Behold the fowls of the air. — Provide not gold in your purse.

IF YOU HELP YOURSELF THEN HEAVEN WILL COME TO YOUR AID

1. *Ask, and it shall be given you; seek, and ye shall find; knock, and it shall be opened unto you: for every one that asketh receiveth; and he that seeketh findeth; and to him that knocketh it shall be opened. Or what man is there of you, whom if his son ask bread, will he give him a stone? Or if he ask a fish, will he give him a serpent? If ye then, being evil, know how to give good gifts unto your children, how much more shall your Father which is in Heaven give good things to them that ask Him? (Matthew, 7: 7-11).*

2. From an earthly point of view the maxim: *Seek and ye shall find* is the same as that other one: *Help yourself and the heavens will come to your aid.* This is the base of the *Law of Work* and consequently the *Law of Progress,* since progress is the child of work, seeing that this puts into action the force of intelligence. During mankind's infancy he only used his intelligence in seeking food, as a means of protection against the climate, and defending himself from his enemies. However, God has given Man something more than He gave to animals, which is *an incessant desire to better himself.* It is this desire which impells him to seek out the best ways of improving his position in life, which duly leads him to make discoveries, to invent things, and to perfect the sciences because it is science which gives him what he lacks. Through Man's research his intelligence heightens and his morals depurate. The needs of the body give way to those of the Spirit. After material nourishment Man needs spiritual nourishment. This is how he passes from savagery to civilization.

But the amount of progress achieved by each person during a single lifetime is very small indeed, in most cases even imperceptible. How then could humanity progress without pre-existence and the *re-existence* of the soul? If the souls who daily leave the Earth were never to return, then humanity would be constantly renewing itself with primitive elements, having everything still to do and learn. There would then be no reason why Man should be more advanced today than he was during the first epochs of the world, because at each birth all intellectual work would have to recommence. On the other hand, by returning with the degree of progress realised and acquiring something more each time, the soul then gradually passes from the barbaric state to that of *materialistic civilization*, and then on to one of *moral civilization* (See chapter 4, item 17).

3. If God had exempted Man from bodily work his limbs would have withered. If He had exempted him from intellectual work then his Spirit would have remained in a state of infancy, or mere animal instinct. This is why He made work a necessity by saying: *Seek and ye shall find; work and ye shall produce.* In this way you are the product of your work; you receive the merit of it and a recompense in accordance with what has been done.

4. It is by virtue of this principle that the Spirits do not help in sparing men the work of research by bringing them discoveries and inventions prepared and ready for use, in such a way that they would have nothing to do but accept what was put into their hands, without any inconvenience whatsoever, nor even to bend down and pick it up, nor yet to think about it. If things were like that then the laziest could enrich themselves and the most ignorant could become wise at the cost of no effort, and both would have merits attributed to them for things they had not done. *No, the Spirits do not come to exempt Man from the Law of Work, but only to show him the goal to be reached and the pathway that leads there, by saying: walk and you will get there.* You will find your path strewn with stones; look upon them and then move them. We will give you the necessary strength if you care to utilize it (See THE MEDIUMS' BOOK, (1) chapter 26, item 291 onwards).

5. From the moral point of view, these words of Jesus signify that if we ask for the light which will show us the way, it will be given; if we ask for strength to resist evil, we shall receive it; if we ask for the assistance of the good Spirits, then they will come to accompany us and, as did the angel of Tobias (2), they will guide us; if we ask for good counsel it will not be refused; if we knock on His door it will be opened. But we must ask with sincerity, faith, confidence and fervour. We must present ourselves with humility and not with arrogance, or else we will be abandoned to our own strength and the falls taken will be punishment for our pride.

This then is what is meant by the words: Seek and ye shall find; knock and it shall be opened.

---

(1) by ALLAN KARDEC
(2) See Book of Tobit, New Jerusalem Bible. (Translator's note.)

BEHOLD THE FOWLS OF THE AIR

6. *Lay not up for yourselves treasures upon Earth, where moth and rust doth corrupt, and where thieves break through and steal: but lay up for yourselves treasures in Heaven, where neither moth nor rust doth corrupt, and where thieves do not break through nor steal: for where your treasure is, there will your heart be also.*

Therefore I say unto you, Take no thought for your life, what ye shall eat, or what ye shall drink; nor yet for your body, what ye shall put on. Is not the life more than meat and the body than raiment?

Behold the fowls of the air: for they sow not, neither do they reap, nor gather into barns; yet your Heavenly Father feedeth them. Are ye not much better than they? Which of you by taking thought can add one cubit unto his stature?

And why take ye thought for raiment? Consider the lillies of the field, how they grow; they toil not, neither do they spin: and yet I say unto you, That even Solomon in all his glory was not arrayed like one of these. Wherefore, if God clothe the grass of the field, which today is and tomorrow is cast into the oven, shall He not much more clothe you, O ye of little faith?

Therefore, take no thought, saying, What shall we eat? or What shall we drink? or, Wherewithal shall we be clothed? (For after all these things do the Gentiles seek:) for your heavenly Father knoweth that ye have need of all these things.

But seek ye first the Kingdom of God, and His righteousness; and all these things shall be added unto you. Take therefore no thought for the morrow: for the morrow shall take thought for the things of itself. Sufficient unto the day is the evil thereof (Matthew, 6: 19-21 & 25-34).

7. In a literal translation these words would be a denial of all providence, of all work and consequently of all progress. With this kind of principle Man would be limited to waiting passively. His physical and intellectual strengths would remain inactive. If such were the normal conditions on Earth we would never have left the primitive state, and if this condition became the law today then it would only remain to live in total idleness. This could not have been the thought of Jesus, since this would be a contradiction of what He said on other occasions and also contradict the Laws of Nature. God created Man without clothes or shelter, but He gave him intelligence so as to be able to make them (See chapter 14, item 6 & chapter 25, item 2).

Consequently these words must not be seen as anything more than the poetical allegory of Providence, which never abandons those who put their confidence in her, but wishes that all work in their turn. If Providence does not always come in the form of material help, then it inspires those ideas from which is found the means of getting out of difficulty (See chapter 27, item 8).

God comprehends our necessities and provides for them when needed. Nevertheless, Man is insatiable in his desires and does not always know how to be content with what he has. Possessing what is necessary is not enough for him; he demands that which is superfluous. Then Providence leaves him to himself. Frequently he becomes unhappy through his own fault, and for having paid no attention to the voice which, through the intermediary of his conscience, has given him warning. In these cases the Lord lets him suffer the consequences so that it may serve as a lesson for the future (See chapter 5, item 4).

8. The Earth will produce sufficient to feed all its inhabitants when Man discovers how to administer the benefits which it offers according to the Laws of Justice, Charity and Love for one's neighbour. When fraternity reigns amongst all peoples, as it does amongst the provincials of any country, then the momentary superfluity of the one will overcome the insufficiency of another, and everyone will have what is necessary. Then the rich man will consider himself as one who possesses a great quantity of seeds. If he shares them with others they will produce a thousandfold for himself and for them. However, if he eats all the seeds himself, or wastes them and allows the surplus from what he ate to be lost, then nothing will be produced and he will take nothing out of this for others. If he hoards the seeds in his barn then the maggots will devour them. Hence Jesus had said: "Do not accumulate treasures on Earth because they are perishable, but accumulate them in Heaven where they are eternal." In other words, do not give material possessions more importance than the spiritual ones, and know how to sacrifice the first for the second (See chapter 16, item 7 onwards).

Charity and fraternity are not decreed under law. If one or the other is not in the heart then selfishness will rule. Consequently it is the task of Spiritism to see that they both penetrate the heart of man.

PROVIDE NOT GOLD IN YOUR PURSE

9. *Provide neither gold, nor silver, nor brass in your purses, nor scrip for your journey, neither two coats, neither shoes, nor yet staves: for the workman is worthy of his meat.*

10. *And in whatsoever city or town ye shall enter, enquire who in it is worthy; and there abide till ye go thence. And when ye come into an house, salute it. And if the house be worthy, let your peace be upon it: but if it be not worthy, let your peace return to you. And whosoever shall not receive you, nor hear your words, when ye depart out of that house or city, shake off the dust of your feet. Verily I say unto you, It shall be more tolerable for the land of Sodom and Gomorrha in the Day of Judgement, than for that city (Matthew, 10: 9-15).*

11. In those days there was nothing unusual in these words which Jesus directed to His apostles, on commanding them to announce the Glad Tidings for the first time. They were in accordance with the patriarchal customs of the

Orient, when the traveller was always made welcome in the tent. But then in those days travellers were very rare indeed. Among modern peoples the development of travel has created new customs. Those of ancient times are only conserved by very distant lands, where the great movement has not yet penetrated. If Jesus were to return today He could no longer tell His apostles to put themselves on the road without provisions.

Apart from their actual meaning, these words hold a very profound moral sense. In proffering them, Jesus was teaching His disciples to have confidence in Providence. What is more, by having nothing, they could not cause covetousness amongst those who received them. This was the way of distinguishing those who were selfish from those who were charitable. This is why He told them to: "Find out who is worthy of putting you up." or rather: who is human enough to clothe a traveller who has nothing with which to pay, as these are the ones who are worthy to receive your words and will be recognisable by their charity.

With regard to those who cared neither to receive them nor to listen to them, did He tell His disciples that they should curse them, that they should impose the teachings upon them, or that they should use violence and force so as to convert them? No, He simply told them to go away and seek others who were willing to listen.

Today Spiritism says the same thing to its followers. Do not violate any consciences. Do not force anyone to leave their faith in order to adopt yours. Do not excommunicate those who do not think as you do. Welcome all who come to join you, and leave in peace all those who are repelled by your ideas. Remind yourselves of the words of Christ. In other times the heavens were taken over by violence, but today they are taken over by mildness (See chapter 4, items 10 & 11).

CHAPTER 26

GIVE FOR FREE WHAT HAS BEEN RECEIVED GRATUITOUSLY

The gift of healing. — Paid prayers. — The moneychangers
expelled from the Temple. — Gratuitous mediumship.

THE GIFT OF HEALING

1. *Heal the sick, cleanse the lepers, raise the dead, cast out devils; freely ye have received, freely give (Matthew, 10: 8).*

2. "Give for free what has been received gratuitously," is what Jesus told His disciples. With this recommendation it is prescribed that no one be charged for something for which nothing has been paid. Now what they had received gratuitously was the faculty of healing those who were sick, and that of expelling devils, that is to say bad spirits. God gave them this faculty gratis for the alleviation of those who suffer and as a means of propagating faith. Jesus, then, recommended that they did not turn this into an object of commercialization, neither speculation, nor a means of livelihood.

PAID PRAYERS

3. *Then in the audience of all the people He said unto His disciples, Beware of the Scribes, which desire to walk in long robes, and love greetings in the markets, and the highest seats in the synagogues, and the chief rooms at feasts; which devour widows' houses, and for a shew make long prayers: the same shall receive greater damnation (Luke, 20: 45-47; also Mark, 12: 38-40 and Matthew, 23: 14).*

4. Jesus also said: Do not make charges for your prayers; do not do as the Scribes who 'on pretext of long prayers, *devoured the homes of widows,'* that is to say, they took possession of their fortunes. Prayer is an act of charity, an ecstasy of the heart. To charge someone for the prayers we direct to God in their name, is to transform oneself into a paid intermediary. Then prayer becomes a mere formula whose length is in proportion to the amount it cost. Moreover only one of the following can be true: either God measures or does not measure His blessings by the number of words used in a prayer. If these were necessary in large numbers, why then are so few said, or even none, for those who cannot pay? This is a lack of charity. If one word is sufficient then an excess of words is useless. How then can we charge for these prayers? This would be a corrupt practice.

God does not sell His benefits; He conceeds them. How then can one who is not an agent and cannot guarantee results, charge for a petition which may produce no results? It is not possible that God makes an act of clemency, kindness and justice, asked for because of His infinite mercy, subject to the payment of a sum of money and that if the sum were not paid, or was insufficient, then the justice, kindness and clemency would be suspended. Reason, good sense and logic tell us it is impossible that God, Who is absolute perfection, could delegate to imperfect beings the right to establish a price for His justice, which is like the Sun: it exists for all, rich and poor alike. As it is considered immoral to trade in the favours of any earthly sovereign, could it then be licit to commercialize those of the Sovereign of the Universe?

Yet another drawback is presented by paid prayers which is that the one who buys them judges themself, in most cases, to be relieved from the need to pray. They consider themselves exonerated, since they gave their money. We know that Spirits are touched by the fervour of the thoughts of those who are interested in them, but what fervour can be felt by one who arranges a third party to pray for them on payment of money? What kind of fervour has this third party when he delegates his task to another, and that one yet another and so on? Does this not reduce the efficiency of prayer to the value of currency?

THE MONEYCHANGERS EXPELLED FROM THE TEMPLE

5. *And they come to Jerusalem: and Jesus went into the temple, and began to cast out them that sold and bought in the temple, and overthrew the tables of the moneychangers, and the seats of them that sold doves; and would not suffer that any man should carry any vessel through the temple. And He taught, saying unto them, Is it not written, My house shall be called of all nations the House of Prayer? But ye have made it a den of thieves. And the Scribes and chief Priests heard it, and sought how they might destroy Him: for they feared Him, because all the people was astonished at His doctrine (Mark, 11: 15-18; and Matthew, 21: 12 & 13).*

6. Jesus expelled the merchants from the temple. With this act He condemned the trading of sacred things *in any form whatsoever,* God does not sell His blessings, neither His pardon, nor the right of entrance into the Kingdom of Heaven. Therefore Man has no right to stipulate a price for such things.

GRATUITOUS MEDIUMSHIP

7. Mediums today (since the Apostles also possessed mediumship) have equally received a faculty gratis from God. This is of being interpreters of the Spirits for the instruction of mankind, to show them the pathway of goodness, conducting them along by means of faith. Not to sell words which do not belong to the mediums, seeing that they are not fruits of *their conception, nor of*

their research, nor of their personal work. God wants the light to reach everyone. He does not want the poorest to be deprived of it so they can say they have no faith because they could not pay for it, nor that they did not have the consolation of receiving encouragement and testimony of affection from those they weep for, because they were too poor. This is why mediumship is not a privilege, and is to be found in all places. To make someone pay for it is to turn it away from its providential objective.

8. Those who understand the conditions in which good Spirits communicate, the feeling of repugnance they have towards everything which shows selfish interest, and know how little it takes to drive them away, could never accept that Superior Spirits are at the disposal of the first who comes along and evokes them, at so much per session. Simple good sense rejects such an idea. Would it not also be profanity to evoke for money those we respect or those who are dear to us? Beyond doubt communications can be obtained in this manner. But who can guarantee their sincerity? Spirits of a frivolous, deceitful, mocking nature, and all the bank of inferior Spirits who are not at all scrupulous, always come running ready to reply to whatever is asked with no regard for the truth. Those then who desire serious communications should before all else ask with seriousness, and following this, should inform themselves of the nature of the sympathies the medium may have with the beings from the Spirit world. Therefore the first conditions necessary to attract the benevolence of the good Spirits are humility, devotion, abnegation, and total disinterest, both *moral and material.*

9. Besides the moral question an effective consideration also presents itself which is no less important. This refers to the actual nature of the faculty itself. Serious mediumship cannot be, and never ever will be a profession; not just because it would be morally discredited and rapidly become mere fortune-telling; but because there is a material obstacle in opposition. Mediumship is a faculty which is essentially unstable, elusive, and variable, whose permanency no one can count upon. It is a very uncertain source for anyone wishing to exploit it, and can fail at the moment it is most needed. A talent acquired by study and work is another matter, and is for this very reason a skill which can be legitmately used to advantage. But mediumship is neither an art nor a skill; therefore it cannot become a profession. It only exists through the co-operation of the Spirits. If they are absent there is no mediumship. The aptitude can exist, but the exercise of it would be annuled. Also there is not a single medium in the world who can guarantee the obtaining of a spiritual phenomenon at any given moment. So then to exploit mediumship is to make use of something which does not really belong to that person. To state the contrary is to deceive the person being charged. What is more, it is not they themself whom the exploiter commands, but rather the concourse of Spirits, the souls of the dead, whose cooperation they put a price on. This idea causes instinctive repugnance. It was the trafficking, the exploitation by charlatans that degenerated into abuse, the ignorance, the incredulity and the

superstition which motivated its prohibition by Moses. Modern Spiritism, understanding the serious nature of this question, has completely discredited this exploitation, so elevating mediumship to the category of a *mission*. (See THE MEDIUMS' BOOK, 2nd part, chapter 28 and also HEAVEN AND HELL (1) 1st part, chapter 11).

10. Mediumship is something sacred which should be practised in a saintly and religious manner, and if there is one type of mediumship which requires this condition even more absolutely than the others, it is that of healing (2). A doctor gives the fruits of his study, which were often gained at the cost of painful sacrifices. A magnetizer gives his own fluids, sometimes even his health. A price can be put upon these. A curing medium however, retransmits healing fluids from the good Spirits, and consequently has no right to sell them. Jesus and His Apostles, although poor, did not charge for the cures they obtained.

So then, those who lack the necessary means of financial support can seek their funds wherever they like, except within mediumship, and if necessary only dedicate their spare time to this work after material needs have been satisfied. The Spirits will take into consideration the devotion and sacrifices, whereas they will turn away from those who expect to turn them into a ladder for material ascension.

---

(1) by ALLAN KARDEC.
(2) In Spiritism the word HEALING is understood to mean restorative work carried out by Spirits using someone, possibly a medium, as their instrument. (Translator's note.)

CHAPTER 27

ASK AND IT SHALL BE GIVEN

The quality of prayers. — The efficacy of prayer. — The action
of prayer. Transmission of thought.— Intelligible prayers. —
Prayer for the dead and for suffering Spirits. — INSTRUCTIONS
FROM THE SPIRITS: The way in which to pray. —Happiness
proportioned by prayer.

THE QUALITY OF PRAYERS

1. *And when thou prayest, thou shalt not be as the hypocrites are: for they love to pray standing in the synagogues and in the corner of the streets, that they may be seen of men. Verily I say unto you, They have their rewards. But thou, when thou prayest, enter into thy closet, and when thou hast shut thy door, pray to thy Father which is in secret; and thy father which seeth in secret shall reward thee openly. But when ye pray, use not vain repetitions, as the heathen do: for they think that they shall be heard for their much speaking. Be not ye therefore like unto them: for your Father knoweth what things ye have need of, before ye ask Him (Matthew, 6: 5-8).*

2. *And when ye stand praying, forgive, if ye have ought against any: that your Father also which is in Heaven may forgive you your trespasses (Mark, 11: 25 & 26).*

3. *And He spake this parable unto certain which trusted in themselves that they were righteous, and despised others: Two men went up into the temple to pray; the one a Pharisee and the other a publican. The Pharisee stood and prayed thus with himself, God, I thank ye, that I am not as other men are, extortioners, unjust, adulterers or even as this publican. I fast twice a week, I give tithes of all that I possess. And the publican, standing afar off, would not lift up so much as his eyes unto Heaven, but smote upon his breast, saying, God be merciful unto me a sinner. I tell you, this man went down to his house justified rather than the other: for everyone that exalteth himself shall be abased; and he that humbleth himself shall be exalted (Luke, 18: 9-14).*

4. Jesus clearly defined the quality of prayer. He said that when you pray you should not make yourself conspicuous, but rather pray in secret. Do not prolong your prayers because it is not by the multiplicity of the words that you will be heard, but by their sincerity. Before praying, if you have anything against another, forgive them, seeing that prayer is not pleasing to God if it does not come from a heart cleansed of all sentiments which are contrary to

charity. Finally, pray with humility, as did the Publican, and not with pride as did the Pharisee. Look at your defects, not at your qualities, and if you compare yourself to others, look for what is bad in yourself (See chapter 10, items 7 & 8).

5. *Therefore I say unto you, What things soever ye desire, when ye pray, believe that ye receive them and ye shall have them (Mark 11: 24).*

6. There are those who contest the effectiveness of prayer on the grounds that, as God knows all our needs, it is useless to enumerate them to Him. Those who think this, then add that seeing that everything in the Universe is linked together by eternal laws, then our petitions cannot change God's decrees.

Beyond all doubt there are natural and immutable laws which cannot be annulled at the caprice of each individual; but from this fact to the belief that all circumstances in life are submitted to fatality is a long step indeed. If it were like that, then Man would be a passive instrument without free-will or initiative. In this hypothesis it would only remain for Man to bow down his head in submission before all occurances, without making any effort to avoid them, and should not try to ward off dangers. God did not grant reason and intelligence for Man not to use them, willpower for him not to desire things, nor activity for him to remain inactive. As Man is free to act one way or the other, for himself and towards others, the consequences depend on what he does or does not do. By his initiative there are events which forcibly escape fatality and yet do not destroy the harmony of the universal laws, just as the quickening or slowing down of the pendulum of a clock does not annul the law of movement upon which the mechanism is based. God then can accede to certain petitions without destroying the immunity of those laws which govern the whole, as consent is always dependant on His Will.

7. From the maxim: "Whatever you ask for through prayer will be granted," it would be illogical to conclude that one can receive just by asking, and unjust to accuse Providence if a request made is not conceded, because it is known what is best for our own good. This is what happens to a prudent father who refuses to give his son certain things which would be against his own interests. Generally, Man only sees the present moment. Meanwhile if the suffering is useful to our future happiness, then God will let us suffer, just as a surgeon allows the patient to suffer an operation which will cure him.

What God will concede if we direct ourselves to Him with confidence is courage, patience and resignation. What He will also concede are the means of resolving situations with the help of ideas suggested to us by good Spirits at God's instigation, whereby we retain the merit for the decisions taken. God helps all those who help themselves according to the maxim: "Help yourself and the Heavens will come to your aid." But He does not help those who, without using their own faculties, wait for outside assistance. Nevertheless in most cases what Man desires is to be helped by miracles, without using any effort of his own (See chapter 25, No. 1 and following items).

8. Let us take an example. A man finds himself lost in the desert. Thirst is torturing him terribly. Fainting, he falls to the ground. He asks God to help him and waits. No angels will come to give him water. However, what does happen is that a good Spirit *suggests* the idea of picking himself up and taking one of the paths that are before him. By pure mechanical movement, uniting what is left of his strength, he gets up, walks and discovers not far away a brook. On sighting this he gains courage. If he has faith he exclaims: "Thank you dear God, for the idea you inspired and for the strength you gave me." If he is without faith he will say: "What a good idea *I had.* How *lucky* I was to take the right-hand path and not the one on the left! Chance sometimes serves one admirably! I must congratulate myself for my courage and for not being defeated!"

But you may ask why the Spirit did not say clearly: "Follow that path and you will find what you need"? Why did the Spirit not show himself, guide him and sustain him in his disanimation? In that way the man would have been convinced of the intervention of Providence. Firstly, so as to teach him that each person must help themself and make use of their strength. Secondly, because the man doubted His existence God put the confidence he had in Him to the test, as well as testing his submission to His will. The man was in the situtation of the child who falls down and because someone is with him starts to cry and waits to be picked up. If the same child saw no one he would make the effort and get up by himself. If the angel which accompanied Tobias had said: "I am sent by God to guide you on your journey and preserve you from all danger," then Tobias could claim no merit. In entrusting himself to his companion he would not even have had to think. This is why the angel only made himself known after the return.

THE ACT OF PRAYER. TRANSMISSION OF THOUGHT

9. Prayer is an invocation through which, by means of thought, Man enters into communication with the being to whom he directed himself. This may be for the purpose of asking for something, giving thanks or as a glorification. We may pray for ourselves or for others, for the living or for the dead. Prayers addressed to God are heard by those Spirits who are charged with the execution of His will. All those addressed to good Spirits are referred to God. When someone prays to beings other than God, these are serving as mediators or intercessors, because nothing can happen without God's wishes.

10. Spiritism makes the act of prayer understandable by explaining how thought is transmitted, either when the Spirit to whom we are praying comes to our help, or when our thoughts raise themselves up to this being. In order to understand what happens in this circumstance, it is necessary to consider all incarnate and discarnate beings as immersed in the Universal Cosmic Fluid which occupies space, as we on Earth are immersed in the atmosphere. This fluid receives an impulse from will-power, which is the vehicle of thought just as air is the vehicle for sound, with the difference that the vibrations of air are circumscribed, whereas those of the Universal Cosmic Fluid extend infinitely.

So when a thought is directed at someone either on Earth or in space, from an incarnate to a discarnate being, or vice-versa, a fluidic current is established between them which transmits the thought from one to the other, just as air transmits sound.

The energy contained in this current remains proportional to the force behind the thought and the desire. This is how the Spirits hear the prayers directed to them wherever they may be. It is also how Spirits communicate amongst themselves, how they transmit their inspirations to us and how contacts are established at a distance between incarnates.

This explanation has in mind especially those who do not understand the utility of completely mystical prayer. It is not meant to seemingly materialise prayer, but rather to make its effect intelligible by showing it can have direct and effective results. But this does not make it any the less subordinate to God's wishes; He being the Supreme Judge of all things, it is only through His wishes that the action of prayer may become effective.

11. It is through prayer that Man obtains the assistance of the good Spirits who come running to sustain him in his good resolutions and inspire wholesome ideas. In this manner he acquires the moral strength necessary to be able to surmount all difficulties, and come back to the straight and narrow path should he at any time stray from it. By these means he can also turn away from himself all the evil which he attracts through his faults. For example: a man loses his health due to his excesses and so leads a life of suffering till the termination of his days. Has he then the right to complain if he does not obtain the cure he so desires? No, because he could have found the strength to resist temptation through the act of prayer.

12. If we divided the evils of life into two parts, one being those which Man cannot avoid and the other those tribulations of which he himself is the principal cause, due to carelessness and excesses, (see chapter 5, item 4) we would see that the number in the second group far exceeds those in the first. So it is evident that Man is the author of the greater part of his afflictions and that they could be avoided if he always behaved with prudence and wisdom.

It is no less certain that these miseries are the result of our infractions against God's Law and that, if we duly observed these Laws, we would be completely happy. If we did not exceed the limit of what is necessary for the satisfaction of our needs, we would not have the sicknesses which are provoked as a consequence of these excesses; nor would we experience the vicissitudes which derive from them. If we put a limit on our ambitions we would not have to fear ruin; if we did not desire to raise ourselves higher than we are able, we would not have to be afraid of falling; if we were humble, we would not suffer the deception of hurt pride; if we practised the law of charity we would not be slanderers, jealous or envious, and so would avoid arguments and fights. If we did no evil to anyone we would not need to fear vengeance, etc.

Admitting that Man can do nothing with respect to other evils, and that prayer would be useless in ridding him of them; would it not mean a great deal to have the possibility of exempting ourselves from those ills which stem from our own behaviour? Here it is easy to conceive the action played by prayer, which aims at attracting wholesome inspirations from the good Spirits, and in asking them for strength to resist our bad thoughts, whose realisation could be disastrous to us. In this case, *what the prayers do is not to remove the wrong from us, but turn us away from our bad thoughts which cause us harm. The prayers in no way prevent the fulfilling of God's laws, nor do they suspend the course of the laws of Nature. They stop us from infringing these laws by guiding our free will.* Yet they act by default, in an imperceptible manner, so as not to subjugate our free-will. Man finds himself in the postion of one who solicits good counsel and then puts it into action; but is always free to follow the advice or not. God desires it to be like this, so that Man can have responsibility for his actions, thereby leaving him the merit of the choice between good and evil. This is what Man can always be sure of obtaining if he asks fervently, and this is the kind of situation where, above all, the words "Ask and it shall be given" can be applied.

Could not the effects of prayer, even when reduced to these proportions, bring immense results? It has been reserved for Spiritism to prove its action through the revelation of the relationship existing between the physical and spiritual worlds. But its effects are not limited just to these results.

Prayer is recommended by all the Spirits. To renounce it is to ignore the benevolence of God; to reject for oneself His assistance and for others the good that we can do.

13. On attending to a request which has been addressed to Him, God desires to recompense the intention, the devotion and the faith of the one who prays. This is why the prayers of a good person have greater merit in God's eyes and are always more effective, because the corrupt and evil person cannot pray with the same fervour and confidence which comes only from a sentiment of true piety. From a selfish heart, the one who prays only from the lips, there can come *only words,* and never a charitable impulse which is what gives force to prayer. So clearly can this be understood, that on asking for the prayers of another person instinctively preference will be given to those whose conduct, it is felt, will be more agreeable to God because they will be more promptly heard.

14. As prayer exercises a type of magnetic action, it could be supposed that its effect would depend on fluidic power. However, this is not so. To be precise, Spirits exercise this action on Man so as to overcome any insufficiency in those who pray, either by direct influence *in his name,* or by giving him momentarily an exceptional force when they judge him deserving of this grace, or when it can be useful to him.

The person who does not consider themself sufficiently good as to exercise a wholesome influence, should not refrain from praying for the good of another because of a mistaken belief of being unworthy to be heard. The consciousness of their own inferiority constitutes a test in humility, which is always pleasing to God, Who then takes into account the charitable intention which animated their intention. Fervour and confidence in God are the first steps in the return to goodness, for which the good Spirits feel themselves blessed in being able to offer stimulation. Prayer is repelled only from *the prideful who deposit faith in their own power and merits, believing it possible to superimpose themselves upon the Will of the eternal Father.*

15. The power of prayer lies in the thought and does not depend on words, the place or the moment in which it is proffered. Therefore it is possible to pray in all places, at any time, alone or with others. The influence of a place or time is only felt according to the circumstances which favour the meditation. *Communal prayer has a more powerful action when all who are praying join together in a heartfelt thought and envisage the same objective,* since it is as if many beseeched together in one voice. But it will do no good for a large number of people to gather together for prayer if each one acts in isolation, on their own account. A hundred people can pray selfishly, whereas two or three joined by the same aspirations, praying like true brothers and sisters in Christ, will give more power to their prayer than would the hundred selfish persons (See chapter 28, items 4 & 5).

INTELLIGIBLE PRAYERS

16. *Therefore if I know not the meaning of the voice, I shall be unto him that speaketh a barbarian, and he that speaketh shall be a barbarian unto me. For if I pray in an unknown tongue, my spirit prayeth, but my understanding is unfruitful. Else when thou shalt bless with the spirit, how shall he that occupieth the room of the unlearned say Amen at thy giving of thanks, seeing he understandeth not what thou sayest? For thou verily givest thanks well, but the other is not edified (I Corinthians, 14: 11, 14, 16 & 17).*

17. The value of prayer comes from the thought to which it is united. So it is impossible to join any thought to something that is not understood, since what is not understood cannot touch the heart. For the great majority of human beings prayers that are said in an unknown language are nothing more than a conglomeration of words which say nothing to the Spirit. In order for prayer to touch one, it is necessary for each word to awaken an idea, and when the words are not comprehended they are unable to do this. It would be merely a simple formula, whose virtue depended on the greater or lesser number of times it was repeated. Many pray from duty, others from obedience to habit; this is why they judge themselves to be exonerated from their duty after having prayed a determined prayer a sufficient number of times, in a certain order. God reads what passes deep in our hearts. He scrutinizes our thought and our sincerity; therefore in judging Him to be more sensitive to the format rather than the depth is to discredit Him (See chapter 28, item 2).

PRAYERS FOR SUFFERING SPIRITS AND THE DEAD

18. Suffering Spirits ask for prayers and these are useful to them, because on recognising that someone thinks of them they feel comforted and less unhappy. However, prayer has a more direct action on them by reanimating them and instilling in them a desire to elevate themselves through repentance, by making amends, and can turn them away from bad thoughts. It is in this sense that prayers can not only alleviate, but can also shorten their suffering (See HEAVEN & HELL, second part — Examples).

19. There are some people who do not accept the offering of prayers for the dead, as according to their belief, the soul has only two alternatives — to be saved or to be eternally condemned to suffering — which would result in prayer being useless in either case. Without discussing the merits of this belief, let us admit for a moment the reality of eternal unpardonable penitence which our prayers are impotent to interrupt. We ask if, even in this hypothesis, it would be logical, charitable or Christian to refuse prayer for the retrobate. However impotent these might be in liberating them, would these prayers not be a demonstration of pity, capable of softening their suffering? On Earth, when a man is condemned to perpetual prison, even if there was not a minimum chance of obtaining a pardon, is it forbidden for a charitable person to help alleviate the weight of the sentence? When someone is attacked by an incurable disease, there being no hope of cure, should we abandon the person without offering some kind of relief? Remind yourselves that amongst the wicked you may find someone who has been dear to you, perhaps a friend, a father or mother, a son or daughter; and ask yourself if, because of your belief that there is no possibility of a pardon, you would refuse a glass of water to mitigate their thirst? Or a balsam which would heal their wounds? Would you not do for them what you would do for one condemned to the galleys? Would you not give them proof of your love and console them? No, this idea would not be Christian. A belief which hardens the heart cannot be allied to one of a God who puts the duty of loving one's neighbour in first place.

The non-existence of eternal punishment does not imply a denial of temporary penalty, given that it is not possible for God in His justice to confound good with evil. In this case to deny the efficiency of prayer would be to deny the efficacy of consolation, encouragement, and good advice. This would be equal to denying the strength we absorb from the moral assistance received from those who wish us well.

20. Others base their ideas on a more specific reason: that of the immutability of Divine decree. God, they say, cannot modify His decisions just when asked by one of His creatures, because if this were so then nothing on Earth would have stability. Therefore Man has nothing to ask of God; it only rests for him to submit and adore Him.

In this idea there is a false interpretation of the principle of the immutability of Divine Law or, better still, an ignorance of this law with regard to future penalties. This law is revealed by the Spirits of the Lord at this time, now that Man is sufficiently mature to understand what, within faith, conforms to or is contrary to the Divine attributes.

According to the doctrine of the absolute eternity of all punishment, the remorse and repentance of the culprit are not taken into account. All desire to better himself is useless, for he is condemned to remain eternally evil. However, if he were condemned for a determined period of time, then the punishment would cease when that time had expired. But who can say that by then he will have improved his sentiments? Who can say, as shown by many who have been condemned on Earth, that on leaving prison he will not be just as bad as before? In the first case, it would be keeping a man under the pain of punishment after he had become good; in the second, it would be the granting of amnesty to one who continues to be guilty. God's law is more provident than that; being always just, impartial and merciful, it places no fixed duration for punishment whatever the case may be. This law can be resumed in the following manner:

21. «Man always suffers the consequences of his errors. There is no infraction of God's laws which does not have its punishment.

«The severity of the penalty is proportional to the gravity of the offence.

«The duration of the penalty for an error is *indeterminate, being subordinate to the repentance of the culprit and his return to goodness;* the penalty lasts as long as the evil. It will be perpetual if the persistance in doing evil is also perpetual; it is of short duration if repentance comes quickly.

«From the moment the culprit cries for mercy God listens and sends hope. But the simple fact of remorse for the evil done is not enough; it is necessary that reparation be made. This then is why the guilty party is submitted to new tests wherein he can, by his own will, do good in reparation for the evil that was done.

«In this manner Man constantly chooses his own destiny. He may shorten his anguish, or prolong it indefinitely. His happiness or unhappiness depends on his will to do good.»

This is the law; the *immutable* law which conforms to the goodness and justice of God.

In this manner the guilty and unhappy Spirit can always save himself, because God's law establishes the condition by which this becomes possible. What the Spirit is lacking in most cases is the will-power, the strength and the courage. If by our prayers we can inspire this will-power; if we uphold the sufferer and encourage him; if by our counsel we give him the enlightenment he lacks, *instead of asking God to annul His law, we turn ourselves into instruments for the execution of His law of love and charity* in which He allows us to participate, so giving us proof of His charity (See HEAVEN & HELL, 1st part, chapters: 4, 7 & 8).

INSTRUCTIONS FROM THE SPIRITS.

THE WAY TO PRAY

22. The first duty of all human beings, the first act which should mark the return to activity each day, is prayer. Most people pray, but only a very few really know how to pray! Of what importance to God are sentences which are mechanically linked together from habit, a duty to perform which weighs as heavily as any other duty?

The prayers of a Christian, of a *Spiritist,* or of whatever cult, must be made as soon as the Spirit returns to the fleshly yoke; it should be raised up to the feet of the Divine Majesty with humility and profundity, in an impulse of gratitude for all the many benefits received till that day; for the night just past during which it was permitted, although without knowing, to get close to friends and guides so as to be able to absorb new strength and more perseverance through this contact. You should lift yourself up humbly to the feet of the Lord, so as to offer up your weaknesses, plead for help, indulgence and mercy. This prayer should be profound, because it is your soul that should raise itself up to the Creator, and in doing so, it should become transfigured, as was Jesus on the mount when He showed the radient splendour of His hope and love.

Your prayer should include a request for His blessings for all those things you really need. Therefore it is useless to ask the Lord to shorten your tests and trials, or to give you happiness and riches.

Preferably ask for more precious items, such as patience, resignation and faith. Do not say, as many do, "It is not worth praying because God does not answer my prayers." In most cases what do your ask Him for? Have you ever remembered to ask Him to help you with your own moral betterment? Oh no! Seldom have you done this. What you most remember to ask for is *success in all your Earthly projects* and then you complain that God does not bother about anyone and that if He did there would not be so many injustices! How foolish! How ungrateful! If you searched deep into your conscience you would almost always find the motive for your suffering. So then, before all else ask that you may become a better person and you will see that you are showered with consolations and blessings (See chapter 5, item 4).

You should pray constantly without seeking your chapel or falling on your knees in public. Daily prayer is the fulfillment of your duty without any exception of any kind whatsoever. Is it not an act of love towards God when you help your brothers and sisters in any moral or physical need? It is an act of gratitude to lift up your thoughts to Him when something happy occurs, when you avoid an accident, or even when some simple triviality grazes our soul. So do not forget to say: *Blessed be my Father in Heaven!* Is it not an act of contrition to humble yourself before the Supreme Judge when you feel yourself weakening, even if only by means of a fleeting thought, so as to say:

*Forgive me, Father, for I have sinned (from pride, selfishness or lack of charity);
give me the strength not to fail again and courage to make reparation for my
fault!*

This is quite apart from regular morning and evening prayer and those for
sacred days. As you see, prayer can be for all moments without interrupting
your activities. On the contrary, in this manner it sanctifies them. You can be
sure that just one of these thoughts, if sent from the heart, is listened to by our
Celestial Father even more than those long repetitious prayers said out of
habit and almost always without any determined motive behind them *only
because the habitual hour is calling mechanically.* — V. MONOD (Bordeaux,
1862).

PRAYER IS A SOURCE OF HAPPINESS

23. Come hither all who wish to believe! The Celestial Spirits are come to
announce great things! My children, God is opening up His treasures so as to
distribute them for your benefit. O incredulous Man! If only you knew what a
great benefit to our hearts is faith and how it induces the soul to repentance
and prayer! Prayer! Ah! . . . How touching are the words which fall from the lips
of one who prays! Prayer is the Divine Dew which lessens the excessive heat of
our passions. Favourite daughter of faith, it leads us along the pathway which
takes us to God. In moments of reclusion and solitude you will find yourselves
together with the Lord. For you the mysteries disappear because He reveals
them to you. Apostles of thought, life is meant for you. Your soul liberates
itself from matter and launches itself into the infinite and etheric worlds which
poor humanity does not know.

March forward! March forward along the path of prayer and you will hear
the voices of the angels! What harmony! No longer the confused noises and
strident sounds of the Earth; but the sound of the lyres of the archangels, the
soft and gentle voices of the Seraphim, which are more delicate than the
morning breeze when it plays among the foliage of the woodlands. Amongst
what delights you will walk! Your earthly language cannot express such bliss,
so quickly does it enter into all your pores, so alive and refreshing is the spring
from which, through prayer, you are able to drink. Sweet voices and heady
perfumes are what the soul hears and breathes when you launch yourself into
prayer, into those unknown and inhabited spheres! All aspirations are divine
when liberated from carnal desires. You too can pray, as did Jesus, while
taking His Cross from Golgotha to Calvary. So take up your burden, and you
will feel sweet emotions which will pass through your soul, even though you
bear the weight of some infamous cross. He was going to die, but only in order
to live the Celestial Life in the House of His Father. — SAINT AUGUSTIN
(Paris, 1861).

CHAPTER 28
A COLLECTION OF SPIRITIST PRAYERS
PREAMBLE

1. The Spirits have always said: "The form means nothing but the thought is everything. Say your prayers in accordance with your convictions and in the manner which is most agreeable to you since a good thought is worth more than numerous words which do not touch the heart."

The Spirits do not prescribe an absolute formula for prayers. When they do give us one it is merely to help us form our ideas and above all to call our attention to certain principles of the Spiritist Doctrine. Or perhaps to offer guidance to those who find it difficult to express their ideas, because there are some who believe they have not prayed properly if they have not been able to formulate their thoughts well.

The collection of prayers contained in this chapter are a selection of some that the Spirits have dictated on several occasions. They could beyond doubt have dictated other prayers, in different terms, appropriate to various ideas and special cases. But the style is of little importance if the thought is essentially the same. The object of prayer is to elevate our soul to God. The diversity of forms should not establish any difference between those who believe in Him and even less between the adepts of Spiritism, because God accepts all of them when they are sincere.

Therefore you should not think of this collection of prayers as an absolute formula, but rather as a varied selection of those received from the Spirits. It is a way of applying the moral principles as taught by Christ which have been developed in this book, a complement to their writings based on our duties before God and our neighbour, in which we are again reminded of all the principles of the doctrine.

Spiritism recognises the prayers of all cults as being good, as long as they come from the heart and not just from the lips. It does not impose them nor does it condemn them. God is far too great, according to Spiritism, to consider repelling a voice which implores Him or which sings His praises, just because it is not done in this or that manner. *Anyone who wants to launch anathema against any prayers which are not within their own formulas will prove they know nothing of the greatness of God.* To believe that God has some kind of attachment to a certain formula is to attribute to Him the smallness and the passions of humanity.

According to Saint Paul, one of the essential conditions of prayer (See chapter 27, item 16) is that it be understandable, so as to move our spirit. Nevertheless, for this it is not enough that it be said in ordinary language, since there are prayers which although they are couched in modern terms, say nothing more to our intelligence than an unknown foreign language does, and for this reason do not touch our hearts. The few ideas which they contain are usually suffocated by the over abundance of words and the mysticism of the language.

The principal quality of a prayer is clarity. It should be simple and concise, without useless phraseology or an excess of adjectives which are nothing more than decoration. Each word should be of value in expressing an idea and in touching a fibre of the soul. In short, it should *cause you to reflect.* This is the only way in which it can reach its objective, since in any other manner it is *nothing but a noise.* However, in most cases it can be seen with what distraction and inconstancy they are said. We see lips which move, but by the expression on the faces, by the sound of the voices, we can verify that it is only mechanical, a solely exterior act, to which the soul remains indifferent.

The prayers in this collection are divided into five categories, as follows: 1) General Prayers. 2) Prayers for oneself. 3) Prayers for the living. 4) Prayers for the dead. 5) Special prayers for the sick and the obsessed.

With the objective of calling special attention to the aims of the various prayers and making their meaning more comprehensive, they are preceded by preliminary comments giving an explanation of the motives behind each one, entitled *preface.*

1 — GENERAL PRAYERS.

THE LORD'S PRAYER

2. PREFACE. — The Spirits recommended that we begin this anthology with the Lord's Prayer, not simply as a prayer, but also as a symbol. Of all the prayers, this one is considered the most important because it came from Jesus Himself (see Matthew, 6: 9-13) and because it can substitute all others, according to the intention and the thoughts that are joined to it. It is the most concisely perfect model; a truly sublime work of art in its simplicity. With effect, in its very reduced form, it manages to summarize all Man's duties before God, before himself and before his neighbour. It includes a mark of faith, an act of adoration and submission, a request for those things necessary to terrestrial life and the principle of charity. Whoever says this prayer for another, asks for them what they would ask for themself.

Nevertheless, because of its shortness, the deep meaning of some of its words escapes most people. This is usually because they say it without thinking of the meaning of each of its phrases. They say it just like a mechanical formula, whose efficiency is proportional to the number of times it is repeated. This number is almost always cabalistic: three, seven or nine, in view of the ancient superstitious belief in the power of numbers and of their practical use in magic.

In order to fill the void often felt by the shortness of this prayer, the Spirits recommended and helped us to add a commentary to each of the phrases which increases their meaning and shows the best way to make use of each one. In accordance with individual circumstances and the time at your disposal at any given moment, you can say the Lord's Prayer in its simple form or in the more developed way.

3. PRAYER:

(1) *Our Father which art in heaven, hallowed be thy name!*

Lord, we believe in thee, because everything about us reveals Your goodness and Your power. The harmony of the Universe is proof of a wisdom, a prudence and a foresight which surpasses all human faculties. The Name of a Being Who is supremely great and wise is written on all the works of Creation, from the humble grass and the smallest insect up to the stars and planets in space. On all sides we see proof of a paternal solicitude. Blind then is the one who does not recognise Your works, prideful is the one who does not worship You, and ungrateful is the one who does not give thanks to You.

(2) *Thy kingdom come!*

Lord, you gave Man laws full of wisdom, which would make him happy if only he observed them. With these laws, justice and peace could be established, and all could help each other instead of causing mutual harm as they do. The strong should uphold the weak instead of crushing them. All the evils which are born of abuses and excesses of all kinds could be avoided. All the miseries of this world stem from the violation of Your laws, because there is not one infraction that does not bring its fatal consequences.

You gave the animals an instinct which traces the limits of their necessities and to which they respond mechanically. But to Man, as well as instinct, You also gave intelligence and reason. Still more, You gave the liberty to keep or to violate those of Your laws which concern each one personally, or rather the faculty to choose between good and bad, so that we have the merit and the responsibility for our acts.

No one can protest ignorance of Your laws, because in Your paternal providence You desired that they be recorded in the consciousness of each one, without distinction as to cults or nationality. In this manner those who violate them do so because they despise You.

The day will come when according to Your promise, all will practise these laws. Then incredulity will have disappeared; all will recognise in You the Supreme Lord of all things and the reign of Your laws will herald Your Reign here on Earth.

Lord, deign to hasten Your accession by giving to Man the necessary enlightenment which will conduct him along the pathway of truth!

(3) *Thy will be done on earth as it is in heaven!*

If submission is the duty of a son towards his father, of the inferior towards his superior, how much greater is that of a being towards his Creator! By the words: 'Your will be done, Lord,' it is for us to observe Your laws and to submit ourselves without lamentations to all Your divine designs. Man will become submissive when he understands You are the source of all wisdom and that without You he can do nothing. Then he will do Your bidding on Earth as do Your elected ones in Heaven.

(4) *Give us this day our daily bread!*

Give us the necessary food for the maintenance of our physical strength and give us also spiritual nourishment for the development of our spirits.

The animals find their pastures, but Man depends on his own activity and his mental resources to produce his food because You gave him freedom.

You have said: "You will earn your bread by the sweat of your brow," and with these words You made work an obligation, which makes us exercise our intelligence in the search for the means to provide our necessities and to attend to our well-being: some by their material work, others by their intellectual work. Without work, Man would remain stationary and could not aspire to the happiness of the Superior Spirits.

Please help those of goodwill, who depend on You for what is necessary, but not those who take pleasure in being lazy and like to receive all things without any effort, nor those who seek superfluity (See chapter 25).

How many succumb throught their own fault, through negligence, through being improvident, through ambition, or through not being content with what You had given them! These are the authors of their own misfortunes and do not have the right to complain, since they are punished according to the manner in which they sinned. But You will not abandon even these because You are infinitely merciful and will extend a providential hand to them, if they return to You with sincerity, like the prodigal son (See chapter 5, item 4).

Before lamenting our bad luck, help us ask ourselves if it is not our own work; at each misfortune which befalls us, help us to verify if we could have avoided it; help us repeat to ourselves that God has given us intelligence so as to be able to get ourselves out of any slough and that it depends on us to put this intelligence to good use.

Seeing that Man is subject to the law of labour here on Earth, give us the courage and the strength to fulfill this law, Give us also prudence and moderation so that we may not lose its fruits.

Give us then, Lord, our daily bread, or rather the means of acquiring our necessities through work, because no one has the right to ask for superfluity.

If we are unable to work, help us have confidence in Your divine providence.

If it is within Your design to test us with great privation, despite our efforts, we accept this as a just expiation for the faults which we have committed in this life or in a previous one, because we know that You are just, and that there are no undeserved penalties since You never punish without cause.

Lord, preserve us from envying those who have what we have not, or of those who have superfluous things at their disposal, when we are wanting in what is necessary. Forgive them, Lord, if they forget the law of charity and of love towards one's neighbour, which You have taught (See chapter 16, item 8).

Withdraw also from our spirit the idea of denying the existence of Your justice when we see evil prosper, and the unhappiness which sometimes falls upon the godly man. Thanks to the new enlightenment which You have given us, we know that Your justice never fails and does not make any exceptions; the material prosperity of one who is evil is as fragile as his bodily existence and he will experience terrible reverses; whereas life will be eternal bliss for those who suffer with resignation (See chapter 5, items 7, 9, 12 & 18).

(5) *Forgive us our trespasses, as we forgive them that trespass against us!*

Lord, each one of our infractions against Your laws is an offence we commit against You, a debt contracted, which sooner or later will have to be paid. We implore that You forgive us through Your infinite mercy, subject to the promise we make to employ all our strength in not contracting others.

You made charity an express law for everyone; but charity does not only consist of helping our fellow beings in all their needs, but also in the forgetfulness and the forgiving of offences. With what right do we demand your indulgence, if we lack charity towards those who have given us motive for complaint?

Dear Lord, give us the strength to stifle within ourselves all resentment, hate and rancour. *Do not let death surprise us with a desire for vengeance in our hearts.* If You approve of our being taken from this world today, help us to be able to present ourself to You completely cleansed of animosity, just like Christ, Whose last words were in favour of His tormentors (See chapter 10).

The persecutions which those who are evil inflict upon us constitute part of our earthly tests; we should accept them without complaint, as we should accept all other tests, without cursing those who by their wrongdoing, open up a pathway for us to eternal happiness seeing that You said, through the intermediary of Jesus: "Blessed be those who suffer for the sake of justice!" Consequently, blessed be the hand that injures and humiliates us, as the mortifications of the body strengthen our soul, and we shall then be raised up from our humiliations (See chapter 12, item 4).

Blessed be Your name Lord, because You have taught us that our destiny is not irrevocably fixed after death; we will find in yet other existences, the means by which we may make atonement and repay all our past debts, and be able to realise in a new life, all those things to help our progress that we were unable to do in this one (See chapter 4; chapter 5, item 5).

In this manner all the apparent irregularities of life are finally explained. The light is cast over our past and our future, as a brilliant sign of Your supreme justice and of Your infinite goodness.

(6) *Lead us not into temptation, but deliver us from all evil.* (1)

Lord, give us the necessary strength to resist all impulses towards evil which will try to divert us from the path of goodness by inspiring us with bad thoughts.

But nevertheless we too are also imperfect Spirits incarnated on Earth so as to expiate our sins and to be able to better ourselves. The cause of evil lies deep within our souls and the bad Spirits only take advantage of these inferior tendencies so as to be able to tempt us. Each imperfection is an open door to their influences; just as they are powerless and give up any attempt against perfect beings. We are only unable to get rid of them as long as we do not put up a decided and unshakable desire for goodness, together with total renunciation of all evil. Therefore it is against ourselves that our strength must be directed and if we do this, the bad Spirits will naturally leave us since it is the evil which attracts them, whereas goodness repels them (See further on in this chapter: Prayers for the obsessed).

Dear Lord, uphold us in our weakness, inspire us through the voices of our Guardian Angels and the good Spirits, with the desire to correct our imperfections so that we may prevent access to our soul by the evil Spirits (See further on, item 11).

Evil is not Your work Lord, because the source of all goodness cannot engender any badness. It is ourselves who create it when we infringe Your laws and through the bad use we make of the liberty You concede to us. When Man has learnt to keep Your laws then evil will disappear from Earth, just as it has already disappeared from more advanced worlds.

Evil does not constitute a fatal necessity for anybody and only appears to be irresistible to those who take pleasure in it. So if we have a desire to practise evil, we can also have a desire to practise good. For this reason, dear God, we beg Your assistance and that of the good Spirits so we may resist temptation.

---

(1) There are some translations of the Bible which say: *do not induce us to temptation* (et nos inducas in tentationem). This sentence gives us to understand that temptation stems from God and that He voluntarily impels Man towards evil; which is a blasphemous idea putting God on an equal basis with Satan and therefore, could not have been in the mind of Jesus. Actually, it is in accordance with the popular idea that exists about the part played by Devils (See HEAVEN & HELL, 1st part, chapter 9 — THE DEVILS).

(7) *So be it!*

O God, may the realisation of our desires be accomplished! But we nevertheless bow down before Your infinite wisdom. In all things that we are unable to understand, may Your blessed Will be done and not ours, since You only desire our improvement and know better than us what is best for us.

We offer You this prayer, Lord, not only for ourselves, but also for all suffering creatures, both incarnate and discarnate, for our friends and our enemies, for all those who demand our help, and especially for X . . . We beseech Your mercy and blessing for all.

(NOTE: Here you can offer thanks to God for all that has been conceded to you and formulate any request you may have, either for yourself or for others (See further on, prayers No. 26 & 27).

SPIRITIST MEETINGS

4. *"For where two or three are gathered together in My name, there am I in the midst of them" (Matthew, 18: 20).*

5. PREFACE — In order to be gathered together in the name of Jesus, our material presence alone is not enough, because it is indispensable to be assembled in the spiritual sense as well, by means of a communion of intentions and thoughts towards goodness. In this way Jesus will be found in your midst, that is to say either He or those pure Spirits who are His representatives. Spiritism enables us to understand the way the Spirits can be with us. This is by means of their fluidic or spiritual body, and if they should make themselves visible they do so with an appearance that allows us to recognise them. The more elevated in the spiritual hierarchy the greater is their power of radiation, so that on possessing the gift of ubiquity, they may be present in various places simultaneously. In order to achieve this it requires merely the emission of a thought.

With these words Jesus wished to show the effect of union and fraternity. It is not the greater or lesser number of people which attract the Spirits, but the sentiment of charity which animates them reciprocally. If it depended on numbers, He would have said some ten or twenty instead of two or three people. Well, for this purpose two persons are enough. But if these two people pray separately, even if they direct themselves to Jesus, there will be no communion of thought between them, especially if they are not motivated by a mutual sentiment of benevolence. If they are animated by mutual prejudice, hate, jealousy or envy, then the fluidic currents of their thoughts will repel each other instead of uniting them in a harmonious impulse of sympathy. So then *they will not be united in the Name of Jesus.* In that case, Jesus will only be the *pretext* for that meeting and not the true motive (See chapter 27, item 9).

This does not mean to say that Jesus will not listen to only one person. However, if He did not say: "I will attend anyone who calls Me." it is because He demands, above all else, the love of one's neighbour, for which it is possible to give greater proof in a group than in isolation, and because all personalized sentiment denies it. It follows then, that in a large meeting, if two or three people joined themselves through their hearts in a sentiment of true charity, while all the others remained isolated, concentrating their ideas on selfish and worldly things, Jesus would be with the first group and not with the rest. It is not then the simultaneity of the words, the songs or the exterior acts which constitute the gathering together in the name of Jesus, but rather the communion of thought according to the true spirit of charity, of which He is the personification (See chapters 10, items 7 & 8, and 27, items 2 & 4).

This should be the character of all serious Spiritist meetings, in which the assistance of the good Spirits is earnestly desired.

6. PRAYER (For the commencement of a meeting):
We beseech You, O Lord God, the All Powerful, to send us the good Spirits to help us and take away all those who may induce us towards error; give us the necessary light so that we may distinguish truth from falsity.

Remove too, the maleficent Spirits, be they incarnate or discarnate, who may try to launch discord amongst us, and so turn us away from charity and love for our neighbours. If some of these Spirits try to enter our ambient, do not allow them access to any of our hearts.

Good Spirits, you see fit to come and teach us, make us yielding to your counselling, turn us away from all thoughts of selfishness, pride, jealousy and envy. Inspire us to indulgence and benevolence towards our fellow beings, present or absent, friends or enemies; lastly, through the sentiments with which we are animated, make us recognise Your beneficial influence.

To those Mediums You chose as transmitters of Your teaching, give awareness of their mandate and the seriousness of the act they are about to practise, so they may perform this act with the necessary fervour and meditation.

If at our meeting, there be any persons present driven by sentiments other than those of goodness, open their eyes to the light and forgive them Lord, as we forgive them, for any evil intentions they may harbour.

We ask especially that the Spirit of X . . ., who is our spiritual Guide, assist us and watch over us.

7. PRAYER (For the closing of the meeting):
We give thanks to the good Spirits who have come to communicate with us, and implore them to help us put into practise the instructions they have given, and also, that on leaving this ambient, they may help us to feel strengthened for the practise of goodness and love towards our fellow beings.

We also desire that Your teachings help all those Spirits who are suffering, ignorant or corrupt, who have participated in our meeting and for whom we implore God's mercy.

FOR THE MEDIUMS

8. *And it shall come to pass in the last days, saith God, I will pour out of My Spirit upon all flesh: and your sons and your daughters shall prophesy, and your young men shall see visions, and your old men shall dream dreams: And on my servants and on my handmaidens I will pour out in those days of My Spirit; and they shall prophesy (Acts, 2: 17 & 18).*

9. PREFACE — God wishes that the light shines for all men and that the voices of the Spirits penetrate to all parts so that everyone may obtain proof of immortality. It is with this objective in mind that the Spirits manifest themselves in all parts of the Globe, and that mediumship is revealing itself in people of all ages and all conditions, in men and in women, in children and in old people. This is one of the signs that the predicted times have arrived.

In order to know the things of the visible world and discover the secrets of material Nature, God has given Man bodily vision, the senses and special instruments. With the telescope his eyes reach into the vastness of space; with the mircoscope he discovers the world of infinite minuteness, and to be able to penetrate the invisible world He has given Man mediumship.

Mediums are interpreters who have undertaken to transmit to mankind the teachings of the Spirits; or rather, *they are the material organs of which the Spirits avail themselves so as to be able to express themselves to Man intelligently.* They fulfill a sacred mission, seeing that the aim is to open up the horizons of eternal life.

The Spirits come to instruct Man as to his destiny, so that he may be led towards the path of goodness, and not to save him from material work which must be fulfilled in this world for his advancement, nor for the furthering of his ambition and covetousness. This is something which must be clearly understood by mediums so that they will not make bad use of their faculty. Those who fully understand the seriousness of the mandate with which they have been invested will carry out this duty religiously. Their conscience will condemn them if by any sacreligious act they transform into a distraction or amusement, *for themselves or for others,* those faculties which were given to them for a serious purpose, which is that of placing them in communication with beings from the other world.

As interpreters for the teachings of the Spirits, mediums should play a very important part in the moral transformation that is in process. The services they are able to offer will be in accordance with the correctness of the orientation they have given to their faculty, because those who follow an incorrect pathway cause more harm than good to the cause of Spiritism. More than one person will delay their progress due to the unfortunate impression these mediums produce. Therefore because of this, all mediums will have to given an account of the use to which they have put their faculty, which was given to them for the purpose of doing good to their fellow creatures.

The medium who desires to be constantly helped by good Spirits will have to work hard towards self-betterment. Those who wish their faculty to grow and be enriched, must therefore enrich themselves morally and abstain from all that can turn them aside from their providential purpose.

If sometimes good Spirits make use of an imperfect medium, it is in order to give good advice, with which they try to make them take the road to goodness. If, however, they meet hardened hearts and their advice is not listened to, they will leave and the field will then be free for the evil Spirits (See chapter 24, items 11 &12).

Experience has proved that on the part of those who do not take advantage of the advice received from the good Spirits, communications which initially showed some brilliance will, little by little, degenerate and finally fall into error, either in the wording or by becoming ridiculous, which are incontestable signs of the retreat of the good Spirits.

To obtain the assistance of the good Spirits and to remove the lying and frivolous ones, must be the aim to which all serious mediums should join forces and without which mediumship becomes a sterile faculty; even capable of causing detriment to the one who possesses it, since it can become the cause of a dangerous obsession.

Any medium who understands their duty and is not proud of a faculty that does not belong to them, seeing that it may be taken away, will always attribute the good things they receive to God. If their communications receive praise, they will not become vain because they know that these are independant of their personal merit. They will give thanks to God for having allowed the good Spirits to be able to manifest through their intermediary. If there is occasion for criticism, they are never offended because the communications are not their own work. On the contrary, they recognize in their inner selves that they were not able to be good instruments and do not possess all the necessary qualities which would obstruct interference from backward Spirits. Therefore, take care to acquire these qualities and implore, by means of prayer, that your strength does not fail.

10. PRAYER:

Almighty God, permit the good Spirits to come and help me in the communication that is solicited. Protect me from the presumption of judging myself to be safe from evil Spirits; from the pride which may induce me to err with respect to the value of what I receive; from all sentiments which are the opposite of charity towards other mediums. If I fall into error inspire someone to alert me of this fact; and give me the humility that will enable me to accept the deserved criticism and to recognise that the advice the good Spirits wish to give through me is not only addressed to others, but primarily to myself.

If I am tempted to abuse in whatever form, the faculty whose bestowal You approved, or to become proud of it, I ask that You take it back rather than it be permitted to stray from its providential objective, which is for the good of all and my own moral betterment.

2 — PRAYERS FOR THE ONE WHO PRAYS.
TO GUARDIAN ANGELS AND PROTECTING SPIRITS

11. PREFACE — From the moment of birth everyone has a good Spirit linked to them who constantly protects. At our side this Spirit carries out the mission of a father to his children which is that of conducting us along the path to goodness and progress, throughout the various tests of life. He feels happy when we respond to his solicitude and suffers when he sees us succumbing.

His name is not important because it is quite possible that it is not known on Earth. So then, we call him by the name of Guardian Angel or our good Spirit. We could also call him under the name of one of the superior Spirits with whom we feel a special sympathy.

Apart form this Guardian Angel, who is always a superior Spirit, we have other Spirit protectors, who although slightly less elevated, are just as good and generous. These are the Spirits of friends and relations, or even people we have not known in the present life. They help us with their advice and quite often intervene in the happenings of our life.

Sympathetic Spirits are those who are linked to us through certain similarities of taste and tendency. They may be either good or bad, according to the nature of those of our inclinations which have attracted them to us.

The seductive Spirits endeavour to turn us aside from the paths of goodness by suggesting bad thoughts to us. They take advantage of all our weaknesses, as if these were so many open doors which give them access to our soul. Some of them hold on to us as if we were their prey, but they *withdraw when they recognise themselves impotent to fight against our will.*

In the form of our Guardian Angel, God has given us a principal and superior guide and in the form of protecting and family Spirits secondary guides, but it is a mistake to believe that *inevitably* we have a bad element at our side to counter-balance the good influences we receive from them. The evil Spirits seek us *voluntarily* as long as they can dominate us by reason of our weakness or our negligence in following the inspirations of the good Spirits, so it is ourselves who attract them. The result is we are never without the assistance of good Spirits, and the withdrawal of the bad Spirits depends entirely on ourselves. Due to his imperfections, Man is the primary cause of all the miseries which afflict him and is, in most cases, his own bad genius (See chapter 5, item 4).

A prayer to Guardian Angels and protecting Spirits should have as its objective the solicitation of their intercession with God, to ask for strength to resist evil suggestions and to ask for help in all of life's contingencies.

12. PRAYER:

Wise and benevolent Spirits, messengers of God, whose mission is to help Man and conduct him towards goodness, uphold me in life's tests; give me the strength to suffer without complaining; turn away from me all evil thoughts, and do not allow me to give access to any bad Spirits who may try to induce me to evil. Clarify my conscience with respect to my defects, and take away the veil of pride from my eyes which can prevent my seeing them and admitting them to myself.

Particularly to X . . ., my Guardian Angel, who watches over me specially; and all the rest of you protecting Spirits who take an interest in me, I beg you to help me to become worthy of your protection. You know my needs; may they be attended to according to the Will of God.

13. PRAYER:

Dear God, allow the good Spirits who accompany me to help me when I am in difficulty and uphold me when I falter. Lord, may they inspire me with faith, hope and charity; may they be a point of support, an inspiration and a testimony of Your mercy. In short, may I always encounter in them the strength that I lack for the tests of life, the strength to resist all evil suggestions, the faith that saves and the love that consoles.

14. PRAYER:

Beloved Spirits and Guardian Angels, who God in His infinite mercy has permitted to assist mankind, be our protectors during all life's tests! Give us the necessary strength, courage and resignation; inspire us towards all that is good, and restrain us from the downward incline to evil; may your sweet influences fill our souls; make us feel that a devoted friend is by our side, who can see our suffering and who participates in all our joys.

And you, my Good Angel, never abandon me because I need all of your protection to be able to support with faith and love the tests that God has sent me.

TO TURN AWAY THE BAD SPIRITS

15. *Woe unto you, Scribes and Pharisees, hypocrites! For ye make clean the outside of the cup and of the platter, but within they are full of extortion and excess. Thou blind Pharisee, cleanse first that which is within the cup and platter, that the outside of them may be clean also. Woe unto you, Scribes and Pharisees, hypocrites! For ye are like unto whited sepulchres, which indeed appear beautiful outward, but are within full of dead men's bones, and of all uncleanness. Even so ye also outwardly appear righteous unto men, but within ye are full of hypocrisy and iniquity (Matthew, 23: 25-28).*

16. PREFACE — Bad Spirits are only found where they can satisfy their perversity. In order to turn them away it is not enough to ask them to go, nor even to order them to go. It is imperative that Man eliminates from within himself that which is attracting them. Bad Spirits discover the ulcers of the soul, the same way that flies discover those of the body. In this manner then, as you cleanse the wound in order to avoid maggots, cleanse also your soul of all its impurities so as to avoid bad Spirits. We live in a world which teems with these Spirits, so the good qualities in the heart do not always make them abandon their attempts on us. But nevertheless, these qualities give us strength to resist them.

17. PRAYER:

In the Name of God the All Powerful, may the bad Spirits turn away from me and the good Spirits defend me from them!

Wicked Spirits, who inspire bad thoughts in men; deceiving and lying Spirits, who delude men; mocking Spirits, who amuse yourselves with mankind's incredulity, I repel you with all the strength within my soul and close my ears to your suggestions; but I also implore that God's mercy be upon you.

Good Spirits, who undertook to accompany me, give me the necessary strength to resist the influence of bad Spirits and the necessary enlightenment so as not to become a victim of their intrigue. Safeguard me from pride and presumption. We beg that you turn aside all thoughts of jealousy, hate, badness, and all sentiments contrary to charity from my heart, which are all as open doors to the bad Spirits.

IN ORDER TO ASK THAT SOME DEFECT WITHIN OURSELVES MAY BE CORRECTED

18. PREFACE — Our bad instincts result from the imperfections of our own Spirit, and not from our physical body. If this were not so then Man would be exempt from all responsibility. Our betterment depends on ourselves, because every person who has all their faculties has in everything the liberty to do or not to do. In order to do good the only thing lacking is will-power (See chapter 15, item 10 and chapter 19, item 12).

19. PRAYER:

Dear Lord, You gave me the necessary intelligence so as to distinguish right from wrong. Thus, on recognising something to be wrong, I am guilty in not struggling to resist the temptation.

Preserve me from pride which can prevent me from perceiving my defects, and also from the bad Spirits, who can incite me to continue in the wrong.

Amongst my imperfections I recognise that I am especially inclined to . . ., and if I am unable to resist, it is because I have already acquired the habit of giving in to it.

Because You are just, You did not create us guilty but with equal aptitude for good and for bad. If I have preferred the bad road it was because of my free-will. But for the same reason that I had the liberty to do wrong, I also have the liberty to do good and therefore to change my pathway.

My actual defects are the remains of the imperfections I brought from my past existences; this is my original sin, from which I may liberate myself through the action of my will and with help from the good Spirits.

Accordingly, protect me kindly Spirits, and above all my Guardian Angel, by giving me the strength to resist evil suggestions and so be victorious in this battle.

These defects are the barrier which separate us from God, and each defect surmounted is a step further along the pathway of progress which will draw us nearer to Him.

O Lord, in Your infinite mercy, You thought fit to concede me this present life so that it would serve for my advancement. Good Spirits, help me to take advantage of this opportunity so that I may not lose it. When it pleases God to remove me from it, help me to leave it in a better condition than on entering (See chapter 5, item 5 & chapter 17, item 3).

TO ASK FOR STRENGTH TO RESIST TEMPTATION

20. PREFACE — Every bad thought can have two origins: our own spiritual imperfection or the action of a harmful influence. In the last case we have the indication of a weakness which exposes us to these influences, and it is for this reason that our soul is imperfect. So that the one who fails cannot offer as an excuse the influence of a strange Spirit, seeing that *this Spirit would not have led them to wrongdoing if they were inaccessible to seduction.*

When we have a bad thought, we can suppose that it was an evil Spirit which suggested the evil, leaving us complete liberty to accede or resist, just as if we were facing a living person. At the same time, we should make a mental picture of our Guardian Angel or protecting Spirit who from his side combats within us the bad influences and anxiously awaits the decision we are going to make. Our hesitation in acting upon the evil suggestions is due to the voice of our good Spirit, who makes himself heard through our conscience.

One recognises a thought is bad when it draws away from charity which is the base of all true morality; or when it comes laden with pride, vanity and selfishness; or when its realization may cause harm to another person: in short, when we are induced by our thoughts to do to others what we would not like someone to do to us (See chapter 28, item 15 & chapter 15 item 10).

21. PRAYER:

All Powerful Lord, do not let me succumb to the temptation to fall into error! Benevolent Spirits who protect me, turn this bad thought away from me and give me the strength to resist this evil. If I succumb, then I will deserve the expiation of my failing in this same life and in the next, because I have free will to make my choice.

THANKSGIVING FOR VICTORY OVER A TEMPTATION

22. PREFACE — Those who resist temptation owe this fact to the assistance given by the good Spirits, whose voice they listened to. So, you should thank God and your Guardian Angel for their help.

23. PRAYER:

My God, I thank You for having permitted me to be victorious in the battle which I sustained against evil. Allow this victory to give me strength to resist new temptations. And you, my Guardian Angel, receive my thanks for the assistance you gave. Allow that my submission to your counsel makes me worthy to receive your protection once again.

TO ASK FOR ADVICE

24. PREFACE — When we are unsure about something we have to do, before anything else, we should ask ourselves the following questions:

1st) Will what I am hesitating about cause harm to anyone?
2nd) Will it be useful to anyone?
3rd) If someone did this to me would I be pleased?

If what we think of doing is of interest only to ourself, it is permissible to weigh the personal advantages or disadvantages which may arise.

If it concerns others and if, in doing good for one person, it redounds in badness for another, it is also equally necessary to weigh the advantages and disadvantages before deciding whether to act or abstain.

Finally, even when dealing with the best of things it is necessary to consider the opportunity and the circumstances being offered, in as much as something that is good in itself can give bad results when put into the wrong hands, or if it is not directed with prudence and circumspection. Before putting it into effect it is best to consult our strength and the means of execution.

In any case, we can always solicit the assistance of our Protecting Spirits, remembering this wise maxim: *When in doubt, do nothing* (See chapter 28, item 38).

25. PRAYER:

In the name of God, the All Powerful One, in my uncertainty, I call upon the good Spirits who protect me to inspire me to make the best decisions. Lead my thoughts always towards goodness and protect me from the influences of those who tempt me to stray.

AFFLICTIONS OF LIFE

26. PREFACE — We can ask God for earthly favours and He will concede them to us when they have a serious purpose. But seeing that we judge their utility from our own point of view and as immediate necessities, we do not always recognise the bad side of what we ask. God, Who can see things in a better perspective than we can and only desires the best for us, may refuse what we ask for, just as a father would refuse his child what he knew would be prejudicial for him. If what we request is refused we should not be disappointed; on the contrary, we should think that to be deprived of our wish is a test or an expiation, and that our recompense will be in proportion to the degree of resignation shown towards what we have to put up with (See chapter 27, item 6 & chapter 2, items 5-7).

27. PRAYER:

God Omnipotent, who sees all our miseries, please deign to hear the supplication we direct to You at this moment. If my request is inconsiderate, forgive me. If it is just and convenient, according to the way You see things, may the good Spirits who execute Your wishes, come to my aid and help me to realise my request.

However it may be, Lord, let Your will be done! If my request is not answered, it will be because it is Your wish that I be tested, and I submit without complaint. Help me not to become disanimated and that neither my faith nor my resignation be shaken.

(Then formulate your request).

THANKSGIVING FOR THE OBTAINING OF A FAVOUR

28. PREFACE — We must not consider as blessed successes only those things which are of great importance. Frequently things that are apparently insignificant are those which most influence our destiny. Man easily forgets the goodness received, preferring to remember only afflictions. If we were to register day by day the many benefits we receive, without even having asked for them, we would be greatly surprised to perceive there are so very many that we have swept from our minds and would feel ashamed of our ingratitude.

On lifting up our soul to God each night, we should remember in our innermost self the many favours that He has granted us during the day and offer thanks for them. But most especially, at the moment we receive the effects of His goodness and protection, we should spontaneously bear witness to our gratitude. For this, it is enough that we direct a thought attributing the benefit to Him, without even interrupting our work.

Benefits from God are not limited to material things. We should also thank Him for the ideas and happy inspirations we receive. Whereas the selfish person attributes all of these things to his own personal merits, and the incredulous person to mere chance, the one who has faith renders thanks to God and the good Spirits. Long sentences are not necessary for this purpose. *"Thank you, dear God, for the inspiration of that good thought"*, says more than a long prayer. The spontaneous impulse which makes us attribute to God what has happened to us, bears witness of an act of thanksgiving and of humility, which will earn us the sympathy of the good Spirits (See chapter 27, items 7 & 8).

29. PRAYER:

Beloved Lord of inifinite goodness, may Your name be blessed for the benefits conceded to me! I would be unworthy if I were to attribute these happenings to mere chance or to my own merit.

Good Spirits, you who execute God's wishes, I thank you and most especially my Guardian Angel. Turn away from me all idea of being proud of what I have received and help me to make use of it exclusively for good. Most of all, I thank . . .

AN ACT OF SUBMISSION AND RESIGNATION

30. PREFACE — When we are suffering an affliction, if we look for the cause, we will always find it in our own imprudence, thoughtlessness or in some past action. As can be seen, in these cases we have to attribute the suffering to ourselves. If the cause of an affliction cannot be found to stem in any way from our own actions, then we are dealing with a test in this life, or an atonement for an error committed in a previous one. In this case, by the nature of the expiation we can know the nature of the error, as we are always punished in the same manner as our sin (See chapter 5, items 4, 6 & subsequent items).

In general, we can only see the evil that is present in our afflictions. We do not see the favourable consequences they may have later on. Goodness is frequently the outcome of a past evil, just as the cure for an illness results from the painful methods used to obtain it. In any case, we must submit to the will of God and courageously support the tribulations of life if we want them to count in our favour. These words of Christ could then be applied to us: "Blessed are those who suffer" (See chapter 5, item 18).

31. PRAYER:

Dear Lord, Your justice is supreme. Therefore all suffering in this world must have a just cause and be of use. I accept the affliction which I am undergoing, or which I have just suffered, as an atonement for my past errors and as a test for the future. Good Spirits who protect me, give me the necessary strength to support this without complaining. Help me to look at it as a providential warning; may it enrich my experience, reduce my pride, diminish my ambition, stupid vanity and selfishness. In short, may it contribute to my progress.

32. PRAYER:

Dear God, I feel the need to ask You for the necessary strength so as to support the test that You have sent me. Allow my Spirit to be enlightened, with the necessary understanding, so that I can appreciate the full extent of a love that afflicts because it desires to save. I submit myself with resignation, dear Lord, but I am so weak I fear I will succumb if You do not uphold me. Do not abandon me, Lord, because without You I am nothing.

33. PRAYER:

I lift up my eyes to You, Eternal Father, and feel fortified. You are my strength, dear Lord, do not abandon me! I am crushed under the weight of my iniquities! Help me! I recognise the weakness of my flesh! Please, do not take Your eyes from me!

I am being devoured by an ardent thirst! Make the spring of living water burst forth to quench this thirst. May my lips open only to sing Your praises and not to complain about my afflictions! I am weak, Lord, but Your love will sustain me.

Eternal Father, only You are great, only You are the reason and the finality of my life! Blessed be Your Name even if You make me suffer, because You are the Lord and I am an unfaithful servant. I bow down before You without complaint because only You are great, only You are the aim of all our lives!

WHEN IN IMMINENT DANGER

34. PREFACE — Through the dangers we run God reminds us of the frailty of our existence. He shows us that our lives are in His hands, and that being held by only a thread, it may break when we least expect it to happen. From this point of view privilege does not exist for anyone because the same alternatives are to be found for both great and small alike.

If we look at the nature and the consequences of danger we will see in most cases that these consequences, if they are verified, will have been a punishment for a misdeed or for an *unfulfilled duty.*

35. PRAYER:

Almight God, and you who are my Guardian Angel, help me! If I must succumb, may God's Will be done. If I am to be saved, may the rest of my life be given to repay the evil I have done, for which I am truly repentant.

THANKSGIVING FOR HAVING ESCAPED A DANGER

36. PREFACE — By the danger we have been through, God shows us that from one moment to another we may be called to give account for the way in which we have utilized our life. This is to alert us to the fact that we should examine ourselves and mend our ways.

37. PRAYER:

Dear God! Dear Guardian Angel! I thank you for the help I received during the danger that threatened me. May this danger be a warning to me and enlighten me with respect to my errors that have brought me this peril. I understand, Lord, that my life is in Your hands and that You may take it away when You see fit. Inspire me then, through the good Spirits who protect me, with the idea of how best to take advantage of the time You grant to me in this world! Guardian Angel! Uphold me in my decision to correct my faults and to do all the good that is within my power to do, so that I may arrive in the spiritual world with fewer imperfections, whenever it pleases God to call me!

AT BEDTIME

38. PREFACE — Sleep is for the purpose of resting the body; however, the Spirit needs no rest. While the physical senses are in a torpid state the soul partly frees itself from the body and enters into the enjoyment of its spiritual faculties. Sleep has been given to Man to enable him to repair both his organic and moral strengths. While the body recuperates the spent energies which have been used during the waking state, the Spirit fortifies itself amongst other Spirits. From all he sees, all he perceives and from the advice he is given, he takes the ideas which occur to him afterwards, in the form of intuitions. This is the temporary return of the exile to his true world, a momentary liberty that is conceded to the prisoner.

But it sometimes happens, as it does in the case of perverse prisoners, that the Spirit does not always take advantage of these moments of liberty for the purpose of progress. If he has bad instincts, instead of seeking the company of the good Spirits, he seeks out those who are like himself and goes to those places where he may give vent to his tendencies.

So then, the person who is convinced of this fact will lift up their thoughts to God before they go to sleep. They will ask for advice from the good Spirits and all those whose memory is dear to them, so they may go to join them for the brief moments of liberty which are conceded to them. On awakening they will then feel fortified against evil and be more courageous when facing adversities.

39. PRAYER:

Lord, for a few short instants my soul will be together with other Spirits. So I beg the good Spirits to come and give me counsel. Guardian Angel, please help me to keep a lasting and beneficial impression of this encounter on awakening!

ON SENSING APPROACHING DEATH

40. PREFACE — During our lifetime to have faith in the future, together with the elevation of our thoughts towards our future destiny helps in the process of rapid liberation of the Spirit because this weakens the links which tie it to the material body. So much so that quite frequently, even before the physical body has expired, the soul being impatient to be free, has already launched itself into the great immensity. The contrary being the case of the person who, having concentrated on all that is material, finds these ties more difficult to break *and the separation more painful and difficult,* to be followed by an awakening full of anxiety and perturbation in the after-life.

41. PRAYER:

Dear God, I believe in You and Your infinite kindness. Therefore, I cannot believe that You have given Man intelligence which allows him to gain knowledge of You and an aspiration for the future, so as to plunge him into nothingness.

I believe that my body is only a perishable covering for my soul and that when I cease to live, I will awaken in the world of the Spirits.

Almighty God, I feel that the ties which hold my soul to my body are breaking and that in a short while I will have to account for the use to which I have put the life that is now slipping away from me.

I know that I will experience the consequences of the good and the bad that I have practised. There will be no possibility of illusions, no subterfuge. My past will unfold before me and I will be judged according to my works.

I will take nothing with me of earthly possessions such as honours, riches, satisfactions of vanity or pride; in short, everything which belongs to the body will remain in this world. Not even the most minute particle of these things will accompany me, nor would they be of use to me in the spiritual world. I will take with me only what belongs to my soul, that is to say, the good and bad qualities I possess, which will be weighed on the balance of strict justice. I know that the judgement will be even more severe according to the number of times I refused the opportunities that were given to me to practise good due to the position I held on Earth (See chapter 16, item 9).

Merciful God, may the depth of the sincerity of my repentance enable it to reach out to You! May You see fit to cast over me Your cloak of indulgence!

If You see fit to prolong my present existence, may I utilize that time to make good, as far as I am able, all the evil that I have done. But if my hour has come, I take with me the consoling thought that I will be permitted to redeem myself by means of new tests, so that one day I may deserve the happiness of the elected ones.

If it is not given to me to enjoy such perfect happiness immediately, which is known only to those who are pre-eminently just, I know nevertheless that I am not denied hope for ever. Sooner or later I will reach my goal, according to the amount of effort I put into working towards that objective.

I know that good Spirits and my Guardian Angel are near to receive me and that soon I shall see them, just as they see me now. I know too, *that if I deserve it,* I will meet again all those I have loved here on Earth, and that those I leave behind will later come to meet me. One day we shall all be united for ever, and until that time arrives I will be able to come and visit them.

I know too, that I will re-encounter those I have offended; may they forgive me for whatever they have to reproach me for, such as my pride, my hardness and my injustices, so that their presence will not overwhelm me with shame!

I forgive all those who have either done or tried to do me harm; I hold no rancour against them and beg You, dear God, to forgive them.

Lord, give me strength to leave all the material pleasures of this world without regret, which are as nothing compared to the healthy and pure delights of the world into which I am about to enter, and where for those who are just, there are no more torments, or miseries, and where only the guilty are subject to suffering. But even they always have the consolation of hope.

Good Spirits and you who are my Guardian Angel, I implore you not to allow me to fail at this supreme moment. If my faith should waver, then cause the Divine Light to shine in my eyes, so that it may be reanimated.

NOTE — See further on, paragraph 5: "Prayers for the sick and obsessed."

3 — PRAYERS FOR OTHERS.
FOR SOMEONE WHO IS AFFLICTED

42. PREFACE — If it is in the interest of the afflicted person to continue their test then any request we might make will not shorten it. But it would be a lack of charity to abandon this person, alleging that our prayer would not be heard. Apart from this, even if the test is not interrupted, they may obtain some degree of consolation that will lessen their suffering. What is really useful for someone who is supporting a test is courage and resignation, without which whatever they are going through will bring them no results, because without these attributes they will have to go through it all again. Therefore, it is with this objective in mind that we should direct our effort towards asking the good Spirits to help them, or by lifting their morale through counselling and encouragement, or even by helping them in a material way, if this is possible. In such cases prayer can have a decisive effect by directing a fluidic current towards them with the intention of fortifying their morale (See chapter 5, items 5 & 27; chapter 27, items 6 & 10).

43. PRAYER:

Dear God of infinite goodness, may it please You to soften the bitterness of the position in which X . . . finds himself, if this be according to Your will.

Good Spirits, in the name of God Almighty, I beseech you to help in his afflictions. If it is not in his interest to be spared this suffering, make him understand that it is necessary for his progress. Give him confidence in God and the future, which will make him less bitter. Also give him strength so that he does not give himself up to despair, which will make him lose the fruits of his suffering and make his future even more painful. Conduct my thoughts to him so that these may help him to maintain his courage.

AN ACT OF THANKSGIVING FOR A BENEFIT RECEIVED BY SOMEONE ELSE

44. PREFACE — Those who are not dominated by selfishness rejoice over the good that comes to their neighbour, even if they did not make a solicitation by means of prayer.

45.PRAYER:

Lord, we thank You for the happiness conceded to X . . . Good Spirits, help him to see that this benefit is the consequence of God's goodness. If the good received constitutes a test, please inspire him with thoughts about how to make the best use of it and not become conceited, so it does not redound to his detriment in the future. You, the good Spirits who protect me and desire my happiness, turn aside from me all sentiment of jealousy or envy.

FOR OUR ENEMIES AND THOSE WHO WISH US ILL

46. PREFACE — Jesus said: *Love your enemies.* This maxim shows us all that is most sublime in Christian charity. But Jesus did not mean to say that we should have the same tenderness for an enemy as we have for a friend. By these words He teaches us to pardon offences, to pardon all evil done to us and to repay all evil with goodness. Apart from the worth that this conduct has in God's eyes, it also serves to show Man the nature of true superiority (See chapter 12, items 3 & 4).

47. PRAYER:

Dear God, forgive X . . . the evil he has done me and still desires to do to me, as I wish You to forgive me; I also ask him to forgive me for the offences I have committed against him. If this person has been put in my pathway as a test, may Your Will be done. Turn me away, dear Lord, from any idea of cursing him and from all other wicked sentiments against him. Do not ever allow me to be happy at any misfortune that may befall him, so as not to blemish my soul with thoughts which are not worthy of a Christian.

Lord, may your mercy extend to him and induce him to harbour better sentiments towards me!

Good Spirits, induce me to forget all evil and remember only the good. May neither hate, rancour nor the desire to pay back evil with evil enter my heart, since sentiments of hate and vengeance belong to bad Spirits, be they incarnate or discarnate! On the contrary, may I be prepared to extend a friendly hand to him, so repaying evil with goodness and help him if it is possible.

So as to test the sincerity of my words, I beg You to give me an opportunity to be useful to him, but above all, Lord, preserve me from doing this out of pride and ostentation, smothering him with humiliating generosity which would only cause me to lose the fruits of my action, since in that case, I would deserve these words of Christ: *You have already received your recompense* (See chapter 13, items 1 & subsequent).

THANKSGIVING FOR BLESSINGS RECEIVED BY OUR ENEMIES

48. PREFACE — To not desire evil towards your enemies is to be only partly charitable. True charity consists in wishing them well and in feeling happy about the good that comes to them (See chapter 12, items 7 & 8).

49. PRAYER:
Dear God, in Your justice You saw fit to make X . . . happy, and on his behalf I thank You, despite the evil he has done to me and still tries to do. If he seeks to use this benefit to humiliate me, I accept this as a test of my capacity for charity.

Good Spirits who protect me, do not let me become regretful because of this. Turn away from me all jealousy and envy, which only degrades. On the contrary, inspire me with the generosity that elevates. Humiliation comes from evil and not from goodness, and we know that sooner or later justice will be done to each one according to their works.

FOR THE ENEMIES OF SPIRITISM

50. *Blessed are the meek: for they shall inherit the Earth.*

Blessed are they which are persecuted for righteousness' sake: for theirs is the Kingdom of Heaven. Blessed are ye, when men shall revile you, and persecute you, and shall say all manner of evil against you falsely, for My sake. Rejoice, and be exceeding glad: for great is your reward in Heaven: for so persecuted they the prophets which were before you (Matthew, 5: 5 & 10-12).

And fear not them which kill the body, but are not able to kill the soul: but rather fear him which is able to destroy both soul and body in hell (Matthew, 10: 28).

51. PREFACE — Of all the liberties, the most inviolable is that of thought, which includes the liberty of conscience. To cast a curse against those who do not think as we do is to demand that liberty for ourself but refuse it to others, which is a violation of the first commandment of Jesus, which is that of charity and love towards one's neighbour. To persecute others for the

beliefs they profess is to attack the most sacred right of Man, which is to believe whatever he wishes and to worship God as he sees fit. To compel him to practise exterior acts similar to those we ourselves practise is to show that we are more attached to the form than the essence and to appearances rather than conviction. Forced renouncement will never produce faith. It can only make hypocrites. It is an abuse of material power, which does not prove the truth. *Truth is sure of itself; it convinces and does not pursue, because there is no need.*

Spiritism is an opinion, a belief; even if it were a religion, why should its adepts not have the liberty to call themselves Spiritists, as do the Catholics, the Jews and the Protestants, or the participants of this or that philosophical doctrine, of this or that economic order? A belief is either true or false. If it is false it will fall by itself, seeing that error cannot stand up against truth when intelligences are enlightened; and if it is true then persecution will not make it become false.

Persecution is the baptism of all new ideas that are great and just. It grows with the development and the importance of the idea. The fury and wrath of its enemies are in direct proportion to the fear it inspires. This is the reason why Christianity was persecuted in the past, and why Spiritism is today, with the difference however that the former was persecuted by the Pagans and the latter by Christians. It is true that the time of bloody persecutions is now past; nevertheless, if today they no longer kill the body, then they torture the soul; attacking it even in its most intimate sentiments, in its most dear affections. Families are divided, exciting mothers against daughters, wives against husbands. Even physical violence is not absent, the body being attacked through the lack of material necessities by taking people away from their means of livelihood, thereby attacking the believer through hunger (See chapter 23, items & subsequent).

Spiritists, do not be upset by the blows that are hurled at you because they are the proof that you have the truth. If this were not so they would leave you in peace and not attack you. It is a test for your faith, since it is through your courage, resignation and perseverance that God will recognise you as being one of His faithful servants, on whom He is counting as from today, to give to each one the part that rests with them according to their works.

Following the example of the first Christians, carry your cross with dignity. Believe in the words of Christ when He said: "Blessed are those who suffer persecution for the love of justice, for theirs is the Kingdom of Heaven. Do not be afraid of those who kill the body, for they cannot kill the soul." He also said: "Love your enemies; do good to those who do you evil and pray for those who persecute you." Show yourselves to be true disciples and that your doctrine is good by doing what He said and did.

The persecution will not last for long. Await with patience for the coming of the dawn, since the morning star is already appearing on the horizon (See chapter 24, items 13 & subsequent).

52. PRAYER

Lord, You have said to us through the lips of Jesus, Your Messiah, "Blessed are those who suffer persecution for love of justice; forgive your enemies; pray for those who persecute you." And He gave us an example of this by praying for His tormentors.

Following this example, O Lord, we beg Your mercy for those who despise Your most sacred precepts, which are the only ones capable of bringing peace to this world and the next. As did Christ, we also say: "Forgive them, Father, for they know not what they do."

Give us strength to support with patience and resignation their mockery, insults, slander and persecutions as a test of our faith and humility; free us from all idea of reprisals, seeing that the hour of justice comes to all, and we await it submitting ourselves to Your holy Will.

PRAYER FOR A CHILD THAT HAS JUST BEEN BORN

53. PREFACE — Only after having passed through the tests offered by physical life can Spirits reach perfection. Those who are in an errant state await God's permission to return to an existance which can offer them progress, either by the expiation of their faults by means of the vicissitudes to which they will be subjected, or by the undertaking of a mission which will benefit humanity. Their advancement and future happiness will be in proportion to the manner in which they employ the time given to them on Earth. The duty of guiding their first steps and of leading them towards goodness is up to their parents, who will have to give an account to God for the degree of fulfillment they gave to this mandate. It was to help them that God made paternal and filial love a Law of Nature, a law which can never be transgressed with impunity.

54. PRAYER (To be said by the parents):
Dear Spirit, who has incarnated in the body of our child, we bid you welcome. We thank You, Almighty God, for the blessing of this child.

We know that this is a trust You have deposited in us and for which one day we will have to give an account. If he (she) belongs to the new generation of Spirits who are to inhabit the Earth, we thank you Lord for this blessing! If it is an imperfect Spirit, it is our duty to help him/her progress towards goodness, by means of counselling and good examples. If he/she falls prey to evil through our fault, we shall be responsible for this, seeing that we shall have failed in our mission.

Lord, uphold us in this task and give us the necessary strength and willpower so as to be able to fulfill it to the best of our ability. If this child has come to test our Spirits, may Your will be done, Lord!

Good Spirits, who have watched over this birth and will accompany this child during the course of his/her new existence, do not abandon him/her. Turn away from him/her all the evil Spirits who will try to tempt him/her into badness. Give this being strength to resist all their suggestions and courage to suffer with patience and resignation the tests which await here on Earth (See chapter 14, item 9).

55. PRAYER:

Dear God, You have entrusted me with the destiny of one of Your Spirits; therefore, Lord, make me worthy of the task You have set me. Grant me Your protection. Illuminate my intelligence so that I may perceive right from the beginning the tendencies of the one it is my duty to prepare for ascension to Your peace.

56. PRAYER:

God of infinite goodness, since You have seen fit to permit the Spirit of this child to come once again to undergo earthly trials, destined to make it progress, give it enlightenment enough so that it may learn to know You, love You and worship You. Through Your omnipotence may this soul regenerate itself from the source of Your Divine Teachings. That, under the protection of its Guardian Angel, its intelligence may develop, amplify and lead it to aspire to move closer to You. May the science of Spiritism be a brilliant light which illuminates it throughout the many choices of life. And finally, may it learn to appreciate the full extension of Your love, which puts us to the test so that we may purify ourselves.

Lord, cast a paternal eye over this family to which You have entrusted this soul, so that it may learn to understand the importance of its mission. May the seeds of goodness within this child germinate till such time as, by its own aspirations, it elevates itself to You.

O Lord, may it please You to answer this humble prayer, in the name of and by the worthiness of He who said: "Let the little children come to me, because the Kingdom of Heaven is for those who resemble them."

FOR ONE WHO AGONIZES

57. PREFACE — Agonizing is the prelude to the separation of the soul from the body. It can be said that at this moment the person has one foot on Earth and the other in the next world. Sometimes this phase is painful for those who are deeply attached to worldly things and who live more for the possessions of this world than those of the next one, or whose conscience is agitated by regrets and remorse. On the other hand, for those whose thoughts seek the Infinite and who are able to disengage themselves from matter, it is less difficult to break the links which tie them to the Earth and there is nothing of pain in these last moments. Only a thin thread links their physical body to their soul, while in the first case there are thick roots which hold them prisoner. In every case, prayer exercises a powerful action in the work of separation (See HEAVEN & HELL, (1) 2nd part, chapter 1 — "The Passing").

58. PRAYER:

Merciful and omnipotent God, here is a soul who is about to leave its terrestrial covering in order to return to the Spirit world, which is the real homeland. May it be given to them to make this passing in peace and may You extend Your mercy to them.

---

(1) By ALLAN KARDEC

Good Spirits, who have accompanied this person on Earth, do not abandon them at this supreme moment. Give them strength to support the last sufferings which they need to pass through in this world, for the good of their future advancement. Inspire them to use any last glimmerings of intelligence or any fleeting awareness they may have, to the consecration of repentance for any faults. Allow my thoughts to act in such a way so as to help them achieve this separation with less difficulty, and may this soul take the consolation of hope with it at the moment of departure from this Earth.

4 — PRAYERS FOR THOSE NO LONGER ON EARTH.

FOR SOMEONE WHO HAS JUST DIED

59. PREFACE — Prayers for those who have just left the Earth are not for the exclusive purpose of showing our sympathy. They also have the effect of helping to release them from their Earthly ties, and in this manner shorten the period of perturbation which always follows the separation, so allowing a more peaceful awakening on the other side. Nevertheless, in this case, as in all other circumstances, the efficacy depends on the sincerity of the thought and not on the quantity of words offered with more or less solemnity in which very frequently the heart does not participate.

Prayers which truly come from the heart encounter a resonance in the Spirit to whom they are directed, whose ideas are still in a state of confusion, as if they were friendly voices come to awaken them from sleep (See chapter 27, item 10).

60. PRAYER:

Almighty God, may Your mercy be shown to the soul of X . . . whom You have just called back from Earth. We beg and implore that the trials suffered here may be counted in their favour and that our prayers may soften and shorten the penalties still to be suffered in the Spirit form!

Good Spirits who came to fetch this soul, and most especially their Guardian Angel, help them to free themself from matter. Give them light and a consciousness of themself so that they may quickly leave the state of perturbation, inherent in the passing from the body back to the spiritual life. Inspire in their Spirit a repentance for all errors and faults committed and a desire to obtain permission to remedy them, so as to quicken their advancement in the direction of the life of those who are eternally blessed.

And you, X . . ., who have just entered into the World of the Spirits, we wish to say that despite this fact, you are still with us; you hear and see us, since you have merely left the perishable physical body, which will quickly be reduced to dust.

You have left the gross envelope which is subject to vicissitudes and death, now retaining only your etheric body which is imperishable and inaccessible to material suffering. If you no longer live through a physical body, you live instead through your Spirit, and the spiritual life is free from those miseries which afflict humanity.

You no longer have over your eyes the veil which hides the splendours of the future existence from us. Now you may contemplate new marvels, while we remain bathed in darkness.

You may travel through space and visit the worlds in all liberty, while we still painfully drag ourselves about here on Earth, prisoner in our material bodies, which are like heavy armour.

The infinite horizons stretch themselves before you, and on seeing their grandeur you will understand the vanity of terrestrial desires, of worldly aspirations and the futility of the so-called joys to which Man delivers himself.

For Man, death is nothing more than a separation from matter, lasting but a few instants. From this place of exile in which we continue to live according to the Will of God, and with the duties we still have to fulfill in this world, we will continue to follow you in thought till the moment when it is permitted for us to join you once again, just as now you are reunited with those who preceded you.

We cannot go to where you are, but you may come here. So come then to those who love you and whom you love; help them in the trials of life; watch over those who are dear to you; protect them as much as you are able; lessen the bitterness of absence by suggesting to them the thought that now you are happier and that one day, for certain, you will again be reunited in a better world.

In the place you are now, you must extinguish all earthly resentments. You must hold yourself inaccessible to them now, for the sake of your future happiness! Therefore forgive all those who may have incurred debts towards you, just as those against whom mistakes were committed now forgive you.

NOTE — To this prayer, which applies to everyone, can be added some special words according to the intimate circumstances of the family, the relationship to the deceased of the one who is praying or the social position of the departed. When dealing with a child, Spiritism teaches us that we are not referring to a Spirit that has been recently created, but to one that has already lived other lives and may even be well advanced. If the last existence has been a short one, then it is because it was needed only to complete a test or trial, or because it was needed as a test for the parents (See chapter 5, item 21).

61. PRAYER (1):

All Powerful Lord, may Your mercy extend over all those brothers and sisters who have just left the Earth! May Your light shine upon them! Remove them from darkness! Open their eyes and ears! May the Good Spirits surround them and let them hear Your words of hope and peace!

---

(1) This prayer was dictated to a medium from Bordeaux at the moment when an unknown funeral procession was passing by their residence.

Lord, even though we are not worthy, we beg and implore Your merciful indulgence for this brother (or sister) who has recently been recalled from exile. Make their return that of the prodigal son. Forget, O Lord, the faults they may have committed and remember only the good they have done. Your justice is immutable, as we know, but Your love is immense. We beseech You therefore, to mitigate Your justice from the fountain of kindness which emanates from You!

You who have just left the Earth, may the light shine brightly before your eyes, my brother! May the good Spirits come to be near you, to surround you and help you to break your earthly chains! Now you can understand and see the grandeur of God: so submit yourself without complaint to His justice; however, never despair of His mercy. Dear brother! (or sister) May a profound examination of your past open the doors of the future, by making you understand the errors you have left behind, as well as the work that awaits, so you may remedy them! May God forgive you and may the good Spirits uphold and animate you! Your brothers and sisters on Earth will pray for you, and ask that you pray for them.

THOSE FOR WHOM WE HAVE AFFECTION

62. PREFACE — How terrible is the idea of nothingness! How deserving of pity are those who think that the voice of one who weeps is lost in a vacuum, without encountering the least sign of response! A pure and saintly affection has never been known by those who think everything dies with the body. They believe that the genius who enlightened their world with vast intelligence, is a mere combination of matter which, as a flame, is extinguished for ever; that of a dearly loved person such as a father, mother or adored child, nothing remains but a handful of dust which time will inevitably disperse.

How can anyone who has a heart remain indifferent to this idea? Why are they not frozen with terror at the thought of absolute annihilation and do not even show a wish that this be not so? If till now reason has been insufficient for them to have been able to dissipate their doubts, behold, Spiritism has come to dispel all uncertainty as to the future, by means of the material proof of survival of the soul and the existence of beings in the beyond that it gives! This is happening to such an extent, that on all sides these proofs are being received with joy. Confidence is reborn, because Man henceforth knows that terrestrial existence is only a brief passage leading to a better life, that work done in this world is not lost and that really pure affections are not shattered beyond hope (See chapter 4, item 18 & chapter 5, item 21).

63. PRAYER:
O Lord, may You see fit to favourably receive this prayer in the name of X... Help them perceive the divine lights that will make their pathway to eternal happiness easier. Permit the good Spirits to take them my words and thoughts.

You who were so dear to me in this world, listen to my voice which calls to offer anew my pledge of affection. God allowed you to be liberated before me and I cannot complain about this without being selfish, because this would be equal to a wish that you be still subject to the sufferings of life. So wait with resignation for the moment of our reunion in this happier world, where you have arrived before me.

I know that this separation is only temporary, and that however long it may appear to be, its duration is nothing compared to the blessed eternity which God has promised to His chosen ones. May His goodness preserve me from doing whatever it might be that could delay this longed for moment, so that I may be saved from the pain of not encountering you when I leave my earthly captivity.

Oh, how sweet and consoling is the certainty that there is nothing between us but a material veil which hides you from my sight! That you can even be here at my side, hear me speak as of old, or perhaps even better than then; to know that you do not forget me as I do not forget you; that our thoughts are constantly intermingling and that your thoughts accompany me and uphold me.

May the peace of the Lord be with you.

FOR SUFFERING SPIRITS WHO ASK FOR PRAYERS

64. PREFACE — So as to appreciate the relief that prayer gives to suffering Spirits, it is necessary to remember by what manner this is achieved, as has been previously explained (See chapter 27, items 9, 18 & subsequent). Those who are convinced of this fact will be able to pray with greater fervour, because of the certainty that they do not do so in vain.

65. PRAYER:
God of clemancy and mercy, may Your goodness extend to all the Spirits we have recommended to You in our prayers, especially the Spirit of X . . .

Good Spirits, whose only occupation is to do good, intercede together with me for their relief. Make a ray of hope shine before their eyes and enlighten them as to the imperfections which maintain them distant from the homes of the blessed. Open their hearts to repentance and the desire to cleanse themselves, so they may accelerate their advancement. Make them understand it is by their own efforts that they may shorten the duration of their trials.

May God, in all His goodness, give them the necessary strength to persevere with their good resolutions!

May these words, infused with benevolence, soften their trials, so showing them that there are on Earth those who sympathize and wish them happiness.

66. PRAYER:

We ask, Lord, that You shower the blessings of Your love and mercy on all who suffer, be they wandering Spirits or incarnates. Have pity for their weaknesses. You made us fallible, but gave us the capacity to resist evil and conquer it. May Your mercy extend to all those who are not able to resist their evil tendencies and still continue to drag themselves along evil pathways. May the good Spirits surround them; may Your light shine in their eyes, and so attracted by the life-giving warmth of this light, may they come to prostrate themselves at Your feet, humbly, repentant and submissive.

Merciful Father, we also ask for those of our brothers and sisters who have not had the strength to resist their earthly trials. Lord, You gave us a burden to carry, to be laid only at Your feet. However, our weaknesses are great and our courage fails us sometimes during the course of the journey. Have pity on these indolent servants who have abandoned the work before time. May Your justice spare them and allow the good Spirits to take them some relief, consolation and hope for the future. The prospect of pardon strengthens the soul; Lord, show this pardon to those guilty ones who have given themselves up to despair, so that upheld by hope they may absorb enough strength from the actual immensity of their failings and sufferings, so they may redeem the past and prepare themselves for the conquest of the future.

FOR AN ENEMY WHO HAS DIED

67. PREFACE — Charity towards our enemies should accompany them into the Beyond. We need to understand that the evil they did was a test for us, which can be useful to our state of advancement, if we know how to take advantage of it. It can be even more beneficial to us than purely material afflications, by the fact of our being allowed to join together courage, resignation, charity and the forgetting of offences (See chapter 10, item 6, & chapter 12, items 5 & 6).

68. PRAYER:

Lord, it pleased You to call the soul of X . . . before You called me. I forgive him the evil he did and the bad intentions nurtured towards me. Maybe he is regretting this now that he no longer feeds off the illusions of this world.

Dear God, may Your mercy descend upon him and turn away from me any idea I might have of rejoicing at his death. If I am in debt towards him for any reason, may he forgive me, as I forget those misdemeanours committed against me.

FOR A CRIMINAL

69. PREFACE — If the efficiency of prayer was proportionate to its length, then the longest ones would be reserved for the most guilty, because they are in more need than those who have lived saintly lives. To refuse prayer to criminals is to lack charity towards them and to be unaware of the mercy of God. To believe they would be useless because a man has committed this or that grave crime would be to prejudge the Almighty's justice (See chapter 11, item 14).

70. PRAYER:

Lord God of Mercy, do not repudiate this criminal who has just left this Earth! Man's justice has condemned him, but this does not exempt him from Your justice, if his heart has not been touched by remorse.

Take away the blind-fold that hides the gravity of his faults! His repentance may deserve Your kindly treatment and soften the sufferings of his soul. Our prayers can also help and the intercession of the good Spirits may offer him hope and consolation. Inspire in him the wish to make amends for his actions in another existence and give him strength so as not to succumb in the new battles which he will undertake!

Lord, have pity on him!

FOR A SUICIDE

71. PREFACE — Man never has the right to dispose of his life, since it is only given to God to retrieve him from captivity on Earth, when He judges opportune. Nevertheless, Divine justice may soften the rigours in accordance with the circumstances, reserving however all severity towards he who wished to evade the trials of life. The suicide is like a prisoner who escapes from prison before he has served his sentence, and who when recaptured is treated with greater severity. The same happens with a suicide who imagines he is escaping from the miseries of the moment, only to plunge into even greater misfortunes (See chapter 5, item 14 onwards).

72. PRAYER:

We know, Lord, the destiny that awaits those who violate Your law, by voluntarily abreviating their days. But we also know that Your mercy is infinite. So please condescend to extend this mercy to the soul of X . . . May our prayers and Your commiseration lessen the harshness of the sufferings they are experiencing for not having had the courage to await the end of their trials.

Good Spirits, whose mission it is to help those who are wretched, take this Spirit under your protection; inspire him to regret the error committed. May your assistance give him strength to support with greater resignation the new trials through which he will have to pass in order to make reparation. Turn aside from him the evil Spirits who are capable of once again impelling him towards that same act and so prolonging his sufferings by making him lose the fruits of future expiations.

We also direct ourselves to you, whose unhappiness is the motive for our prayers, to offer a wish that our commiseration may diminish the bitterness and help to create within you the hope for a better future. This future lies in your hands; believe in the goodness of God, whose bosom opens to accept all repentance and only remains closed to hardened hearts.

FOR REPENTANT SPIRITS

73. PREFACE — It would be unjust to include in our category of evil Spirits the suffering and repentant ones who ask for prayers. They may have been bad; nevertheless, they no longer are, ever since they recognised the error of their ways and deplore them; they are only unhappy. Some of them have even begun to enjoy relative happiness.

74. PRAYER:

God of Mercy, who accepts the sincere repentance of the sinner, be they incarnate or discarnate, here is a Spirit who has taken pleasure in evil, who recognises his errors and is entering into the good pathway. Condescend, Lord, to receive him like the prodigal son and forgive him.

Good Spirits, whose voices he did not pay attention to but now wishes to hear, permit him to glimpse the happiness of the elected ones of the Lord, so that he may persist in his desire to purify himself in order to be able to reach them. Uphold him in all his good intentions and give him the necessary strength to resist his bad instincts.

To the repentant Spirit of X . . ., we offer our congratulations for the inner changes you have made and we thank the good Spirits who have helped you to do this.

If you previously took pleasure in evil, it was because you did not understand how sweet is the enjoyment of doing good, and also because you felt too lowly to be able to manage to do it. But, from the moment you placed your first step on the path of goodness a new light shone in your eyes. Then you began to enjoy an unknown happiness and hope entered your heart. This is because God always hears the prayer of a sinner who repents; He never repels anyone who seeks Him.

So to be once again completely within God's grace, you must apply yourself from now on to not only never again committing evil but to doing good, and above all else to repair the evil that you have done. Then you will satisfy God's justice; each good action you practise will wash away all past errors.

The first step has been taken; so now as you continue to advance by this path it will become easier and more agreeable. Persevere then, and one day you will have the glory of being counted amongst the good Spirits and those who are blessed.

FOR HARDENED SPIRITS

75 PREFACE — The bad Spirits are those who have not yet been touched by repentance, who delight in evil and who feel no regrets for this. They are insensitive to reprimands, repel prayer and frequently blaspheme in God's name. They are those hardened Spirits, who after death seek vengeance upon men for the suffering they had endured and pursue with hate all who practised evil against them during their existence, by either obsessing them or by exercising all kinds of disastrous influences over them (See chapter 10, item 6, and chapter 12, items 5 & 6).

There are two distinct categories of perverse Spirits: those who are plainly evil and those who are hypocrites. It is infinitely easier to bring the first ones back to goodness than the last ones. The first, more often than not, have brutal and coarse natures, just as is seen in men; they practise evil more from instinct than from calculation and do not seek to appear better than they are. However, there is in them a latent germ that needs to open up, which is usually achieved by means of perseverance; firm benevolence, counselling, reasoning and prayer. It has been noticed that in automatic-writing these Spirits have difficulty in writing the name of God, which is a sign of an instinctive fear, an intimate voice of conscience which tells them they are unworthy. It is at this point that they are ready to convert themselves and we can have high hopes for them; we only need to find the vulnerable point in their hearts.

Hypocritical Spirits are almost always very intelligent. But they do not have a grain of sensitivity in their hearts; nothing touches them. They simulate all the good sentiments so as to gain confidences and are happy when they encounter those who are foolish enough to accept them as good Spirits, because then they can control them as they like. The name of God, far from inspiring the least tremor of fear, serves them as a mask to cover their vileness. In both the invisible and visible worlds, the hypocrites are the most dangerous of beings because they act in the shadows, without anyone suspecting; they have only apparent faith, never real faith.

76. PRAYER:

Lord, may it please You to cast a kindly glance over the imperfect Spirits who find themselves in the obscurity of ignorance and so do not know You, especially the Spirit of X . . .

Good Spirits, help us to make them understand that by inducing men towards evil, obsessing them and tormenting them, they only prolong their own sufferings. Make the example of the happiness You enjoy into an encouragement for them.

Spiritual brother, you who still take pleasure in the practise of evil, listen to the prayer we offer for you; it should convince you that we only desire to help you and not to do you harm.

You are unhappy, because it is not possible to be happy while practising evil. So why do you remain in suffering when the possibility of avoiding it depends on yourself? Look at the good Spirits surrounding you at this moment and see how blessed they are! Would it not be more agreeable for you to enjoy the same happiness?

You say this is impossible; however, nothing is impossible to he who wants something, since God gave you, as He did all His creatures, the liberty to choose between good and evil, happiness and wretchedness, and no one is condemned to practise evil. Just as you have the will to do evil, you may also find the will to do good and be happy.

Cast your eyes back towards God. Direct your thoughts for an instant to Him and a ray of divine light will illuminate you. Say these simple words together with us: *Dear God, I repent, forgive me!* Try to repent and do good instead of doing bad things, and you will soon see His mercy descending upon you and an indescribable feeling of well-being will substitute the anguish you experience now.

Once you have taken the first step along the path to goodness the rest of the way will be easy to follow. You will understand then what a long period of happiness you have lost through your own fault. Nevertheless, a radiant future full of hope will open before you and make you forget your miserable past, full of perturbation and moral tortures, which would be hell for you if they were to last for eternity. The day will come when these tortures will be such that you will desire to make them cease at any price. Nevertheless, the longer you leave it the more difficult this will be.

Do not believe that you will always remain in your present state; no, this is not possible. You have two prospects before you: to suffer very much more than you have done until now, or to be blessed as are the good Spirits who surround you. The first is inevitable if you persist in being obstinate, when a simple effort on your part would be sufficient to take you out of the bad situation in which you find yourself. So hurry, seeing that each day you delay is a lost day of happiness!

Good Spirits, permit these words to echo in the mind of this backward soul so they may help him to approach God. We ask this in the name of Jesus Christ, Who has such great power over evil Spirits.

5 — PRAYERS FOR THE SICK AND OBSESSED.
FOR THOSE WHO ARE SICK

77. PREFACE — Illness belongs to the tests and vicissitudes of earthly life. It is inherent in the grossness of our material nature and in the inferiority of the world we inhabit. Passions and excesses of all kinds create unhealthy conditions in our organism, which are sometimes transmitted by heredity. In worlds that are more advanced in both physical and moral aspects, the human organism, being more purified and less material, is no longer subject to the same infirmities and the body is not secretly undermined by the corrosives of passions (See chapter 3, item 9). In this manner we must resign ourselves to the consequences of the ambient in which our inferiority places us, until we deserve to pass on to a better one. However, while we are waiting this does not prevent us from doing whatever we can to improve our present situation. But if despite our best efforts we do not manage this, then Spiritism teaches us to support our passing miseries with resignation.

If God had not wished that in certain cases bodily sufferings be dissipated and softened, He would not have put the possibility of cure within our reach. His solicitude in this respect, being in conformity with the instinct of self-preservation, indicates that it is our duty to seek these means and apply them.

Apart from ordinary medication elaborated by Science, magnetism allows us to know the power of fluidic action, and Spiritism reveals another powerful force in *the mediumship of healing* and the influence of prayer (See below PREFACE 81, the note about the mediumship of healing).

78. PRAYER (To be said by the sick person):

Lord, You are all justice. The illness You saw fit to send me must be deserved, because You never impose suffering without just cause. Therefore I entrust my cure to Your infinite mercy. If it pleases You to restore my health, may Your Name be blessed! If on the contrary it is necessary for me to suffer more, may You be blessed just the same. I submit without complaint to Your wise purpose, since what You do can only be for the good of Your creatures.

Dear God, let this infirmity be a timely warning to me, which will cause me to meditate upon myself. I accept it as an expiation for my past and as a test of my faith and submission to Your blessed will (See prayer No. 40).

79. PRAYER (For the sick person):

Dear God, Your designs are impenetrable and in Your wisdom You have sent this affliction to X . . . I implore You, Lord, to cast a glance of compassion over his sufferings and if You see fit, to terminate them.

Good Spirits, you who are ministers of the Almighty, I beseech you to second my request to alleviate his sufferings; direct my thought so that a balsam may be poured over his body and consolation poured into his soul.

Inspire him with patience and submission to God's Will. Give him enough strength to support the pain with Christian resignation, so that the fruits of this test may not be lost (See prayer No. 57).

80. PRAYER (To be said by the Healer):

Dear God, if it pleases You to use me as an instrument, although I am unworthy, may I cure this infirmity if You so desire, because I have faith in You. But I know I can do nothing alone. Permit the good Spirits to concentrate their beneficial fluids in me, so that I may transmit them to the sick person and free me from all thought of pride and selfishness, which might alter their pureness.

FOR THOSE WHO ARE OBSESSED

81. PREFACE — Obsession is the persistant action which an inferior or bad Spirit exercises over an individual. It may present many varied characteristics, from a simple moral influence with no perceptible exterior signs, to a complete organic and mental perturbation. It may obstruct all mediumship faculties. In automatic-writing this may be shown by the insistance of one Spirit in communicating, to the exclusion of all other Spirits.

Bad Spirits encircle the Earth, due to the moral inferiority of its inhabitants. Their malevolent action forms part of the afflictions which face humanity. Obsessions, just as much as infirmities and all life's tribulations, must be considered as tests and atonements and accepted as such.

In the same manner that sicknesses are the result of our physical imperfections, which make the body accessible to pernicious exterior influences, obsession is always the result of moral imperfections, which allow the access of a bad Spirit. Physical causes pit themselves against physical forces; a moral cause must be opposed by a moral force. In order to prevent infirmities we fortify our bodies; to exempt ourselves from obsession it is necessary to fortify the soul, which means that the obsessed person must work for their own betterment, which is frequently sufficient to relieve them of the obsession without resorting to help from others. When an obsession degenerates into subjugation and possession, then the help of other people becomes indispensable, because not infrequently the patient loses their will-power and their free-will.

Obsession almost always manifest the vengeance that a Spirit desires, which is frequently rooted in the relationship they had with this person in a previous life (See chapter 10, item 6 and chapter 12, items 5 & 6).

In the case of a grave obsession, the person being obsessed is enveloped and impregnated by pernicious substances, so neutralizing the action of healthy fluids and repelling them. It is very important to free the person from these negative vaporous fluids. However, a bad fluid cannot be eliminated by other bad fluids. By a similar action to that exercised by a healer in the case of illness, it is necessary to expel the bad substances with the help of better ones, which in a certain way produces the effect of a reaction. This may be called a mechanical action, but it is not sufficient alone. It is also necessary and most important, to act upon this intelligent being by speaking with authority, which can only be acheived through moral superiority. The greater this is, the greater will be the authority.

This is not all however. In order to guarantee liberation from the obsessor it is also necessary to induce the perverse Spirit to renounce their bad designs, to awaken repentance in them and a desire to do good. This can be done through the means of skillfully directed instruction, given during special private meetings for this purpose, with the objective of offering moral education to this Spirit. Then it may be possible to have the double satisfaction of liberating an incarnate Spirit and converting a discarnate one at the same time.

This task is made easier when the obsessed person, understanding their situation, joins in with the prayers and adds their cooperation in the form of a desire to recuperate. The same does not happen when, being seduced by the obsessing Spirit, the person remains deluded as to the qualities of the entity who dominates them, even taking pleasure in the errors this Spirit induces them to commit. In this case, instead of helping, he repels all assistance offered. This is what happens in cases of fascination, which are infinitely more rebellious to treatment than even the most violent case of subjugation (See THE MEDIUMS' BOOK, (1) chapter 23). In all cases of obsession, prayer is the most powerful means of help in the action against an obsessing Spirit.

82. PRAYER (To be said by the person being obsessed):
   Dear God, permit the good Spirits to liberate me from the malefic Spirit which has linked itself to me. If this Spirit is seeking vengeance as a consequence of wrongs I might have practised against him in other existences, then You have permitted this, Lord, and I suffer for my own faults. May my

_____

(1) by ALLAN KARDEC.

repentance make me worthy of Your pardon and of my liberation! But whatever the motive, I beseech Your mercy for he who persecutes me. Lord; help him to find the pathway to progress, which will turn him away from the practise of evil. May I, on my part, repay evil with goodness, so inducing him to better sentiments.

But dear God, I also know that it is my own imperfections which make me accessible to the influences of imperfect Spirits. Give me the necessary light so I may recognise these imperfections and above all, remove the pride in me which makes me blind to my own defects.

How great must be my unworthiness to allow a malefic being to dominate me!

Dear God, may this blow to my vanity be a lesson for the future. May it fortify the resolution I have made to cleanse myself by means of the practise of goodness, charity and humility, so that as from now I may put up a barrier against all bad influences.

Lord, give me strength to support this test with patience and resignation. I understand that, just as with all other tests, it will aid my progress if I do not spoil the fruits with my complaining, because it offers me an opportunity to demonstrate my submission and to practise charity towards an unhappy brother by forgiving him the evil he has done me (See chapter 12, items 5 & 6; chapter 28, item 15 and subsequent, also items 46 & 47).

83. PRAYER (For the one who is obsessed):

Almighty God, may it please You to give me the power to liberate X . . . from the influence of the Spirit that is obsessing him. If it be in Your designs to put an end to this test, concede me the grace of speaking to this Spirit with the necessary authority.

I ask all good Spirits who help me, and you, his Guardian Angel, to give me your assistance; help me to free this sufferer from the impure fluids which envelop him.

In the name of Almighty God, I urge the malefic Spirit which torments this person to retire!

84. PRAYER (For the obsessing Spirit):

Lord of infinite goodness, I implore Your mercy for the Spirit who is obsessing X . . . Help him to see the Divine Light so that he may recognise the falsity of the path he follows. Good Spirits, help me make him understand that he has everything to lose by the practise of evil, and everything to gain by the practise of good.

To the spirit who is tormenting X . . ., I beg you to listen to me since I speak to you in the name of God!

If you would but reflect, you would understand that evil can never outdo goodness and that it is not possible to be stronger than God and the good Spirits.

It is possible for them to protect X . . . from your attacks; if this has not been done already it is because he had to go through this test. But when this test reaches its end, then all action against him will be blocked. The evil that you have done, instead of causing harm, will have contributed towards his progress and happiness. In this manner, your wickedness will be a total loss for you and will only rebound upon yourself.

God, Who is all powerful, and the Superior Spirits who are His delegates, being more powerful than you, are capable of putting an end to this obsession whenever they wish, and your tenacity will fall before this supreme authority. But because He is good, God wants to leave you the merit for having ceased of your own will. It is a respite that is being offered to you, and if you do not take advantage of it you will suffer deplorable consequences. Great punishment and cruel suffering will await. You will be forced to plead for mercy and for the prayers of your victim, who has already forgiven you and prays for you, which constitutes a great merit in the eyes of God and hastens their liberation.

So reflect while there is still time, seeing that God's justice will fall upon you as it does on all rebellious Spirits. Consider that the evil you do now necessarily has a limit, whereas, if you persist in being obstinate, you will only increase the extension of your own sufferings.

When you were upon Earth, did you never consider it stupid to sacrifice a great goodness for a small momentary satisfaction? It is the same now you are a Spirit. What will you gain by what you are doing? The misguided pleasure of tormenting someone, which does not stop you being wretched even if you do not admit it, only leaves you even more unhappy.

On the other hand, see what you are missing! Look at the good Spirits around you and tell me if their lot is not preferable to yours. The happiness they enjoy can also be yours whenever you like. What do you have to do for this? Beseech God, and instead of doing evil, do good. I know that you cannot transform yourself immediately, but God does not demand the impossible; He only asks for good-will. Try, and we will help you. Make an effort so that very soon we may offer up in your name the prayer for those who are repentant (No. 73), and no longer rank you amongst the bad Spirits, while we await the moment when we can count you among the good Spirits.

(See also No. 75 — Prayers for Hardened Spirits).

REMARKS: The cure of grave obsessions requires much patience, perseverance and devotion. It also demands tact and ability in order to direct those who are frequently perverse, hardened and astute, towards being good Spirits, since there are those who are extremely rebellious. In the vast majority of cases we must be guided by the circumstances. Nevertheless, whatever the characteristics of the Spirit, it is an incontestable fact that nothing is obtained by either constraint or threats; all influence resides in moral superiority. Another truth, equally well proven by experience as well as logic, is of the complete ineffectiveness of exorcism, formulas, sacremental words, amulets, talismans, exterior practises or any kind of material symbols.

Prolonged obsessions may cause pathological disorders, which frequently demand simultaneous or consecutive treatment, be it magnetic or medical, so as to be able to restore organic health. When the cause has been destroyed, it remains for the effects to be remedied (See THE MEDIUMS' BOOK, 2nd part, chapter 23 — "Obsession" — also REVUE SPIRITE, February and March, 1864 & April, 1865 — examples of cures for obsession).

BIOGRAPHICAL SKETCHES OF SOME OF THE SPIRIT COMMUNICANTS WHOSE MESSAGES ARE PUBLISHED IN THIS BOOK

ERASTUS (A disciple of Paul) — Treasurer of Corinth, he was a disciple of Paul of Tarsus, having accompanied him on his mission to Ephesus. He is cited in the book of Acts, 19:22. — "So he sent into Macedonia two of them that ministered unto him, Timotheus and Erastus; but he himself stayed in Asia for a season." In the book of Romans, 16:23. — "Gaius mine host, and of the whole church, saluteth you. Erastus the chamberlain of the city saluteth you, and Quartus a brother." In 2 Timothy, 4:20. — "Erastus abode at Corinth: but Trophimus have I left at Miletum sick."

FÉNELON, François de Salignac de la Mothe — A French prelate born in 1651 who discarnated in 1715. He belonged to a family famous in the field of arms and diplomacy. An ordained Priest, he dedicated himself to his ministry despite the intolerance of the epoch. For his royal pupils he wrote a didatic work entitled "The Fables," "Dialogue with the dead" and "Telemaco." This last book fell out of favour due to the question of Quietism, which was a doctrine preached by Madame Guyon. Fénelon defended Quietism, whereas Bossuet condemned it. Later on he was condemned by the Pope, so becoming just a simple priest again. He left many literary works, mostly on matters of politics, religion and education.

GIRARDIN, Delfina de — To be exact her maiden name was Delphine Gay. On marrying Emile de Girardin, a politician and a man of letters, she became Mrs Emile de Girardin. She published many poetical works under the name of Delphine Gay. In 1827, when she was twenty-three, she found herself acclaimed in the Capitolian when journeying through Italy. After her marriage she published various poems and romances. She was most certainly a great inspirational medium. On 6th September, 1853, she disembarked on the Isle of Jersey for the purpose of spending a short time with the family of Victor Hugo, where she held numerous mediumship sessions by means of the 'talking-tables'.

HAHNEMANN, Samuel-Chrétien-Fréderic — Of German origin he was born in Meissen on 10th April, 1755. Graduating in Medicine from Erland University in 1779 he exercised his profession till 1789 when he abandoned his medical practice due to a great dissatisfaction with the total lack of guidance at that time in the administration of remedies. He finally discovered Homoeopathy about 1790 and continued to research and experiment in this area, managing to survive by translating books. In 1796 he presented his discovery to the world in the form of a monograph, going on to practise his new found discovery. As Homoeopathy was very rational it soon became a success which caused him to suffer persecution from his ex-colleagues and so was given protection by the reigning duke of Anhalt-Coehen where he went to live in 1821. But the hate followed him and the local doctors incited the people against him and on one occasion his house was stoned. Despite this he continued to live there and became rich and greatly sought after for his treatments. In 1835 he moved to Paris and in 1843 returned to the spiritual world at the age of eight-eight. He was laid to rest in the Montmartre Cemetery. In 1900 his mortal remains were transferred, by members of the International Homoeopathic Congress, to a monument erected by his disciples in the Pére Lachaise Cemetery. On the same day and time in Washington, President Mackinley of the United States of America inaugurated a statue to Hahnemann which had cost American Homoeopathic doctors seventy thousand dollars.

HEINE, Henri — He was a German poet born in Düsseldorf in 1797, discarnating in Paris in 1856. He was the author of poems of a painfully melancholic nature (*Intermezzo, Sketches of a Journey and Song; Essays on Modern German Literature, The Romantic School and Germany*) all written with sparkling brilliance but tainted with profound scepticism.

JOHN THE EVANGELIST — The Apostle of Jesus Christ, son of Zebedee and brother to the Apostle James. He was the author of the fourth Gospel and three epistles. While exiled on the Greek island of Patmos he received, through the means of mediumship, the Apocalypse. He lived almost one hundred years. Together with the Apostles Peter and James the Elder, he was invariably called upon by Jesus to witness the most important events which occured during His mission.

LACORDAIRE, Jean-Baptiste-Henri — This is the Priest Lacordaire referred to in the *Revue Spirite,* the Spiritist magazine initiated by Allan Kardec in 1858. He also had a brother of some note, Jean-Théodore Lacordaire who was a naturalist, teacher and journalist, born in 1801. It is certain that we are dealing with the first brother, born in 1802 and discarnated in 1861. He was a Dominican, a brilliant preacher and disciple of Lamennais, with whom he broke off relations in 1834. He was vicar of Notre-Dame and after five years of retreat entered the Dominican Order in 1839. He was a member of the French Academy, his principle works being two very different lectures: 'The Life of Saint Domingos' and 'Considerations on the Philosophical system of M. de Lamennais'.

LAMENNAIS, Félicité Robert de — Born in Saint-Malo in 1782 he discarnated in Paris in 1854. He was ordained a priest in 1816. The following year he published 'Essays on religious indifference and its bearing on political and civil order' which was a translation of 'Imitation of Jesus Christ'; and also 'Modern Slavery'. He founded the newspaper *'L'Avenir'* (The Future) in which he extolled the alliance of the Church with Liberty. The Pope, Gregory XVI, denied his authority to hold such opinions in a circular letter entitled *Mirari vos* (Looking at Ourselves). Following this he published 'Words of a Believer', which was condemned in the circular *Singulari nos*. But he continued without interruption with 'The Tasks of Rome', 'The Book of the People', 'An Outline of a Philosophy', etc. In 1840 he was condemned to prison. In 1848 he was elected to the National Assembly. He asked that he be buried amongst the poor.

MORLOT, François Nicolas Madeleine — A French prelate and Archbishop of Paris and Cardinal. Born in 1795 he discarnated in 1862.

PAUL, THE APOSTLE — Born in the flourishing town of Tarsus in Cilicia, possibly in the year 10 or 12 of this epoch; he was martyrized in Rome in the year 67 AD. Nicknamed 'The Apostle of the Gentiles,' he was one of the most outstanding disseminators of Christian ideas, taking the word of Jesus Christ to the great centres of population of that time, these being Antioch, Athens, Ephesus, Corinth, Macedonia, Jerusalem and Rome. He wrote a great number of Epistles, which are contained in the book of 'The Acts of the Apostles' where many elucidative descriptions of his Apostlehood and his incomparable activities in favour of the birth of Christianity are also to be found. His original name was Saul, which was later changed to Paul. Although he was not one of the Apostles of Jesus he deserves the title of Apostle due to the magnificent tasks which he accomplished.

PASCAL, Blaise — He was a French geometrician, physicist, philosopher and writer, born in Clermont in 1623 he discarnated in Paris in 1662. When he was eleven years old he composed a treatise on sound; at twelve he discovered the thirty-second theorem of the first book of Euclid. At sixteen he wrote his "Essay on conics." At nineteen, in order to help the mathematical work of his father, he conceived his machine for mathematics which took him ten years. He also wrote works on space, on calculations of possibility and, after a period of time spent living a worldly life, he then returned to religion and dedicated himself to the production of works of a metaphysical and spiritual nature. He was in fact one of the great exponents of religious and philosophical thought of his time.

SAINT AUGUSTIN, (Aurelius Augustinus, 354-430 AD) — Bishop of Hipona, he was a theologist, philosopher, moralist and dialectician. After a disturbed boyhood he was attracted to a religious life by the Spirit of the enlightened Ambrose. On the insistence of his mother, Monica, he left Africa to go to Italy hoping to seek a more promising career in the Roman Empire. He wrote many sermons, helped the poor and, during the second part of his life, maintained the firm objective of serving the Church and Christ. He became the most celebrated of all the doctors of the Catholic Church. He sought to harmonize the doctrine of Plato with the Catholic dogmas, and intelligence with faith. His chief works were "The City of God," "Confessions" and a treatise on grace.

SAINT LOUIS (Louis IX) — A King of France, he lived from 1215 until 1270. He began his reign under the tutorship of his mother, Blanche de Castille. He took part in the seventh and eighth Crusades and discarnated as a victim of a plague on disembarking in Cartagus. He was a good and pious man and was cannonised by the Catholic Church in 1297. He is constantly cited in the *Revue Spirite* thanks to the numerous communications received from his Spirit.

SAINT VINCENT DE PAUL (1576-1660) — He was a French priest celebrated for his acts of charity. He was the instigator of the creches and hospitals of charity. When the provinces of Lorrain, Picardi and Champagne were devastated by war and famine, this apostle of charity gave all he had in order to minimize the hardships of the population of those regions.

VIANNEY, Jean Marie Baptiste — He lived from 1786 till 1859. While on Earth, he was the vicar of Ars. During the past century he gained great popularity due to the numerous cures he managed to realise and for the brotherly attention he dispensed to the sick of whatever nature, who sought him out in his obscure village. He protected his parish through the sheer force of mediumship phenomena, for which he was the intermediary, and which the people saw as authentic miracles. His fame caused the other priests to feel inferior, even though his parish was considered one where 'there was not even place to rest one's head'. They said: 'He is an illiterate who was ordained out of commiseration and charity. He does not know even three words of Latin and nothing of theology, who dares to offer confession to the multitudes and frequently treats complex and dangerous cases," and with these accusations they prohibited his followers from visiting him. The Abbot of Borjon wrote to him: "Dear Vicar, when you have as little theology as you have, you should be reluctant to enter into a confessionary." — On receiving this letter the Vicar of Ars broke into sobs and exclaimed: "It is true, it is true!" On replying to this critic he pondered: "My very venerable brother, I have so much reason to love you! You are the only one who has known me well. Please help me to obtain the grace that I have been asking for, for so long, so that on being substituted in my position, in whose exercise I do not consider myself worthy due to my great ignorance, I might retire to some small village where I can weep over my poor life."

(Permission to include the translation of these brief biographical sketches in this book was kindly given by the SPIRITIST FEDERATION OF THE STATE OF SAO PAULO, BRAZIL, as taken from the same book pages 15 to 19, published in 1982 under the title 'O EVANGELHO SEGUNDO O ESPIRITISMO.)

THE HEADQUARTERS PUBLISHING COMPANY LIMITED is one of the foremost publishers in the psychic sphere, publishing two monthly Spiritualist magazines:-

"TWO WORLDS"
"HERE AND THERE"

Other books published by the Headquarters Publishing Company:-

PRINCIPLES OF SPIRITUALISM by Harold Vigurs
ASPECTS OF HEALING by Chloris Morgan
THE TWO WORLDS OF WILLIAM REDMOND
by Chloris Morgan
MY GUIDE SAYS by Claire Ross

THE SPIRITUALIST HYMN BOOK

THE ROCK OF TRUTH by Arthur Findlay
ON THE EDGE OF THE ETHERIC by Arthur Findlay
THE WAY OF LIFE by Arthur Findlay
WHERE TWO WORLDS MEET by Arthur Findlay
THE UNFOLDING UNIVERSE by Arthur Findlay
THE TORCH OF KNOWLEDGE by Arthur Findlay
LOOKING BACK by Arthur Findlay
THE PSYCHIC STREAM by Arthur Findlay
THE CURSE OF IGNORANCE by Arthur Findlay

For details of any of the above publications send a s.a.e. to the publishers.

THE HEADQUARTERS PUBLISHING CO. LTD.
5 ALEXANDRIA ROAD
LONDON W13 0NP